I0049870

Google Cloud Associate Cloud Engineer Certification Guide

A comprehensive guide to implementing, managing, and monitoring Google Cloud solutions

Arijit Sarkar

bpb

www.bpbonline.com

First Edition 2025

Copyright © BPB Publications, India

ISBN: 978-93-65894-141

All Rights Reserved. No part of this publication may be reproduced, distributed or transmitted in any form or by any means or stored in a database or retrieval system, without the prior written permission of the publisher with the exception to the program listings which may be entered, stored and executed in a computer system, but they can not be reproduced by the means of publication, photocopy, recording, or by any electronic and mechanical means.

LIMITS OF LIABILITY AND DISCLAIMER OF WARRANTY

The information contained in this book is true and correct to the best of author's and publisher's knowledge. The author has made every effort to ensure the accuracy of these publications, but the publisher cannot be held responsible for any loss or damage arising from any information in this book.

All trademarks referred to in the book are acknowledged as properties of their respective owners but BPB Publications cannot guarantee the accuracy of this information.

To View Complete
BPB Publications Catalogue
Scan the QR Code:

www.bpbonline.com

Dedicated to

My wife, **Sudeshna Sarkar**

About the Author

Arijit Sarkar is a Data & AI enthusiast. He started his career as an ETL Developer and is currently working as a Lead Architect - Google Cloud in Data & AI consulting practice. He has been using Google Cloud since 2019 and has completed four certifications on this. He always likes to explore new technologies and platforms and implement those in real-world use cases.

About the Reviewers

❖ **Avik Sarkar** is a seasoned Cloud Solution Architect with extensive expertise in Google Cloud Platform (GCP) and multi-cloud environments. With over 20 years of experience in IT, he specializes in cloud migrations, enterprise application design, and digital modernization; he has led large-scale enterprise solutions across AWS, Azure, and GCP. His expertise spans multiple domains, including banking, insurance, manufacturing, and logistics, with extensive experience working in India and Switzerland.

Avik plays a pivotal role in designing and implementing solutions in financial crime detection, insurance modernization, and digital transformation. His technical acumen includes architecting high-availability, scalable, and secure cloud solutions, leveraging technologies such as Kubernetes, Kafka, Redis, and AI-driven analytics.

Avik's professional journey includes impactful tenures at Cognizant and IBM, where he contributed to cloud-based data lake solutions, enterprise data ingestion frameworks, and banking infrastructure modernization. His deep understanding of agile methodologies, project management, and security frameworks enables him to drive strategic initiatives and innovation.

Holding multiple industry-recognized certifications—including Microsoft Azure Security Engineer Associate, TOGAF 9, and Google Associate Cloud Engineer—Avik continues to push the boundaries of cloud technology. With a passion for optimizing performance and security in large-scale cloud environments, he remains a thought leader in enterprise cloud solutions.

Beyond his technical pursuits, Avik is multilingual, fluent in English, Hindi, and Bengali, and actively shares knowledge within the tech community.

❖ **Vibhor Malik** is a backend engineer at one of the Fortune 500 companies with a strong interest in technical literature and artificial intelligence. He holds a GCP Associate Developer certification and a Master's in Machine Learning and AI from Liverpool John Moores University, combining academic knowledge with industry experience. In his reviews, he focuses on exam-related content and certification insights to help readers better understand complex topics. Outside of work, he enjoys coding and cooking—because, as he believes, if you are good at cooking, you are probably a great coder too!

❖ **Karanbir Singh** is a seasoned Engineering Leader with over 8 years of experience in AI/ML, distributed systems, and backend engineering. Currently a Senior Software Engineer at Salesforce, he specializes in backend technologies and AI applications. He is a recognized thought leader, having spoken at major conferences like AAAI, ICLR, the WebConference, and Google Developer Groups, and has been featured on the Data Neighbours podcast alongside AI experts like Josh Starmer (StatQuest).

Previously, as Engineering Manager at TrueML, he led teams deploying ML models in production, boosting development velocity, client engagement, and operational efficiency. His leadership directly influenced revenue growth and cost optimization. He also held impactful engineering roles at Lucid Motors and Poynt, contributing to product innovation and system integration.

Karanbir holds a Master's in Computer Software Engineering from San Jose State University and is a Silicon Valley Innovation Challenge winner. Passionate about mentoring, he continues to contribute to the global tech community through public speaking and knowledge sharing.

Acknowledgement

There are a few people I would really want to thank for the continued and ongoing support they have given me during the writing of this book. First and foremost, I would like to thank my wife, my brother and my colleagues for continuously encouraging me to write this book.

I am grateful to the courses, tutorials, blogs, and the companies which gave me support throughout the learning process of Google Cloud. Thank you for all the support you provided.

My sincere gratitude also goes to the team at BPB Publications for being supportive throughout the journey.

Preface

Mainly due to the exponential growth of data, organizations need to scale up their IT infrastructure to maximize their business outcome. With the emergence of cloud computing, organizations are moving their workloads to public cloud in order to reduce the capital expenditure towards on-premises IT infrastructure and Google Cloud Platform is one of the major public cloud platforms present today.

This book will guide you to prepare for Google Cloud Associate Cloud Engineer certification with detailed explanation and pictorial demonstrations of GCP services. It contains 16 Chapters and 2 Practice Tests.

Chapter 1: Cloud Computing with GCP - This will introduce the readers to cloud computing with GCP, why cloud computing is needed, the drawbacks of on-premises infrastructure, what are public, private and hybrid cloud, and what are the major public cloud providers available in the market. It will also include Google Cloud Platform's history and list of services GCP provides. It will set the foundation to learn GCP.

Chapter 2: Overview of Google Cloud Associate Cloud Engineer Certification - This will include the details about the Google Cloud Associate Cloud Engineer Certification, how much time, how many questions, questions covering the parts of services etc.

Chapter 3: Understanding GCP Console, Cloud Shell, Billing and APIs - This will introduce the readers to the GCP Console, it will make them familiar with different portions of the console and show how to use those effectively with pictorial examples. It will also show how to enable API and Billing and finally how to use Cloud SDK from the command prompt/ or Cloud Shell.

Chapter 4: Identity and Access Management in GCP - This chapter will include the Identity and Access Management in GCP. It will introduce IAM roles, service accounts, different types of access control mechanisms, IAM best practices etc.

Chapter 5: Storage Solution in GCP (Block, Network File and Objects) - This chapter will discuss Google Cloud Object Storage service, public and private access, object life cycle and versioning. Access using console and Python Programming language.

Chapter 6: Understanding Different Databases in GCP - This chapter will introduce the SQL and NoSQL databases in GCP. It will also help you to identify the correct database choice for different types of requirements.

Chapter 7: Google Compute Engine - This chapter introduces the readers to the first compute services of GCP. Here we will learn about configuring VMs and understand the managed instance group.

Chapter 8: Cloud Run - This chapter introduces the service to build and deploy scalable containerized apps written in any language (including Go, Python, Java, Node.js, .NET, and Ruby) on a fully managed platform.

Chapter 9: Google Kubernetes Engine - This chapter will include the Kubernetes service inside GCP. We will learn about creating and managing the Kubernetes cluster and deploying services into it.

Chapter 10: Cloud Functions - We will study App Engine which is a fully managed, serverless platform for developing and hosting applications at scale.

Chapter 11: App Engine - This chapter will introduce a new concept called Functions as a Service in GCP with Cloud Functions. It is a serverless scalable service that offers event driven processing.

Chapter 12: Networking in GCP – Networking is a very important topic in Computer Science. It deals with communication between two systems. In Google Cloud Platform, Networking takes place via VPC, i.e., Virtual Private Cloud. It is the backbone of various services in GCP to stay connected among each other and communicate internally or outside of GCP.

Chapter 13: Networking in GCP Firewall Rules, Load Balancing, DNS, CDN and NAT– In this part 2 of Networking in GCP, here we are going to learn about Firewall Rules and load balancers and will see how these help in movement of network traffic in Google Cloud Platform along with Cloud DNS, CDN and NAT.

Chapter 14: Big Data Processing, AI, Deployment and Monitoring in GCP - This chapter covers the basic details around some of the services related to Big Data processing, artificial intelligence, deployment and monitoring in GCP. In various industries, Google Cloud Platform is the preferred choice for Bigdata and artificial intelligence. We are going to cover the basic understanding of these services.

Chapter 15: End-to-End Application Lifecycle in GCP Design, Build, Test, Deployment and Monitoring - This chapter covers the End-to-End Application lifecycle in Google Cloud Platform. We will start with requirement gathering and finish with monitoring of an application.

Chapter 16: Specific Topics for GCP ACE Exam - This chapter covers some of the specific topics required for GCP ACE certification exam.

Chapter 17: Practice Test 1- 20 Practice Questions on Certification exam.

Chapter 18: Practice Test 2- 20 Practice Questions on Certification exam.

Code Bundle and Coloured Images

Please follow the link to download the
Code Bundle and the *Coloured Images* of the book:

https://rebrand.ly/wiy52el

The code bundle for the book is also hosted on GitHub at
https://github.com/bpbpublications/Google-Cloud-Associate-Cloud-Engineer-Certification-Guide.
In case there's an update to the code, it will be updated on the existing GitHub repository.

We have code bundles from our rich catalogue of books and videos available at
https://github.com/bpbpublications. Check them out!

Errata

We take immense pride in our work at BPB Publications and follow best practices to ensure the accuracy of our content to provide with an indulging reading experience to our subscribers. Our readers are our mirrors, and we use their inputs to reflect and improve upon human errors, if any, that may have occurred during the publishing processes involved. To let us maintain the quality and help us reach out to any readers who might be having difficulties due to any unforeseen errors, please write to us at :

errata@bpbonline.com

Your support, suggestions and feedbacks are highly appreciated by the BPB Publications' Family.

Did you know that BPB offers eBook versions of every book published, with PDF and ePub files available? You can upgrade to the eBook version at www.bpbonline. com and as a print book customer, you are entitled to a discount on the eBook copy. Get in touch with us at :

business@bpbonline.com for more details.

At **www.bpbonline.com**, you can also read a collection of free technical articles, sign up for a range of free newsletters, and receive exclusive discounts and offers on BPB books and eBooks.

Piracy

If you come across any illegal copies of our works in any form on the internet, we would be grateful if you would provide us with the location address or website name. Please contact us at **business@bpbonline.com** with a link to the material.

If you are interested in becoming an author

If there is a topic that you have expertise in, and you are interested in either writing or contributing to a book, please visit **www.bpbonline.com**. We have worked with thousands of developers and tech professionals, just like you, to help them share their insights with the global tech community. You can make a general application, apply for a specific hot topic that we are recruiting an author for, or submit your own idea.

Reviews

Please leave a review. Once you have read and used this book, why not leave a review on the site that you purchased it from? Potential readers can then see and use your unbiased opinion to make purchase decisions. We at BPB can understand what you think about our products, and our authors can see your feedback on their book. Thank you!

For more information about BPB, please visit **www.bpbonline.com**.

Join our book's Discord space

Join the book's Discord Workspace for Latest updates, Offers, Tech happenings around the world, New Release and Sessions with the Authors:

https://discord.bpbonline.com

Table of Contents

CHAPTER 1
Cloud Computing with GCP

Introduction

This chapter will cover the introduction of cloud computing with **Google Cloud Platform** (**GCP**). We will understand why cloud computing is needed, the drawbacks of on-premises infrastructure, the meaning of public, private, and hybrid cloud infrastructure, and the major public cloud providers available in the market. It will also include GCP's history and the types of services it provides. We will also learn a brief description of most of the services in GCP. This chapter will set the foundation for learning the GCP.

Structure

The chapter covers the following topics:

- Cloud computing
- On-premise infrastructure and its drawbacks
- Public, private, and hybrid cloud
- Major public cloud providers
- IaaS, PaaS, and SaaS
- Introduction to GCP

- Google Cloud Platform resource hierarchy
- Brief introduction about different GCP services

Objectives

By the end of this chapter, you will be able to understand the cloud computing concepts, the difference between cloud computing and on-premise-based computing, the drawbacks of on-premise-based infrastructure, the difference between **Infrastructure as a Service (IaaS)**, **Platform as a Service (PaaS)**, **Software as a Service (SaaS)**, a brief about various GCP services solving challenges around storage, computing, artificial intelligence, etc.

Cloud computing

Cloud computing is the on-demand availability of computing resources like storage, infrastructure, etc., without actually owning any of these. It is very much like renting the services which are required. In this way, the capital expenditure towards hardware can be minimized, and users can focus more on the application than on managing and monitoring the hardware infrastructure.

On premise infrastructure and its drawbacks

On-premise infrastructure means owning the computing resources. It requires upfront investment towards hardware, which leads to higher capital expenditure before even focusing on the actual product. Secondly, managing the infrastructure and monitoring these needs specialized resources, which again increases IT expenditure. Upgradation and licensing of this hardware again fall under the IT department of the organization, along with the need for scalability with the exponential growth of data and digital initiatives.

Public, private, and hybrid cloud

In cloud computing, when we are using multi-tenant platforms (hardware) for storage, infrastructure, etc., then it is called a public cloud. To be precise, multiple organizations use the same shared platform (hardware).

When the usage of the cloud service provider's hardware is single-tenant, then it is a private cloud; that is, only a single organization is using the hardware that is rented, and no other organizations are using it.

Sometimes, organizations need to keep their data movement within on-premises hardware due to security restrictions or the governing body's policy. At that time, both on-premises and public cloud are used to deliver a particular business application or solution. This type of arrangement is called a hybrid cloud.

Major public cloud providers

There are many cloud service providers at this moment, but the majority of the market share is with AWS from Amazon, Azure from Microsoft, and GCP from Google. Take a look at the following figure:

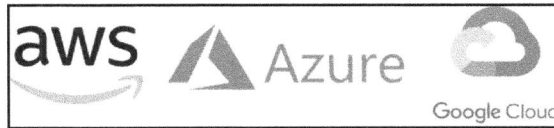

Figure 1.1: *Major public cloud providers*

IaaS, PaaS, and SaaS

Starting with IaaS. It is a cloud computing model where you rent the infrastructure. The infrastructure can be **virtual machine** (**VMs**), storage, network, etc. The service provider takes care of hosting and maintaining the infrastructure, and you need to take care of the operating system, data, and applications.

When it comes to PaaS, Cloud service providers will provide a platform, and they will manage the backend infrastructure completely. You do not have to worry about the infrastructure. You just need to write the code for your application and manage the data and applications.

SaaS is a software distribution model that connects its customers mostly by internet. It normally comes with a subscription-based software services. Examples of SaaS are very common to us, like Dropbox, Workplace, Netflix, YouTube, Salesforce etc.

Introduction to GCP

GCP is a cloud computing platform offered by Google. It started its journey in April 2008 with **App Engine** as its first service which was generally available in November 2011.

GCP offers various services, which can be categorized as storage, computing, database, networking, data analytics, security, AI, monitoring and logging, API, etc. It has 11% of the market share at the start of 2023, and it is growing daily.

Google Cloud Platform resource hierarchy

For GCP resources, the hierarchy is **Organization** | **Folders** | **Projects** | **Services**. The organization is like a company, say *abc.com*. Folders are specific to the area of services the company provides or the actual products of the company or features. Under a folder, there are different projects, mostly for various environments. These can be defined as per the organization's needs and choices. Take a look at the following figure:

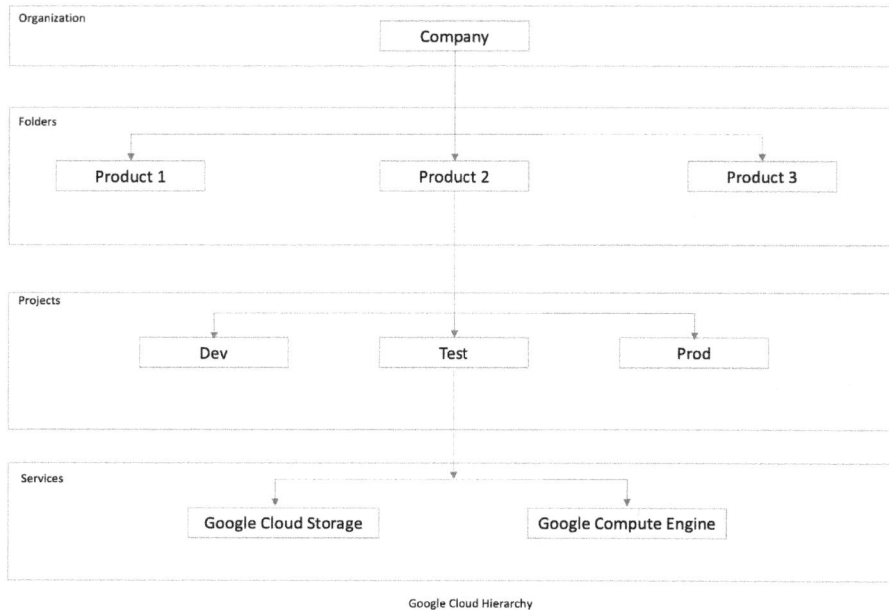

Google Cloud Hierarchy

Figure 1.2: *GCP resource hierarchy*

Brief introduction about different GCP services

Let us understand each service one by one. For ease of understanding, we are going to categorize the services in different areas like storage, compute, network, etc.

Storage related services

The storage services are as follows:

- **Google Cloud Storage:** Google Cloud Storage is an object storage service. It can store any type or any amount of data. It is good for building Data Lakes and static content delivery websites like images, video streaming, etc. You can retrieve the data any time you want. It can also be used as a low-cost archival solution.

- **Persistent Disk:** It is a block storage service mainly used with Compute Engines/ VMs and GCP's Kubernetes service **Google Kubernetes Engine** (**GKE**). It can be a storage solution attached to VMs as Disks. It can also be used as storage for installed databases.

- **Filestore:** It is a fully managed service mainly used for file storage for application migration.

- **Data transfer services**: It is a service that transfers data between one cloud service provider to GCP or from on-premises to GCP. The data transfer services are as follows:

- **Transfer appliance:** It is used to collect and move data from limited connectivity areas or bandwidth-constrained locations.

- **Local SSD**: It is an ephemeral locally attached block storage for VMs and containers.

- **Google Cloud Backup and disaster recovery (DR):** It is a service for managed backup and DR to protect file systems, databases, and VMs. It can also be used to keep a backup of on-premise workloads to GCP.

- **Artifact registry:** It is used as a centralized repository of container images, OS, and language packages. It is mostly used with CI/CD pipelines in various environments.

Compute related services

The compute services are as follows:

- **Compute Engine:** It is a general-purpose VM. It can be used for web server hosting, **Extract, Transform, Load** (ETL) and application servers. It can integrate with various GCP services. It can be used as a replica of an on-premises VM.

- **Google Kubernetes Engine:** It is a Google-managed implementation of Kubernetes, which is actually an open-source container orchestration platform. It is a reliable and secure way to deploy containerized applications.

- **Cloud Run:** It is a highly scalable service to deploy containerized applications. It comes with two versions, one is fully managed Cloud Run, and another is Cloud Run for Anthos. We will discuss this in more detail in later chapters.

- **App Engine:** It is a fully managed and serverless platform to build applications using common programming languages.

- **Batch:** It is a fully managed and dynamically scalable batch service to schedule, queue, and execute containerized or script-based batch jobs on Compute Engine.

Database related services

The database services are as follows:

- **Cloud SQL:** A fully managed MySQL or PostgreSQL or SQL Server database. It can used as a regular RDBMS application database.

- **AlloyDB for PostgreSQL**: It is a PostgreSQL compatible GCP's database service.

- **Spanner:** Cloud Spanner is a very highly scalable global cloud native database with 99.999% of availability.

- **Bigtable:** It is a highly scalable, fully managed and NoSQL database service for larger workloads with 99.999% availability.

- **Firestore:** Highly scalable and massively popular document database service for mobile, web, and server development that offers rich and fast querying and high availability up to 99.999%.

- **Memorystore:** It is a fully managed in-memory database (**Redis and Memcached**) for sub-milliseconds of data access. Memorystore for **Redis Cluster** is a fully managed service that can scale up to TBs of keyspace and tens of millions of operations per second.

- **BigQuery:** It is a serverless, highly scalable and cost-effective cloud data warehouse designed for business agility and offers up to 99.99% availability.

- **Partner solution databases:** There are partner solution databases available in Google Cloud, like MongoDB Atlas, Neo4j Aura, etc.

Network services

The network services are as follows:

- **Virtual Private Cloud (VPC):** VPC is used to provision, connect, and isolate GCP resources using global network of Google. It defines the networking policies ingress, egress and within GCP. It includes the creation of subnets using IP range selection, routing, firewalls, Cloud VPN, etc.

- **Cloud Domain Name Systems (DNS):** It is a domain naming system service provided by GCP. It translates domain names to IP addresses. Its features include domain registration and management, authoritative DNS lookup, and anycast name server.

- **Private service connects:** It connects applications running within a VPC inside GCP with third-party applications and other Google Services. It also helps secure the application data transfer by keeping it inside the Google Cloud's network.

- **Cloud Content Delivery Network (CDN):** Cloud CDN accelerates content delivery for different websites and applications inside Compute Engine using Google's globally distributed edge caches. Cloud CDN lowers network latency, offloads origins, and reduces overall serving costs. It delivers the content globally with anycast IP.

- **Cloud load balancing:** It is used for application and network load balancing. It quickly scales up applications based on demand. It distributes load-balanced compute resources in single/multiple regions and nearer to the users while achieving high-availability requirements. It can put resources behind a single anycast IP, scale up or down using intelligent autoscaling and integrate with Cloud CDN.

- **Cloud armor**: It usually works with an application load balancer and provides defense against infrastructure DDoS attacks. It supports hybrid and multi-cloud deployments. It provides geo-based and IP-based access control.

- **Cloud IDS:** Cloud IDS is an **intrusion detection service** that provides threat detection for different attacks on the network like intrusions, malware, spyware, and command-and-control. It provides full visibility into network traffic.

- **Cloud NAT**: Google Cloud's managed network address translation service enables us to provision application instances without any public IP addresses while allowing controlled and efficient internet access. Outside resources cannot directly access any of the private instances behind the Cloud NAT gateway, helping keep the Google Cloud VPC completely isolated and secure.

- **VPC service controls:** It helps users to define a security perimeter for the API-based services like Cloud Storage buckets, Cloud Bigtable instances, and BigQuery datasets to help resolving data exfiltration risks. It also enables enterprises to keep their sensitive data private while leveraging Google Cloud's fully managed storage and data processing solutions.

- **Network connectivity center:** The network connectivity center provides a unique ability to connect on-premises, Google Cloud, and other cloud enterprise networks and manage them with a single, centralized, logical hub on GCP.

- **Service directory:** It provides a single place to publish, discover, and connect all application's services and reduces management and operations complexity.

- **Network intelligence center:** The network intelligence center provides complete network status and keeps on monitoring along with proactive network verification.

- **Network service tiers:** It delivers the traffic on Google's high-performance global network, runs cost-sensitive workloads and helps in choosing the right tier for the workload etc.

Data analytics services

The data analytics services are as follows:

- **Dataproc:** Dataproc is a fully managed and highly scalable service for running Apache Hadoop, Apache Spark, Apache Flink, Presto, and various open source tools and frameworks. We can use Dataproc for processing petabytes of data present in data lakes, streaming sources, complex ETLs, spark based machine learning and etc.

- **Dataplex**: Dataplex is an intelligent data fabric that enables organizations to centrally discover, manage, monitor, and govern data across different data lakes, data warehouses, and data marts. It provides access to trusted data and empowers analytics and AI at scale. It also helps in reducing data silos within the same organization.

- **Cloud data fusion:** It is a fully managed and cloud-native data integration solution. It removes bottlenecks by enabling nontechnical users using a code-free graphical interface that provides point-and-click data integration. Data fusion is built using an open-source project CDAP.

- **Dataflow:** It is a unified stream and batch data processing. It is a serverless, fast, and cost-effective service for data processing. Dataflow is a fully managed service. That means Google manages all of the resources needed to run Dataflow. When you run a Dataflow job, the Dataflow service allocates a pool of worker VMs to execute the pipeline. You do not need to provision or manage these VMs.

- **Cloud composer:** It is a fully managed workflow orchestration service built on top of Apache Airflow. Cloud composer's managed nature allows you to focus on authoring, scheduling, and monitoring your workflows as opposed to provisioning resources. You need to use Python for writing Airflow DAGs.

- **Dataprep:** Dataprep is an intelligent data related service by Trifacta for visually exploring and cleaning structured and unstructured data, making it ready for analysis, reporting, and machine learning. Dataprep is serverless and works at any scale.

- **Pub/Sub:** Pub/Sub is an asynchronous and scalable messaging service that separates services producing messages from the services processing those messages. It allows services to communicate asynchronously, with latencies in the order of 100 milliseconds.

- **BigQuery:** BigQuery is a serverless and cost-effective enterprise data warehouse that works across clouds and scales with your data. Use built-in ML/AI and BI for insights at scale. It is a database solution as well and using BigQuery based SQL, you can create BigQuery Proc to perform various transformations within data.

Security and identity services

The security and identity services are as follows:

- **Identity and access management (IAM):** It allows the administrators to authorize a person who can take action on specific resources/services, giving the full control and visibility to manage Google Cloud resources centrally. For enterprises with complex organizational structures, hundreds of workgroups, and many projects, IAM provides a unified view of security policy across the entire organization, with built-in auditing mechanism to ease the compliance processes.

- **Secret manager:** Secret manager is a secure and convenient storage system for API keys, certificates, passwords, and other sensitive information. Secret manager provides a central place and single source of truth to manage, access, and audit secrets across GCP.

- **Security command center:** It is a built-in security and risk management service for GCP. It helps in identifying configuration issues and vulnerabilities, it points out cyber risks and helps in remediation. It can detect threats to the Google Cloud resources, monitor and manage regulatory compliance.

- **Cloud identity:** A unified identity, access, app, and **endpoint management (IAM/EMM)** platform. It gives users easy access to apps with single sign-on. The **multi-factor authentication (MFA)** protects user and company data and Endpoint management enforces policies for personal and corporate devices.

- **Identity aware proxy (IAP):** It provides a single point of control for managing the user access in web applications and cloud resources. It can also protect access to applications hosted on Google Cloud, other clouds, and on-premises.

- **Cloud data loss prevention:** Cloud **data loss prevention (DLP)** provides automated sensitive data discovery and classification, sensitive data intelligence for security assessments, De-identification, masking, tokenization, and bucketing.

AI and machine learning services

The artificial intelligence and machine learning services are as follows:

- **Vertex AI:** Vertex AI is a ML platform that provides you the opportunity to train and deploy ML models and AI applications. Vertex AI combines data engineering, data science, and ML engineering workflows, enabling users to collaborate using a common toolset.

- **Vertex AI Workbench:** Vertex AI Workbench is a Jupyter notebook-based development environment for the complete data science workflow. You can interact with Vertex AI and other GCP services from within a Vertex AI Workbench instance's Jupyter Notebook. Its integrations and features can make it easier to access data, process data faster, schedule notebook runs, etc. Vertex AI Workbench provides a managed notebooks option with built-in integrations that help you set up an end-to-end notebook-based production environment.

- **AutoML:** AutoML enables developers with limited machine learning expertise to train high-quality models specific to their business needs. You can quickly build your own custom machine learning model.

- **Vision AI:** It is a fully managed development environment Vertex AI Vision to create your own computer vision applications or derive insights from images and videos with pre-trained APIs, AutoML, or custom models.

- **Natural language AI:** Derive insights from unstructured text using Google machine learning.

- **Dialogflow:** It is a conversational AI as virtual agents. It is a comprehensive development platform for chatbots and voicebots.

- **Video AI:** Enable powerful content discovery and engaging video experiences.
- **Speech-to-text and text-to-speech:** Accurately convert speech into text or vice versa with an API powered by the best of Google's AI research and technology.

Operations related services

The services related to operations are as follows:

- **Cloud logging:** It is a fully managed real-time log management with storage, search, analysis, and alerting capabilities at an exabyte scale.
- **Cloud monitoring:** Using this service, you will gain visibility into the performance, availability, and health of your applications and infrastructure.
- **Cloud trace:** Cloud Trace is a distributed tracing system for Google Cloud that collects latency data from applications and displays it in near real-time in the GCP console.

API related services

The services related to API are as follows:

- **Apigee:** A fully managed comprehensive offering from Google to build, manage, and secure APIs. Managing high value/volume of APIs with enterprise-level security.
- **API gateway:** It is a fully managed service to create, deploy, and manage APIs built using Compute Engine, App Engine, Cloud Functions, and Cloud Run.
- **Apigee hybrid:** An API management solution for use in any kind of environment on-premises or any cloud. It is used to maintain and process API traffic in the Kubernetes cluster.
- **Cloud endpoints:** It is a customer-managed service to run co-located gateway or private networking. It is used to manage gRPC services with a locally hosted gateway for private networking.

Developer tools

Developer tools are as follows:

- **Cloud Code:** Cloud Code is a set of IDE plugins for popular IDEs that make it easier to create, deploy, and integrate applications with Google Cloud.
- **Cloud Build:** It is a serverless CI/CD platform to build, test and deploy applications within GCP. It can scale up and down with no infrastructure to set up, upgrade, or scale. It is used to run builds in a fully managed environment in Google Cloud with connectivity within the private network (**https://cloud.google.com/build/docs/private-pools/private-pools-overview**)

- **Cloud Deploy:** Cloud Deploy creates deployment pipelines for GKE, Cloud Run, and Anthos. It is a fully managed continuous delivery service for easy scaling.

- **Cloud Scheduler:** Cloud Scheduler is a fully managed enterprise-grade cron job scheduler. It helps to schedule virtually any job, including batch, Big Data jobs, cloud infrastructure operations, etc.

- **Cloud Deployment Manager:** Google Cloud Deployment Manager is an infrastructure deployment service that automates the creation and management of GCP resources. You can write flexible templates and configuration files and use them to create deployments for a variety of Google Cloud services, such as Cloud Storage, Compute Engine, and Cloud SQL, configured in such a way to work together.

- **Cloud Software Development Kit (SDK):** This combination of libraries and tools for interacting with Google Cloud products and services. It integrates APIs using client libraries for Java, Python, Node.js, Ruby, Go, .NET, PHP, and ABAP.

- **gcloud command line interface (CLI):** The **gcloud CLI** manages authentication, local configuration, developer workflow - CI/CD, and other interactions with Google Cloud resources. It is used to create a Compute Engine VM instance, manage a GKE cluster, deploy an App Engine application, etc.

- **Cloud Shell**: Cloud Shell is an online development and operations environment accessible anywhere within the browser. GCP resources can be managed with its online terminal preloaded with gcloud command-line tool, kubectl and more. You can also develop, build, debug, and deploy your cloud-based apps using this online Cloud Shell Editor.

Conclusion

We have reached the end of the chapter. This was an introduction to most of the Google Cloud services which we need to encounter while working on GCP regularly, but there are many other services apart from these that cater to more specific needs, sometimes specific to the functional domain like Healthcare or technical areas like IoT or Blockchain, etc.

Join our book's Discord space

Join the book's Discord Workspace for Latest updates, Offers, Tech happenings around the world, New Release and Sessions with the Authors:

https://discord.bpbonline.com

CHAPTER 2
Overview of Google Cloud Associate Cloud Engineer Certification

Introduction

This chapter of the book will co ver an overview of Google Cloud Associate Engineer Certification, the exam guide, topics, how to set up an exam, and more. It will help the students become familiar with the certification examination.

Structure

This chapter covers the following topics on GCP Associate Cloud Engineer Certification:

- Cloud engineer
- Exam details
- Target audience
- Mode of exam
- Syllabus
- How to set up an exam
- Preparation strategy

Objectives

By the end of this chapter, you will be able to understand the exam, the number of questions, the mode of questions, the topics, and how to prepare and register for the exam.

Cloud engineer

The role of cloud engineers in any organization is to deploy applications, monitor operations, and manage enterprise solutions in the cloud environment. For GCP-based solutions, they need to use Google Cloud Console and the command-line interface to perform common platform-related tasks in order to manage deployed solutions on Google Cloud. Due to the above responsibilities, the Associate Cloud Engineer exam assesses your ability to:

- Set up a cloud environment in GCP
- Configure a cloud solution
- Implement and deploy the solution in Google Cloud
- Configure access and security policies in GCP for an organization
- Monitoring an application in the GCP environment

Exam details

Length of this associate level exam is 2 hours, registration fee is $125 + tax (at the time of writing this book), aspirants can appear in English, Japanese, Spanish and Portuguese languages. There will be 50 to 60 questions in the exam. Effective from October 1, 2022 the Associate Cloud Engineer certification is valid for three years from the date of certification.

Target audience

Let us understand who should take this certification exam:

- Cloud engineers started working in GCP or other cloud providers.
- On premise engineers is where GCP migration is planned in an enterprise.
- Students planning to start their cloud journey.
- Professionals willing to gain knowledge on Google Cloud Platform.

Mode of exam

This exam can be given in two ways: one is in an online proctored environment, and another is by going to an exam center.

Syllabus

Here, we will look into the topics which we are going to study in upcoming chapters. These can be thought as syllabus for this certification exam.

Setting up cloud environment

In this book, the following topics will be discussed:

- **Projects, accounts, CLI, gcloud, and SDK:**
  o   Creating resource hierarchy
  o   Applying the organizational policies to the resource hierarchy
  o   Granting IAM roles within a project
  o   Managing users and user related groups in Cloud Identity (manually and automated)
  o   Enabling the APIs
  o   Provisioning and setting up services in Google Cloud's operations suite
  o   **Command line interface (CLI)** and Cloud SDK

- **Billing configuration**:
  o   Creating billing accounts
  o   Linking projects to the billing account
  o   Establishing budgets and alerts for billing
  o   Billing exports

Planning and configuring a cloud based solution

In this book, we will discuss the following topics:

- **Compute resources:**
  o   Appropriate compute choices for workloads
  o   Preemptible virtual machines and custom machine types
  o   Pricing calculator

- **Data storage options**:
  o   Cloud SQL, BigQuery, Firestore, Cloud Spanner, Cloud Bigtable
  o   Storage options

- **Network resources**:
  o   Load balancing

o   Identifying resource locations in a network for availability

o   Configuration of Cloud DNS

Deploying and implementing a cloud based solution

In this section, we will learn how to deploy and implement cloud based solution:

- **Compute engine:**
  o   Launching of a compute instance via Google Cloud console and Cloud SDK

  o   Assign disks, availability policy, SSH keys for Compute Engine VMs

  o   Autoscaling of managed instance group using an instance template

  o   Custom SSH key for VM instances

  o   Installation and configuration of Cloud Monitoring and logging agent

- **Google Kubernetes Engine resources:**
  o   Enabling kubectl

  o   Different configurations like AutoPilot, regional clusters, private clusters, etc.

  o   Deploying a containerized application

  o   Configuring monitoring and logging

- **Cloud Run and Cloud Functions resources:**
  o   Deploying an application, configuring scaling, versions, and traffic splitting

  o   Deploying an application that receives Pub/Sub or GCS events

- **Data solutions:**
  o   Cloud SQL, Firestore, BigQuery, Cloud Spanner, Pub/Sub, Cloud Bigtable, Dataproc, Dataflow, Cloud Storage, etc.

  o   Different data loading techniques

- **AI solutions:**
  o   Understanding various AI related services

- **Networking resources:**
  o   VPC with subnets

  o   Custom-mode VPC and shared VPC

  o   Internal-only IP address, Google private access, static external and private IP address, network tags

  o   Spinning up resources under VPC

- o Ingress and egress firewall rules for a VPC
- o Cloud VPN
- o Global HTTP(S) load balancer, Global SSL Proxy load balancer, Global TCP Proxy load balancer, regional network load balancer and regional internal load balancer

- **Cloud Marketplace:**
  - o Cloud Marketplace options
  - o Deployment of a Cloud Marketplace solution

- **Infrastructure as code:**
  - o Cloud Foundation Toolkit templates
  - o Config Connector in Google Kubernetes Engine in order to create, update, delete, and secure resources

Ensuring successful operation of a cloud based solution

In this section, we will ensure the successful operation of a cloud based solution:

- **Compute Engine resources:**
  - o Managing a VM instance
  - o Remote connection to the VM
  - o Attaching a GPU
  - o VM inventory details
  - o Create a snapshot/image from a VM, view snapshots/images, delete a snapshot/image
  - o Working with instance groups like setting up autoscaling parameters, assigning instance templates, creating an instance template, removing instance group

- **Google Kubernetes Engine resources:**
  - o Cluster inventory (nodes, pods, services)
  - o Docker images and viewing their details in the GCP's Artifact Registry
  - o Working with node pools, pods, and services
  - o Working with stateful applications like. persistent volumes, stateful sets
  - o Horizontal and vertical autoscaling configurations

- **Cloud Run resources:**
  - o Traffic splitting and autoscaling parameters
  - o Cloud Run vs. Cloud Run for Anthos
- **Storage and database solutions:**
  - o Cloud Storage buckets
  - o Object life cycle in Cloud Storage bucket,
  - o Executing queries in various database solutions (e.g., Cloud SQL, BigQuery, Cloud Spanner, Datastore, Cloud Bigtable)
  - o Estimating costs for various data storage resources
  - o Backing up and restoring database instances like Cloud SQL, Datastore
  - o Running jobs and monitoring in Dataproc, Dataflow, or BigQuery
- **Networking resources:**
  - o Adding subnet to an existing VPC
  - o Expanding subnet to have more IP: addresses
  - o Reserving static external or internal IP addresses
  - o Cloud DNS, Cloud NAT, load balancers, and firewall rules
- **Monitoring and logging:**
  - o Cloud Monitoring alerts
  - o Cloud Monitoring custom metrics
  - o Log sinks, exporting logs
  - o Log routing
  - o Viewing and filtering logs in Cloud Logging
  - o Cloud Trace and Cloud Debug

Configuring access and security

In this section, we will configure access and security:

- **Identity and access management (IAM):**
  - o IAM policies
  - o Role types and custom IAM roles.
- **Service accounts and monitoring audit logs:**
  - o Creating service accounts
  - o Using service accounts in IAM policies with minimum permissions
  - o Assigning service accounts to resources

- o Managing IAM of a service account
- o Managing service accounts
- o Creating and managing short-lived service account credentials
- o Viewing audit logs.

How to set up an exam

The following are the steps to set up an exam:

1. Navigate to **https://cloud.google.com/learn/certification/cloud-engineer**

Associate Cloud Engineer

Associate Cloud Engineers deploy applications, monitor operations, and manage enterprise solutions. They use Google Cloud Console and the command-line interface to perform common platform-based tasks to maintain one or more deployed solutions that leverage Google-managed or self-managed services on Google Cloud.

The Associate Cloud Engineer exam assesses your ability to:

✓ Set up a cloud solution environment

✓ Plan and configure a cloud solution

✓ Deploy and implement a cloud solution

✓ Ensure successful operation of a cloud solution

✓ Configure access and security

Register   View FAQs

Figure 2.1: Associate Cloud Engineer Exam

2. Click on **Register**, and a new tab will be opened (**https://webassessor.com/googlecloud**):

Ready to start?

Dear candidate,

The following guidelines will help streamline your registration and testing experience.

- Register for your exam as far in advance as possible.
  - Appointments are set up for every 15 minutes around the clock.
  - Top of the hour appointments tend to fill up first. Consider scheduling your exam on the quarter hour.
- Appointments at the end of the month are in high demand. Scheduling your exam earlier in the month provides the best chance at your first-choice time slot.
  - Consider scheduling your exam at a test center if remote delivery options are limited.
  - If you need to reschedule your appointment, do so as soon as possible to maximize appointment options and to avoid late reschedule fees.
- When registering, ensure that your first and last name (surname) exactly matches your government ID.
  - If the information does not match exactly, you will not be able to test.
  - You may incur additional rescheduling fees if the discrepancy is discovered on your test day.
- If you are testing online, confirm you have sufficient administrative rights on your device to download all required software.
  - Ensure your internet connection is reliable, your camera is working, and your desk surface is clear.
  - See Kryterion Support for resources to help you prepare for your exam.

Google Cloud certification team

Please log in with your Google Cloud Webassessor account to see our catalog and register for an exam.

| Login |
| Password |

Forgot password?

LOGIN

Figure 2.2: Login to the portal

3. Log in to the Google Cloud Webassessor account. If you do not have an account, create a new one:

Google Cloud   Powered By **kryterion** by DRAKE INTERNATIONAL

Receipts   Register For An Exam   My Assessments   **Home**

You last logged in 19 June 2022 at 4:14AM MST.

Make sure you review the retake policy and recertification eligibility criteria before you take an exam. There is a limit on the number of times you can take an exam and a waiting period between attempts (even if you are taking the same exam in a different language). It is your responsibility to adhere to these terms and conditions to avoid possible suspension or rejection of exam results.

Launching your online exam? Due to high volume, you may experience additional wait time (15-20 mins) before connecting with a proctor. Do not disconnect. We appreciate your patience!

REGISTER FOR AN EXAM

Kryterion, Inc. uses cookies to track session reliability, maintain session security, and understand user interaction with our website. By browsing our website, you consent to our use of cookies and other tracking technologies. For more information please see our Privacy Policy.

Privacy Policy | Terms of Service   © 2023   KRYTERION, Inc. and KRYTERION, Limited - All Rights Reserved.   kryterion

Figure 2.3: Register for the exam

4. Click on **REGISTER FOR AN EXAM**:

Official identification is verified at the time of your exam and must match the information in your user profile. To register, please select an exam from a menu below.

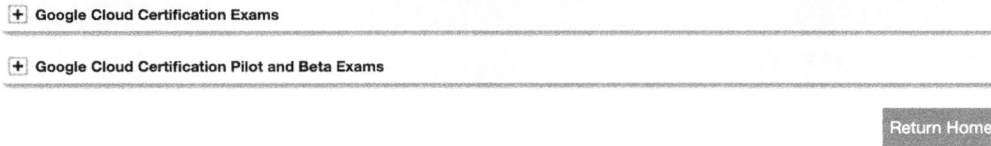

⊞ **Google Cloud Certification Exams**

⊞ **Google Cloud Certification Pilot and Beta Exams**

Return Home

Figure 2.4: Choose the exam

5. Expand Google Cloud Certification Exams:

Google Cloud Certified - Associate Cloud Engineer (English)	This is the Google Cloud Certified - Associate Cloud Engineer exam. Please refer to the exam guide for current topics that may appear on the exam. You may attempt an exam at a test center or online and each attempt regardless of delivery method or language counts toward the total permissible attempts and the waiting period between attempts still applies (see our Retake Policy).	multiple		
Google Cloud Certified - Associate Cloud Engineer (English)	Pre-requisites:: Retake Policy :		Onsite Proctored	USD 125.00
Google Cloud Certified - Associate Cloud Engineer (English)	Pre-requisites:: Retake Policy :		Remote Proctored	USD 125.00

Figure 2.5: Choose the mode of the exam

6. Select the one based on your convenience.

7. Choose the date and time and follow the instructions to set up an exam.

8. For Remote Proctored Exam, please install required software package as instructed if any and it is best to appear the exam from personal laptop where you have all the access privileges.

Preparation strategy

To clear the exam, you need to have a solid preparation in both theoretical and practical aspects. For a beginner, it is better to have 3 months of time preparation plan.

1. Understand the syllabus.

2. Create a personal GCP account. It will have $ 300 credit for three months

3. From the next chapter onwards, read the topics and practice the same using your personal GCP account.

4. Two hours daily for three months, during which one-hour theory and one-hour practical are advised.

5. At the end of every chapter, there will be practice questions; try to solve those.

6. At the end of the book, solve all the question sets at least two times each.

7. On the exam day, just relax and appear for the exam.

8. All the best.

Conclusion

We have reached the end of our first section of the book i.e. Introduction to cloud computing with GCP and we have covered the overview of the Associate Cloud Engineer exam. Now, from the next chapter onwards, we will learn about various services present in GCP, and we will put emphasis on the portions of the services which are present in the exam syllabus.

Sample questions

There will be multiple choice single select and multiple choice multi select questions in the exam. We will see examples of all these types in this section.

Multiple choice single select questions

1. **The CFO of your company feels you are spending too much on BigQuery. You are finding that a few long-running queries are costing more than they should. You would like to experiment with different ways of writing these queries. You'd like to know the estimated cost of running each query without running them. How will you achieve this?**

a. Use –dry-run option with a bq query command

b. Use Pricing Calculator provided by GCP

c. Use estimate cost option with bq command

d. Use estimate cost option with gcloud command

2. **You need to create a Kubernetes cluster for a high availability set of applications. Which cluster type would you choose?**

a. Regional

b. Multi Zonal

c. Single Zone

d. Multi Regional

Answers

1.a

2.d

Multiple choice multi select questions

1. **You need to create a backend service using serverless GCP based computing   service, which compute options will you select? (Multiple answers)**

   a.   Compute Engine

   b.   Cloud Run

   c.   GKE

   d.   App Engine

   e.   Cloud Functions

2. **Your organization has appointed a third-party auditor for GCP usage within the organization. They have asked for access to any audit logs available in GCP. What type of audit logs are available for each project, folder, and organization? (Multiple answers)**

   a.   Data Access

   b.   Admin Activity

   c.   Policy Access

   d.   User Login Information

   e.   System Event

Answers

   1.   b, d

   2.   a, b, e

Note: These questions are given here as examples of Google Cloud - Associate Cloud Engineer certification examination, detailed explanations will be available in subsequent chapters.

Join our book's Discord space

Join the book's Discord Workspace for Latest updates, Offers, Tech happenings around the world, New Release and Sessions with the Authors:

https://discord.bpbonline.com

CHAPTER 3

Understanding GCP Console, Cloud Shell, Billing, and APIs

Introduction

This chapter will take you inside **Google Cloud Platform** (**GCP**). It will certainly help you to get started with GCP by setting up the project, billing, Cloud Shell etc. These are the foundation steps to dive inside the GCP. Services, billing, APIs are part of projects. For different projects, you need to enable these separately and these are completely separated from one project to another. This chapter will provide the knowledge about various regions and zones in GCP.

Structure

The chapter covers the following topics:

- Creating a GCP project
- Understanding GCP console
- Cloud Shell
- gcloud Command Line Interface
- Regions and zones
- Cloud Billing
- Cloud APIs
- Cloud SDK

Objectives

By the end of this chapter, you will have a complete understanding of the GCP console. You will learn how to navigate to different services in GCP. You will be able to activate Cloud Shell for GCP projects, configure billing and APIs. Usage of Cloud SDK and **Command Line Interface (CLI)** will be shown. You will become friendly with gcloud commands.

Creating a GCP project

GCP project is the entry point to use any of the services in GCP. In order to create a project in GCP please follow the below steps:

1. Go to **https://cloud.google.com/?hl=en** . Click on **Get started for free**:

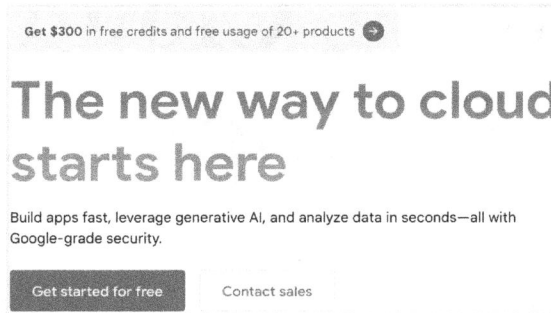

Figure 3.1: Getting started with GCP

2. Provide the required information and payment information:

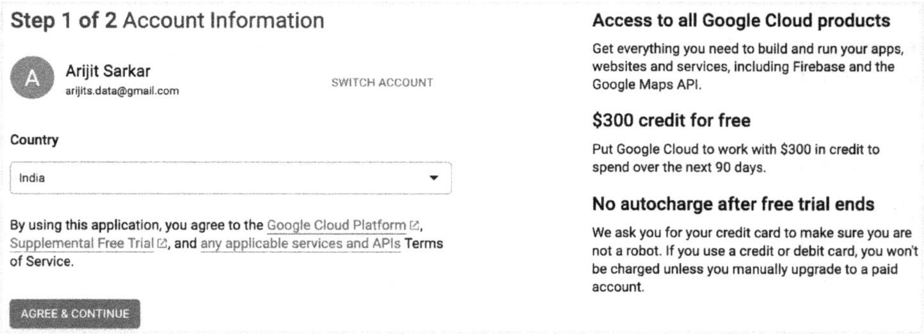

Figure 3.2: Account information in GCP

3. After completing all the steps, **My First Project** will be created:

Figure 3.3: My First Project

4. Click on the drop down beside **My First Project** in the above image, and the below screen will appear:

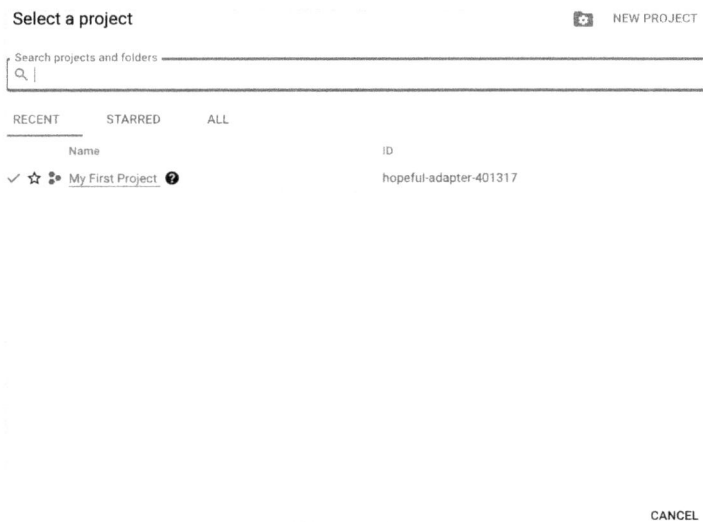

Select a project   📷 NEW PROJECT

Search projects and folders
🔍 |

RECENT   STARRED   ALL

Name   ID
✓ ☆ :• My First Project ❓   hopeful-adapter-401317

CANCEL

Figure 3.4: Project selection page

5. Click on **New Project** to create a new GCP project and provide a suitable name based on your choice:

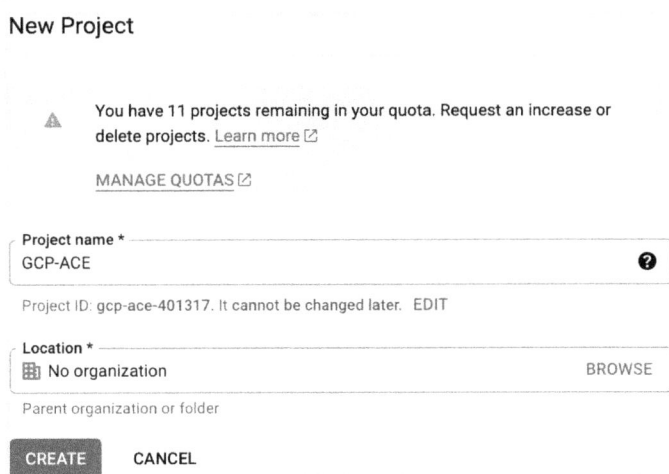

New Project

⚠ You have 11 projects remaining in your quota. Request an increase or delete projects. Learn more ☐

MANAGE QUOTAS ☐

Project name *
GCP-ACE   ❓

Project ID: gcp-ace-401317. It cannot be changed later.   EDIT

Location *
🎫 No organization   BROWSE

Parent organization or folder

CREATE   CANCEL

Figure 3.5: Create new project

6. A new project named **GCP-ACE** has been created:

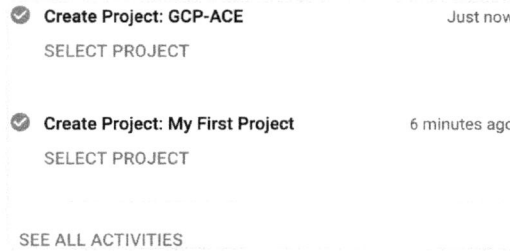

Figure 3.6: New project got created

7. You can activate your full account based on how you are going to practice:

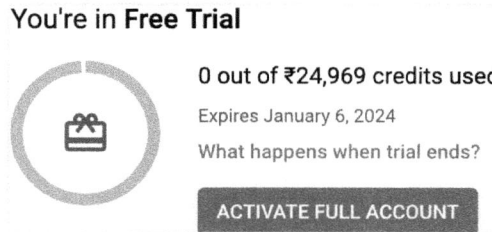

Figure 3.7: Credits usage

8. From the project selection drop down select the new project:

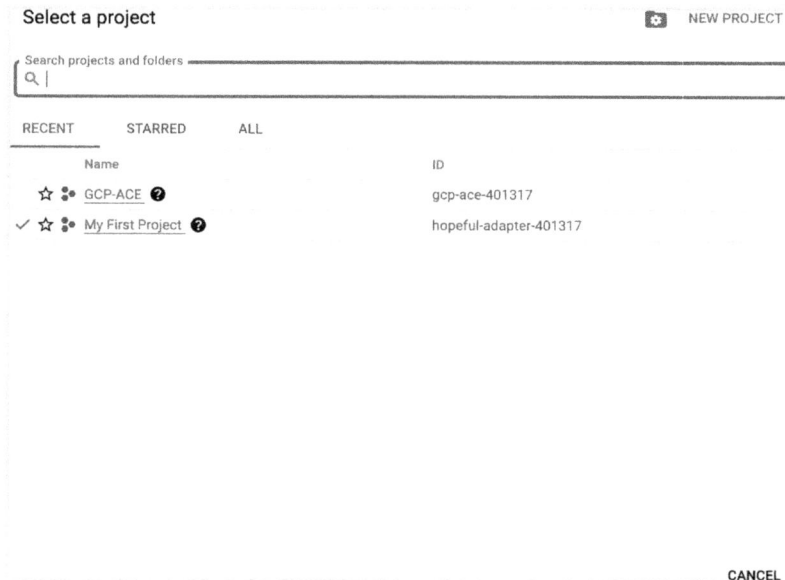

Figure 3.8: Select the new project

9. Once you select the project, you will see the new project in the console:

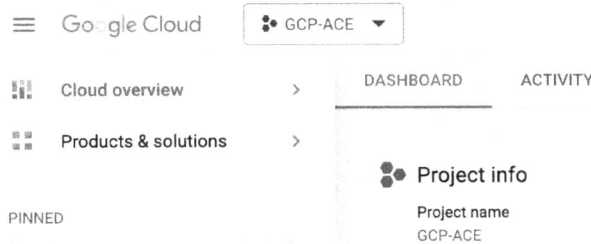

Figure 3.9: *Confirm the project selection*

Understanding GCP console

Let us understand different portions of the GCP console, which will be essential to understand and work in GCP.

1. The following is the GCP console after the initial setup:

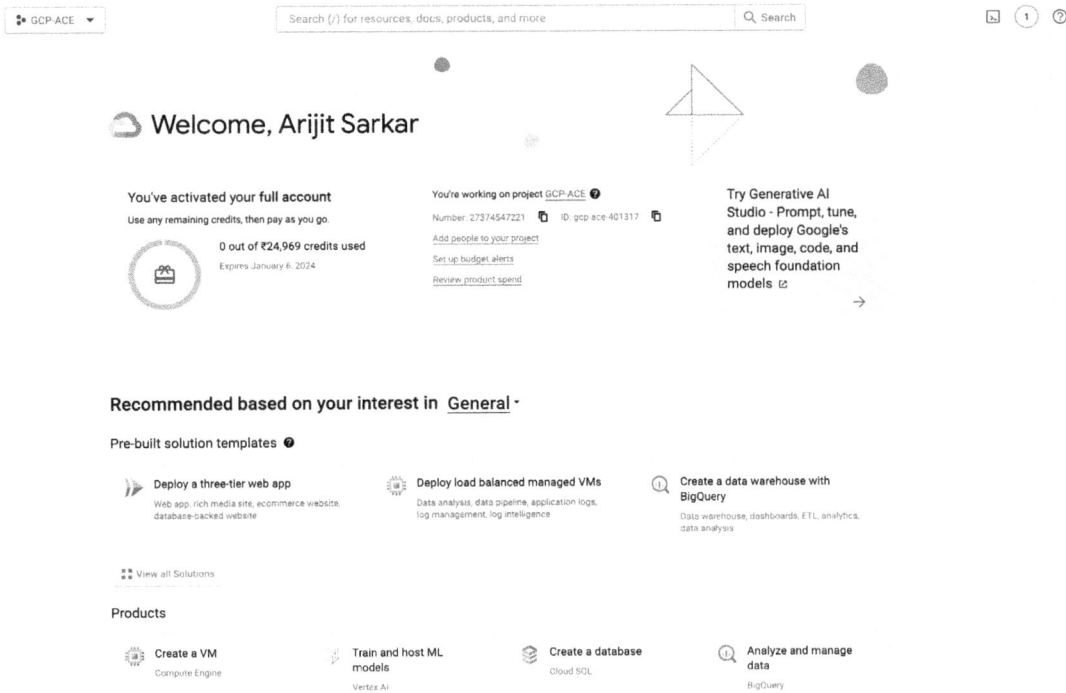

Figure 3.10: *GCP console*

2. The navigation menu for different services is present in the top left corner. You can pin the services which you use regularly:

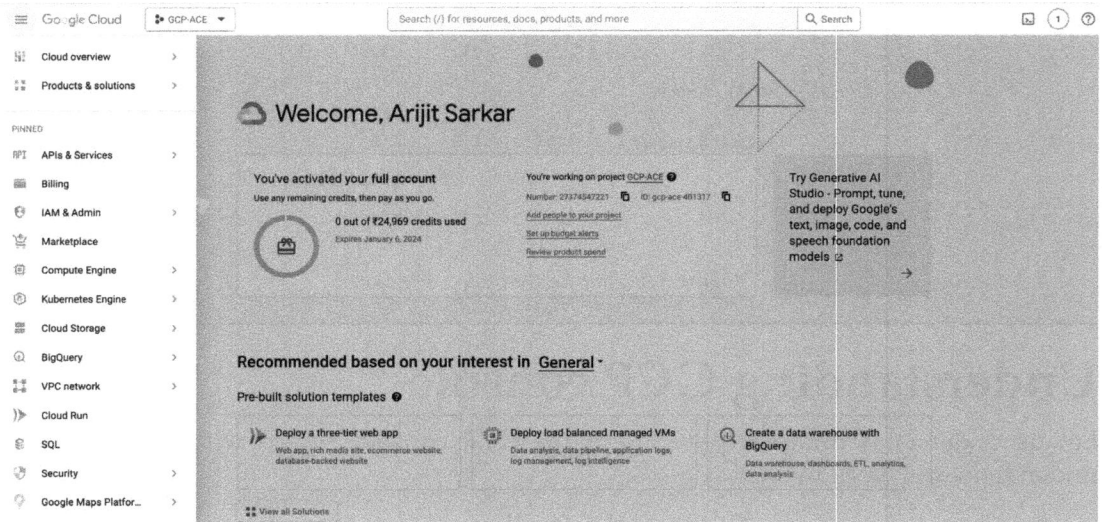

Figure 3.11: Navigation menu

3. Account details, project, and billing settings, and activation of the Cloud Shell button are present in the top right corner:

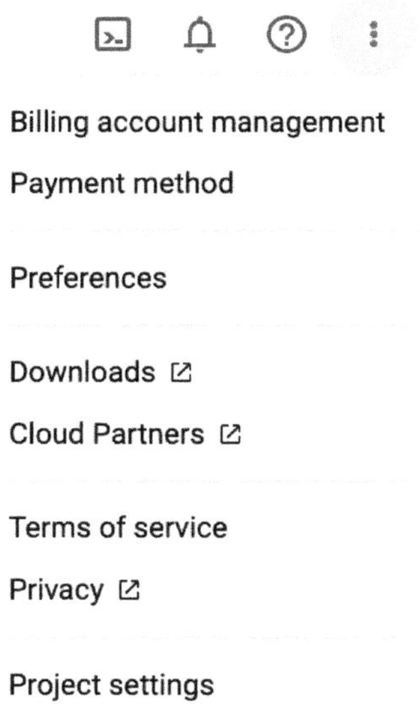

Billing account management

Payment method

Preferences

Downloads ☐

Cloud Partners ☐

Terms of service

Privacy ☐

Project settings

Figure 3.12: GCP project settings

4. You can search for various services, docs, etc., in the search box present in the top middle:

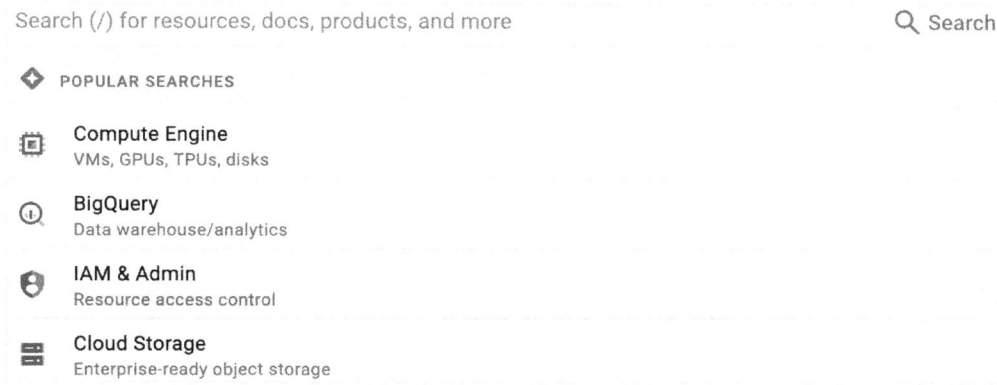

Figure 3.13: Search in GCP console

5. Dashboard from Cloud Overview Menu will provide a quick glance of your elected project. On the right-hand side, you will get the sections like **Billing, Monitoring,** and **Error Reporting**. In the middle, you will get **APIs** and **Project info** and **Resources** section.

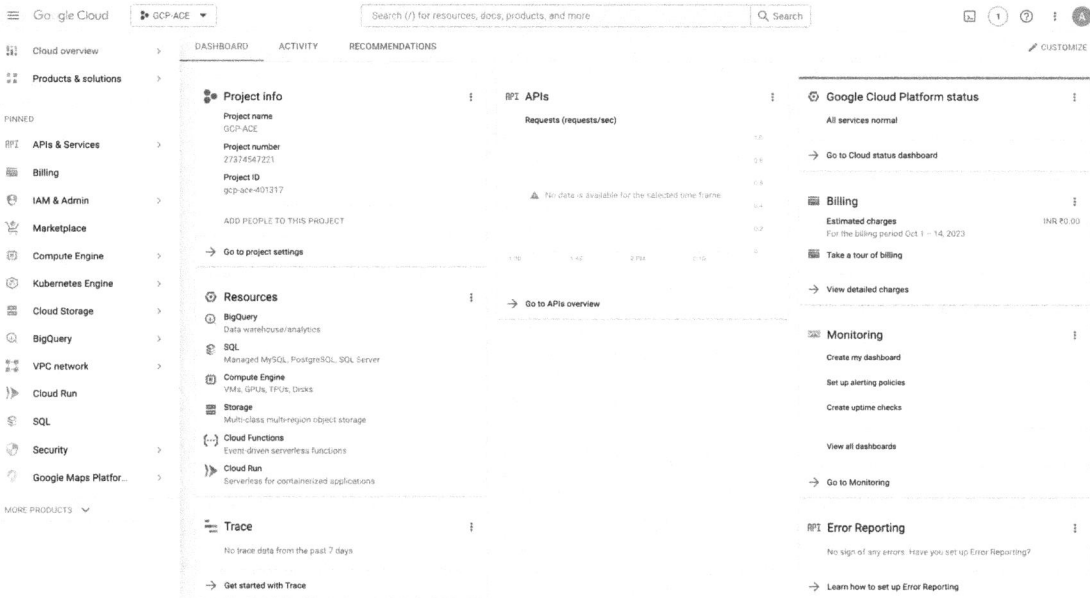

Figure 3.14: Dashboard view

Cloud Shell

Cloud Shell can be activated from the **Activate Cloud Shell** option present in the top right corner of the GCP console, as shown in the following figure:

✎ CUSTOMIZE

Figure 3.15: Activate Cloud Shell

Once it is authorized and activated, the below screen will appear:

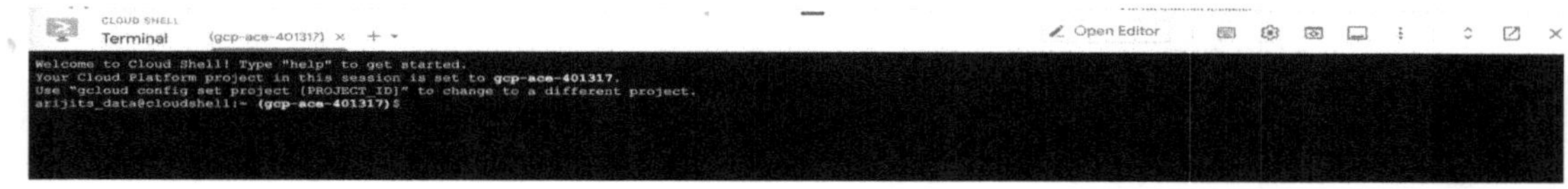

Figure 3.16: Cloud Shell within GCP console

Cloud Shell is a Debian-based VM with 5 GB available space in the home directory, which makes it easy to manage GCP resources inside the project. The gcloud command line tool and other utilities are pre-installed within Cloud Shell environment.

gcloud Command Line Interface

The Google Cloud CLI is a set of tools to manage Google Cloud resources. You can use it to perform many regular tasks in GCP from the command line like:

- Compute Engine VM instances and other resources
- Cloud SQL instances
- Google Kubernetes Engine clusters
- Dataproc clusters and jobs
- Cloud DNS managed zones and record sets
- Cloud deployment manager deployments
- And many more.

For example, **gcloud config set project PROJECT_ID** is used to set a project in Cloud Shell.

The gcloud CLI manages the authentication, local configuration, developer workflow, and interactions with Google Cloud APIs. You can run **gcloud cheat-sheet** command and explore various gcloud commands. We will learn more commands when we discuss different services in detail.

Regions and zones

Regions allow us to locate the cloud resources close to the customers. The closer your customers are to the region where the cloud resources are located, the faster and better their experience will be.

A zone is the deployment area for Google Cloud resources within a single region. Zones should be considered as a single failure domain within a region. To deploy fault-tolerant applications with high availability and help protect against unexpected failures, deploy applications across multiple regional zones.

GCP has 39 regions and 118 zones. Each region is mostly divided into three zones. For example, asia-south1 (Mumbai) has three zones: asia-south1-a, asia-south1-b, asia-south1-c:

Refer to the GCP regions and zones in the following figure:

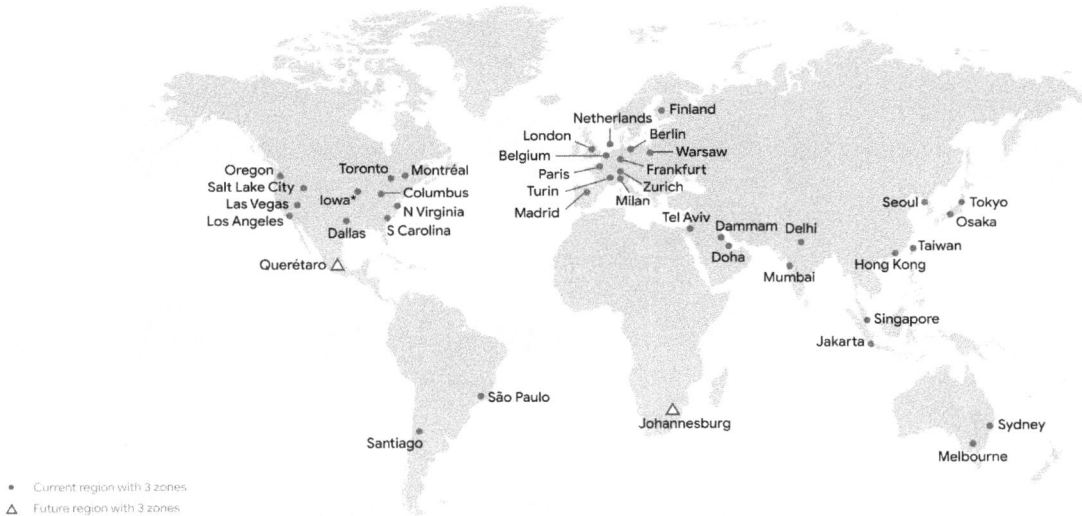

Figure 3.17: GCP regions

Cloud Billing

Cloud Billing is a collection of tools that helps in tracking Google Cloud spending, paying bills, and optimizing the costs.

A Cloud Billing account defines who is responsible for payment for a given set of GCP resources. To use GCP services, you need to have a valid Cloud Billing account, and it must be linked to the Google Cloud projects. GCP project's usage is charged to the linked billing account.

Note: You need to have a valid Cloud Billing account even if you are in your free trial period, i.e., 3 months currently, or if you are only using Google Cloud resources, those are part of GCP's free tier.

- You can navigate to the **Billing** section from the navigation menu:

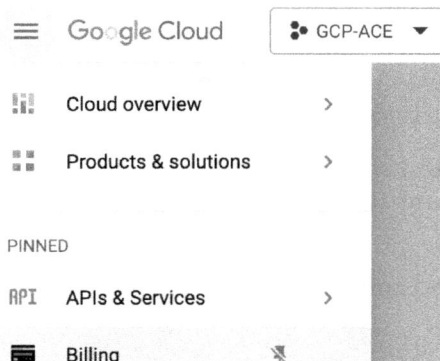

Figure 3.18: Navigate to GCP Billing

- The overview page describes the billing account overview and payment overview:

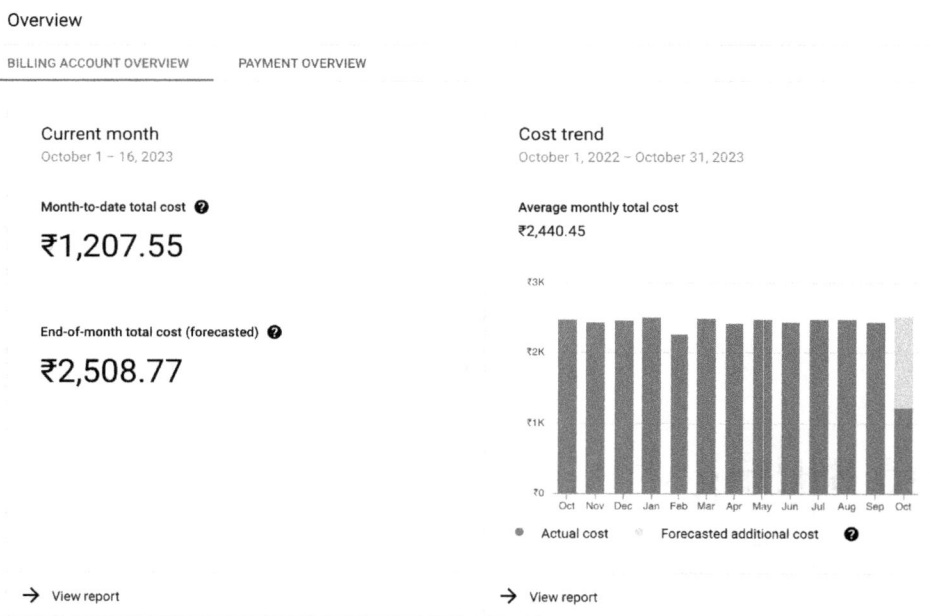

Figure 3.19: Billing account overview

- The report section provides a detailed report on the billing account and its usage for various services:

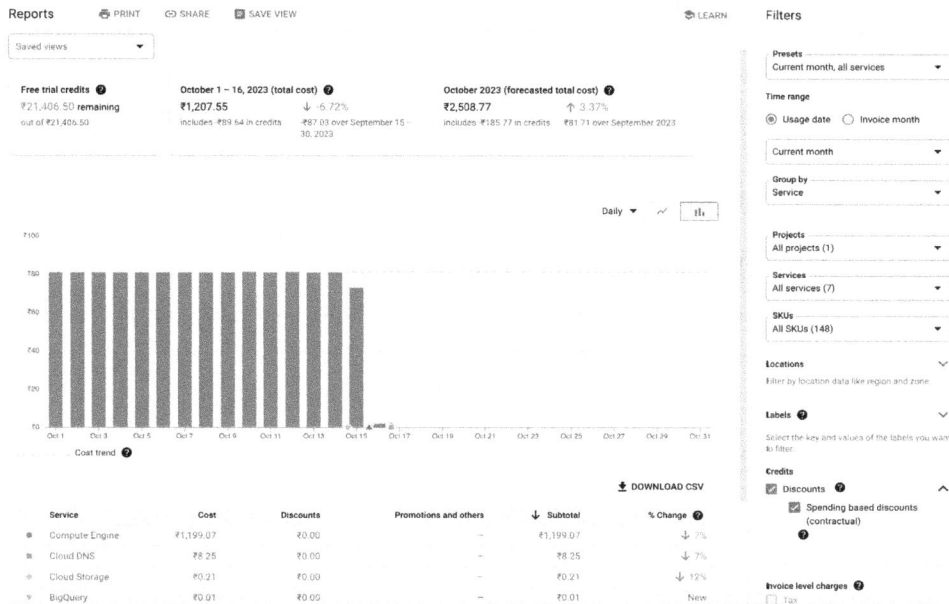

Figure 3.20: *GCP project billing report*

- You can create a budget and alert within billing account. You can set the trigger alerts at 50%, 90%, 100% etc. The following figure provides an example:

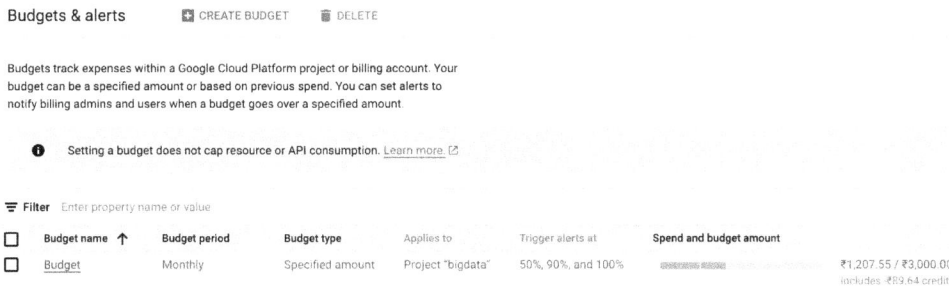

Figure 3.21: *Budget and alert*

- You can export the billing data to BigQuery for analysis.
- These sections, like Committed Use Discounts, FinOps Hub, etc, make your work easier for the GCP.

Cloud APIs

Google Cloud APIs are programmatic interfaces to GCP services. They are the key parts of the GCP, allowing us to easily add the power of everything from computing to networking to storage to machine-learning to the applications.

Cloud APIs are exposed as network API services to the customers. Each Cloud API runs on one or more subdomains of googleapis.com and provides both JSON based HTTP and gRPC interfaces to the clients over public Internet and **virtual private cloud (VPC)** networks. Clients can communicate via HTTP and gRPC requests to Cloud API endpoints directly or by using client libraries.

All the Cloud APIs present in GCP accept only secure requests using TLS encryption.

Example usage

As an example, let us understand how to use Google BigQuery APIs using Python Client. Execute the below lines based on your operating system.

Installation

For Windows, install the BigQuery Python library using the below steps in command prompt.

```
pip install virtualenv
virtualenv <your-env>
<your-env>\Scripts\activate
<your-env>\Scripts\pip.exe install google-cloud-bigquery
```

For Mac/Linux, install the BigQuery Python library using the below steps in the terminal.

```
pip install virtualenv
virtualenv <your-env>
source <your-env>/bin/activate
<your-env>/bin/pip install google-cloud-bigquery
```

Please use Python 3.7 or above for this example:

```
1. from google.cloud import bigquery
2.
3. client = bigquery.Client()
4.
5. QUERY = ('SELECT col1 FROM `project.dataset.
   table` WHERE col2 = "ABC" LIMIT 100')
6. query_job = client.query(QUERY)  # API request
7. rows = query_job.result()  # Waits for query to finish
8.
9. for row in rows:
10.    print(row.column1)
```

Cloud SDK

Cloud **software development kit (SDK)** provides language specific client libraries supporting each language's conventions and styles. This makes it easier for us to interact with Google Cloud APIs in any language. Client libraries handle authentication, reduce the amount of necessary initial coding, and provide helper functions for the pagination of large datasets and asynchronous handling of long-running operations. Cloud SDK is available at no charge for users with a Google Cloud account.

Installation in MacOS

Follow the below steps to install Cloud SDK on MacOS:

- Confirm that Python 3.8 / 3.9 is installed.
- Visit this URL **https://cloud.google.com/sdk/docs/install#mac**
- Click on the package required based on platform.
- Open the `.tar.gz` file.

Installation in Windows

Follow the below steps to install Cloud SDK in Windows.

- Visit this URL **https://cloud.google.com/sdk/docs/install#windows**
- Download the installer.
- Launch it and follow the prompts.

Initializing the gcloud CLI

Run the command `gcloud init` to initialize the gcloud CLI. Follow the prompts, and finally, you will be authenticated, and the project you chose will be selected in your terminal or command prompt window.

Authorize the gcloud CLI

Authorization can be done in two ways: one is a user account, and another is a service account.

A user account is recommended if you are going to use the gcloud CLI from the command line or writing scripts with the gcloud CLI for use on a single machine.

Command:
`"gcloud auth login"`

A service account is recommended if you are going to install and set up the gcloud CLI as part of a production process, or on Compute Engine VM instances where all users have access to root.

Command:
`gcloud auth login --cred-file="Service Account File"`

Conclusion

We have reached the end of this chapter. In this, we have learned about the essential components of Google Cloud, which we need to be aware of to perform our daily tasks on GCP. We will leverage this chapter's knowledge in upcoming chapters when we go through the services in detail. In the next chapter we will get to know about identity and access management in GCP.

Multiple choice questions

1. **gcloud command to set the Project ID?**

   a. gcloud configure set project PROJECT-ID

   b. gcloud config set project PROJECT-ID

   c. gcloud config assign project PROJECT-ID

   d. None of These

2. **GCP Region covers more area than zone?**

   a. True

   b. False

3. **GCP provides trial account for how many months?**

   a. 3 months

   b. 6 months

   c. 9 months

   d. 12 months

4. **In GCP, in order to communicate with Google Cloud APIs, clients need to send requests via which protocol?**

   a. HTTP

   b. gRPC

   c. Both

   d. None of these

Answers

1. b

2. a

3. a

4. c

Chapter 4

Identity and Access Management in GCP

Introduction

In this chapter, we will understand the **identity and access management (IAM)** in **Google Cloud Platform (GCP)**. It is a fundamental service and the first step towards securing your applications, virtual machines, databases, environments etc. in Google Cloud. It is used as an access control mechanism in GCP for both human and non-human (like service accounts) users.

Structure

The chapter covers the following topics:

- Principals
- Resources, permissions, roles, and policies
- Inside IAM in GCP console
- Service account
- Custom role
- IAM best practices

Objectives

By the end of this chapter, you will have a complete understanding of the IAM module in GCP. It will help in understanding various principals, roles, permissions, and policies. You will be able to secure the platform and, more importantly, your applications by implementing access control. You will be able to create service accounts for programmatic usages and assign permissions and roles to these. You will gain knowledge about how to create custom IAM roles and best practices of IAM.

Principals

The principal is an identity, which is nothing but a user or an entity who has some privileges to perform any operation in GCP. There are seven types of principals as follows:

Google account

Google account is a Google wide username and password which can be used to access different Google products like Gmail, Google Drive etc. For an example, we user our Google account for logging into Gmail.

Service account

Service accounts are non-human privileged accounts used to execute applications and run automated services, virtual machine instances, and other processes. This is mainly used for automated authentication before any operation on GCP.

Google group

Google groups help in managing users at scale. Each member of a Google group inherits the IAM roles granted to that group. This inheritance means you can use the membership of a group to manage user roles instead of providing IAM roles to individual users.

Google workspace account

Similar to the Google account, Google workspace account is used to access various Google products, Google workspace is normally a paid business service, and the account is associated with Google workspace.

Cloud Identity domain

Users having Cloud Identity accounts can also be called principal. It is similar to the Google Workspace Account, not having access to Workspace products. It is associated with a domain.

All authenticated users

The is a special type of identifier that represents all the service accounts and all the users on the internet who have been authenticated with a Google account. Personal Gmail accounts are not included.

All users

This grants public access. The value all users is a special type of identifier that represents anyone who is on the Internet, including authenticated and unauthenticated users.

Resources, permissions, roles, and policies

These are important concepts for IAM section in Google Cloud. Understanding these in detail will help you in working with access control in GCP. Let us understand these in detail.

Resources

Resources are objects in GCP using which we perform different types of operations. We can think of Cloud Storage Bucket or Compute Engine as resources. In GCP, resource hierarchy is defined as **Organization | Folders | Projects | Resources**. You can set the IAM policy at the organization level, folder level, project level, or resource level. Resources always inherit the policies from the parent resource. If you set a policy at the organization level, it is then inherited by all of its child folders and project-level resources, and if you are setting a policy at the project level, it is automatically inherited by all its child resources (**Organization | Folders | Projects | Services**).

Permissions

Permissions in GCP are required to allow access to a specific type of resource. For example, `compute.instances.create` is a permission allowing to create an instance. Another example would be `bigquery.datasets.create` to create datasets in BigQuery.

Roles

A role contains a set of IAM permissions that allow us to perform specific actions on the GCP resources. To make the permissions available, you need to grant roles to the principals.

There are mainly three types of roles in IAM:

- **Basic roles**, which include the owner, editor, and viewer roles.
- **Predefined roles,** managed by Google Cloud, it is more granular to use particular services.
- **Custom roles,** which provide access based on user-specified list of permissions.

Policies

IAM policy specifies access controls for GCP resources. It is a collection of bindings. A binding normally binds one or more members i.e. principals, to a single specified role. For some of the types of Google Cloud resources, a binding can also specify a certain condition, which is nothing but a logical expression which allows access to the resource only if that expression evaluates to true.

Inside IAM in GCP console

Let us discuss IAM module in GCP console. Search for "IAM" in the search box in GCP console and select **IAM & Admin** under **Products & Pages**. You will be redirected to the IAM section of GCP:

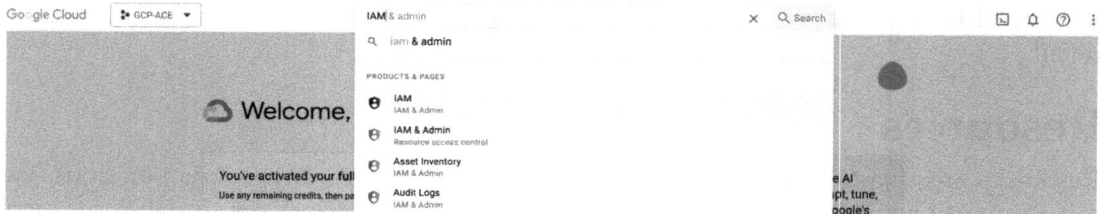

Figure 4.1: *Search for IAM section*

Let us understand the different parts of IAM module:

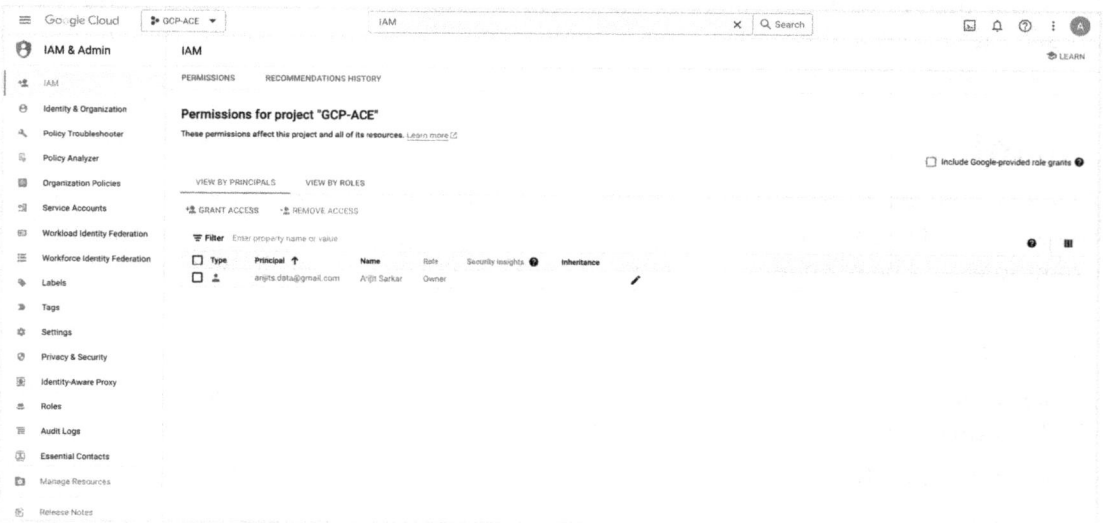

Figure 4.2: *IAM Section (View by Principals)*

To grant access to a principal, we need to click on **GRANT ACCESS**, Enter the principal (like Google account, service account etc.) and select the required role. To remove access from a principal, we need to select that principal, click on **REMOVE ACCESS** and remove the role which is required to be removed from that principal.

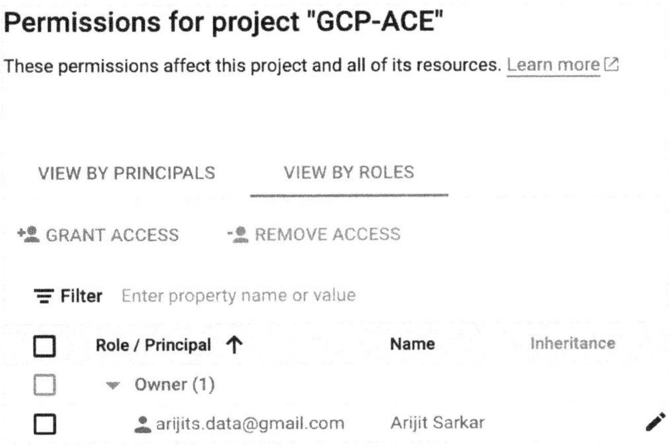

Figure 4.3: View by roles

Service accounts

Service accounts is a type of principal used for programmatic access in GCP. Let us understand how to work with service accounts in GCP:

1. Navigate to **Service accounts** section.

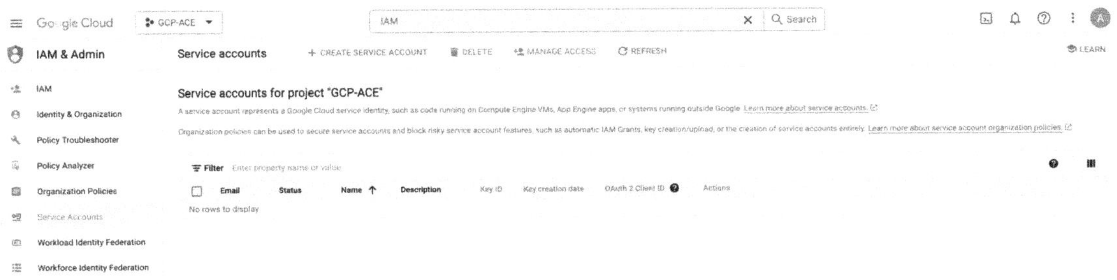

Figure 4.4: Service accounts section

2. Click on **Create service account** and fill up the details:

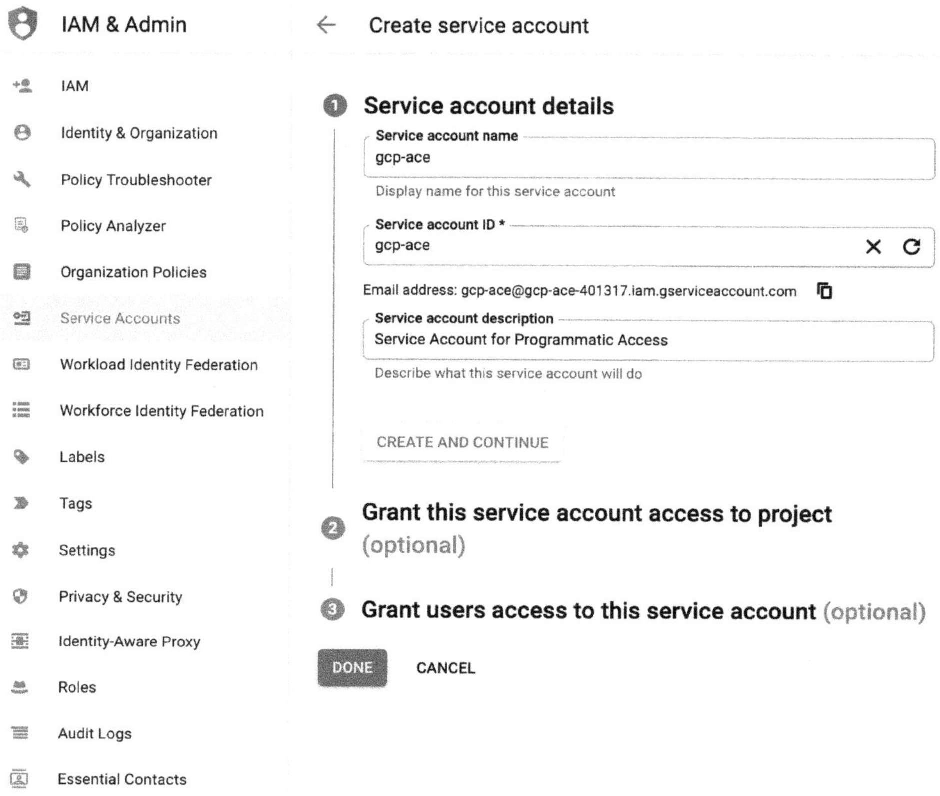

Figure 4.5: Create service account

3. Once you click on **Done**, a service account will be created.

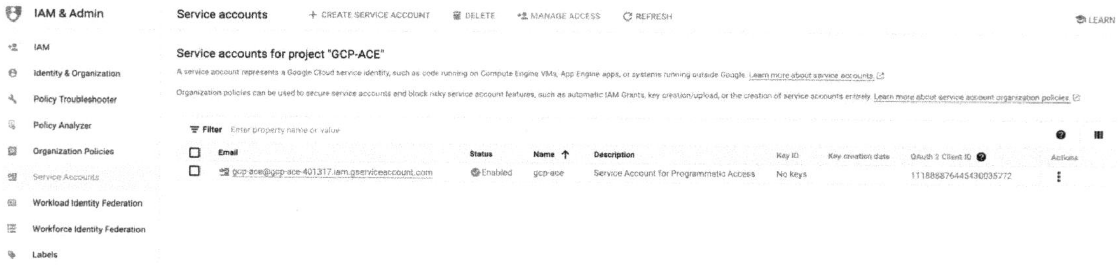

Figure 4.6: Created a service account

4. Grant access to this newly created service account on IAM page:

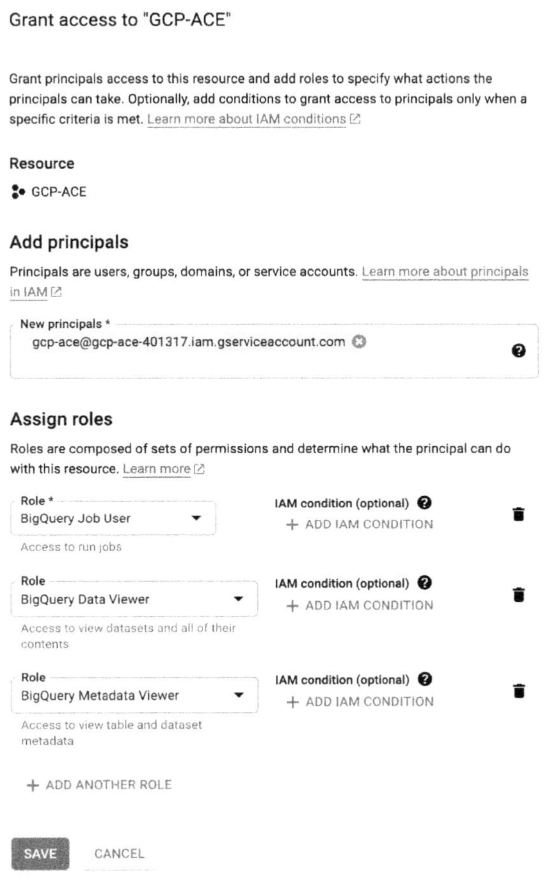
Grant access to "GCP-ACE"
Grant principals access to this resource and add roles to specify what actions the principals can take. Optionally, add conditions to grant access to principals only when a specific criteria is met. Learn more about IAM conditions
Resource
GCP-ACE
Add principals
Principals are users, groups, domains, or service accounts. Learn more about principals in IAM
New principals *
gcp-ace@gcp-ace-401317.iam.gserviceaccount.com
Assign roles
Roles are composed of sets of permissions and determine what the principal can do with this resource. Learn more
Role *
BigQuery Job User
Access to run jobs
IAM condition (optional)
+ ADD IAM CONDITION
Role
BigQuery Data Viewer
Access to view datasets and all of their contents
IAM condition (optional)
+ ADD IAM CONDITION
Role
BigQuery Metadata Viewer
Access to view table and dataset metadata
IAM condition (optional)
+ ADD IAM CONDITION
+ ADD ANOTHER ROLE
SAVE
CANCEL

***Figure 4.7:** Granting access to the service account*

5. Confirm the access details on the IAM page:

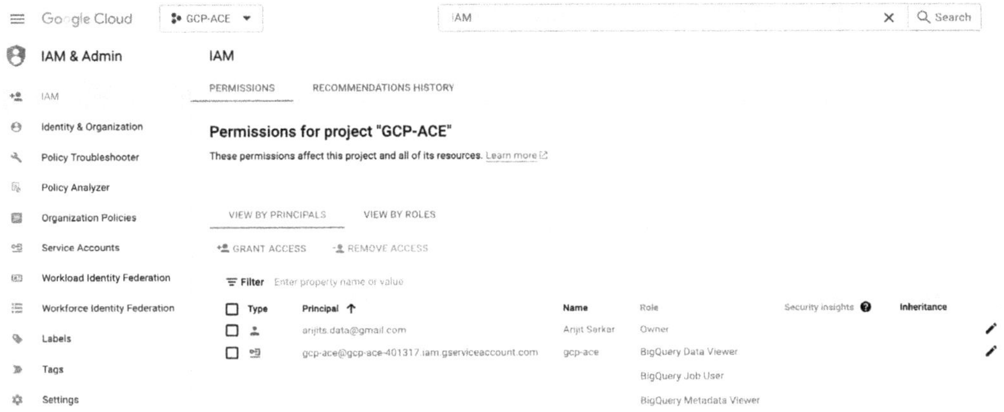
Google Cloud
GCP-ACE
IAM
Search
IAM & Admin
IAM
PERMISSIONS
RECOMMENDATIONS HISTORY
IAM
Identity & Organization
Policy Troubleshooter
Policy Analyzer
Organization Policies
Service Accounts
Workload Identity Federation
Workforce Identity Federation
Labels
Tags
Settings
Permissions for project "GCP-ACE"
These permissions affect this project and all of its resources. Learn more
VIEW BY PRINCIPALS
VIEW BY ROLES
GRANT ACCESS
REMOVE ACCESS
Filter Enter property name or value
Type
Principal
Name
Role
Security insights
Inheritance
arijits.data@gmail.com
Arijit Sarkar
Owner
gcp-ace@gcp-ace-401317.iam.gserviceaccount.com
gcp-ace
BigQuery Data Viewer
BigQuery Job User
BigQuery Metadata Viewer

***Figure 4.8:** Verify the access details*

6. Generate a JSON key for this service account. Go to **Actions** and select **Manage keys**:

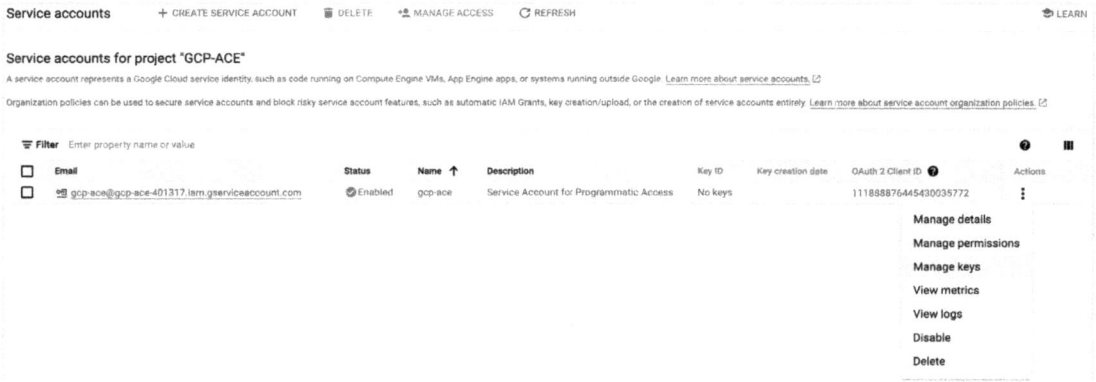

Figure 4.9: Manage keys for service account

7. Click on **Create new key**:

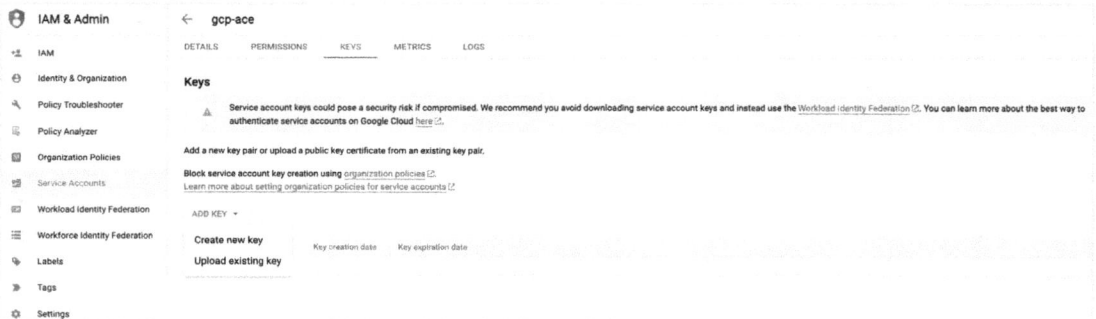

Figure 4.10: Create a new key for the service account

8. Click on **Create new key**, and you will get the below options: JSON (Key value pair for private key and other identity details) and P12 (Binary format for keeping certificate chain along with private key).

Figure 4.11: Generate key in JSON format

9. Use this generated key in Python environment:
   1. `import os`
   2.
   3. `os.environ['GOOGLE_APPLICATION_CREDENTIALS']='Path to JSON key file'`

10. The service account key needs to be kept in a secure place. It can be deleted from the console as well:

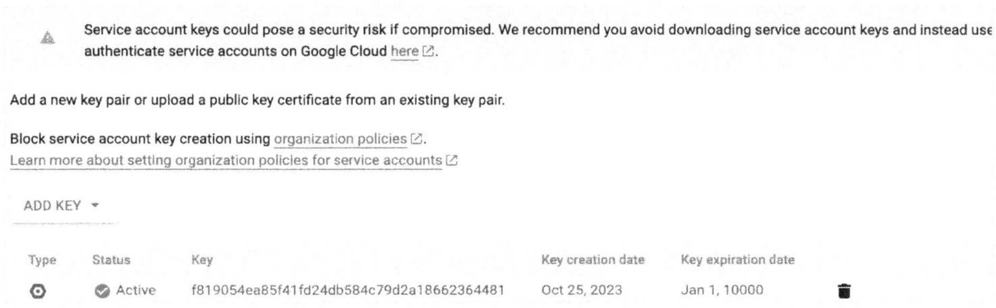

⚠ Service account keys could pose a security risk if compromised. We recommend you avoid downloading service account keys and instead use authenticate service accounts on Google Cloud here ⧉.

Add a new key pair or upload a public key certificate from an existing key pair.

Block service account key creation using organization policies ⧉.
Learn more about setting organization policies for service accounts ⧉

ADD KEY ▾

Type	Status	Key	Key creation date	Key expiration date	
⊙	✅ Active	f819054ea85f41fd24db584c79d2a18662364481	Oct 25, 2023	Jan 1, 10000	🗑

Figure 4.12: Generated service account key

Custom role

Custom roles will allow you to group various permissions and assign them to principals in a project or organization. You can either manually select permissions or import permissions from other roles.

1. Navigate to **Roles** section under **IAM and Admin**:

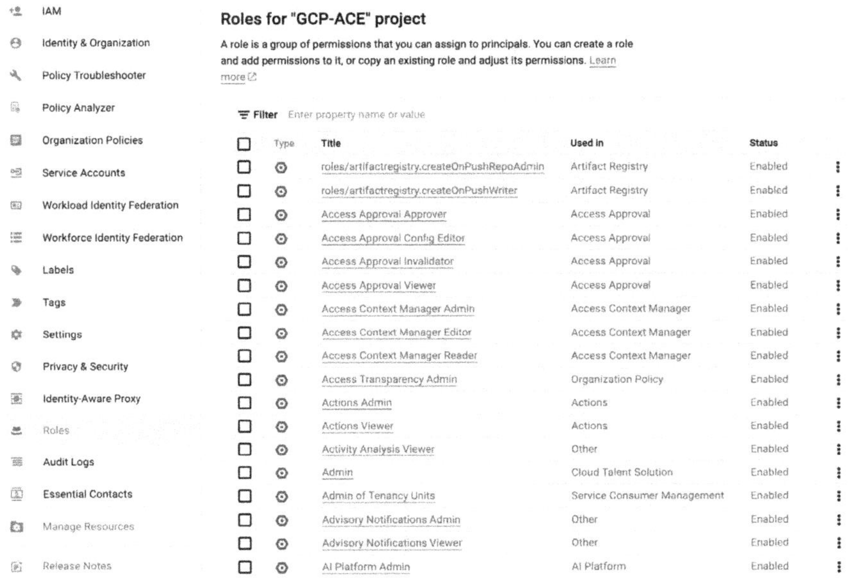

Figure 4.13: Roles

2. Click on **CREATE ROLE**:

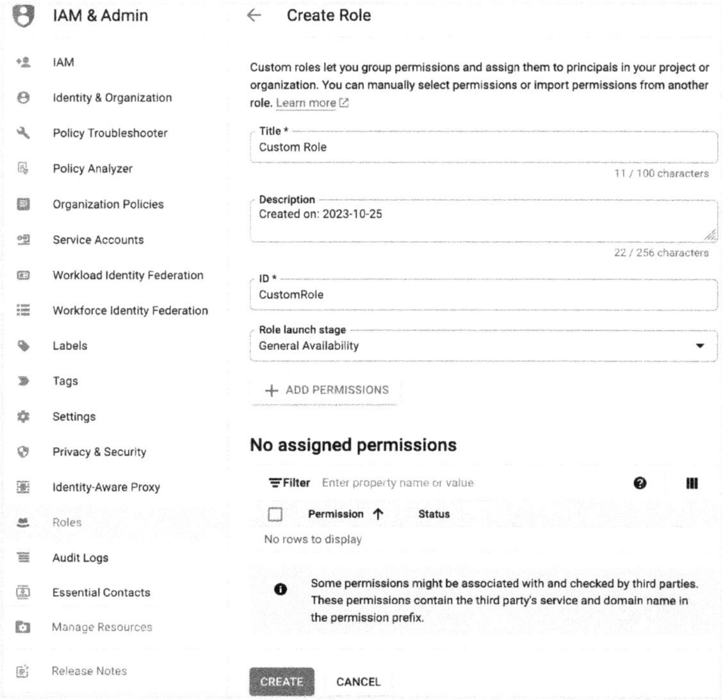

Figure 4.14: Create Role

3. Fill in the details and click on **ADD PERMISSIONS** to provide permissions to the required services along with specific actions:

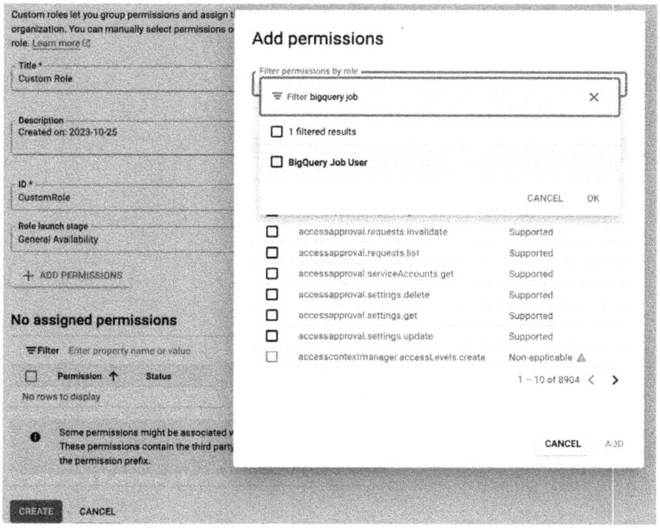

Figure 4.15: Filter by role

4. Select required permissions:

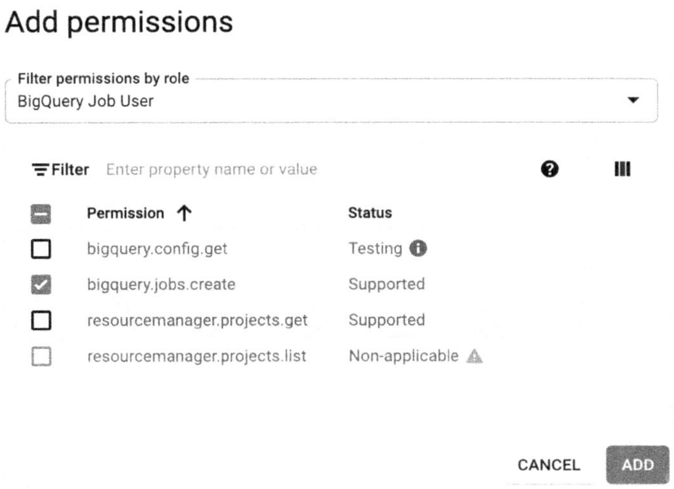

Figure 4.16: *Add permission from a predefined role*

5. Continue the selection for another permission:

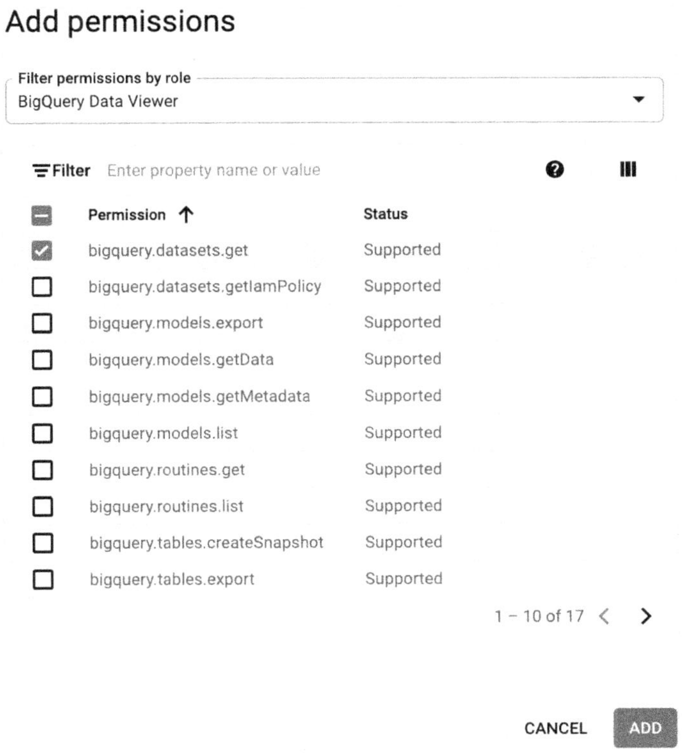

Figure 4.17: *Add another permissions from another predefined role*

6. Assigned permissions:

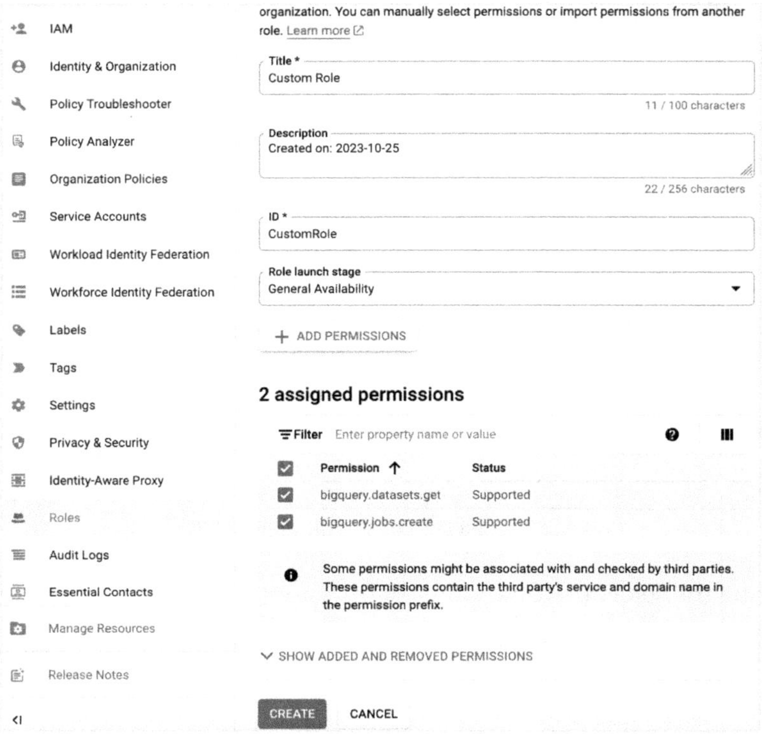

Figure 4.18: Assigned permissions

7. Finally, role is created:

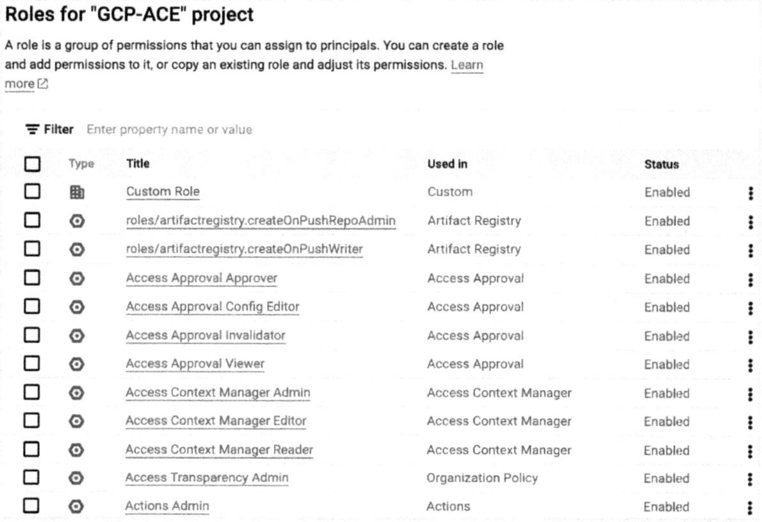

Figure 4.19: Created a custom role

IAM best practices

It is important to follow best practices while working with IAM module in GCP. Let us point out some of the best practices:

- Always go for the least privileged access.
- Use predefined roles as much as possible.
- Use custom roles only when predefined roles do not meet the requirement.
- Basic roles should be used in a limited environment.
- Use service accounts for programmatic access. Do not use individual user identities for applications running in multiuser environments.
- Create a group and assign roles to the group and then add users to that group in a multiuser environment.
- Do not add service accounts to groups.
- Use policies to control access and attach these to the correct level of hierarchy to use inheritance.
- Use Audit logs to track changes in IAM policies related to access and store them in a persistent storage service like GCS bucket or BigQuery.

Conclusion

We have reached the end of the chapter as well as at the end of section 2. In this chapter, we have learnt about various IAM concepts which will help us in designing the access control patterns in GCP. With the end of this chapter, we have completed our learning towards GCP essentials. From the next chapter onwards, we are going to learn about various Google Cloud services in detail.

Multiples choice questions

1. **Which is not a principal in GCP?**
   a. Google account
   b. IAM role
   c. Google group
   d. Service account

2. **In which format below a service account key can be generated in GCP?**
   a. TSV
   b. CSV

c. JSON

d. None of these

3. **When should we use Custom Role?**

   a. When we need to connect any system outside GCP.

   b. When we need to have specific permissions which are not easily available in predefined roles.

   c. When we need specific permissions to be given to a group of users.

   d. None of these

4. **Which is not a best practice in IAM?**

   a. Use predefined roles as much as possible.

   b. Always go for a least privileged access.

   c. Add service accounts to the group.

   d. None of these

5. **What is the correct Hierarchy in GCP?**

   a. Organization >> Folders >> Projects >> Resources.

   b. Organization >> Projects >> Folders >> Resources.

   c. Organization >> Folders >> Resources >> Projects.

   d. None of these

6. **What is the difference between roles and permissions?**

   a. Roles are set of various permissions.

   b. Permissions are set for various roles.

   c. We cannot relate roles and permissions.

   d. None of these

Answers

1. b
2. c
3. b
4. c
5. a
6. a

CHAPTER 5

Storage Solutions in GCP (Block, Network File and Object)

Introduction

In this chapter, we will understand storage solutions in **Google Cloud Platform** (**GCP**). We will learn about GCP's block storage solutions, i.e., Local SSDs and persistent disks, file storage solutions, i.e., Filestore and object storage service **Google Cloud Storage** (**GCS**). These solutions can store any type of file/data. Let us understand these in detail.

Structure

The chapter covers the following topics:

- Block storage: Local SSDs and persistent disks
- Network file storage: Cloud Filestore
- Comparison between block and file storage
- Object storage: Google Cloud Storage
- Working with Google Cloud Storage
- Practice questions

Objectives

For this chapter, our main objective will be to gain a complete understanding of GCP storage solutions to design a solution for the specific storage requirements. We will also understand buckets, object versioning, object lifecycle, various storge classes, different types of encryptions while going through the GCS service. We will also learn how to upload or download data from GCS bucket programmatically using Python programming language, via GCP console and using gsutil commands.

Block storage: Local SSDs and persistent disks

Block storage is a technology used for storing files on **storage area networks (SAN)**. In GCP there are two ways to achieve block storage. One is Local SSDs, and another is persistent disks.

Local SSDs

Local SSDs are an ephemeral locally attached storage system for virtual machines and containers. We can achieve higher **input/output operations per second (IOPS)** and lower latency using these compared to using other types of block storage options. The data stored in these are available till the associated compute instance is running.

Persistent disks

Persistent disk is a fully managed block storage service in GCP. It can be attached to a Compute Engine or a Google Kubernetes Engine. We can take back up and resize easily the persistent disks. It supports simultaneous reads. Persistent disks are encrypted by default in rest and in transit. They normally stay independent from virtual machines, so it can be detached from the VM easily without losing the data. You can create snapshots to take the back up of data from the zonal or regional persistent disks and snapshots are geo-replicated by default available for restoration in all regions.

Comparison between Local SSDs and persistent disks

Let us draw a comparison between Local SSDs and persistent disks:

Characteristics	Local SSDs	Persistent disks
Location	It is attached locally with VMs	It is available regional and zonal.

Operational Efficiency	It has higher I/O ops and lower latency.	It has higher durability.
Encryption	Compute Engine will automatically encrypt the data while writing it to Local SSDs.	Persistent disks are automatically encrypted.
Availability	Data of these Locals SSDs are available till the time the hosting VM is running.	Persistent disks are independent of any VM instances.
As GCP Service	It is ephemeral and locally attached block storage.	It is independent and fully integrated block storage with other GCP services.

Table 5.1: Local SSD vs persistent disks

Network file storage: Cloud Filestore

Network file storage is similar to **network attached storage (NAS)**. It provides file-level access to applications for reading and updating information that can be shared across multiple VMs. Cloud Filestore is a fully managed GCP service that offers network file storage. It can be used with applications running in Compute Engine VMs and Google Kubernetes clusters. Filestore offers two performance tiers: one is standard, and another is premium. Both tiers offer consistent performance and predictable costs.

The following are the benefits of network file storage:

- Managed service by GCP.
- Ready to use NFS v3 based NAS storage in the cloud.
- Standard and premium options

The following are the considerations of network file storage:

- Size limited to 64 TiB for basic version.
- Backup facility is manual.
- No guaranteed SLAs.
- Backup or snapshot functionality.

Comparison between block and file storage

In block storage, data is normally stored in blocks (i.e., chunks), whereas, in file storage, data is usually stored as files in a single place. A block is not a complete file, so the integration is not a property of a block, but in the case of file storage, you can integrate the data in different folders. You can access the block storage data over any OS, which is not in the case of file storage. Block storage is like a **hard disk drive (HDD)** in the server, making it more flexible than file storage. File storage is simpler and easier to manage. Block storage is popular as networking architecture used for business-critical applications, while file storage is good for data sharing within a smaller set of teams.

To understand these better, let us elaborate on two more concepts: SAN and NAS:

- A **storage area network (SAN)** is a dedicated high-speed network or subnetwork that interconnects and presents shared pools of storage devices to multiple servers.

- A NAS is a shared repository that will make a file or data accessible from different computers connected over a network. File storage solutions are most relevant when data sharing needs to be done within a small team.

Object storage: Google Cloud Storage

Object storage, also known as **object-based storage,** is a type of data storage architecture mainly designed for handling and storing large volumes of unstructured data. It considers data as distinct or separate units, combined with metadata and a unique identifier that is used to locate and access each unit of data. Object storage has become the preferred way of storing static content.

Cloud Storage is the object storage service in GCP. Within a GCP project, there can be multiple **Cloud Storage Buckets**, which are nothing but containers to store the objects, for simplicity, think the object is a file containing some data, image, or video.

Tools for Google Cloud Storage

Here are some basic ways you can interact with Cloud Storage:

- **Console**: The GCP console provides an interface to manage your data in a browser window.

- **Gcloud CLI**: It allows us to interact with Cloud Storage through a terminal using gsutil commands.

- **Client libraries**: The Cloud Storage client libraries allow us to manage data using programming languages like C++, C#, Go, PHP, Python, Java, Node.js and Ruby.

- **REST APIs**: Manage data using the JSON or XML API.

- **Terraform**: Terraform is an Infrastructure as Code tool which is used to provision the infrastructure for Cloud Storage.

Here are some benefits of using Object Storage.

- **Massive scalability**: It is easier to scale up due to flat architecture.

- **Reduced complexity**: It has no folders or directories, making it easier to access.

- **Searchability**: Metadata is part of an object, so searching and navigation become easier with this. We can tag the objects as well to a particular type.

- **Resiliency**: Object storage can replicate data automatically across geographical regions, this property helps it to protect against outages.

- **Cost efficiency**: It is less costly than other storage types for large amounts of data.

Working with Google Cloud Storage

Let us understand how to work with Cloud storage using the GCP console:

1. Navigate to **Cloud Storage** by typing the same in the search box present in the console.

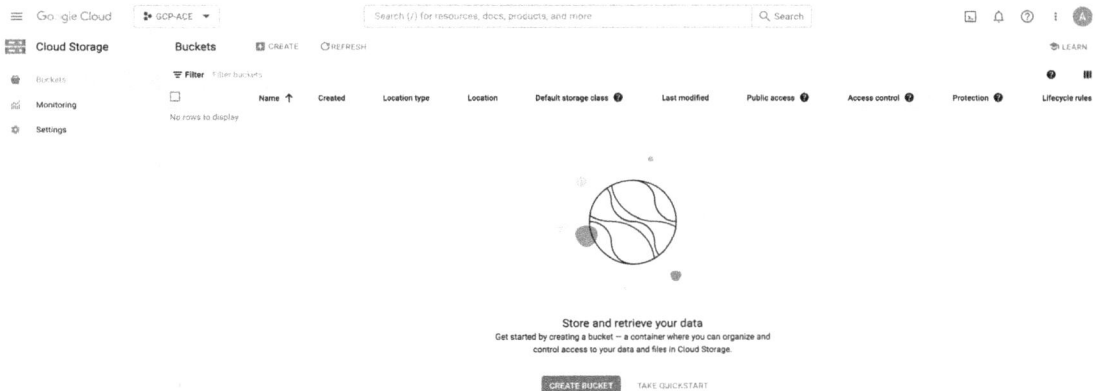

Figure 5.1: Cloud Storage

2. Click on create a bucket and provide a globally unique name like **gcp-ace-data** in this case.

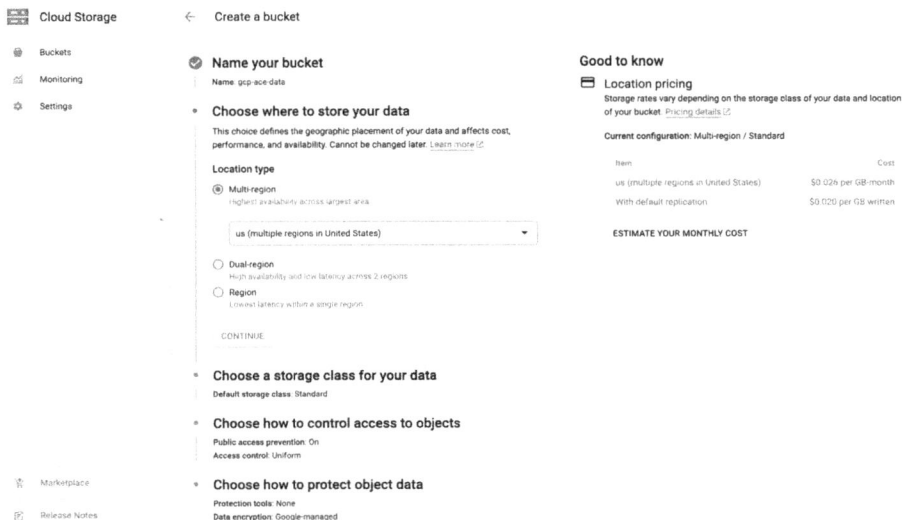

Figure 5.2: Creating a bucket

You can choose the region based on your requirements. In case you are building a customer centric application, frequent bucket access is required; it is preferred to have the bucket created in the same region where most of your customer resides.

It may also be needed for some regulatory requirements where data should be present within a region only.

For higher availability, we need to choose dual or multi-region types.

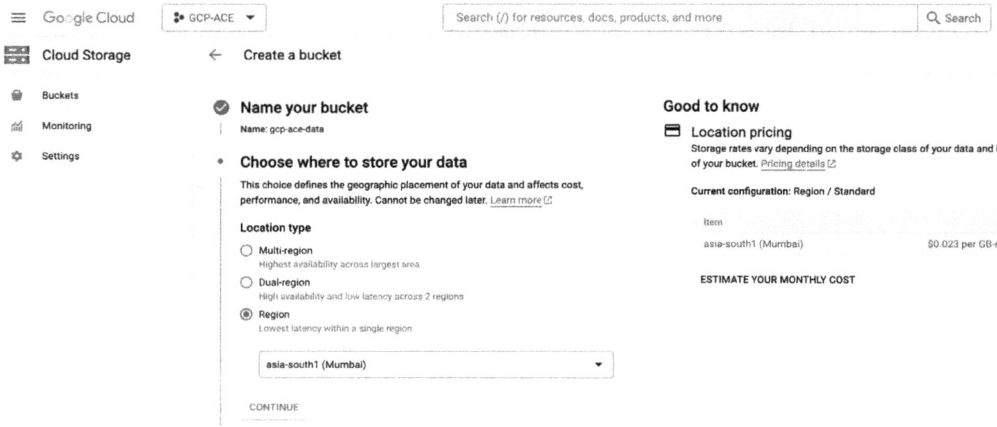

Figure 5.3: Selecting location type

3. Next, we need to select the storage class for the bucket:

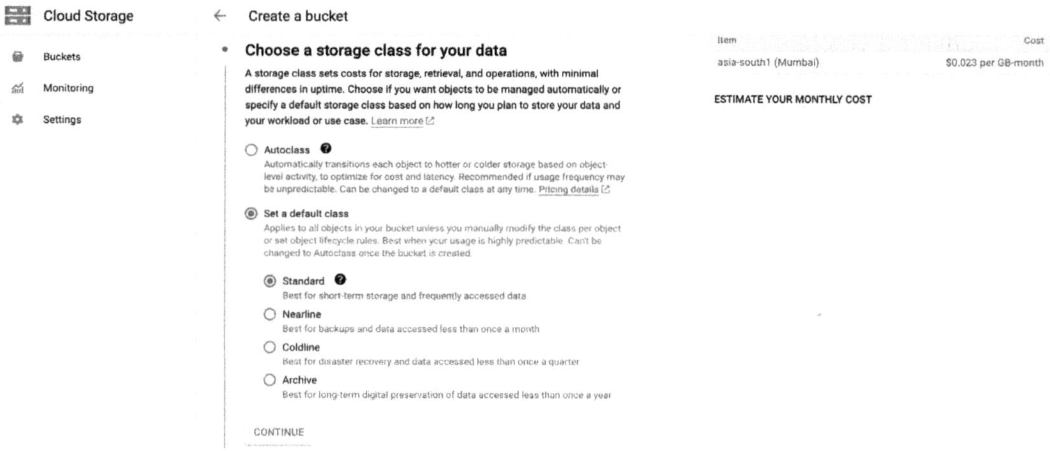

Figure 5.4: Selecting storage class

Note: [**Standard: For frequent data access, Nearline: For one-time data access more than a month but less than a quarter (30 < access day < 90), Coldline: For one-time data access more than a quarter but less than a year (90 < access day < 365), Archive: For one-time data access more than a year (access day > 365)]**

4. We need to select Protection Tools and Data Encryption, initially, let us keep it None as Protection Tools and Data Encryption as Google Managed Encryption.

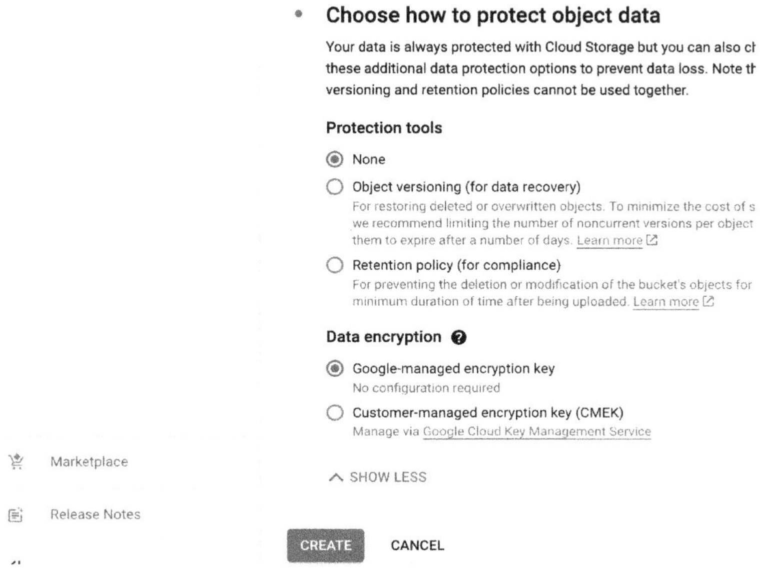

Figure 5.5: Selecting Protection Tools and Data Encryption method

We need to keep this public access prevented unless we are hosting any publicly available files or static web content for public use.

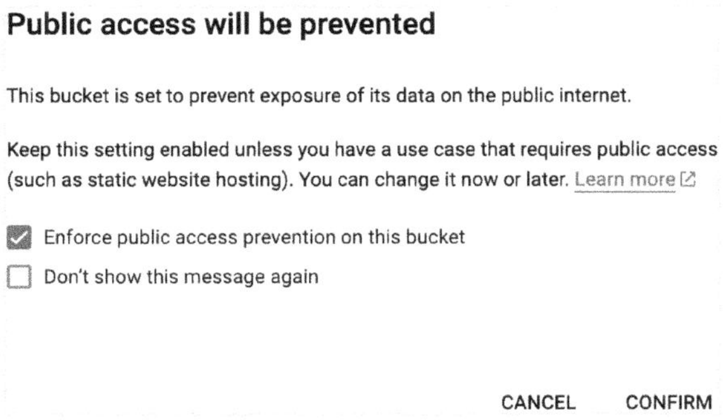

Figure 5.6: Public access prevention on bucket

Upon successfully creating a bucket, we can see the bucket in the console:

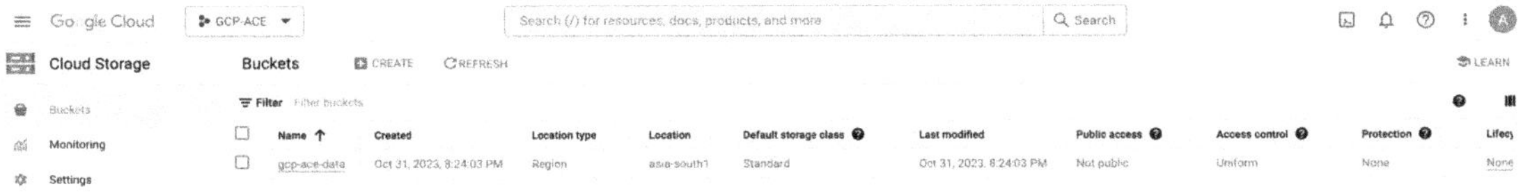

Figure 5.7: Bucket created

If we click on the bucket name, we can get to see many options as below:

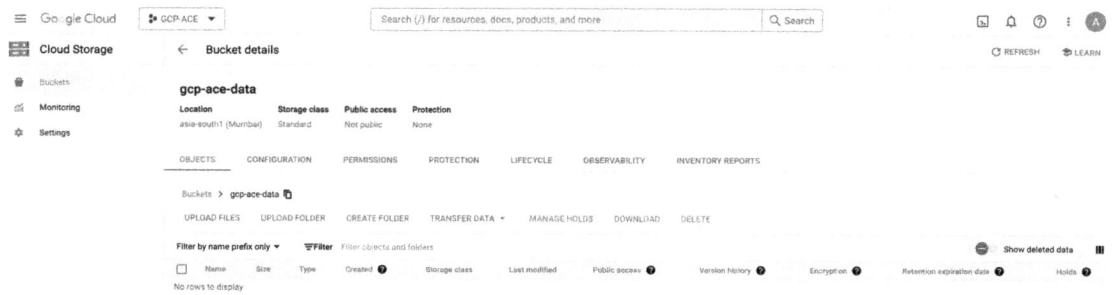

Figure 5.8: Inside created bucket

5. Create a folder named as **2023-10-31** by clinking on **Create Folder** option:

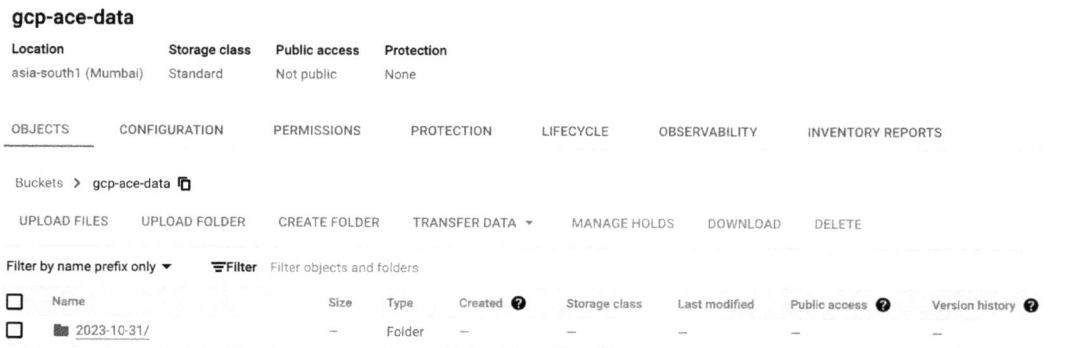

Figure 5.9: Created folder inside the bucket

Let us upload a file inside this folder by clicking on **Upload Files** option:

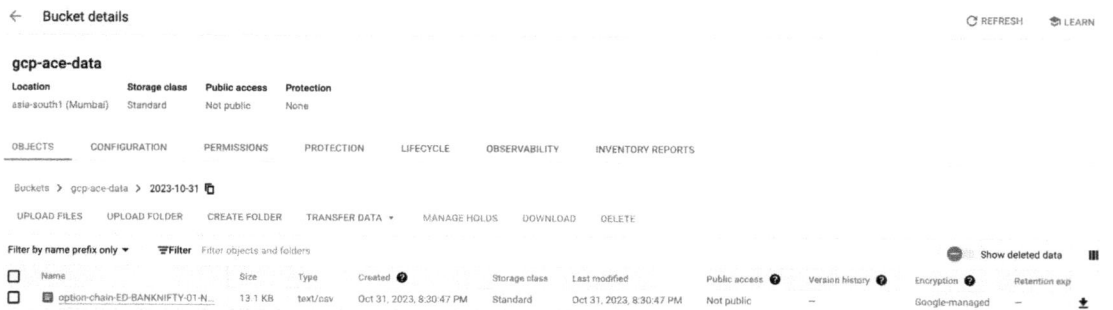

Figure 5.10: Uploaded a file

We can delete a file by selecting that object and pressing **Delete** option.

Delete 1 object?

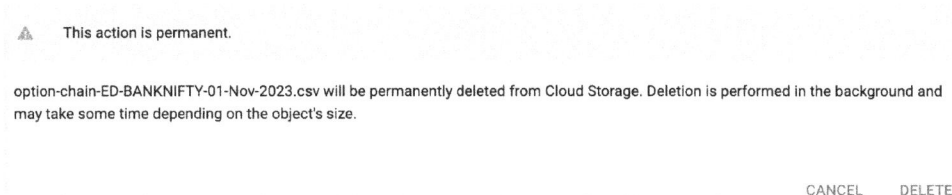

⚠ This action is permanent.

option-chain-ED-BANKNIFTY-01-Nov-2023.csv will be permanently deleted from Cloud Storage. Deletion is performed in the background and may take some time depending on the object's size.

CANCEL   DELETE

Figure 5.11: *Deleting a file*

We can keep the object versioning "ON" to preserve the non-current versions in case the file is deleted:

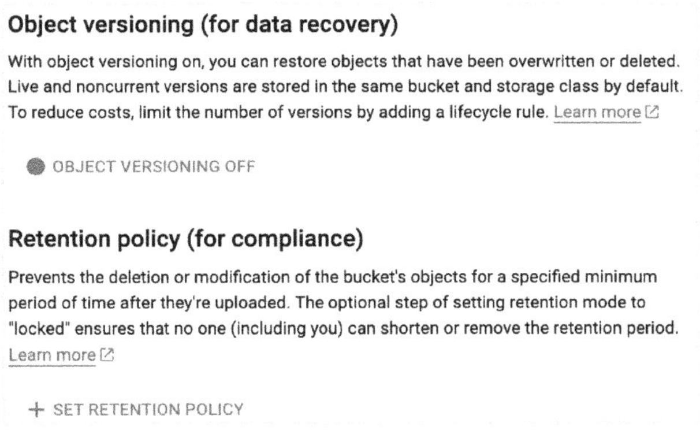

Object versioning (for data recovery)

With object versioning on, you can restore objects that have been overwritten or deleted. Live and noncurrent versions are stored in the same bucket and storage class by default. To reduce costs, limit the number of versions by adding a lifecycle rule. Learn more ☑

⬤ OBJECT VERSIONING OFF

Retention policy (for compliance)

Prevents the deletion or modification of the bucket's objects for a specified minimum period of time after they're uploaded. The optional step of setting retention mode to "locked" ensures that no one (including you) can shorten or remove the retention period. Learn more ☑

+ SET RETENTION POLICY

Figure 5.12: *Object versioning and retention policy*

By clicking the **object versioning** option, we can switch the object versioning "ON":

Turn on object versioning?

With object versioning on, live and noncurrent versions will be stored in the same bucket and storage class by default.

Save on version costs by adding lifecycle rules

Object lifecycle rules keep versioning costs under control. Without any lifecycle rules, versioning will be unlimited. Rules can be added or modified at any time. Learn more ☑

☐ Add recommended lifecycle rules to manage version costs

CANCEL   CONFIRM

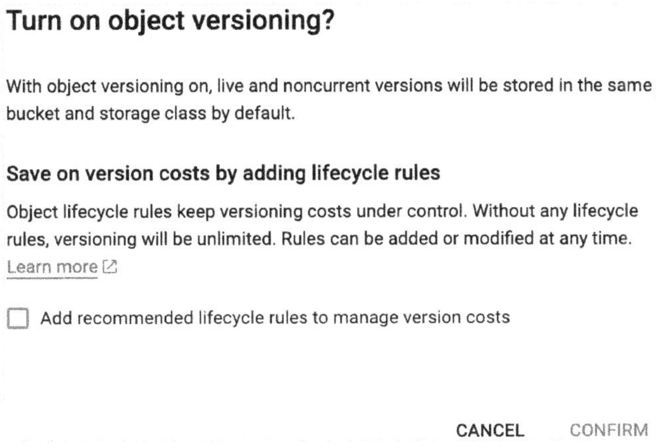

Figure 5.13: *Turning on object versioning*

If we delete a file, its non-current version will be preserved, as shown below:

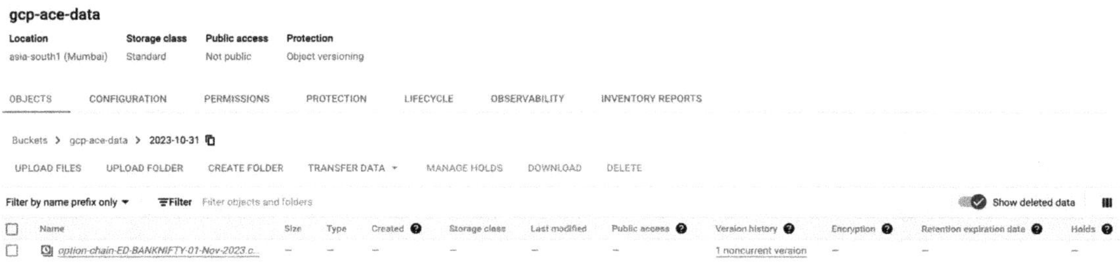

Figure 5.14: Non-current version after deletion

If we want to set a retention policy for any object within a bucket, we can configure it under the **PROTECTION** tab.

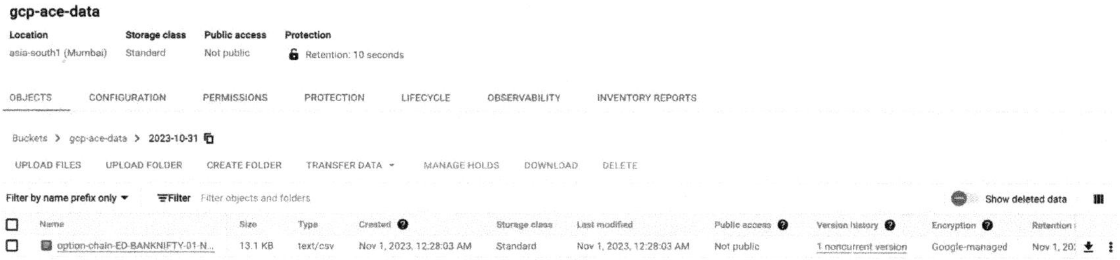

Figure 5.15: Retention policy set

This bucket has 10 10-second retention policy by which any file cannot be deleted within the first 10 seconds of its creation.

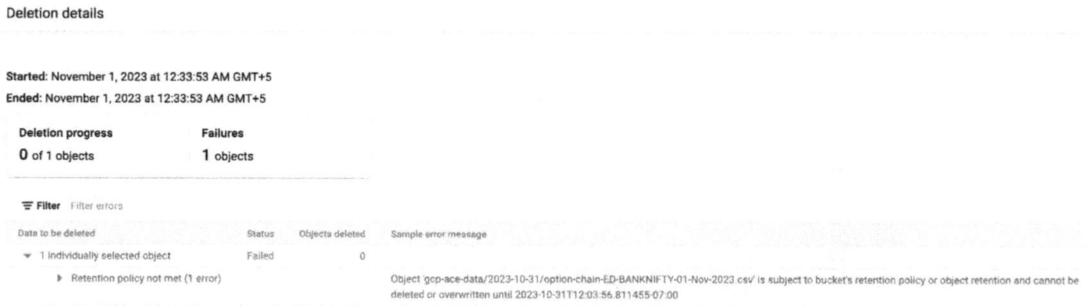

Figure 5.16: Unable to delete due to retention policy

We can select an object lifecycle rule using **LIFECYCLE** tab:

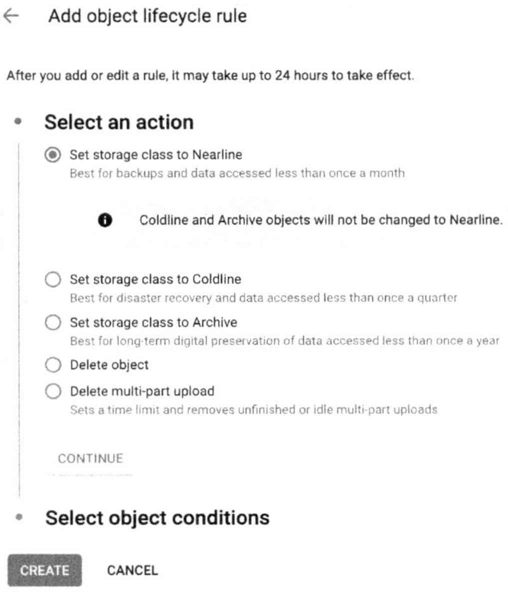

← Add object lifecycle rule

After you add or edit a rule, it may take up to 24 hours to take effect.

• **Select an action**

◉ Set storage class to Nearline
Best for backups and data accessed less than once a month

ℹ Coldline and Archive objects will not be changed to Nearline.

○ Set storage class to Coldline
Best for disaster recovery and data accessed less than once a quarter

○ Set storage class to Archive
Best for long-term digital preservation of data accessed less than once a year

○ Delete object

○ Delete multi-part upload
Sets a time limit and removes unfinished or idle multi-part uploads

CONTINUE

• **Select object conditions**

CREATE   CANCEL

Figure 5.17: *Lifecycle*

We can view the IAM permissions on the bucket using **PERMISSIONS** tab:

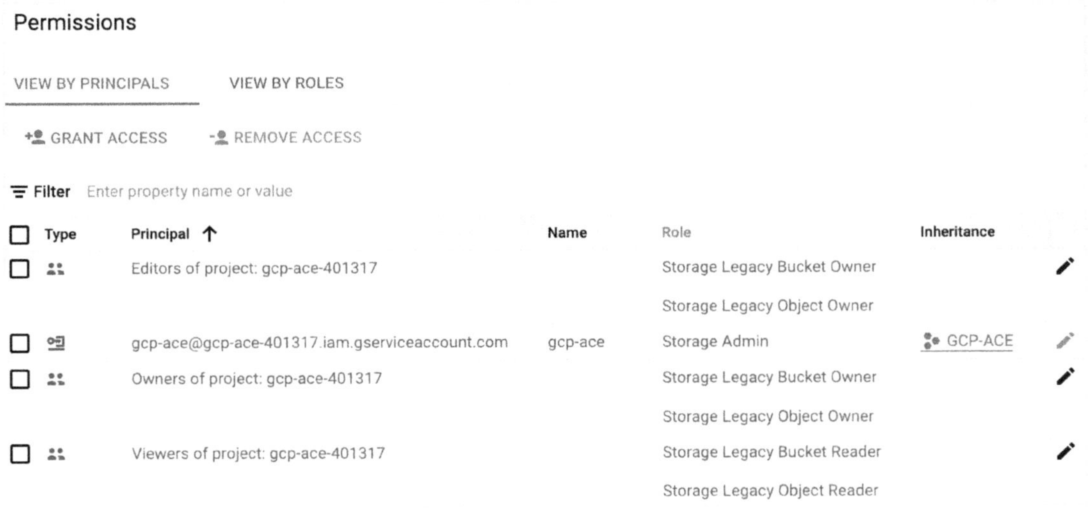

Permissions

VIEW BY PRINCIPALS   VIEW BY ROLES

+👤 GRANT ACCESS   -👤 REMOVE ACCESS

≡ **Filter**   Enter property name or value

Type	Principal ↑	Name	Role	Inheritance	
👥	Editors of project: gcp-ace-401317		Storage Legacy Bucket Owner		✏
			Storage Legacy Object Owner		
🔑	gcp-ace@gcp-ace-401317.iam.gserviceaccount.com	gcp-ace	Storage Admin	👥 GCP-ACE	✏
👥	Owners of project: gcp-ace-401317		Storage Legacy Bucket Owner		✏
			Storage Legacy Object Owner		
👥	Viewers of project: gcp-ace-401317		Storage Legacy Bucket Reader		✏
			Storage Legacy Object Reader		

Figure 5.18: *Permissions*

In order to have object-level permission, we can use **PERMISSIONS** tab in the Access Control area. We can change the access method to "Fine-grained" and specify object-wise access:

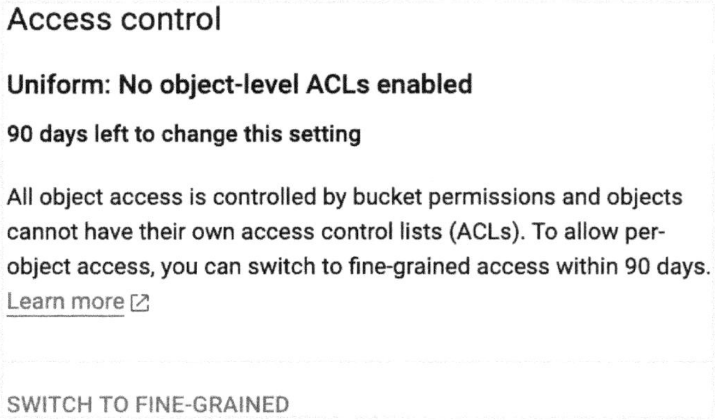

Access control
Uniform: No object-level ACLs enabled
90 days left to change this setting
All object access is controlled by bucket permissions and objects cannot have their own access control lists (ACLs). To allow per-object access, you can switch to fine-grained access within 90 days.
Learn more
SWITCH TO FINE-GRAINED

Figure 5.19: *Object-level access*

You can click on three dots at the right side of an object in the console and modify the access:

OBJECTS
CONFIGURATION
PERMISSIONS
PROTECTION
LIFECYCLE
OBSERVABILITY
INVENTORY REPORTS
Buckets > gcp-ace-data > 2023-10-31
UPLOAD FILES
UPLOAD FOLDER
CREATE FOLDER
TRANSFER DATA
MANAGE HOLDS
DOWNLOAD
DELETE
Filter by name prefix only
Filter
Filter objects and folders
Show deleted data
Name
Size
Type
Created
Storage class
Last modified
Public access
Version history
Encryption
Retention ex
option-chain-ED-BANKNIFTY-01-N...
13.1 KB
text/csv
Nov 1, 2023, 11:25:12 PM
Standard
Nov 1, 2023, 11:25:12 PM
Not public
Google-managed
Open object overflow menu

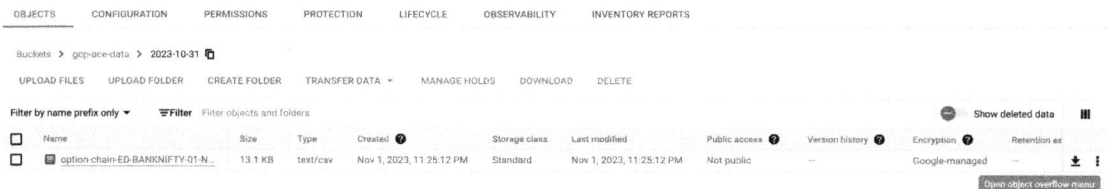

Figure 5.20: *ACL Access - 1*

Click on **Edit access**:

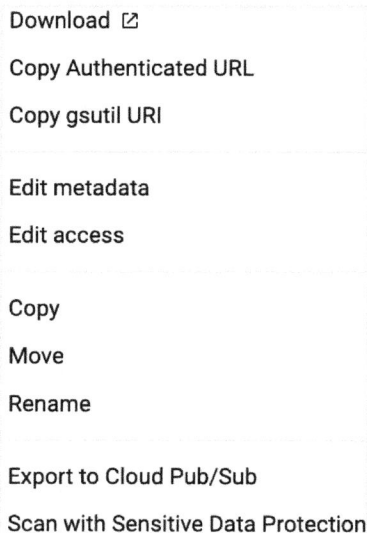

Download
Copy Authenticated URL
Copy gsutil URI
Edit metadata
Edit access
Copy
Move
Rename
Export to Cloud Pub/Sub
Scan with Sensitive Data Protection

Figure 5.21: *ACL Access – 2*

You can modify the access as needed:

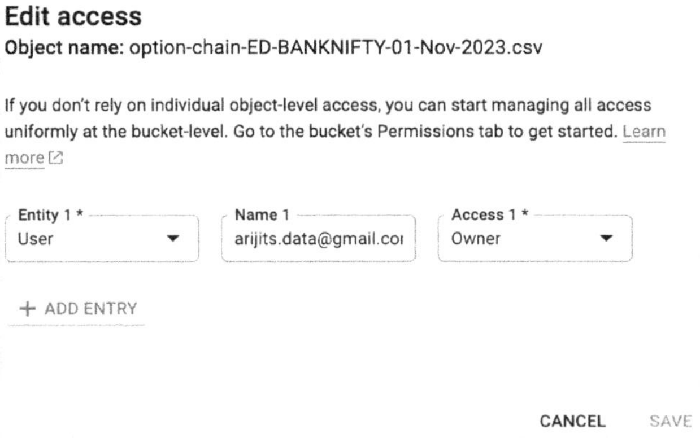

Edit access
Object name: option-chain-ED-BANKNIFTY-01-Nov-2023.csv

If you don't rely on individual object-level access, you can start managing all access uniformly at the bucket-level. Go to the bucket's Permissions tab to get started. Learn more ⬀

Entity 1 *	Name 1	Access 1 *
User ▼	arijits.data@gmail.coi	Owner ▼

+ ADD ENTRY

CANCEL   SAVE

Figure 5.22: ACL Access – 3

Access Google Cloud Storage using Python

Let us go through the process of accessing cloud storage buckets using Python:

1. Install **google-cloud-storage** module in Python environment using **pip install google-cloud-storage** command in Windows/MacOS/Linux.

   Execute the following code:

```
1. from google.cloud import storage
2. import os
3.
4. os.environ['GOOGLE_APPLICATION_CREDENTIALS'] = 'Path to Service
   Account JSON key file'
5.
6. client = storage.Client()
7. bucket = client.get_bucket('gcp-ace-data')
8. blob = bucket.get_blob('2023-10-31/option-chain-ED-BANKNIFTY-01-
   Nov-2023.csv')
9.
10. print(blob.download_as_string())
```

Access Google Cloud Storage using gsutil commands

The installation of gcloud is discussed in *Chapter 3, Understanding GCP console, Cloud Shell, Billing and APIs*. gsutil is a part of gcloud, and version 5.0 and above requires Python 3.

- Authenticate using `gcloud auth login` command.
- Set the Project ID using `gcloud config set project PROJECT_ID` command.
- Set the bucket using `BUCKET='gs://gcp-ace-data'`
- Command like `gsutil ls $BUCKET` will list the items inside the bucket.
- There are plenty of gsutil commands which are useful to work with GCS buckets.
- `gcloud storage cp gs://gcp-ace-data/2023-10-31/option-chain-ED-BANKNIFTY-01-Nov-2023.csv` is used to copy the file from GCS location to local machine's current path.

Cost calculation

We can use the GCP cost calculator to calculate the usage cost for Cloud Storage.

Link for GCP Calculator: **https://cloud.google.com/products/calculator**

Assumptions

Let us consider the below scenario for cost calculation:

- Amount of Storage 10 GiB (1 GB = 0.93 GiB)
- Class A Operations 0.5 million per month
- Class B Operations 0.1 million per month
- Inter Region Egress – Asia: 1 GiB
- Multi Region Egress – Asia: 1 GiB
- Intra Region Egress – North America and Asia: 1 GiB

Calculated cost based on the above assumptions:

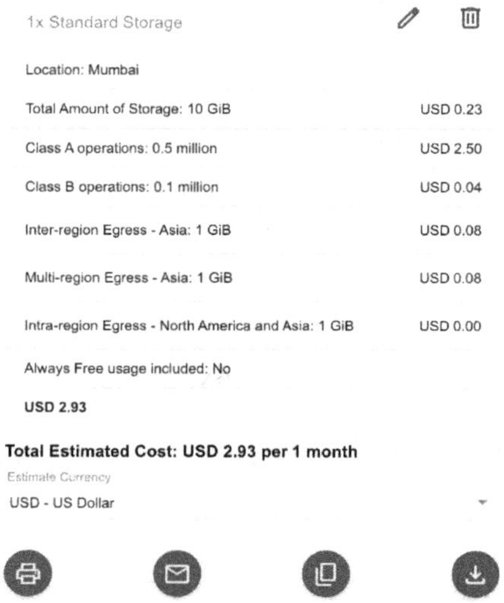

1x Standard Storage	
Location: Mumbai	
Total Amount of Storage: 10 GiB	USD 0.23
Class A operations: 0.5 million	USD 2.50
Class B operations: 0.1 million	USD 0.04
Inter-region Egress - Asia: 1 GiB	USD 0.08
Multi-region Egress - Asia: 1 GiB	USD 0.08
Intra-region Egress - North America and Asia: 1 GiB	USD 0.00
Always Free usage included: No	
USD 2.93	

Total Estimated Cost: USD 2.93 per 1 month

Estimate Currency
USD - US Dollar

Figure 5.23: Cost calculation for GCS bucket

Data Encryption in Cloud Storage

GCP provides multiple ways to handle encryption for objects in buckets; these are:

- Google managed
- Customer managed
- Customer supplied
- Client-side encryption

Conclusion

We have reached the end of the chapter. We have learned about various storage systems in Google Cloud and examined Cloud Storage in detail; this is an essential service in GCP and an important topic for the Associate Cloud Engineer exam. The next two chapters will explain SQL and NoSQL databases in GCP.

Multiple choice questions

1. **If my customers are spread across geographically and they need to use the Cloud Storage bucket randomly, which type of location I would prefer?**

    a. Regional

    b. Dual region

    c. Multi region

    d. None of these

2. **Which storage class is preferable when one-time data access is more than a quarter but less than a year?**

    a. Standard

    b. Nearline

    c. Coldline

    d. Archive

3. **Within the retention period of a bucket, objects cannot be deleted.**

    a. True

    b. False

4. **Which is a choice of encryption method for objects in Cloud Storage Buckets?**

    a. Customer managed

    b. Google managed

    c. Customer supplied

    d. All of these

Answers

1. c
2. c
3. a
4. d

Join our book's Discord space

Join the book's Discord Workspace for Latest updates, Offers, Tech happenings around the world, New Release and Sessions with the Authors:

https://discord.bpbonline.com

CHAPTER 6
Understanding Different Databases in GCP

Introduction

Business leaders say that **data is the new oil**. It is true, as this gives us a complete understanding of the process, starting from generating new leads for businesses, customer behavior, various logs generated from different system processes, and so on. To use the data, you need to store it in place from where you can retrieve it as and when required; and this brings the concept of databases, which will store data in a sophisticated manner. Databases are primarily categorized as SQL or NoSQL, which we will discuss in this chapter. Google Cloud has various types of database options, for different types of data requirements.

We will be discussing each of these concepts in detail.

Structure

The chapter covers the following topics:

- SQL versus NoSQL databases
- SQL databases in GCP
- NoSQL databases in GCP
- In-memory database in GCP
- Database for analytics

Objectives

By the end of this chapter, we will be able to choose the database based on a particular requirement or use case. We will also be discussing the concept of SQL and NoSQL databases and exploring various database options in the **Google Cloud Platform** (**GCP**).

SQL versus NoSQL databases

Databases can generally be categorized into two major types: **Structured Query Language (SQL)**, and **Non-SQL (NoSQL)**. SQL Databases are relational in nature and offer **Relational Database Management System** (**RDBMS**) capability, which relies on **Atomicity, Consistency, Isolation, and Durability** (**ACID**) properties, while NoSQL databases follow the **Consistency, Availability, and Partition tolerance** (**CAP**) theorem. SQL databases are designed to store structured data, and NoSQL databases are designed to store semi-structured (documents, key-value pairs, etc.) and unstructured (URL, images, logs, etc.) data.

Comparative study between SQL and NoSQL databases

Let us understand the differences between SQL and NoSQL databases:

Property	SQL	NoSQL
Relational	SQL databases are relational in nature, supporting structured data.	NoSQL databases are non-relational in nature supporting semi structured and unstructured data.
Schema flexibility	Database schema is fixed in nature, so new columns are to be added separately before data population.	It has dynamic schema; so new key data can be populated easily.
Use cases	Transactional use cases where data is frequently inserted, updated or deleted.	Big Data use cases where semi-structured and unstructured data is stored.
Complex querying	These databases are best when complex querying is required.	These are not suitable for complex querying.
Scalability	It is vertically scalable.	It is horizontally scalable, can be imagined as a distributed database.

Working property	It follows ACID property.	It follows CAP theorem.
Types and examples	**Transactional**: Oracle, MySQL, SQL Server, Cloud SQL, Amazon RDS **Analytical**: BigQuery, Snowflake, Teradata, Redshift, Hive	**Document**: MongoDB **Column**: Cassandra, HBase **Key-value pair**: Couchbase **Graph**: Neo4j **In memory key-value**: Redis, Memcached

Table 6.1: SQL versus NoSQL databases

SQL databases in GCP

Let us understand the SQL or relational databases in Google Cloud. This type of database normally stores structured data. Cloud SQL, Alloy DB for PostgreSQL, and Cloud Spanner are SQL databases in GCP.

Cloud SQL

Cloud SQL is a fully managed relational database service, for popular RDBMS choices like MySQL, PostgreSQL, and SQL Server. It takes care of the database administration work seamlessly so that you can focus on the applications and manage their data.

Cloud SQL has an SLA of 99.95%.

Let us try to understand the components of Cloud SQL, and how they are configured with each other:

- Each Cloud SQL instance is configured with a virtual machine running on host GCP service.

- Each VM runs a database-related program, such as MySQL's server, PostgreSQL's server, or SQL Server, and service-related agents that help in supporting services, like logging and monitoring.

- The **High Availability (HA)** option provides a standby VM, in another zone with similar configurations to the primary VM.

- The actual database is on a scalable and durable network storage device called a **persistent disk,** which is attached to the VM.

- A static IP address, in front of each VM, ensures that the IP address gets connected, and stays throughout the entire session of the Cloud SQL instance.

Use cases for Cloud SQL

It is used mainly as the backend database for use cases:

- **Enterprise Resource Planning (ERP)**
- Online transactions
- **Customer Relationship Management (CRM)**
- E-commerce

Key features

Let us understand the key features of Cloud SQL database:

- **Fully managed**: Cloud SQL manages the databases so that the business can run without any disruption. It automates all the backups, replications, patches, encryption, and storage-capacity increases to give the applications more reliability, scalability, and security.

- **Open and standards-based**: Cloud SQL supports popular open-source and commercial engines, like MySQL, PostgreSQL, and MS SQL Servers, with rich support for extensions, configuration flags, and popular developer toolsets. It is easy to start, the database can be created with just a few clicks in the console (**https://console.cloud.google.com/sql/instances?pli=1&invt=AbuMAg**), and connected to the application.

- **Cost-effective:** According to an **IDC study**, in three years, Cloud SQL customers can achieve an ROI of around 246% and a payback period of around 11 months. You can scale as the application grows, customize the machine types, and choose different levels of performance and availability, with up to 99.99% availability of SLA. Committed use discounts can offer additional savings for up to three years.

- **Supports Gen-AI:** You can extend the database applications to build AI-powered experiences using the pgvector PostgreSQL extension, LangChain, and **large language models** (**LLMs**). Cloud SQL for PostgreSQL makes it easier to store vector embeddings for machine learning models (for applications like similarity search, etc.).

- **Easy migrations:** Database located whether on-premises, on Compute Engine, or in other cloud service providers, can migrate securely using **Database Migration Service** (**DMS**), with minimal downtime. DMS leverages the native replication capabilities of the source database, to maximize the reliability of the migration activity. It is available with no additional charges, for migrations to Cloud SQL.

- **Integrated:** Cloud SQL easily integrates with other Google Cloud services such as Compute Engine, Cloud Run, and GKE, allowing application developers to build and deploy the applications with ease. You can provision the database through APIs and third-party tools, to use the federated queries in BigQuery and to replicate low-latency databases using Datastream, enabling the near real-time data capture, on operational data-related use cases.

- **High Availability:** You can configure the built-in HA with automatic failover across zones, (with the click of a button) to provide isolation from various types of infrastructure, hardware, and software failures. You can optimize the database costs depending upon your applications, and choose a 99.99% availability SLA for business-critical transactional workloads, or a 99.95% availability SLA, to cut down the costs.

- **Data protection and compliance**: You can configure the backups for data protection and restore the instance to an earlier point in time, with a retention period of up to 35 days. You can also configure your data storage location to comply with the data residency or data locality requirements. Cloud SQL automatically encrypts the data, SSAE 16, ISO 27001, and PCI DSS compliant, and supports HIPAA compliance.

- **Secure access and connectivity**: Cloud SQL data is completely encrypted when within Google's internal networks and when stored in DB tables, temp files, and backups. It supports private connectivity to the **virtual private cloud** (**VPC**), and every Cloud SQL instance includes a network firewall, which allows you to control the public network access requirements.

- **Scalability**: It can easily scale up as the data grows, by adding processor cores, required RAM, and storage units, and scale out, by adding more read replicas, to handle the increasing read traffic. Cloud SQL can scale up the storage capacity when approaching the limit. The read replicas support the HA. Cloud SQL can have its read replicas, which can be located across regions and platforms.

- **Near zero downtime for maintenance**: Cloud SQL offers nearly zero downtime (approximately less than 10 seconds for planned maintenance). It also offers a flexible maintenance window, with features like advanced email notification and the ability to reschedule it by 28 days; you can pick specific times for maintenance and even deny maintenance for up to 90 days.

- **Data cache**: Cloud SQL can automatically accelerate the applications that use its built-in performance management procedures. Cloud SQL for MySQL uses flash memory on the database instance to lower the read latency and improve the throughput by smartly caching data within memory and providing high-speed storage.

- **Change data capture and replication:** You can stream data from various databases, storage, and applications reliably with minimal latency, using Datastream. You can scale up or down with the serverless architecture, with no other resources required, to provision or even manage.

AlloyDB for PostgreSQL

AlloyDB for PostgreSQL is a fully managed PostgreSQL-compatible database service for most of the relational workloads in an organization. It brings the best of Google with PostgreSQL, superior performance, scalability, and availability. It is built on the fundamental principle of disaggregation of the compute and storage and is designed to use disaggregation at every layer of the stack. It begins by separating the DB layer from the storage and introducing a new intelligent storage service, which is optimized for PostgreSQL. This finally reduces I/O bottlenecks and allows AlloyDB to offload several DB operations to the storage layer using the use of a log-processing mechanism. The storage service also disaggregates the compute and storage, allowing the block storage to scale up or scale down, separately from the log processing mechanism.

Use cases for AlloyDB for PostgreSQL

It is used mainly as backend database for the following use cases:

- ERP
- Online transactions
- CRM
- E-commerce
- Backend database in **Software as a Service (SaaS)**
- As RDBMS in financial services

Key features

Let us understand the key features of AlloyDB for PostgreSQL database:

- **Fully managed database service**: AlloyDB is a fully managed PostgreSQL-compatible database service with industry-leading performance, availability, and scalability. It automates administrative tasks, like taking backups, data replication, database patching, and capacity management, and uses adaptive algorithms and machine learning techniques for PostgreSQL vacuum management, storage and memory management, data tiering, and acceleration of analytics, so you can focus on building your applications.

- **Fast transactional processing**: AlloyDB is 4 times faster than a standard PostgreSQL, in carrying out transactional or OLTP workloads. It is suitable for enterprise workloads, including the ones that require high transactional throughput, large data volumes, or multiple read replicas. Read connections can scale horizontally, backed by low lag, it can scale out read replica pools and support cross-region replicas.

- **High Availability**: AlloyDB offers 99.99% of uptime SLA, including maintenance. It can automatically detect and recover most database failures within a span of 60 seconds, irrespective of the database size and load. The architecture supports a non-disruptive instance resizing capability and database maintenance.

- **Real-time business insights**: AlloyDB is 100 times faster than the standard PostgreSQL to carry out analytically complex queries; with zero impact on the operational performance, offering reporting, **Hybrid Transactional and Analytical Workloads (HTAP)**. It is integrated with Vertex AI, (Google's AI platform), allowing you to call machine learning models, including generative AI models, directly in the query or a transaction without the need to write any kind of application code.

Cloud Spanner

Cloud Spanner is an enterprise-grade, distributed globally (multi-region). With a highly scalable and strongly consistent database that offers 99.999% availability, built specifically to mix the benefits of relational DB with non-relational or NoSQL's horizontal scaling. It has a unique database that combines ACID transactions, SQL-based querying, and relational structure with scalability, which is normally present with non-relational or NoSQL databases. So, Spanner is best used for gaming, payment solutions, global financial ledgers, retail banking, and inventory management that require the ability to scale limitlessly with consistency and very HA.

Use cases for Cloud Spanner

It is used mainly as the backend database for the below use cases:

- Order and inventory management
- Online banking payments and ledger
- Gaming: player profiles and gameplay data
- Electronic medical records

Key features

Let us understand the key features of Cloud Spanner database:

- **Write and read scalability with no limits**: Spanner decouples compute resources from the data storage, making it easier to transparently scale in and out, processing resources. Each additional compute system can process both, reads and writes, providing effortless horizontal scalability. Spanner optimizes the performance by automatically handling sharding, replication, and transaction processing.

- **Automated maintenance**: It can significantly reduce operational costs and improve reliability, for databases of any size. Synchronous replications and maintenance, are automatic and built-in. It provides 100% online schema changes and maintenance, serving traffic with zero downtime.

- **PostgreSQL interface**: You get PostgreSQL's interface along with Spanner's reliability and scalability; preventing the need to learn a new way of working, migrating from standard PostgreSQL to Spanner.

- **Automatic database sharding**: No need to worry about manually resharding the database again. Its built-in capability for sharding automatically distributes the data, to optimize the performance and availability. It can automatically scale up and scale down, without interruption.

- **High-performance and workload-isolated query processing**: Cloud Spanner's data boost enables users to run analytical queries, batch processes, or data export operations much faster, without affecting existing OLTP workloads. Fully managed by Google Cloud, data boost does not require any prior, capacity planning or management. It is always ready to process user queries, directly on the data stored in Spanner's distributed storage system, named **Colossus**. This on-demand and independent compute resource, allows users to easily handle mixed workloads and data sharing.

- **Strong transactional consistency**: Spanner relies on industry-leading external consistency, without compromising scalability or availability.

- **Single-region and multi-region configurations**: Users can be anywhere on the globe, and applications backed by the Spanner can read and write strongly consistent data, globally. Additionally, your database is completely protected against regional failure while running a multi-region instance, offering an industry-leading 99.999% of availability.

- **Enterprise-grade security and controls**: Spanner provides **customer managed encryption keys (CMEK)**, data-layer encryption, integration with IAM access and controls, and an efficient audit logging mechanism. It has support for VPC service control, access transparency, and access approvals. The fine-grained access control allows you to authorize access to the Spanner data at the table, and even at the column level.

NoSQL databases in GCP

Let us understand the NoSQL or non-relational databases in Google Cloud. This type of database normally stores semi-structured data.

Firestore

Firestore is a serverless document database, which can scale on demand-basis. It is highly consistent, offering 99.999% availability and acting on the backend as a service. Its Database is a service, which is optimized for building web and mobile applications. It is perfect for all general-purpose use cases like e-commerce, gaming, IoT, and real-time dashboards. In Firestore, users can interact and collaborate, with live and offline data making it useful for real-time apps.

Use cases for Firestore

It is used mainly as backend database for the below use cases:

- Web and mobile apps
- News feeds and social chats
- Gaming - player profiles and game saves
- Retail catalogs and point of sales

Key features

Let us understand the key features of Firestore:

- **Serverless**: Firestore is a fully managed and serverless database, which can effortlessly scale up or down, to meet the demand, without any maintenance window or downtime.

- **Powerful query engine**: Firestore allows us to run sophisticated ACID transactions (though not an SQL database) against the document data. This gives us more flexibility to structure the data.

- **AI Integrations**: Useful extensions can. be integrated with popular AI products, with a few clicks. This enables use cases, such as auto language translations, image classification, etc.

- **Data share between Firestore and BigQuery**: You can capture the changes on your documents stored in Firestore, and. easily replicate the changes on BigQuery. Furthermore, you can pull data from BigQuery, put it in Firestore with ease, and add analytics to the apps.

- **Security**: Firestore integrates with *Firebase Authentication* and *Identity Platform*, to provide customizable and identity-based security access controls, which enables data validation using configuration language.

- **Multi-region replication**: Using automatic multi-region replication and strong consistency, the data is safe and guaranteed a 99.999% availability, even when disasters strike.

- **Live synchronization and offline mode**: Firestore has a built-in live synchronization and an offline mode of operation, making it easier to build, multiuser collaborative apps on mobile, web, and IoT devices; including workload consisting of live activity tracking, real- time analytics, media, product catalogs, communications, various social user profiles, and gaming leaderboards.

- **Libraries for popular languages**: You can focus on application development, using the Firestore client-side development libraries for Web, iOS, Flutter, Android, C++, and Unity. It also supports the traditional server side of development libraries in Node.js, Go, Ruby, Java, and PHP.

- **Datastore mode**: Firestore supports Datastore API, requiring no changes in the existing Datastore apps. You get the same performance and pricing, with stronger consistency. The existing Cloud Datastore databases will automatically be upgraded to Firestore in 2021.

Cloud Bigtable

Cloud Bigtable can scale billions of rows and columns, enabling us to store petabytes of data. It is ideal for large amounts of single key-based data, with very low latency. It supports high read or write throughput, at sub millisecond latency, and is an ideal data source for MapReduce based operations. It supports HBase API (open source) standards, to easily integrate Apache ecosystem like HBase, Beam, Hadoop and Spark along with GCP services.

Use cases for Cloud Bigtable

It is used mainly as the backend database for the below use cases:

- Realtime analytics
- IOT, clickstream, time series
- Financial markets
- Batch unstructured data processing
- Feature stores, operational Datahub, and data fabrics

Key features

Let us understand the key features of Cloud Bigtable:

- **High throughput and low latency at petabyte scale**: Bigtable is a key value and wide column store database, ideal for fast access to large amounts of structured, semi-structured, or unstructured data, with very high read or write throughput. It empowers core Google services like YouTube, Google Analytics, Google Search, Google Ads, Drive, and Maps.

- **Cluster resizing without downtime**: It can seamlessly scale millions of reads or writes per second. Its throughput can dynamically be adjusted by adding or removing the cluster node, without any downtime. It can also automatically scale the cluster, based on the changes in demand so that we can maintain the performance, cost-effectively.

- **Flexible, automated replication to optimize workload**: Once you write the data, it will automatically replicate where needed with consistency, providing you the control for HA, and isolation of read or write workloads. No manual steps are needed to ensure consistency, repair data, and, or synchronize the writes and deletes. You can benefit from a HA SLA of 99.999% for instances with multi-cluster routing, in 3 or more regions (99.9% for single-cluster instances).

- **Easy migrations from HBase and Cassandra to Bigtable**: Live migrations enable, fast and easy migrations from HBase to Bigtable, ensuring accurate data migration, reducing migration effort, and providing a better experience. HBase Bigtable replicates the library, allowing no downtime for live migrations. Import Tools easily load HBase snapshots into the Bigtable, and Validation Tools ensure accurate data migration. The Dataflow templates simplify migrations from Cassandra to Bigtable.

- **Enterprise grade security and controls**: Customer-managed encryption keys with External Key Manager support, IAM for access and controls, VPC service control, and comprehensive audit logging, all ensure the data is protected and complies with all the regulations.

In-memory database in GCP

Memorystore is a fully managed in-memory data store service for *Redis* and *Memcached* in Google Cloud. It is best suited for In-memory and transient data stores, and it automates complex tasks of provisioning, replication, failover, and patching so that more time can be spent on coding. Its extremely low latency and high performance, make it suitable for web and mobile apps, gaming or leaderboard, social, chat, and news feed apps.

Use cases for Memorystore

It is used mainly as a database for the below use cases:

- Database caching
- Session store
- Jobs and queues
- Leaderboards
- Fast data ingestion

Key features

Let us understand the key features of Memorystore:

- **Choice of engines**: You can choose from popular, open-source caching engines to build your applications. Memorystore supports Redis Cluster, Redis, and Memcached, and is fully protocol compatible.

- **Connectivity**: Memorystore for Redis Cluster is available with **Private Service Connect** (**PSC**) to simplify management and offer secure, private, and granular connectivity with minimal IP consumption.

- **Security**: Memorystore is protected from the internet, using a VPC network and private IP. It comes with IAM integration to protect the data. The systems are monitored 24/7, to ensure the protection of applications and data.

- **Fully managed**: Provisioning, replication, failover, and patching are completely automated, reducing the DevOps time significantly.

- **Highly scalable**: Memorystore for Redis Cluster provides no downtime, scales up to 250 nodes, terabytes of keyspace, and 60 times more throughput with microsecond latencies. Memorystore for Redis and Memcached can scale, based on demand, with minimal downtime.

- **Monitoring**: You can monitor your instance and set up custom alerts, with Cloud Monitoring. You can also integrate it with Open-Census, to get additional insights on client-side metrics.

- **Highly available**: Memorystore for Redis Cluster offers 99.99% SLA, with an automatic failover. Shards are automatically distributed in different zones, for maximum availability. Standard tier Memorystore for Redis instances provides a 99.9% SLA with automatic failover to ensure that the instance is highly available. You get the same SLA availability for Memcached instances, as well.

- **Migration:** Memorystore is fully compatible with the open-source protocols, making it easier to switch applications with zero code changes. You can take advantage of the import or export feature, to migrate Redis Cluster, Redis and, or Memcached instance to GCP.

Database for analytics

BigQuery is Google Cloud's fully managed, petabyte-scale, cost-effective, analytics data warehouse, that allows you to run analytics over a huge amount of data in near real-time. With BigQuery, there is no infrastructure to set up or manage, allowing you to focus on finding meaningful insights using Google SQL, and take full advantage of the flexible pricing models (with on-demand and flat-rate options).

We will learn more about this in the *Big Data and Artificial Intelligence* section of this book.

Use cases for BigQuery

It is mainly used for the following use cases:

- Enterprise data warehouse
- Data mesh
- Highly scalable analytics
- Persistent data storage for reporting platforms
- Fast data ingestion

Key features

Let us understand the following key features of BigQuery:

- **Data storage and analysis**: Petabyte scale data storage for Bigdata analysis, Data warehouse, etc.
- **Data Stewardship**: Data profiling and governance.
- **Petabyte scale data processing**: Bigdata processing.
- **Faster data ingestion**: Bigdata Ingestion, support for streaming ingestion, etc.

Conclusion

In this chapter, we have discussed about various database options in Google Cloud, investigated the use cases for these databases, and understood their key features. This brings us to the end of this chapter.

In the next section, we will learn about different computing options in Google Cloud.

Multiple choice questions

1. **Which of the following is an SQL or relational database?**

   a. Spanner

   b. Cloud Bigtable

   c. MongoDB

   d. None of these

2. **Which of the following is a NoSQL or Non-relational database?**

   a. AlloyDB

   b. Firestore

   c. Cloud SQL

   d. None of these

3. **Which of the following is used as an analytical database?**

   a. Spanner

   b. Cloud SQL

   c. BigQuery

   d. None of these

4. **Which of the following is used as an In-Memory database?**

   a. Memorystore

   b. HBase

   c. Cassandra

   d. None of these

5. **Which of the following is best suited for an IoT use case?**

   a. Spanner

   b. Cloud SQL

   c. Cloud Bigtable

   d. None of these

6. **NoSQL databases follow which one of the following rules?**

   a. CAP Theorem

   b. ACID property

   c. Both a and b

   d. None of these

7. **Firestore is best suited for mobile and apps.**

   a. True

   b. False

8. **Which database is best suited for online payments and ledger systems?**

   a. Cloud SQL

   b. Cloud Bigtable

   c. Spanner

   d. None of these

9. **SQL databases are usually vertically scalable.**

   a. True

   b. False

Answers

1.	a
2.	b
3.	c
4.	a
5.	c
6.	a
7.	a
8.	c
9.	a

CHAPTER 7
Google Compute Engine

Introduction

A developer writes a program using a programming language and runs it locally, on their laptop or computer; the program runs on top of the local machine's operating system and uses the machine's processor (CPU) and RAM to get executed. However, this program remains within this local machine itself. Now, if any of us need to run the same program, then it should not be present inside one person's machine, rather it should be in a central place or an environment, from where we all can execute the program. We need an infrastructure to run the program, which has at least a CPU, some amount of RAM, an operating system, and the necessary minimum hard disk space, which can be accessed. When a company provides the **infrastructure as a service (IaaS)** to its clients, it is called IaaS. Compute Engine is one such IaaS tool provided by Google Cloud.

Structure

The chapter covers the following topics:

- Understanding Google Compute Engine
- Creation of Compute Engine VM instance
- Custom SSH keys
- Managed instance groups
- Working in a Compute Engine VM instance

Objectives

We will understand the concept of Google Compute Engine in this chapter. We will see how to create or spin up a virtual machine using the Google Cloud console and using gcloud commands. We will also learn about advanced IaaS features that Google Cloud provides using Compute Engine. Finally, we will execute some codes inside a VM.

Understanding Google Compute Engine

Google Compute Engine is a computing and hosting service that lets you create and run virtual machines on Google infrastructure. It offers scale, performance, and value that lets you easily launch large compute clusters on Google's infrastructure. It is an IaaS offered by Google Cloud.

Key features

Some of the key features of Google Compute Engine service are as follows:

- **Live migration for VMs:** Compute Engine VMs can live migrate between host systems without the need to reboot, which keeps the applications running even if the host systems need maintenance.

- **VM manager**: VM manager is a set of tools that are used to manage the operating systems for large virtual machine fleets running in Windows or Linux on Compute Engine.

- **Batch**: It is a fully managed batch-based service, that helps jobs to be scheduled, queued, or auto-scaled and executed on Compute Engine instances.

- **Confidential VMs**: Confidential VMs are a breakthrough technology that allows us to encrypt the data in use, while it is getting processed. It is simpler and easier in deployment which doesn't compromise on the performance.

- **Sole-tenant nodes**: They are the physical Compute Engine servers that are dedicated exclusively for the customer's use. It simplifies deployment for the **bring-your-own-license** (**BYOL**) applications. It gives access to similar machine types and VM configuration options as regular VM instances.

- **Custom machine types**: You can create a VM with a customized machine type that best fits your needs. By changing a custom machine type to the specific needs, you can get significant savings.

- **Predefined machine types**: Compute Engine offers you predefined virtual machine configurations for every need from a small general-purpose instance to a highly large memory-optimized instance, with up to 11.5 TB of RAM or faster highly compute-optimized instances with up to 60 vCPUs.

- **Spot VMs**: These are affordable compute instances highly suitable for batch jobs / fault-tolerant workloads. Spot VMs provide a significant saving of up to 91% while getting the same performance and capabilities as regular VMs.

- **Instance groups**: An instance group is a collection of VMs running a single application. It automatically creates and deletes VMs to meet the workload demand, repairs the workload from failures, and runs necessary updates.

- **Persistent disks**: As discussed in the previous chapter, it is durable and high-performance block storage for VM instances. Compute Engine offers two types of persistent disks: Google Cloud Hyperdisk and persistent disk. You can create persistent disks either in HDD or in SSD formats. You can take a snapshot and create a new persistent disk from that snapshot. If a VM instance is terminated, its persistent disk still retains data, and this can be attached to another VM instance.

- **Local SSD**: Compute Engine provides always encrypted local **solid-state drive** (**SSD**) storage. Local SSDs are normally physically attached to the server which hosts the virtual machine instance for very high **input or output operations per second** (**IOPS**) and a very low latency compared to the persistent disks.

- **GPU accelerator**: GPUs can be added to accelerate intensive workloads like machine learning, Simulation of a process, and virtual workstation-based applications. You can add or remove GPUs to a VM when the workload changes and pay only for GPU resources time you have used.

- **TPU Accelerators**: Cloud TPUs can be added with VMs to accelerate machine learning and artificial intelligence applications. The Cloud TPUs can be reserved or used on-demand or made available as preemptible VMs (Older versions of Spot VMs).

- **Per-second billing**: Google bills in second-level increments. You need to pay only for the compute time that you use.

Creation of Compute Engine VM instance

We will create VM instances in two ways, using the GCP console and via the command line approach in this book. You can create VM instances using **infrastructure as code (IaC)** tools like Terraform, let us start using GCP console first.

Using GCP console

Let us complete this using a step-by-step process as follows:

- Search for **Compute Engine** in the GCP console and navigate to the same:

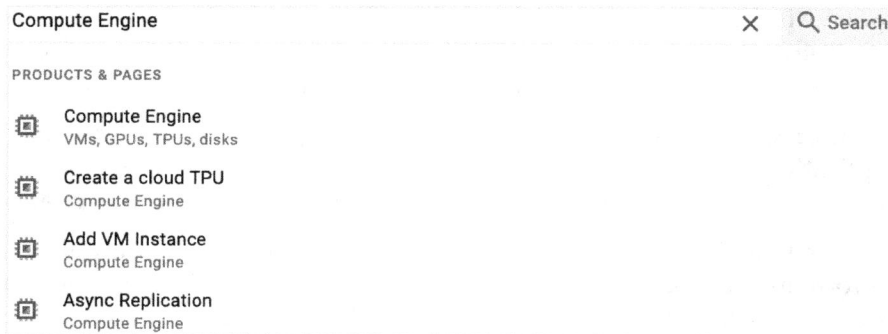

Figure 7.1: Compute Engine

- Enable **Compute Engine API**:

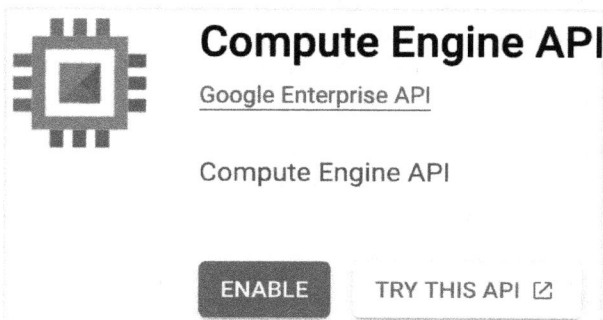

Figure 7.2: Enable Compute Engine API

- Click on **Create Instance**:

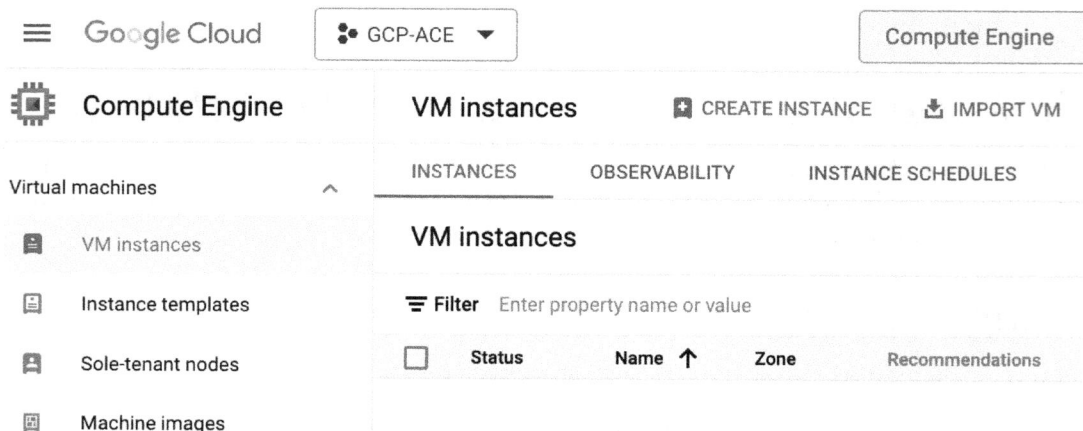

Figure 7.3: Create an instance

- You can create a VM using any of the following options:

  New VM instance
  Create a single VM instance from scratch

  New VM instance from template
  Create a single VM instance from an existing template

  New VM instance from machine image
  Create a single VM instance from an existing machine image

  Marketplace
  Deploy a ready-to-go solution onto a VM instance

Figure 7.4: Create an instance from any of these options

- Let us explore the creation of a VM from scratch:
- Choose instance **Name**, **Region**, and **Zone**:
- You can select **machine configurations** based on your needs:
- On the right-hand side, you can see the **monthly estimate** based on your selections:

Name *
instance-1

∨ MANAGE TAGS AND LABELS

Region *   Zone *
us-central1 (Iowa)   us-central1-a
Region is permanent   Zone is permanent

Monthly estimate
$25.46
That's about $0.03 hourly
Pay for what you use: no upfront costs and per second billing

Item	Monthly estimate
2 vCPU + 4 GB memory	$24.46
10 GB balanced persistent disk	$1.00
Total	$25.46

Compute Engine pricing ↗
∧ LESS

Machine configuration

✓ General purpose | Compute optimized | Memory optimized | GPUs

Machine types for common workloads, optimized for cost and flexibility

	Series ❓	Description	vCPUs ❓	Memory ❓	Platform
○	C3	Consistently high performance	4 - 176	8 - 1,408 GB	Intel Sapphire Rapids
○	C3D	Consistently high performance	4 - 360	8 - 2,880 GB	AMD Genoa
◉	E2	Low cost, day-to-day computing	0.25 - 32	1 - 128 GB	Based on availability
○	N2	Balanced price & performance	2 - 128	2 - 864 GB	Intel Cascade and Ice Lake
○	N2D	Balanced price & performance	2 - 224	2 - 896 GB	AMD EPYC
○	T2A	Scale-out workloads	1 - 48	4 - 192 GB	Ampere Altra Arm
○	T2D	Scale-out workloads	1 - 60	4 - 240 GB	AMD EPYC Milan
○	N1	Balanced price & performance	0.25 - 96	0.6 - 624 GB	Intel Skylake

Figure 7.5: Region, Zone, Machine configuration

- Based on your previous selection, you can choose **vCPU**, **cores**, and **memory**:

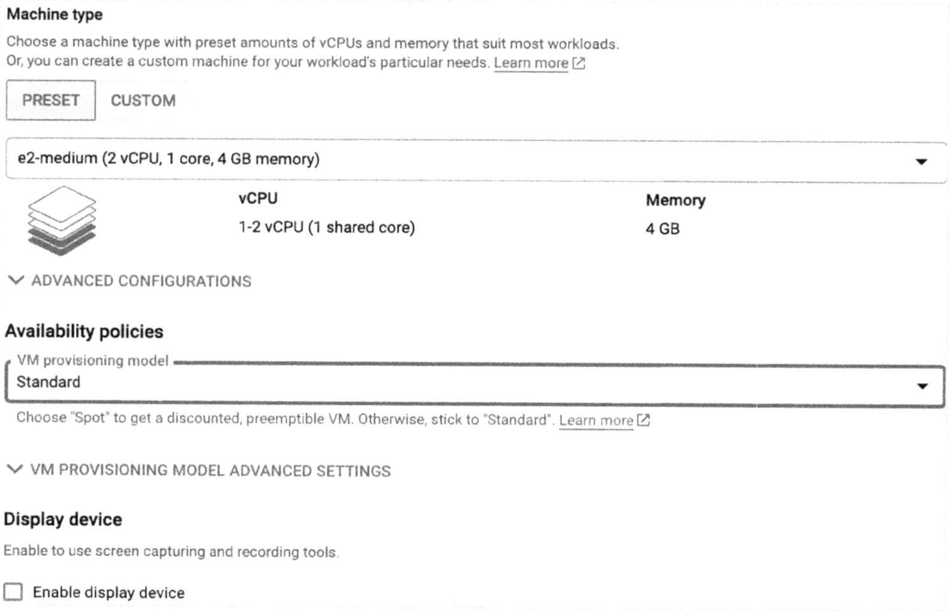

Machine type

Choose a machine type with preset amounts of vCPUs and memory that suit most workloads.
Or, you can create a custom machine for your workload's particular needs. Learn more ☑

PRESET	CUSTOM

e2-medium (2 vCPU, 1 core, 4 GB memory)	▼

	vCPU	Memory
	1-2 vCPU (1 shared core)	4 GB

ⅴ ADVANCED CONFIGURATIONS

Availability policies

VM provisioning model
Standard	▼

Choose "Spot" to get a discounted, preemptible VM. Otherwise, stick to "Standard". Learn more ☑

ⅴ VM PROVISIONING MODEL ADVANCED SETTINGS

Display device

Enable to use screen capturing and recording tools.

☐ Enable display device

Figure 7.6: Machine type and Availability policies

- Then you can choose the **Boot disk** required for your VM:

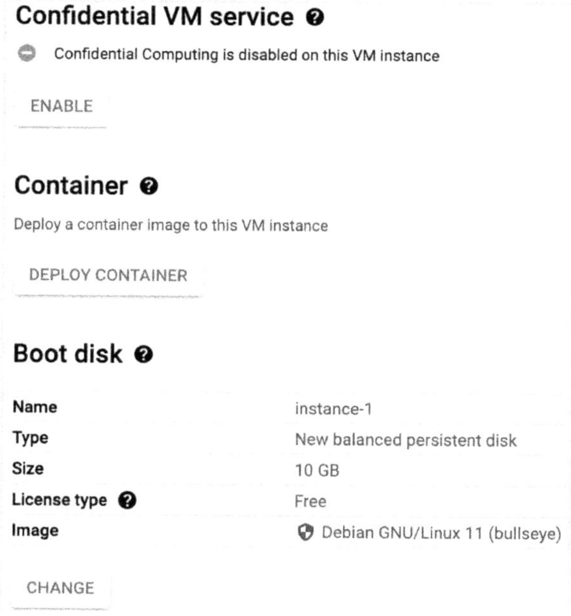

Confidential VM service ❷

⊖ Confidential Computing is disabled on this VM instance

ENABLE

Container ❷

Deploy a container image to this VM instance

DEPLOY CONTAINER

Boot disk ❷

Name	instance-1
Type	New balanced persistent disk
Size	10 GB
License type ❷	Free
Image	🛡 Debian GNU/Linux 11 (bullseye)

CHANGE

Figure 7.7: Boot disk

- You can select from various options as follows:

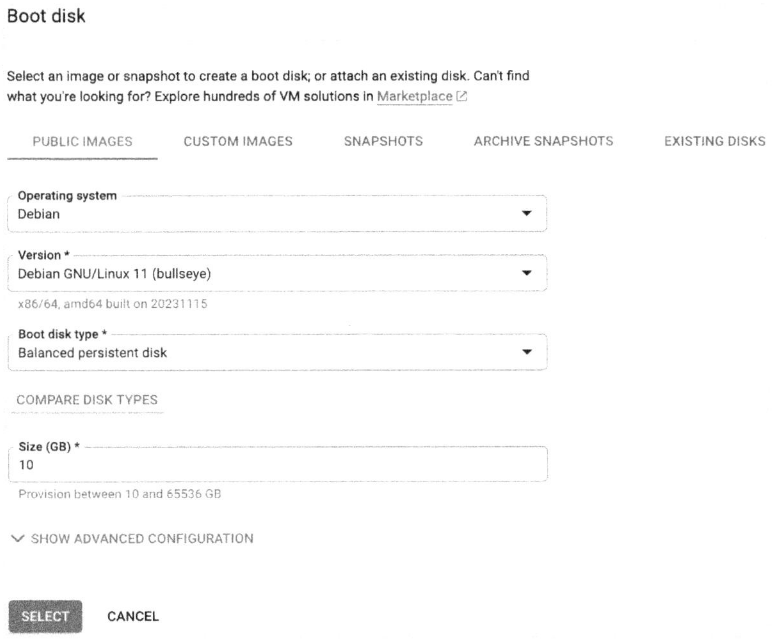

Boot disk

Select an image or snapshot to create a boot disk; or attach an existing disk. Can't find what you're looking for? Explore hundreds of VM solutions in Marketplace

| PUBLIC IMAGES | CUSTOM IMAGES | SNAPSHOTS | ARCHIVE SNAPSHOTS | EXISTING DISKS |

Operating system
Debian

Version *
Debian GNU/Linux 11 (bullseye)

x86/64, amd64 built on 20231115

Boot disk type *
Balanced persistent disk

COMPARE DISK TYPES

Size (GB) *
10

Provision between 10 and 65536 GB

∨ SHOW ADVANCED CONFIGURATION

SELECT   CANCEL

Figure 7.8: Boot disk options

- Finally choose the **Service account**, **Access scopes**, **Firewall** configurations, and create the VM:

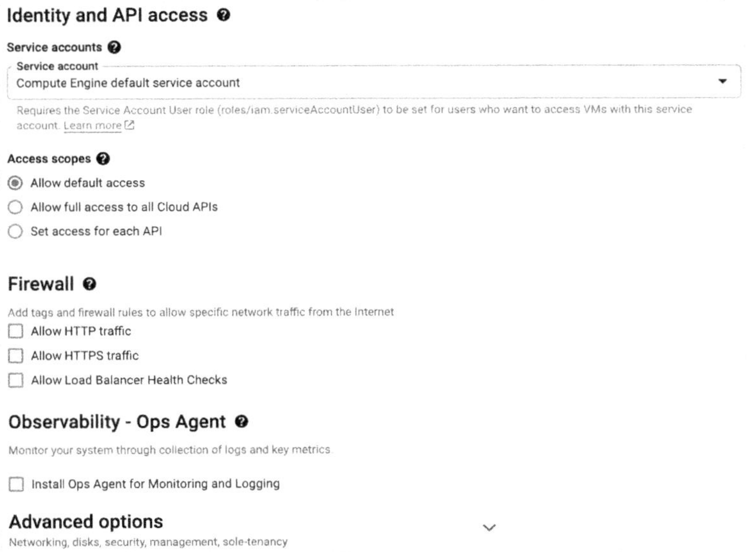

Identity and API access ❷

Service accounts ❷
Service account
Compute Engine default service account

Requires the Service Account User role (roles/iam.serviceAccountUser) to be set for users who want to access VMs with this service account. Learn more

Access scopes ❷
◉ Allow default access
○ Allow full access to all Cloud APIs
○ Set access for each API

Firewall ❷
Add tags and firewall rules to allow specific network traffic from the Internet
☐ Allow HTTP traffic
☐ Allow HTTPS traffic
☐ Allow Load Balancer Health Checks

Observability - Ops Agent ❷
Monitor your system through collection of logs and key metrics

☐ Install Ops Agent for Monitoring and Logging

Advanced options   ∨
Networking, disks, security, management, sole-tenancy

Figure 7.9: Service account, Access scope, and Firewall

- Click on **CREATE** to create the VM instance with the aforementioned configuration settings:

- After the instance is created, you will be able to see it, as follows:

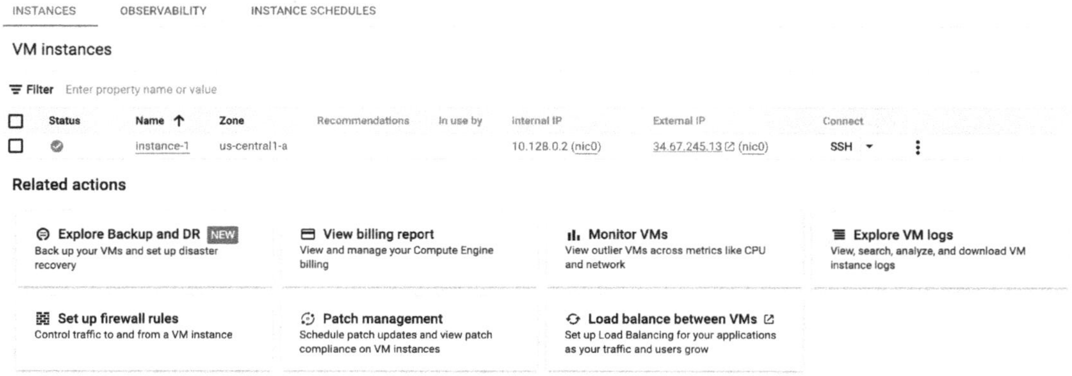

Figure 7.10: Created VM instance

Using command line

Let us create a VM instance using a command line. To create an instance using the latest *Red Hat Enterprise Linux 8* image available, run the following command in Cloud Shell:

```
gcloud compute instances create instance-2 --image-family=rhel-8 --image-project=rhel-cloud --zone=us-central1-a
```

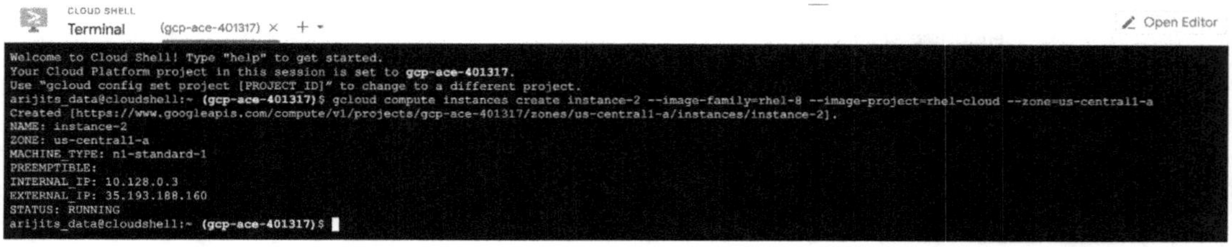

Figure 7.11: Create VM instance using command line

- See it in the console:

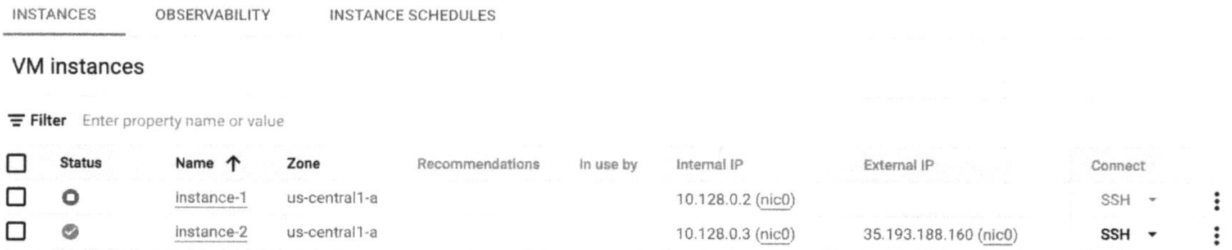

Figure 7.12: Created VM instanced using a command line, verifying from the console

- Basic or default configurations:

DETAILS	OBSERVABILITY	OS INFO	SCREENSHOT

Basic information

Name	instance-2
Instance Id	4394403252411872823
Description	None
Type	Instance
Status	✅ Running
Creation time	Dec 13, 2023, 6:58:57 AM UTC+05:30
Zone	us-central1-a
Instance template	None
In use by	None
Reservations	Automatically choose (default)
Labels	None
Tags ❓	—
	✏️
Deletion protection	Disabled
Confidential VM service ❓	Disabled
Preserved state size	0 GB

Machine configuration

Machine type	n1-standard-1
CPU platform	Intel Haswell
Minimum CPU platform	None
Architecture	x86/64
vCPUs to core ratio ❓	—
Custom visible cores ❓	—
Display device	Disabled
	Enable to use screen capturing and recording tools
GPUs	None
Resource policies	

Figure 7.13: Defaulted configurations – 1

Networking

Public DNS PTR Record	None
Total egress bandwidth tier	—
NIC type	—

→ VIEW IN NETWORK TOPOLOGY

Firewalls

HTTP traffic	Off
HTTPS traffic	Off
Allow Load Balancer Health checks	Off

Network tags

None

Network interfaces

Name ↑	Network	Subnetwork	Primary internal IP address	Alias IP ranges	IP stack type	External IP address	Networ
nic0	default	default	10.128.0.3		IPv4	35.193.188.160 (Ephemeral)	Premiu

Storage

Boot disk

Name ↑	Image	Interface type	Size (GB)	Device name	Type	Architecture	Encryption	Mode	Wh
instance-2	rhel-8-v20231115	SCSI	20	persistent-disk-0	Standard persistent disk	x86/64	Google-managed	Boot, read/write	Del

Figure 7.14: Defaulted configurations – 2

- You can delete the VM once your tutorial-related work is completed otherwise it will incur unwanted costs.

Custom SSH Keys

To work inside a VM instance you need to login to the **VM from Putty (Windows)** or **Terminal (MacOS)**. Now to do this, we need to generate and add SSH keys to the GCP Project's Compute Engine metadata:

- Run the following command:

  ssh-keygen -t rsa -f ~/.ssh/my-ssh-key -C arijits_data -b 2048

- The command will generate one private key and one public key, **my-ssh-key** (private key) and **my-ssh-key.pub** (public key).

- Now copy the content of this public key and add it to GCP Project's Compute Engine metadata.

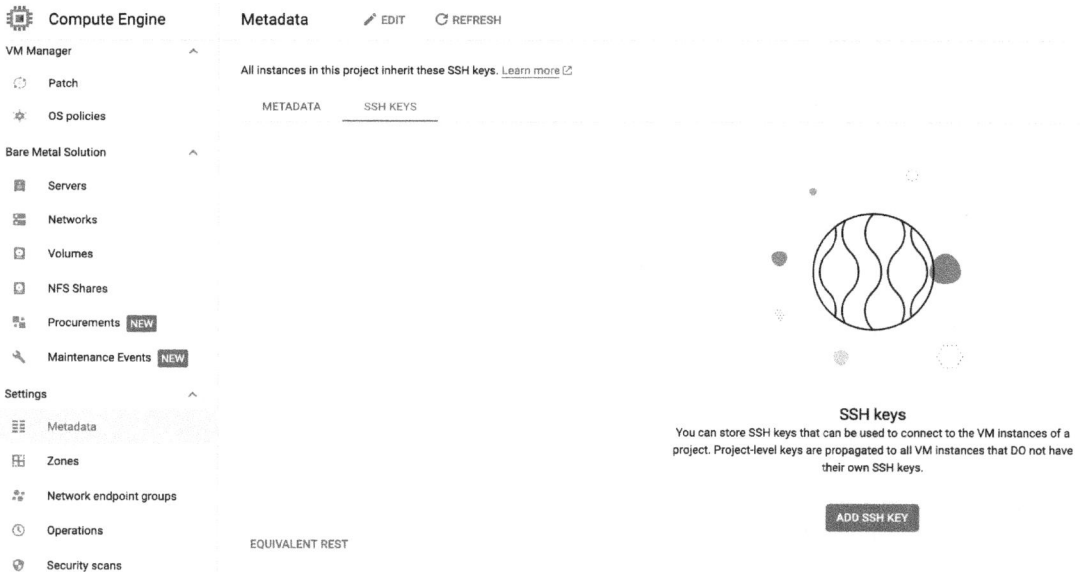

Figure 7.15: Compute Engine's metadata

- Inside the metadata section go to **SSH KEYS** and add the content of the public key generated in *Figure 7.15*.

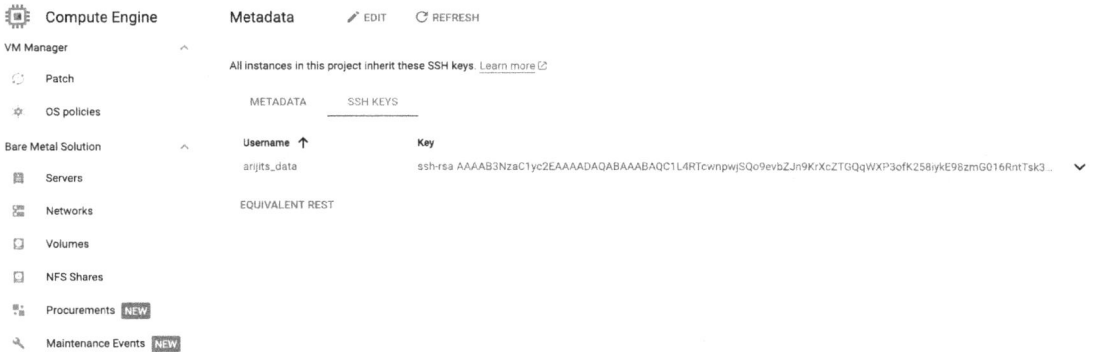

Figure 7.16: Added Public Key

- Now you access log in to the VM using the private key, **ssh -i my-ssh-key arijits_data@35.184.196.111**

- **arijits_data** is the user on the compute engine which is also used while generating public and private keys.

- **35.184.196.111** is the external IP address of the VM.

Managed instance groups

It will allow you to operate applications on multiple identical VMs. You can make your workload scalable and highly available by taking advantage of automated MIGs, including autoscaling, auto-healing, regional (multiple zones) deployment, and automatic updating.

Scenarios

Let us understand in which scenarios it is better to switch to managed instance groups.

- Stateless serving workloads, such as a website frontend

- Stateless batch, high-performance, or high-throughput compute workloads, such as image processing from a queue

- Stateful applications, such as databases, legacy applications, and long-running batch computations with checkpointing

Benefits

There are some certain benefits you can get via managed instance groups.

- **High availability**: It is highly available as it is a group of VM instances.

- **Scalability**: It can spin up instances as load increases and vice versa.

- **Automated updates**: You can apply VM configuration updates automatically.

- **Support for stateful workloads**: It supports batch jobs which run for hours maintaining the state of application and data, another example for stateful workload is database application on managed instance group.

Working in a Compute Engine VM instance

To build an application that will be hosted on a Compute Engine VM instance, we need to log in to the VM and start playing around the Native Operating System. Let us explore this from the console:

- Navigate the Compute Engine section.

VM instances

Figure 7.17: Listed VMs in the console

- Click on **SSH** present under the **Connect** section against **instance-1** VM.
- Once clicked, it will open a browser window and ask for authorization:

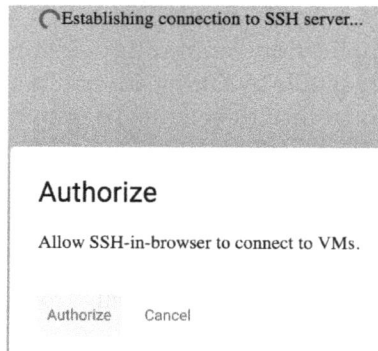

Figure 7.18: Authorize the access to the VM

- Inside the VM, you will be able to see the following screen:

```
Linux instance-1 5.10.0-26-cloud-amd64 #1 SMP Debian 5.10.197-1 (2023-09-29) x86_64

The programs included with the Debian GNU/Linux system are free software;
the exact distribution terms for each program are described in the
individual files in /usr/share/doc/*/copyright.

Debian GNU/Linux comes with ABSOLUTELY NO WARRANTY, to the extent
permitted by applicable law.
Last login: Wed Dec 13 02:20:28 2023 from 182.69.5.227
arijits_data@instance-1:~$
```

Figure 7.19: Inside the VM

- You can execute commands and build or deploy applications like you normally do in any other VMs:

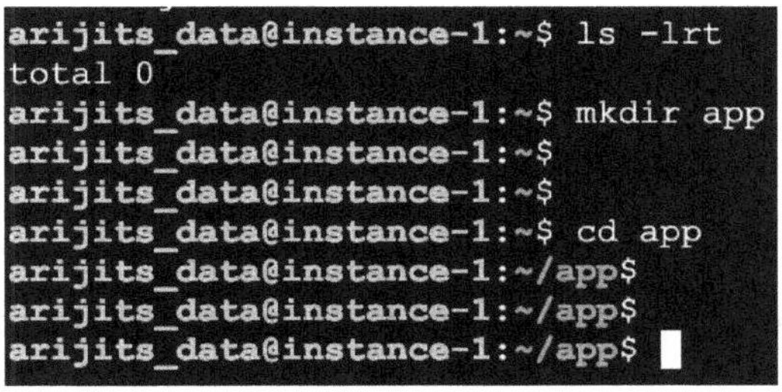

Figure 7.20: *Executing Linux commands on the VM*

Conclusion

In this chapter, we have learned how to set up the compute engine VM in the Google Cloud Platform. Compute Engine VMs are used widely for various types of computing workloads across industries.

We discussed how SSH keys are configured to the VM. Moreover, we saw how we can log in and execute commands in the VM's operating system. Additionally, we have discussed the key features, along with different types of Compute Engine VMs in this chapter.

We will learn about another GCP computing service called *Cloud Run* in the next chapter.

Multiple choice questions

1. **Which of the following is not an advantage of MIGs?**
   a.   High availability
   b.   Scalability
   c.   Automatic updates
   d.   None of these

2. **To login to a GCP VM from a local machine you normally connect to:**
   a.   Internal IP address
   b.   External IP address
   c.   Both
   d.   None of these

3. While creating Google Cloud Platform's compute engine VM, which of the following gcloud command is used?

       e.   gcloud compute instances create.

       f.   gcloud compute instances add.

       g.   gcloud compute instances configure.

       h.   None of these

4. For SSH key-based login, which type of key's content is added in Compute Engine's metadata?

       a.   Private key

       b.   Public key

       c.   Both

       d.   None of these

Answers

1.	c
2.	b
3.	a
4.	b

Join our book's Discord space

Join the book's Discord Workspace for Latest updates, Offers, Tech happenings around the world, New Release and Sessions with the Authors:

https://discord.bpbonline.com

CHAPTER 8
Cloud Run

Introduction

In the last chapter, we discussed Compute Engine, which is an **infrastructure as a service (IaaS)** offering from the Google Cloud Platform. To execute a program, a compute platform is required. Now, if that compute platform needs scaling, to process a huge amount of computing tasks in a quick time, then it needs a powerful processor and a higher volume of RAM; so basically, an organization needs to spend a large amount of money upfront to meet the processing need. But if this scaling is needed for a short span of time, then the rest of the time the heavy processor and the RAM need to stay idle, which results in the wastage of money and resources. Now, if we can get a computing system or a platform which can scale up and down automatically based on the need, then it becomes quite easy for the organization to manage its workload. In this chapter, we will learn how to solve this scaling problem using container-based approach, using Cloud Run.

Structure

The chapter covers the following topics:

- Understanding platform as a service
- Difference between PaaS and IaaS
- Introduction to Cloud Run

- Introduction to containerized applications
- Container or artifact registry
- Creating a REST API using Cloud Run

Objectives

In this chapter, we will understand Cloud Run. We will understand how to set up Cloud Run using Google Cloud Console and gcloud commands. Moreover, we will discuss about platform as a service concept and how we can implement the same using Cloud Run. We will discuss containers in this chapter and understand how to create Docker container and deploy it using Cloud Run, to create a REST API.

Understanding platform as a service

Platform as a service (PaaS) is a category of cloud computing that allows customers to provision, initiate, instantiate, run, deploy, and manage a modular bundle comprising a computing platform and one or more applications without worrying about the complexity of building and maintaining the infrastructure, normally associated with developing and launching the application(s), and allows the developers to create, develop, and package such software bundles.

Difference between PaaS and IaaS

Let us understand the difference between IaaS and PaaS from User and cloud provider's perspective, as follows:

Characteristics	Infrastructure as a service (IaaS)	Platform as a service (PaaS)
Data and configurations	Managed by User	Managed by User
Application code	Managed by User	Managed by User
Scaling	Managed by User	Managed by User and Cloud Provider both
Runtime	Managed by User	Managed by Cloud Provider
Operating system	Managed by User	Managed by Cloud Provider

Virtualization	Managed by Cloud Provider	Managed by Cloud Provider
Hardware	Managed by Cloud Provider	Managed by Cloud Provider

Table 8.1: Difference between PaaS and IaaS

Introduction to Cloud Run

Cloud Run is a managed compute platform that allows you to run containers directly on top of Google's scalable infrastructure. You can deploy the written code using any programming language on Cloud Run, if you are able to build a container image from it. For *Go, Node.js, Python, Java, .NET Core*, or *Ruby,* you can use the source-based deployment option, which builds the container using the best practices for the language in use. Cloud Run integrates with other Google Cloud services easily, which makes the application development easier in GCP. Cloud Run allows developers to utilize their time in writing their code, and very little time on operating, configuring, and scaling their Cloud Run service. Moreover, there is no need to create a cluster or manage infrastructure to be productive with Cloud Run.

Ways of using Cloud Run

The following are the two ways of using Cloud Run:

- **Cloud Run services:** It runs the code, responds to web requests or events, and it runs continuously.

  Its use cases are as follows:

  o Websites and web applications

  o APIs and microservices

  o Streaming data processing

- **Cloud Run jobs:** It is used to run the codes to perform certain work, and once the execution or work is completed, it quits.

  Its use cases are as follows:

  o Script or tool

  o Array job

  o Scheduled job

Features of Cloud Run

The following are the features of Cloud Run:

- **Any language, any library, any binary**: You can write code using your favorite language, framework, and libraries, package it up as a container, run `gcloud run deploy`, and your app will be live provided with everything it needs to run in production.

- **Fast autoscaling**: Whether you own event-driven, long running services or deploy containerized jobs to process data, Cloud Run automatically scales your containers up and down from zero. This means you only pay when your code is running.

- **Automatically build container images from your source**: Cloud Run can also automate how you get to production, using buildpacks to enable you to deploy directly from source, without having to install Docker on your machine. You can automate your builds and deploy your code whenever new commits are pushed to a given branch of a Git repository.

- **Run scheduled jobs**: Cloud Run jobs allow you to perform batch processing with instances running parallel. Execute run-to-completion jobs that do not respond to HTTP requests, all on a serverless platform. Let your jobs run for up to 24 hours.

- **Direct VPC connectivity**: You can enable your Cloud Run service or job to send traffic to a VPC network by using **Direct VPC egress** with no serverless **VPC Access connector** required.

Introduction to containerized applications

In this section, we will learn about containerized applications:

- **Docker container**: A Docker container is a standard unit of software that packages up code and all its dependencies so the application runs quickly and reliably from one computing environment to another.

- **Docker container image**: A Docker container image is a lightweight, standalone, executable package of software that includes everything needed to run an application: code, runtime, system tools, system libraries, and settings.

You can use Docker images and containers in combination with each other when you create and deploy software. Ideally, you will create containers from images as follows:

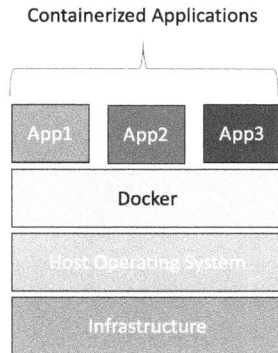

Figure 8.1: Containerized applications

A host operating system runs on the underlying infrastructure and, the Docker software runs on the host operating system; and multiple applications as Docker containers, run on top of them.

Container or artifact registry

A Container Registry is used to store container images. Artifact registry enables us to centrally store artifacts and build dependencies as part of an integrated Google Cloud experience. It provides a single location for storing and managing your packages and Docker container images. It expands on the capabilities of Container Registry and is the recommended Container Registry, for Google Cloud.

Features

The following are the features:

- Container Registry stores container images.
- You can store artifacts from Cloud Build in the artifact registry.
- It deploys artifacts to Google Cloud runtimes, including GKE, Cloud Run, Compute Engine, etc.
- Manage container metadata and scan for container vulnerabilities with Artifact analysis.
- Protect repositories in a VPC service control security perimeter.
- Enforce deployment policies with binary authorization.

Creating a REST API using Cloud Run

In this section, we will understand how to create a simple REST API using Cloud Run, a containerized application. Starting from creating a Docker file to deploy the application to

Cloud Run, we are going to learn all the required steps to build a full-fledged REST API. We are going to use Python based flask library in this case, using the following steps:

1. Activate Cloud Shell in a **GCP** project and check whether Docker is present or not, as follows:

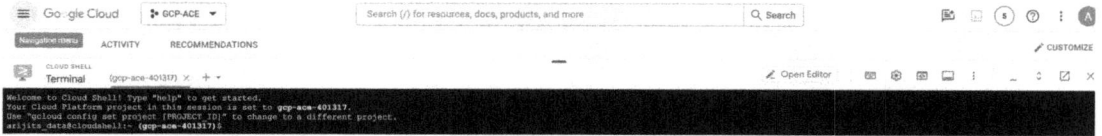

Figure 8.2: Cloud Shell

Check the Docker version by running a command **docker version** in command line prompt:

Command:

docker version

Figure 8.3: Docker version

2. Create a directory named **deploy**, as follows:

Command:

mkdir deploy

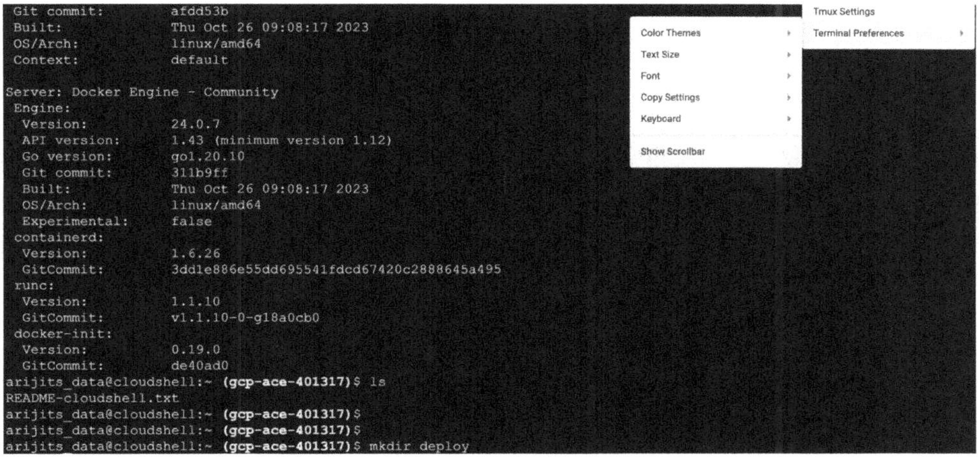

Figure 8.4: Creating directory called deploy

3. Create a simple application as follows and name it **app.py** in side **deploy** folder:

Command:

cd deploy

vi app.py

Contents of app.py:

```
from flask import Flask

app = Flask(__name__)

@app.route("/")
def func():
        return {"value": "Yes"}

if __name__ == "__main__":
        app.run(host="0.0.0.0")
```

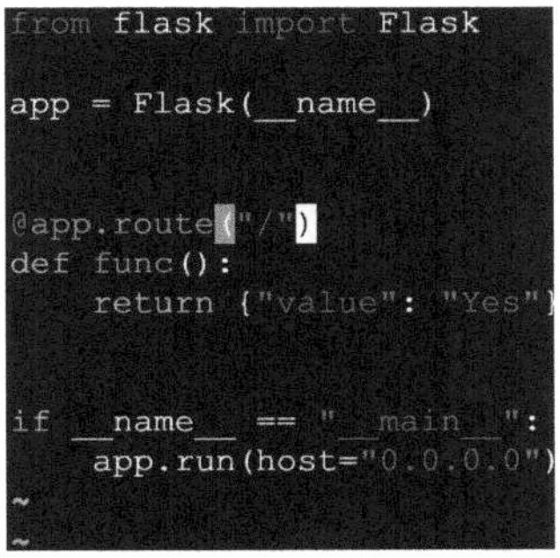

Figure 8.5: Simple flask application

4. Run it locally, as follows:

Command:

```
python app.py
```

```
arijits_data@cloudshell:~/deploy (gcp-ace-401317)$ python app.py
 * Serving Flask app 'app'
 * Debug mode: off
WARNING: This is a development server. Do not use it in a production deployment. Use a production WSGI server instead.
 * Running on all addresses (0.0.0.0)
 * Running on http://127.0.0.1:5000
 * Running on http://10.88.0.3:5000
Press CTRL+C to quit
```

Figure 8.6: Flask application running locally in Cloud Shell

5. You can preview it, as follows:

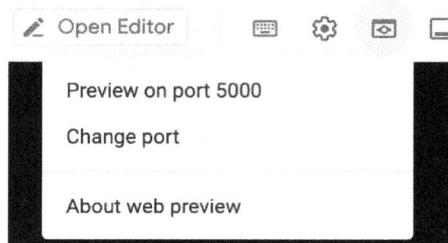

Figure 8.7: Preview the application

You can change the port if it is running on a different port to see the preview:

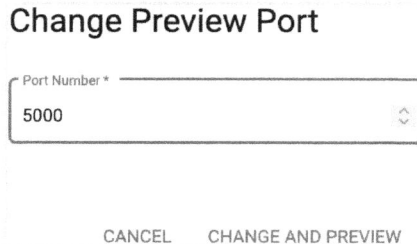

Figure 8.8: Change the port to see the Preview Port

Response is obtained as follows:

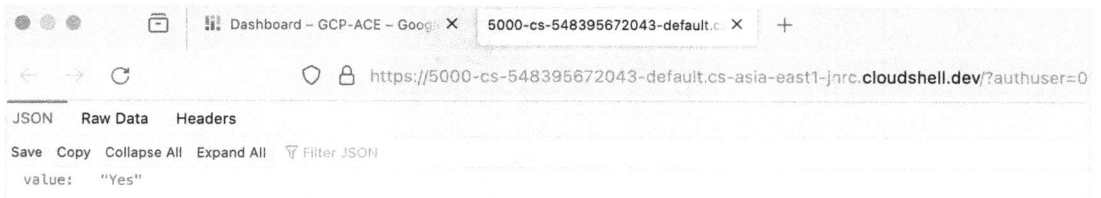

Figure 8.9: Application preview

You will receive a **Response code 200**.

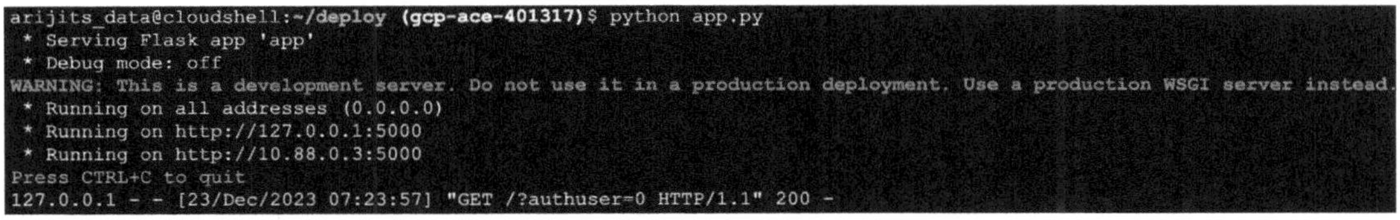
arijits_data@cloudshell:~/deploy (gcp-ace-401317)$ python app.py
* Serving Flask app 'app'
* Debug mode: off
WARNING: This is a development server. Do not use it in a production deployment. Use a production WSGI server instead.
* Running on all addresses (0.0.0.0)
* Running on http://127.0.0.1:5000
* Running on http://10.88.0.3:5000
Press CTRL+C to quit
127.0.0.1 - - [23/Dec/2023 07:23:57] "GET /?authuser=0 HTTP/1.1" 200 -

Figure 8.10: Response Code – 200, after preview

6. Create a Docker file named **Dockerfile** as follows at the same location:

   Command:

   vi Dockerfile

   Contents of Docker file:

```
FROM python:3.7-slim
RUN pip install flask
WORKDIR /working
COPY app.py /working/app.py
CMD [“python”, “/working/app.py”]
```

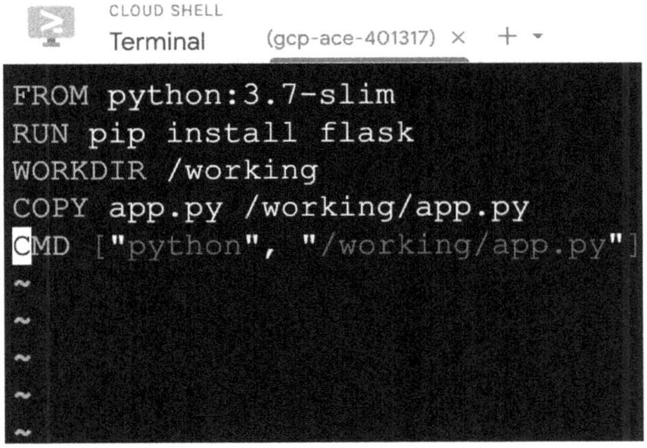
CLOUD SHELL
Terminal
(gcp-ace-401317)
FROM python:3.7-slim
RUN pip install flask
WORKDIR /working
COPY app.py /working/app.py
CMD ["python", "/working/app.py"]

Figure 8.11: Docker file

7. You can verify the same using **ls** command as follows:

   Command:

   ls

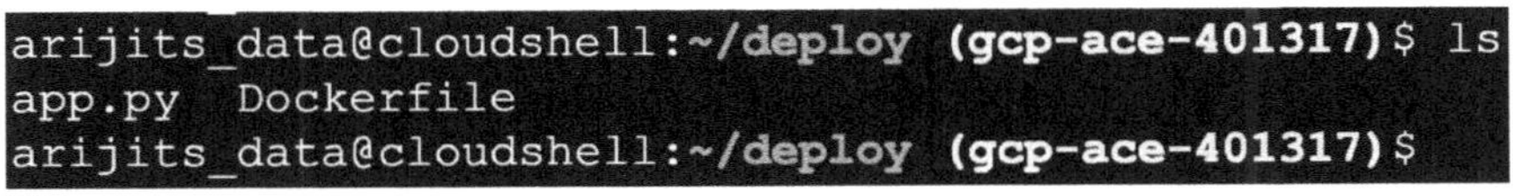
arijits_data@cloudshell:~/deploy (gcp-ace-401317)$ ls
app.py Dockerfile
arijits_data@cloudshell:~/deploy (gcp-ace-401317)$

Figure 8.12: Current directory

8. Build the Docker image, as follows:

Command:

```
docker build -t gcr.io/gcp-ace-401317/flask-image:v1.0 .
```

Figure 8.13: Image building

9. Verify the created **Docker image**, as follows:

Command:

```
docker images
```

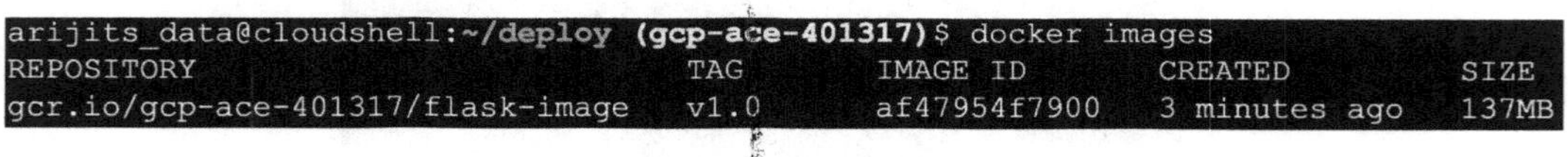

Figure 8.14: Images created

10. Execute the image as container locally, as follows:

Command:

```
docker run -p 7000:5000 gcr.io/gcp-ace-401317/flask-image:v1.0
```

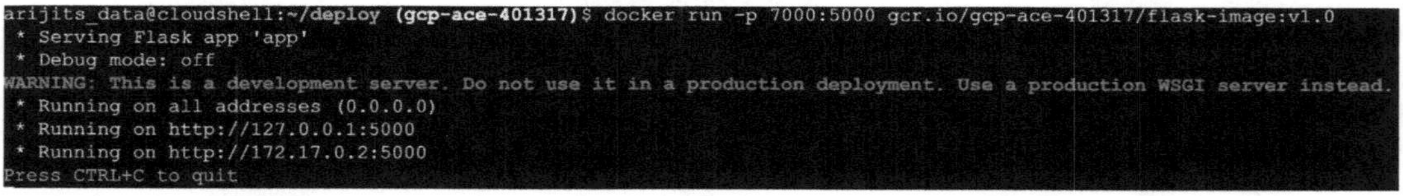

Figure 8.15: Running the image as container

11. Authorize by configuring to Docker, to push the image to Container Registry, as follows:

Command:

`gcloud auth configure-docker`

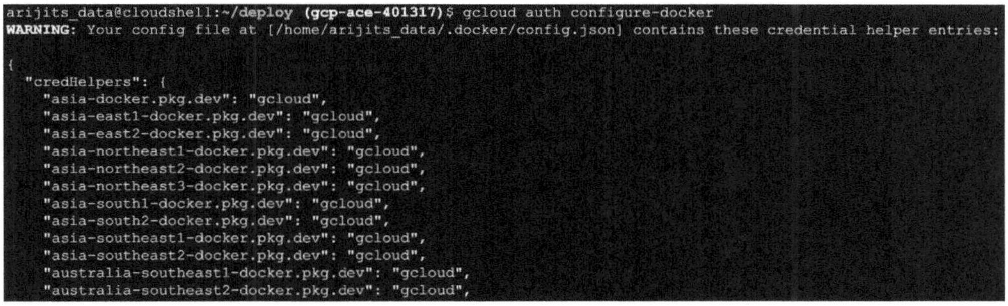

```
arijits_data@cloudshell:~/deploy (gcp-ace-401317)$ gcloud auth configure-docker
WARNING: Your config file at [/home/arijits_data/.docker/config.json] contains these credential helper entries:

{
  "credHelpers": {
    "asia-docker.pkg.dev": "gcloud",
    "asia-east1-docker.pkg.dev": "gcloud",
    "asia-east2-docker.pkg.dev": "gcloud",
    "asia-northeast1-docker.pkg.dev": "gcloud",
    "asia-northeast2-docker.pkg.dev": "gcloud",
    "asia-northeast3-docker.pkg.dev": "gcloud",
    "asia-south1-docker.pkg.dev": "gcloud",
    "asia-south2-docker.pkg.dev": "gcloud",
    "asia-southeast1-docker.pkg.dev": "gcloud",
    "asia-southeast2-docker.pkg.dev": "gcloud",
    "australia-southeast1-docker.pkg.dev": "gcloud",
    "australia-southeast2-docker.pkg.dev": "gcloud",
```

***Figure 8.16:** Docker authorization*

12. Push the image to Container Registry as follows:

    Command:

    `docker push gcr.io/gcp-ace-401317/flask-image:v1.0`

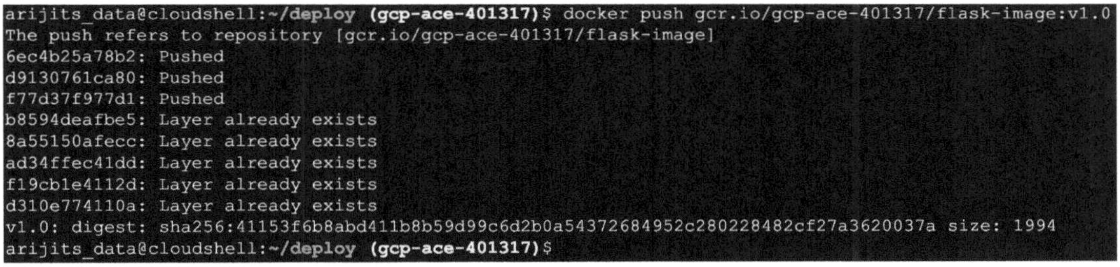

```
arijits_data@cloudshell:~/deploy (gcp-ace-401317)$ docker push gcr.io/gcp-ace-401317/flask-image:v1.0
The push refers to repository [gcr.io/gcp-ace-401317/flask-image]
6ec4b25a78b2: Pushed
d9130761ca80: Pushed
f77d37f977d1: Pushed
b8594deafbe5: Layer already exists
8a55150afecc: Layer already exists
ad34ffec41dd: Layer already exists
f19cb1e4112d: Layer already exists
d310e774110a: Layer already exists
v1.0: digest: sha256:41153f6b8abd411b8b59d99c6d2b0a54372684952c280228482cf27a3620037a size: 1994
arijits_data@cloudshell:~/deploy (gcp-ace-401317)$
```

***Figure 8.17:** Pushing the Docker image to Container Registry*

13. Verify the image pushed to **Container Registry**, as follows:

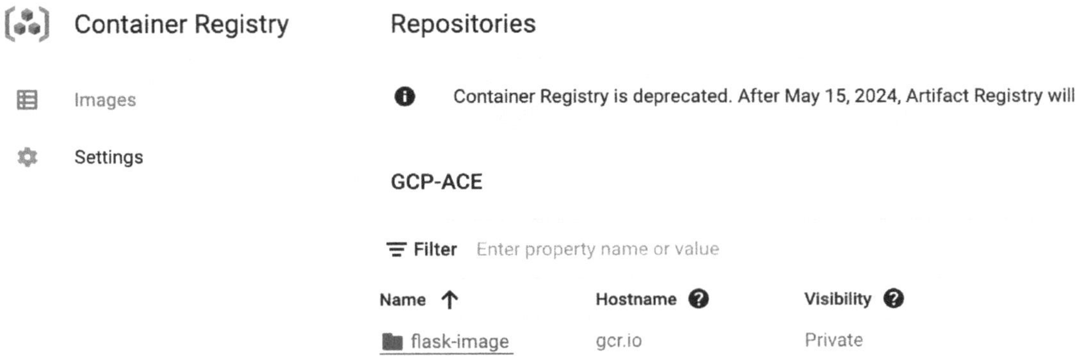

***Figure 8.18:** Image pushed to Container Registry in GCP*

You can deploy to different compute services from the image also:

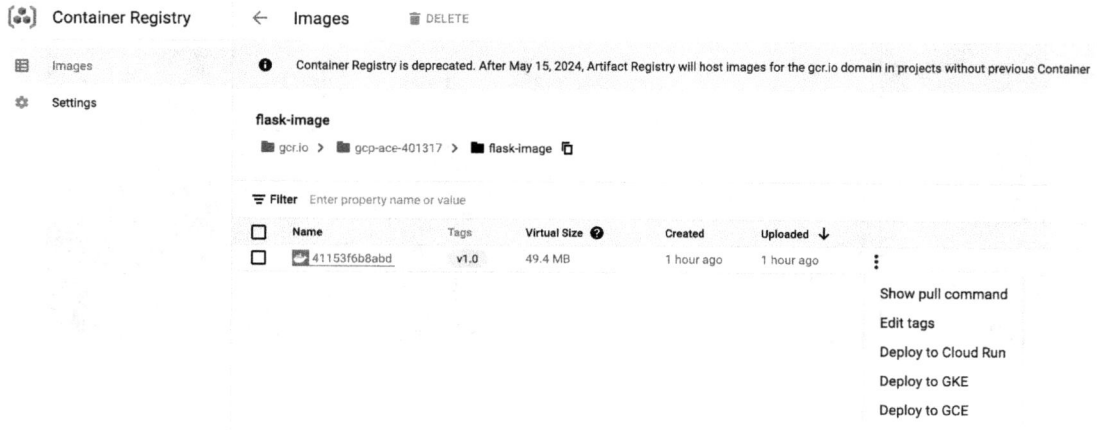

Figure 8.19: Image in Container Registry

14. Now let us deploy the image as container in Cloud Run, and search for `cloud run`, as follows:

Figure 8.20: Search Cloud Run in search bar

15. Check the **Cloud Run** page, as follows:

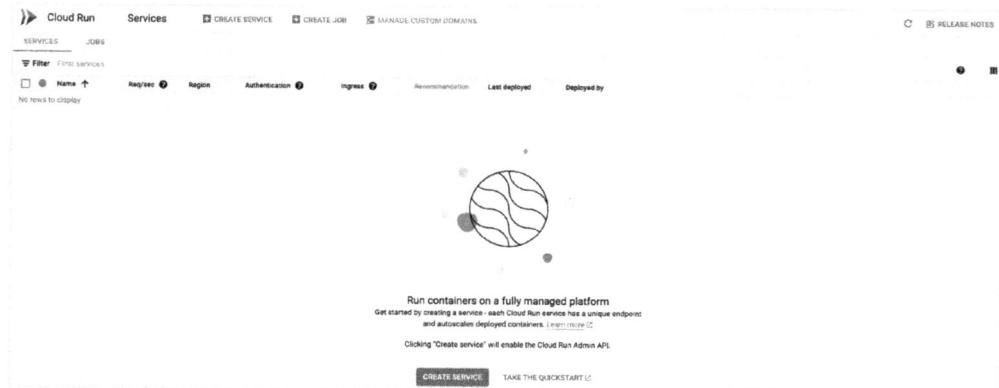

Figure 8.21: Inside Cloud Run

16. Click on **CREATE SERVICE** to start, as follows:

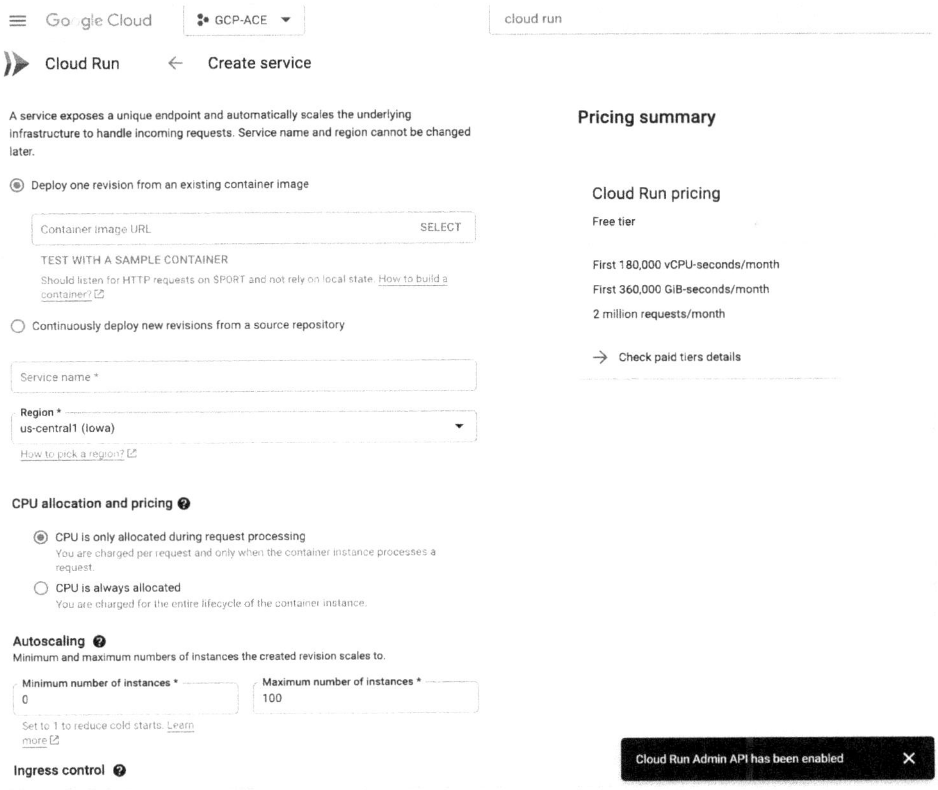

Figure 8.22: Creating Cloud Run Service

17. Select the **image**, as follows:

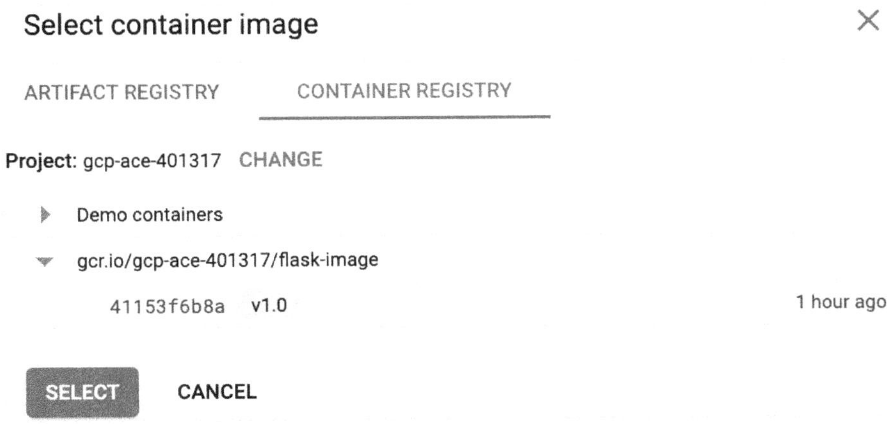

Figure 8.23: Selecting the image for Cloud Run service

Other Cloud Run configurations are as follows:

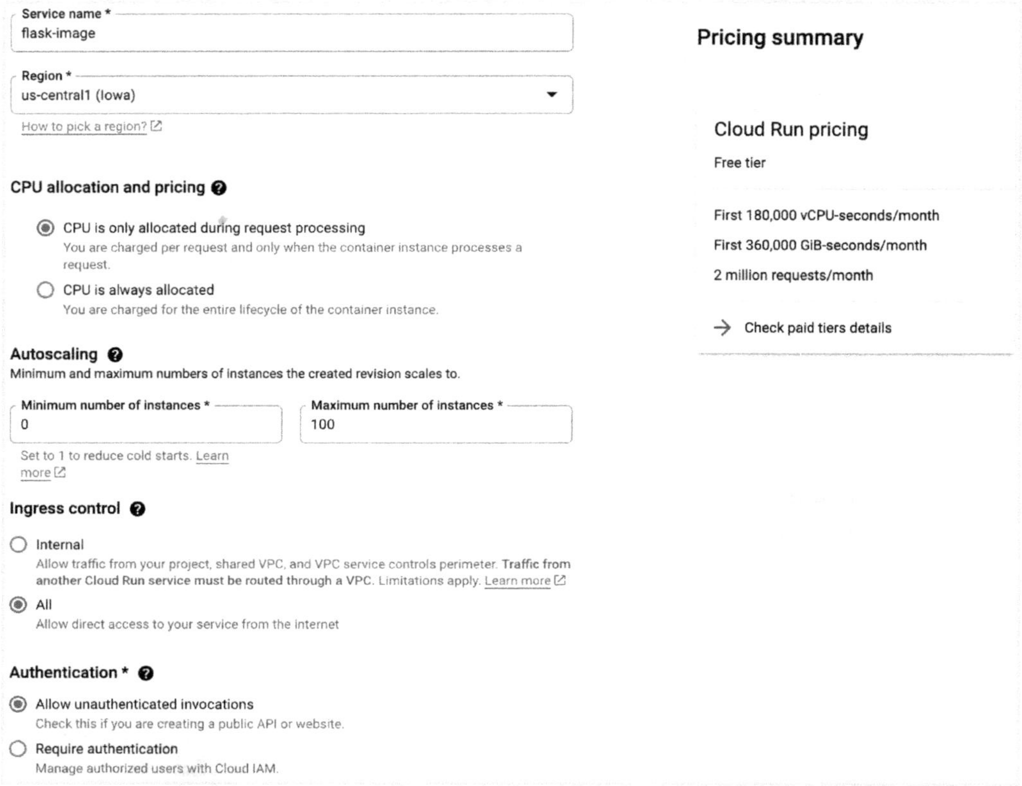

Figure 8.24: Creating Cloud Run service more settings, port, networking, etc.

18. Cloud Run service is ready to be consumed:

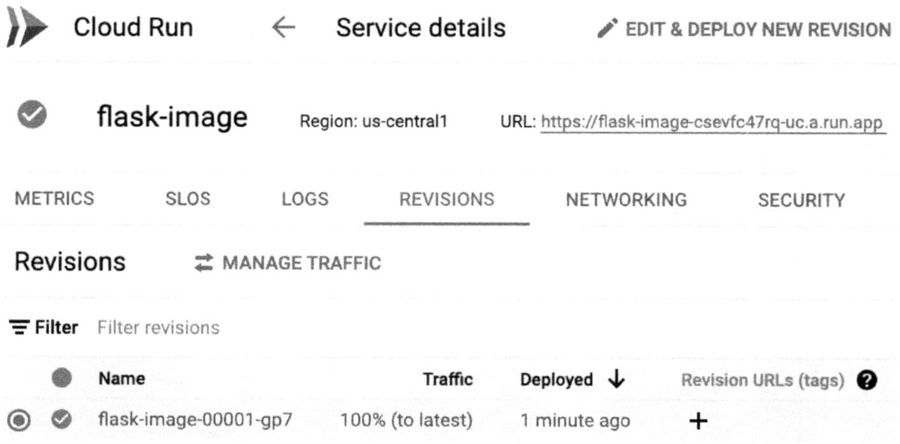

Figure 8.25: Service is ready

Details of the Cloud Run service are as follows:

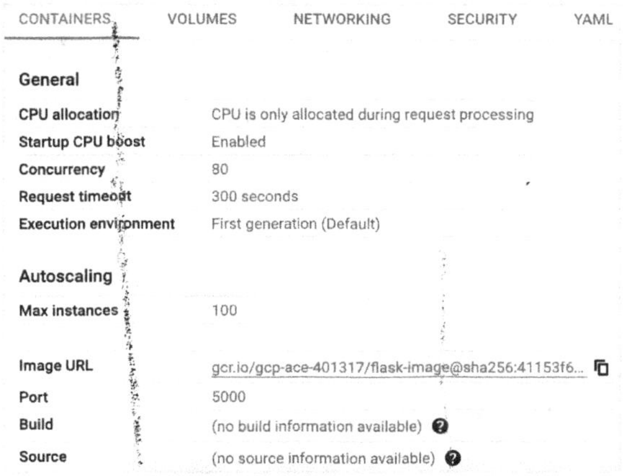

Figure 8.26: Cloud Run service details

19. After the service is ready, you can test it by logging into the Cloud Run service URL, as follows:

Figure 8.27: Testing the URL

Edit the deployment and revise the service to create another revision of Cloud Run service, and for this, we will change the return statement from "value": "Yes" to "value": "No".

20. Return statement will be changed as follows:

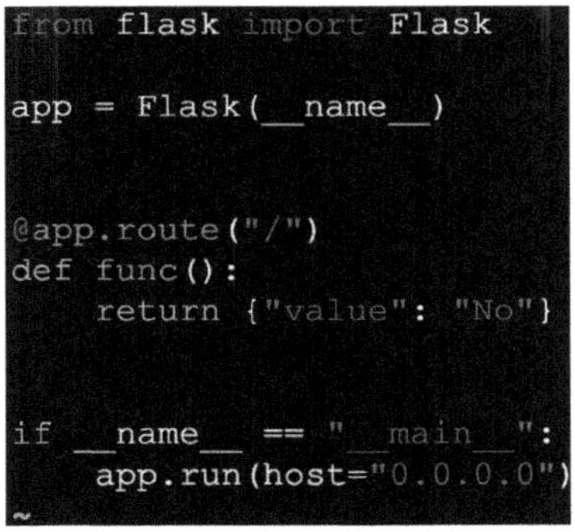

```
from flask import Flask

app = Flask(__name__)

@app.route("/")
def func():
    return {"value": "No"}

if __name__ == "__main__":
    app.run(host="0.0.0.0")
~
```

Figure 8.28: Changing the application code

21. Build the image as *version 2.0* under the same image name, as follows:

Figure 8.29: Built the image again as version 2.0

22. Pushing the new image version to Container Registry, as follows:

Figure 8.30: Pushed the new image to Container Registry

23. Both **images** can be verified in the console, as follows:

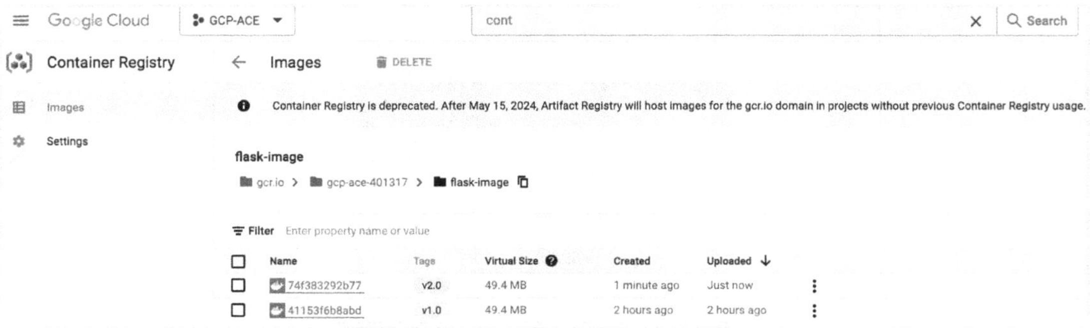

Figure 8.31: Version 1 and Version 2 images

24. Edit the deployment in Cloud Run and point the new image version, as follows:

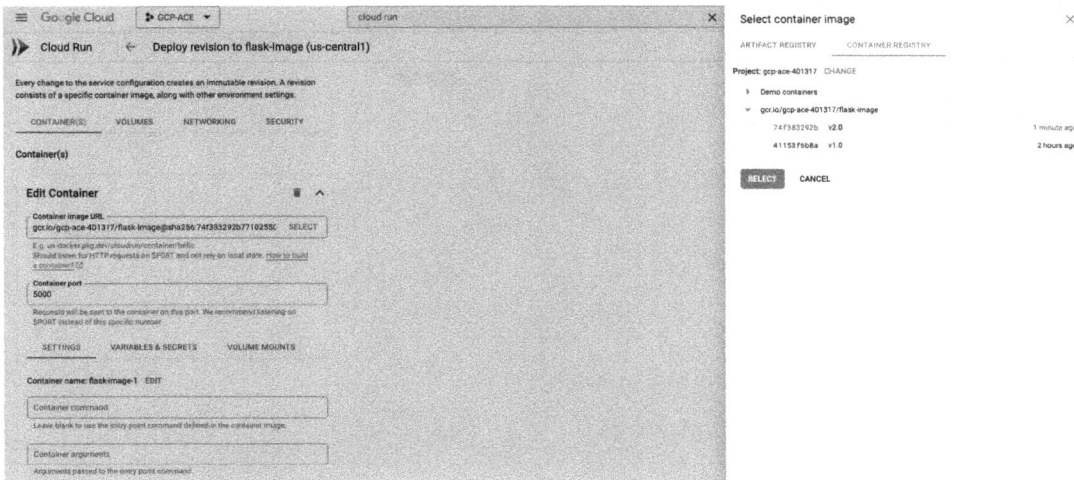

Figure 8.32: *Edit the deployment service to reflect the new image*

25. Uncheck the **Serve this revision immediately** option (otherwise complete traffic will be pointed to this new revision) and deploy this revision by clicking on **DEPLOY** button, as follows:

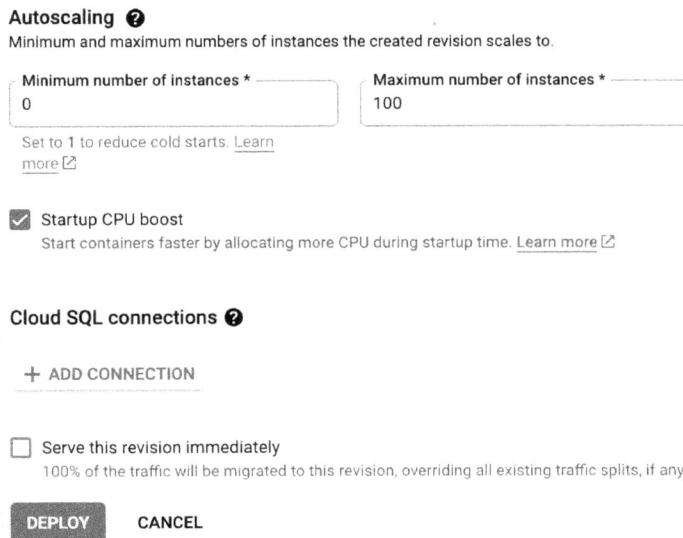

Autoscaling ❓
Minimum and maximum numbers of instances the created revision scales to.

Minimum number of instances *
0

Maximum number of instances *
100

Set to 1 to reduce cold starts. Learn more ☑

☑ Startup CPU boost
Start containers faster by allocating more CPU during startup time. Learn more ☑

Cloud SQL connections ❓

➕ ADD CONNECTION

☐ Serve this revision immediately
100% of the traffic will be migrated to this revision, overriding all existing traffic splits, if any.

DEPLOY   CANCEL

Figure 8.33: *Serving the new image*

26. You can click on **MANAGE TRAFFIC** to redirect the traffic, to correct versions by splitting the **traffic** percentage as follows:

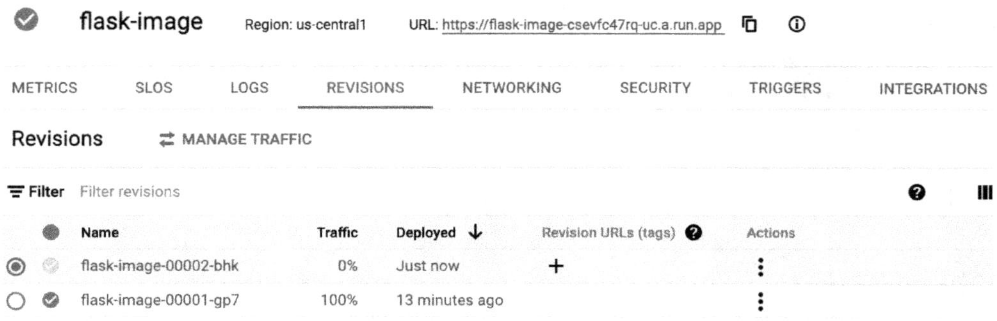

✓ **flask-image**   Region: us-central1   URL: https://flask-image-csevfc47rq-uc.a.run.app 🗗 ①

| METRICS | SLOS | LOGS | REVISIONS | NETWORKING | SECURITY | TRIGGERS | INTEGRATIONS |

Revisions   ⇄ MANAGE TRAFFIC

⇅ Filter   Filter revisions   ❷   ▥

	Name	Traffic	Deployed ↓	Revision URLs (tags) ❷	Actions
◉ ◌	flask-image-00002-bhk	0%	Just now	✛	⋮
○ ✓	flask-image-00001-gp7	100%	13 minutes ago		⋮

Figure 8.34: Deployed the revision

Split the traffic based on requirement:

Manage traffic

Revision 1 *	Traffic 1
flask-image-0... ▼ Serving	50 ↕ % (Currently: 100%)

Revision 2 *	Traffic 2
flask-image-00002-bhk ▼	50 ↕ % (Currently: 0%)

✛ ADD REVISION

CANCEL   **SAVE**

Figure 8.35: Split the traffic between two versions

27. Testing the URL once, to redirect to *version 1* image, as follows:

← → ⟳   ○ 🔒 https://flask-image-csevfc47rq-uc.a.run.app

JSON   Raw Data   Headers

Save Copy Collapse All Expand All ▽ Filter JSON

   value: "Yes"

Figure 8.36: Version 1 output

28. Testing the URL once, to redirect to *version 2* image, as follows:

← → ⟳   ○ 🔒 https://flask-image-csevfc47rq-uc.a.run.app

JSON   Raw Data   Headers

Save Copy Collapse All Expand All ▽ Filter JSON

   value: "No"

Figure 8.37: Version 2 output

Testing the same URL two times resulted two different outputs based on image versions and traffic splits.

Conclusion

In this chapter, we discussed about PaaS and how containerized applications are deployed in GCP's managed service called Cloud Run and invoked from outside. Additionally, we discussed about Docker images, container etc. In the next chapter, we will discuss the Google Kubernetes Engine and deploy the images to it.

Multiple choice questions

1. **In PaaS, scaling of an application is managed by whom?**

   a. User

   b. Cloud Service provider

   c. Both a and b

   d. None of these

2. **Cloud Run offerings include:**

   a. Services

   b. Jobs

   c. Both a and b

   d. None of these

3. **Cloud Run Service URL cannot be accessed without authentication**

   a. True

   b. False

4. **You can have two versions of Cloud Run service deployed at the same time**

   a. True

   b. False

5. **Cloud Run is suitable for Microservice based applications**

   a. True

   b. False

Answers

1.	c
2.	c
3.	b
4.	a
5.	a

Join our book's Discord space

Join the book's Discord Workspace for Latest updates, Offers, Tech happenings around the world, New Release and Sessions with the Authors:

https://discord.bpbonline.com

CHAPTER 9
Google Kubernetes Engine

Introduction

In the previous chapters, we discussed Compute Engine, which is an **infrastructure as a service (IaaS)** offering, and Cloud Run, which is a **platform as a service (PaaS)** offering from Google Cloud Platform. In Cloud Run, we have seen how containerized applications are deployed. Now, when the number of containerized applications increases and their internal communication and scalability requirement increases, then we need some container orchestration system which can take care of the orchestration needs like scalability, fail-over, internal communication, etc. Kubernetes comes to the rescue, and Google Kubernetes Engine is Google Cloud Platform's container orchestration offering. It has two types: standard and autopilot.

Structure

This chapter covers the following topics:

- Container orchestration
- Understanding Kubernetes
- Google Kubernetes Engine
- Working with Google Kubernetes Engine

Objectives

In this chapter, we will understand about container orchestration, Kubernetes, and its terminologies. We will also discuss about Google Kubernetes Engine, compare it with Cloud Run and, work with Kubernetes to deploy microservices.

Container orchestration

Container orchestration provisions, deploys, scales, manages, and monitors containerized applications automatically. Kubernetes is a popular container orchestration engine.

Functioning of container orchestration

When you deploy new containers, the platform automatically schedules the containers and finds the most appropriate host based on the predetermined requirements defined in the configuration file, like CPU, memory, proximity to other machines, or even the metadata.

Once the containers start running, container orchestration tools automate the life cycle management and operational tasks based on the container definition file, including:

- Provisioning or deployment
- Scaling containers up or down and load balancing
- Allocating resources between the containers
- Moving the containers to another machine to ensure availability, a shortage of resources, or an unexpected outage occurs
- Monitoring the performance and health of the applications
- Service discovery

Container orchestration can be used in any computing environments that supports containers, from traditional on-premises servers to the public, private, hybrid or multi-cloud computing environments.

In this chapter, we will understand container orchestration using Google Cloud Platform's offering of Kubernetes, i.e. Google Kubernetes Engine.

Understanding Kubernetes

Kubernetes, also known as **K8s**, is an open-source system for automating deployment, scaling, and managing containerized applications. There are various flavors are present across the public cloud platforms.

Features of Kubernetes

Let us discuss the following features of Kubernetes:

- **Automated rollouts and rollbacks**: Kubernetes rolls out changes to the application or its configuration, while monitoring the application health to ensure it doesn't kill all the instances at the same time. If something goes wrong or does not work appropriately, Kubernetes will rollback the changes. You can take advantage of a growing ecosystem of deployment solutions via Kubernetes.

- **Service discovery and load balancing**: There is no need to modify the application, to use an unfamiliar service discovery pattern. Kubernetes provides Pods their own IP addresses and, a single DNS name for a set of Pods, and it can load-balance across them.

- **Storage orchestration:** It can automatically mount the storage system of choice, whether a local storage, a public cloud provider, or a network storage system, like **NFS**.

- **Self-healing**: It restarts the containers that fail, automatically replaces and reschedules containers when nodes die or fail, kills the containers that do not respond to the user-defined health check, and does not advertise containers to the clients until they are ready to work.

- **Secret and configuration management:** It deploys and updates the Secrets and application configuration without bothering about rebuilding the image and without exposing the Secrets in the stack configuration.

- **Automatic bin packing**: It automatically places the containers based on their resource requirements and other constraints, while not sacrificing the availability. Mix the critical and best-effort workloads to drive up the utilization and save more resources.

- **Batch execution**: In addition to the services, Kubernetes can manage the batch and CI workloads, replacing the containers that fail if desired.

- **Horizontal scaling:** It can scale the application up and down with simple commands, with a UI, or automatically based on the CPU usage.

- **IPv4/IPv6 dual stack:** Allocation of IPv4 / IPv6 addresses to the Pods and services.

- **Designed for extensibility:** Add features to the Kubernetes cluster without changing the upstream source code.

Kubernetes terminologies

Let us understand different terminologies in Kubernetes as follows:

- **Containers**: A containerized application can be thought of as an application that has been packaged in one or more containers. You can think of a container as a box which includes everything it needs to run the application inside it.

- **Pods**: Pods are the core building block in Kubernetes. They host and manage the containers which are needed to run the applications.

- **Nodes**: Nodes are physical or virtual machines which are used to run pods. In Kubernetes, there are two types of nodes, master and worker nodes.

- **Master node**: The master nodes host the control plane, which is required to manage the state of a Kubernetes cluster.

  The following are the components of the master node:
  - API server
  - Scheduler
  - Controller manager
  - etcd

- **Worker node**: Worker nodes are required to run the containers. We do not interact with the worker nodes directly. We send the instructions to the control plane, and then the control plane delegates the task of creating and maintaining the containers to the worker nodes.

  The following are the components of the worker node:
  - Kubelet
  - Kube-proxy
  - Container runtime

- **Cluster:** A Kubernetes cluster is a group of nodes required to run containerized applications. It consists of master node components and worker node components.

- **Controllers**: Controllers are control loops which watch the state of the cluster and accordingly make or request changes whenever needed. Each controller tries to move the current state of the cluster closer to the desired state.

- **ReplicaSets**: A ReplicaSet's purpose is to maintain the stable set of replica Pods running at any given time. It guarantees the availability of specified number of identical Pods.

- **Deployments**: A Deployment provides the declarative updates for the Pods and ReplicaSets. We describe a desired state in a deployment, and then the deployment controller changes the actual state to the desired state in a controlled rate. You can define the deployments to create new ReplicaSets, or to remove the existing deployments and adopt all the resources with new deployments.

- **Services**: In Kubernetes, a service is a way to expose network applications which are running as Pods inside the cluster. A key aim of services in K8s is that you do not need to modify the existing application to use any unfamiliar service discovery pattern. You can run the code inside Pods, whether it is designed for a cloud-native world, or an older application that was containerized. We normally use a service to make a set of Pods available on the network so that the clients can communicate with it.

- **Kubectl**: Kubectl is a command line tool for communicating with Kubernetes cluster's control plane using the Kubernetes API.

  Some of the command examples include:

  o **kubectl logs**: Displays the logs from a container in a Pod.

  o **kubectl exec**: Executes a command on a container in a Pod.

Google Kubernetes Engine

Google Kubernetes Engine (**GKE**) is the Google Cloud's version of Kubernetes.

Additional features of GKE are as follows:

- **Load balancing:** As we will see when we expose the containers as services, we will use a GCP load balancer to distribute the traffic amongst Pods.

- **Node Pools:** It is a group of nodes within a cluster, having the same configuration. For example, we may need to schedule the addition a group of more powerful nodes for some certain events.

- **Autoscaling:** We can take advantage of Google's scaling capabilities to keep the app responsive.

- **Logging and monitoring:** All the logs and metrics are pushed to the GCP dashboard.

- **Automatic upgrades:** Nodes will be kept up to date.

- **Node Auto-repair:** If the node becomes unhealthy, it is taken out of circulation and replaced.

Cloud Run vs Google Kubernetes Engine

Cloud Run and GKE, both can be used to execute containerized applications inside Google Cloud Platform, let us understand the use cases as follows:

- If managed service is needed, Cloud Run is a better choice than GKE.

- If the application needs local storage, GKE is better than Cloud Run.

- Cloud Run supports a maximum of 10 containers in a single service using a sidecar pattern, and GKE is the option above this limit.

- If the service does not meet the container contract, GKE is a better choice.

Cloud Run for Anthos

There is an option to deploy Cloud Run into Anthos GKE cluster. Cloud Run for Anthos abstracts away the complexity of Kubernetes, making it easy to build and deploy your serverless workloads across hybrid and multi cloud environments.

Anthos is Google's managed applications platform, that lets you run Kubernetes and other workloads consistently, across on-premises data centers and multiple public clouds.

Working with Google Kubernetes Engine

Let us create the application using GKE, from the GCP console with the following steps:

1. Create a **new project** in GCP console as follows:

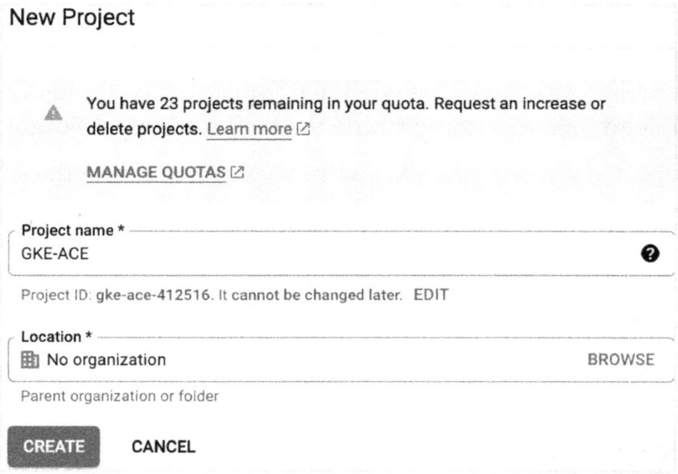

New Project

⚠ You have 23 projects remaining in your quota. Request an increase or delete projects. Learn more ⧉

MANAGE QUOTAS ⧉

Project name *
GKE-ACE   ❓

Project ID: gke-ace-412516. It cannot be changed later.   EDIT

Location *
🏢 No organization   BROWSE

Parent organization or folder

CREATE   CANCEL

Figure 9.1: Create a new GCP project

2. Select the newly created **project** as follows:

Select a project   ⚙ NEW PROJECT

🔍 Search projects and folders

RECENT   STARRED   ALL

Name	ID
☆ ⦂• GKE-ACE ❓	gke-ace-412516
✓ ☆ ⦂• My First Project ❓	hopeful-adapter-401317

Figure 9.2: Select the new GCP project

3. Search for Kubernetes Engine in the **Search** box in GCP console, as follows:

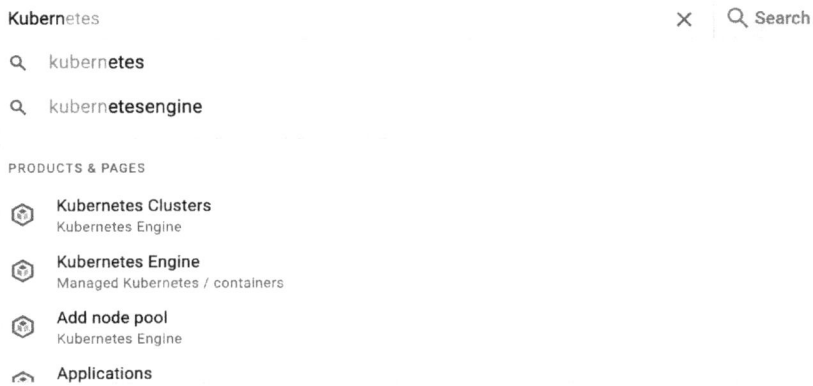

Figure 9.3: Search for GKE

4. **Enable** the **Kubernetes Engine API** as follows:

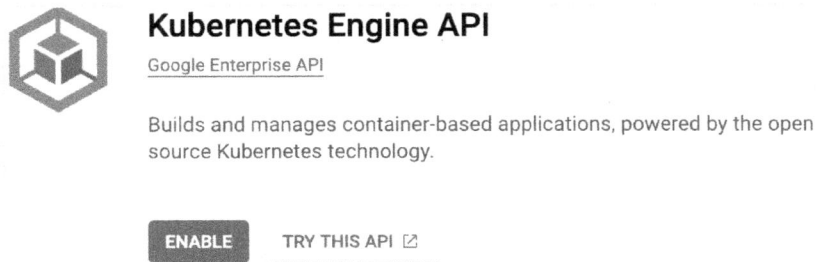

Figure 9.4: Enable the API

5. Click on **CREATE** to create a Kubernetes cluster as follows:

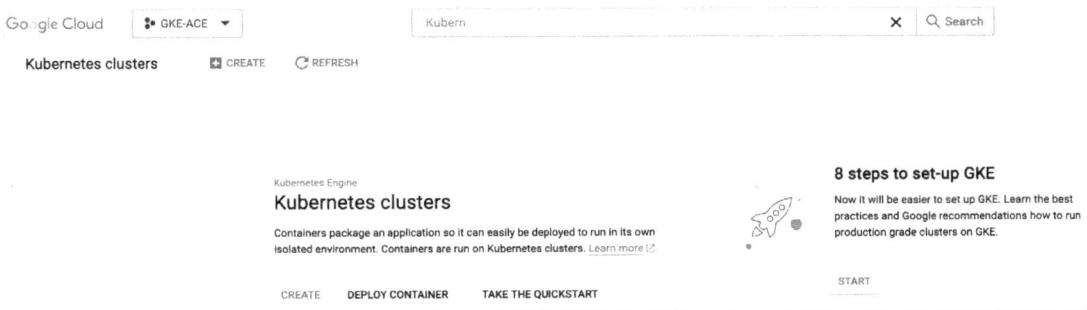

Figure 9.5: Create GKE cluster

6. Click on the **SWITCH TO STANDARD CLUSTER** option, as follows:

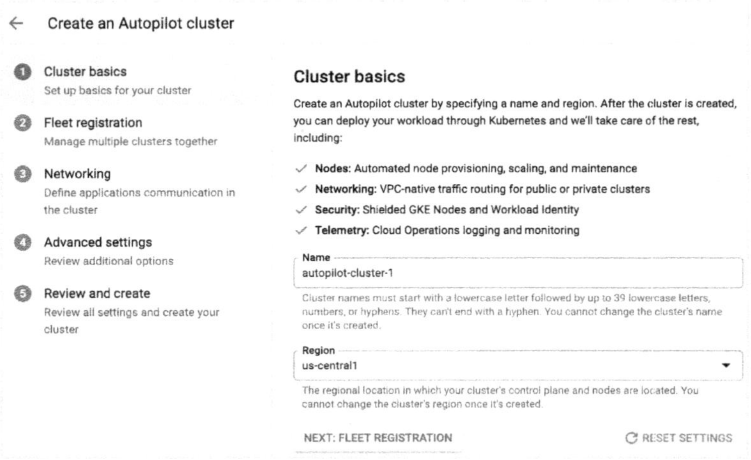

Figure 9.6: Switch to standard cluster

7. Click on **SWITCH TO STANDARD CLUSTER** option, as follows:

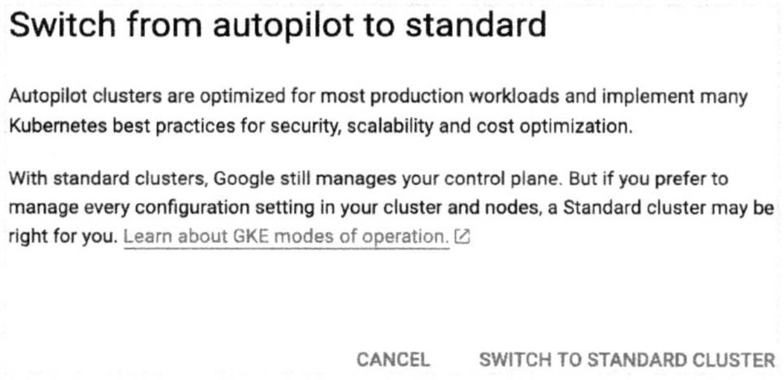

Figure 9.7: Switch to standard cluster (2)

8. Provide a name for the cluster, and for the demo, we are making the cluster **Zonal**:

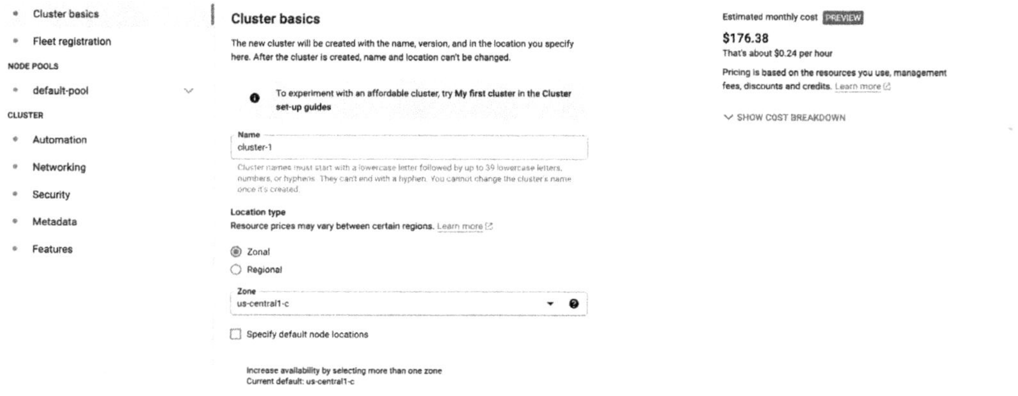

Figure 9.8: Cluster configurations

9. Let us keep the control plane version static and keep the default option as follows:

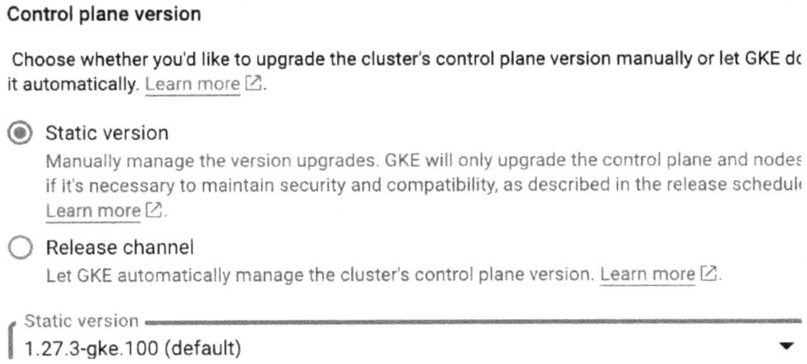

Control plane version

Choose whether you'd like to upgrade the cluster's control plane version manually or let GKE do it automatically. Learn more ☑.

◉ Static version
Manually manage the version upgrades. GKE will only upgrade the control plane and nodes if it's necessary to maintain security and compatibility, as described in the release schedule Learn more ☑.

○ Release channel
Let GKE automatically manage the cluster's control plane version. Learn more ☑.

Static version
1.27.3-gke.100 (default) ▼

Figure 9.9: Cluster configurations (2)

10. Keep the following settings as the default:

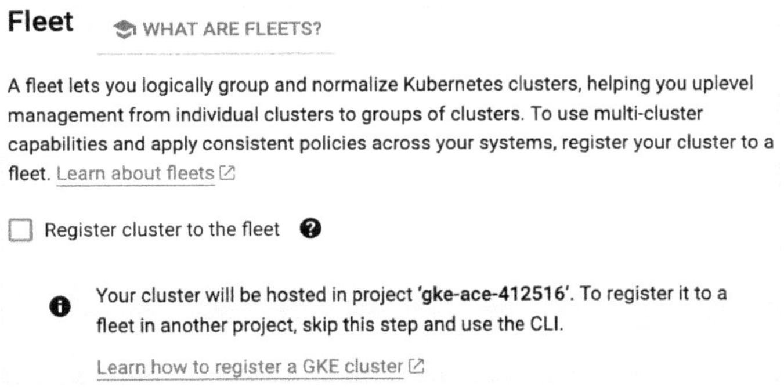

Fleet 🎓 WHAT ARE FLEETS?

A fleet lets you logically group and normalize Kubernetes clusters, helping you uplevel management from individual clusters to groups of clusters. To use multi-cluster capabilities and apply consistent policies across your systems, register your cluster to a fleet. Learn about fleets ☑

☐ Register cluster to the fleet ❷

ⓘ Your cluster will be hosted in project '**gke-ace-412516**'. To register it to a fleet in another project, skip this step and use the CLI.

Learn how to register a GKE cluster ☑

Figure 9.10: Cluster configurations (3)

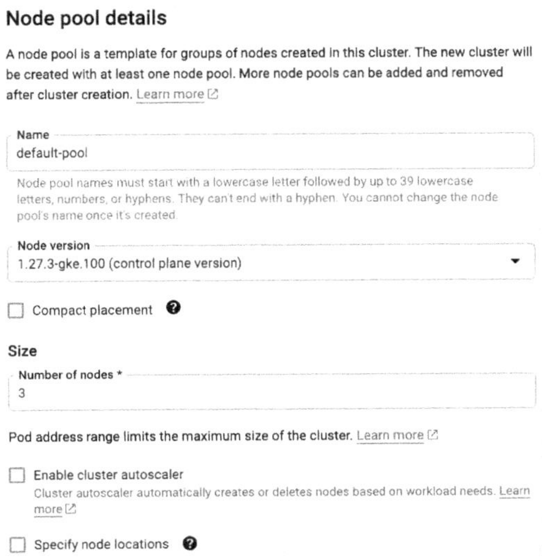

Node pool details

A node pool is a template for groups of nodes created in this cluster. The new cluster will be created with at least one node pool. More node pools can be added and removed after cluster creation. Learn more ☑

Name
default-pool

Node pool names must start with a lowercase letter followed by up to 39 lowercase letters, numbers, or hyphens. They can't end with a hyphen. You cannot change the node pool's name once it's created

Node version
1.27.3-gke.100 (control plane version) ▼

☐ Compact placement ❷

Size
Number of nodes *
3

Pod address range limits the maximum size of the cluster. Learn more ☑

☐ Enable cluster autoscaler
Cluster autoscaler automatically creates or deletes nodes based on workload needs. Learn more ☑

☐ Specify node locations ❷

Figure 9.11: Cluster configurations (4)

The following are the cluster configurations:

Automation

☑ Automatically upgrade nodes to next available version
Keep nodes up-to-date with the cluster's control plane version. Learn more ☑

☑ Enable auto-repair ❓

Node pool upgrade strategy ❓

◉ Surge upgrade
Faster and more cost-effective for stable workloads. Upgrades nodes one at a time in place.
By default, a temporary additional node is created when upgrading each node. To reduce
cost (with a greater risk of disruption), set Max surge = 0 and Max unavailable = 1. Learn
more ☑

Max surge *		Max unavailable *	
1	❓	0	❓

○ Blue-green upgrade `NEW`
Reduce risk for workloads that are sensitive to disruptions. This creates a new node pool
and temporarily keeps old nodes. It has flexible upgrade pacing through batch requests and
simple rollbacks. Higher cost than surge upgrades. Learn more ☑

Figure 9.12: Cluster configurations (5)

Configure node settings

These node settings will be used when new nodes are created using this node pool.

Image type
Container-Optimized OS with containerd (cos_containerd) (default) ▾

Choose which operating system image you want to run on each node of this cluster. Learn
more ☑

⚠ The default Linux node image for newly created clusters and node pools with
version 1.27.3-gke.100 or later is Container-optimized OS with containerd.
For Windows node pools using version 1.21 or later, containerd is also the
recommended runtime. Since Dockershim is being deprecated by
Kubernetes project, GKE will deprecate Docker node images ☑. We
recommend that you migrate to containerd node images ☑ as soon as
possible. Learn more ☑.

Machine configuration

Choose the machine family, type, and series that will best fit the resource needs of your cluster.
You won't be able to change the machine type for this cluster once it's created. Learn more ☑

| ✓ General purpose | Compute optimized | Memory optimized | GPUs |

TPUs `NEW`

Machine types for common workloads, optimized for cost and flexibility

	Series ❓	Description	vCPUs ❓	Memory €
○	C3	Consistently high performance	4 - 176	8 - 1,408 GB
○	C3D	Consistently high performance	4 - 360	8 - 2,880 GB
◉	E2	Low cost, day-to-day computing	0.25 - 32	1 - 128 GB
○	N2	Balanced price & performance	2 - 128	2 - 864 GB
○	N2D	Balanced price & performance	2 - 224	2 - 896 GB
○	T2A	Scale-out workloads	1 - 48	4 - 192 GB

Figure 9.13: Cluster configurations (6)

Keep the following settings as the default:

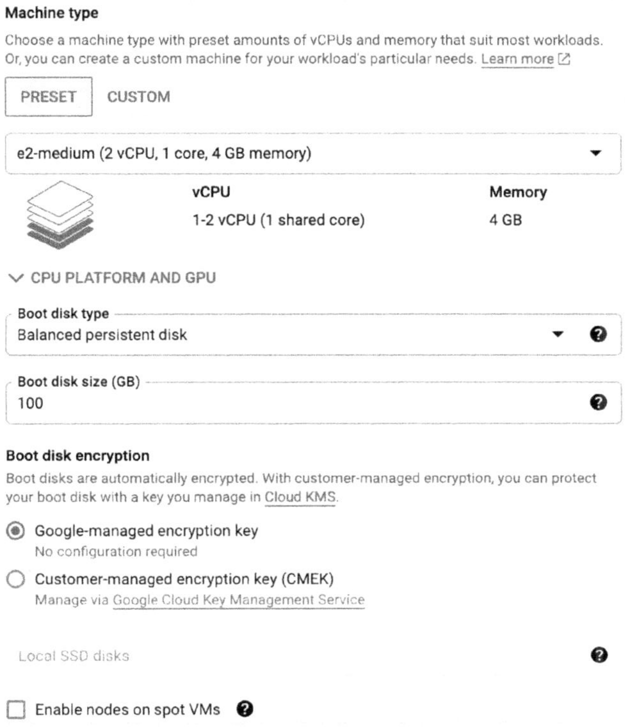

Machine type

Choose a machine type with preset amounts of vCPUs and memory that suit most workloads. Or, you can create a custom machine for your workload's particular needs. Learn more ☑

PRESET	CUSTOM

e2-medium (2 vCPU, 1 core, 4 GB memory)   ▼

	vCPU	Memory
	1-2 vCPU (1 shared core)	4 GB

∨ CPU PLATFORM AND GPU

Boot disk type
Balanced persistent disk   ▼   ❷

Boot disk size (GB)
100   ❷

Boot disk encryption

Boot disks are automatically encrypted. With customer-managed encryption, you can protect your boot disk with a key you manage in Cloud KMS.

⦿ Google-managed encryption key
   No configuration required

◯ Customer-managed encryption key (CMEK)
   Manage via Google Cloud Key Management Service

Local SSD disks   ❷

☐ Enable nodes on spot VMs ❷

Figure 9.14: Cluster configurations (7)

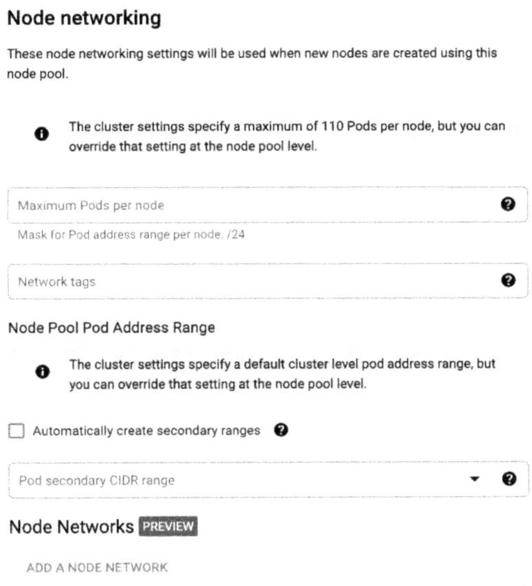

Node networking

These node networking settings will be used when new nodes are created using this node pool.

ⓘ The cluster settings specify a maximum of 110 Pods per node, but you can override that setting at the node pool level.

Maximum Pods per node   ❷
Mask for Pod address range per node. /24

Network tags   ❷

Node Pool Pod Address Range

ⓘ The cluster settings specify a default cluster level pod address range, but you can override that setting at the node pool level.

☐ Automatically create secondary ranges ❷

Pod secondary CIDR range   ▼   ❷

Node Networks `PREVIEW`

ADD A NODE NETWORK

Figure 9.15: Cluster configurations (8)

Keep the following settings as the default:

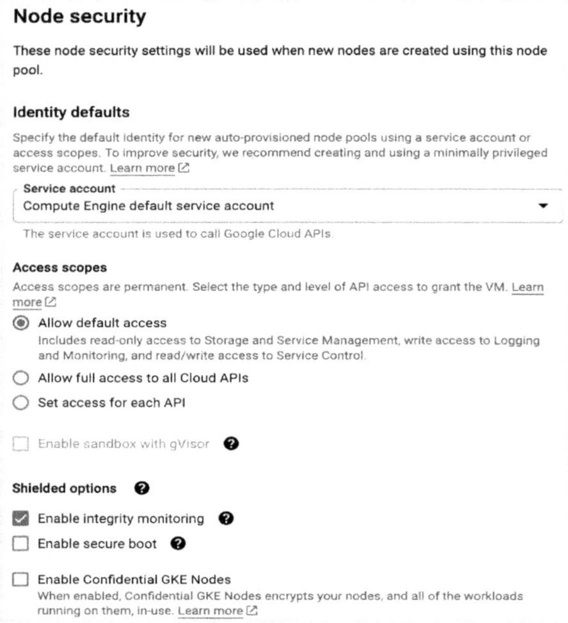

Node security

These node security settings will be used when new nodes are created using this node pool.

Identity defaults

Specify the default identity for new auto-provisioned node pools using a service account or access scopes. To improve security, we recommend creating and using a minimally privileged service account. Learn more ⬚

Service account
Compute Engine default service account ▼

The service account is used to call Google Cloud APIs.

Access scopes

Access scopes are permanent. Select the type and level of API access to grant the VM. Learn more ⬚

⦿ Allow default access
   Includes read-only access to Storage and Service Management, write access to Logging and Monitoring, and read/write access to Service Control.

◯ Allow full access to all Cloud APIs

◯ Set access for each API

☐ Enable sandbox with gVisor ❓

Shielded options ❓

☑ Enable integrity monitoring ❓

☐ Enable secure boot ❓

☐ Enable Confidential GKE Nodes
   When enabled, Confidential GKE Nodes encrypts your nodes, and all of the workloads running on them, in-use. Learn more ⬚

Figure 9.16: Cluster configurations (9)

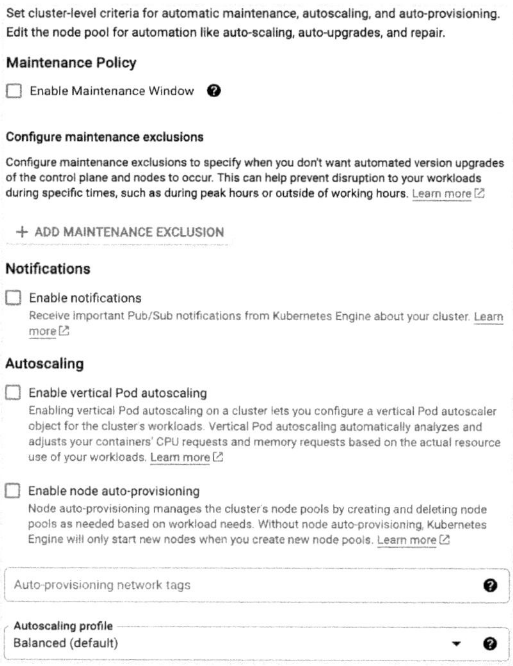

Set cluster-level criteria for automatic maintenance, autoscaling, and auto-provisioning. Edit the node pool for automation like auto-scaling, auto-upgrades, and repair.

Maintenance Policy

☐ Enable Maintenance Window ❓

Configure maintenance exclusions

Configure maintenance exclusions to specify when you don't want automated version upgrades of the control plane and nodes to occur. This can help prevent disruption to your workloads during specific times, such as during peak hours or outside of working hours. Learn more ⬚

➕ ADD MAINTENANCE EXCLUSION

Notifications

☐ Enable notifications
   Receive important Pub/Sub notifications from Kubernetes Engine about your cluster. Learn more ⬚

Autoscaling

☐ Enable vertical Pod autoscaling
   Enabling vertical Pod autoscaling on a cluster lets you configure a vertical Pod autoscaler object for the cluster's workloads. Vertical Pod autoscaling automatically analyzes and adjusts your containers' CPU requests and memory requests based on the actual resource use of your workloads. Learn more ⬚

☐ Enable node auto-provisioning
   Node auto-provisioning manages the cluster's node pools by creating and deleting node pools as needed based on workload needs. Without node auto-provisioning, Kubernetes Engine will only start new nodes when you create new node pools. Learn more ⬚

Auto-provisioning network tags ❓

Autoscaling profile
Balanced (default) ▼ ❓

Figure 9.17: Cluster configurations (10)

Keep the following settings as the default:

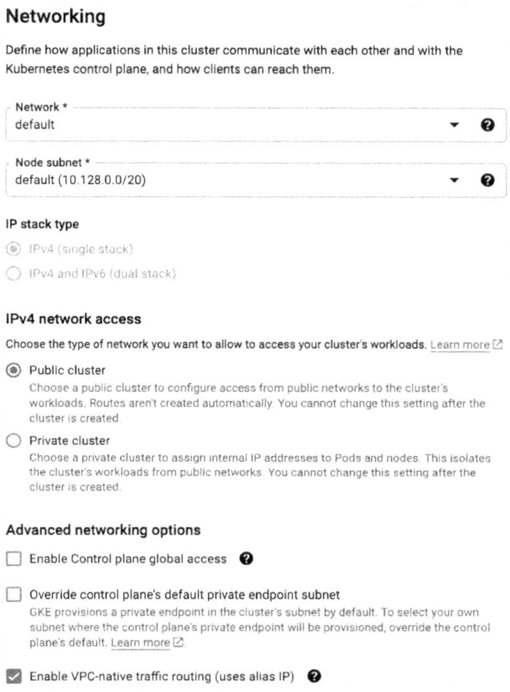

Networking

Define how applications in this cluster communicate with each other and with the Kubernetes control plane, and how clients can reach them.

Network *
default ▼ ❓

Node subnet *
default (10.128.0.0/20) ▼ ❓

IP stack type

⦿ IPv4 (single stack)

◯ IPv4 and IPv6 (dual stack)

IPv4 network access

Choose the type of network you want to allow to access your cluster's workloads. Learn more 🔗

⦿ Public cluster
Choose a public cluster to configure access from public networks to the cluster's workloads. Routes aren't created automatically. You cannot change this setting after the cluster is created.

◯ Private cluster
Choose a private cluster to assign internal IP addresses to Pods and nodes. This isolates the cluster's workloads from public networks. You cannot change this setting after the cluster is created.

Advanced networking options

☐ Enable Control plane global access ❓

☐ Override control plane's default private endpoint subnet
GKE provisions a private endpoint in the cluster's subnet by default. To select your own subnet where the control plane's private endpoint will be provisioned, override the control plane's default. Learn more 🔗

☑ Enable VPC-native traffic routing (uses alias IP) ❓

Figure 9.18: Cluster configurations (11)

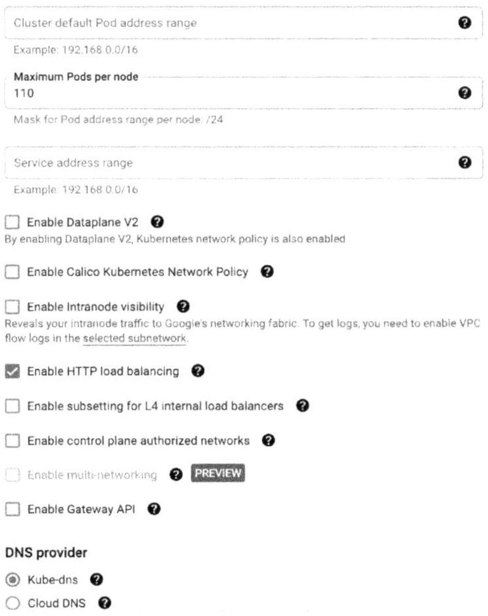

Cluster default Pod address range ❓
Example: 192.168.0.0/16

Maximum Pods per node
110 ❓
Mask for Pod address range per node: /24

Service address range ❓
Example: 192.168.0.0/16

☐ Enable Dataplane V2 ❓
By enabling Dataplane V2, Kubernetes network policy is also enabled

☐ Enable Calico Kubernetes Network Policy ❓

☐ Enable Intranode visibility ❓
Reveals your intranode traffic to Google's networking fabric. To get logs, you need to enable VPC flow logs in the selected subnetwork.

☑ Enable HTTP load balancing ❓

☐ Enable subsetting for L4 internal load balancers ❓

☐ Enable control plane authorized networks ❓

☐ Enable multi-networking ❓ PREVIEW

☐ Enable Gateway API ❓

DNS provider

⦿ Kube-dns ❓

◯ Cloud DNS ❓

Figure 9.19: Cluster configurations (12)

The following are the cluster configurations:

Security

For features not in beta, defaults are set according to the Security hardening guide ⬈.
Security includes cluster authentication handled by IAM and Google-managed encryption by default.

☐ Enable Binary Authorization ❓

☑ Enable Shielded GKE Nodes ❓

☐ Enable Confidential GKE Nodes
   When enabled, Confidential GKE Nodes encrypts your nodes, and all of the workloads running on them, in-use. Learn more ⬈

☐ Encrypt secrets at the application layer ❓

☐ Enable Workload Identity ❓

☐ Enable Google Groups for RBAC ❓

☑ Configuration auditing ❓

☐ Workload vulnerability scanning ❓

Legacy security options

☐ Enable legacy authorization ❓

☐ Issue a client certificate
   To maximize security, do not select. You cannot change this setting once the cluster is created. Clients use this base64-encoded public certificate to authenticate to the cluster endpoint. Certificates don't rotate automatically and are difficult to revoke. You can still authenticate to the cluster using Identity and Access Management (IAM) or with basic authentication, which is not recommended. Learn more ⬈.

Figure 9.20: Cluster configurations (13)

11. Finally, click on **CREATE** to create the cluster. You will see cluster created as follows:

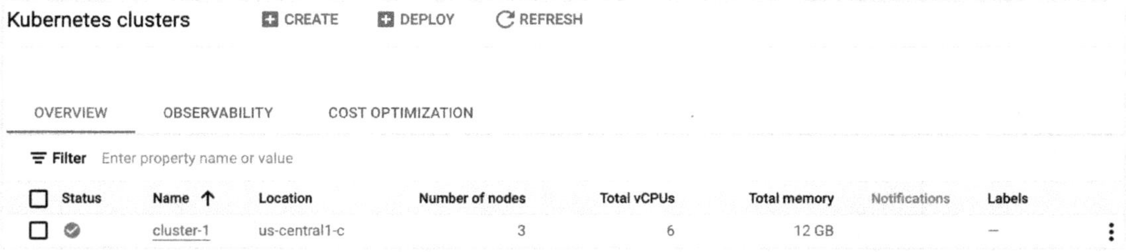

Kubernetes clusters   ➕ CREATE   ➕ DEPLOY   ↻ REFRESH

OVERVIEW   OBSERVABILITY   COST OPTIMIZATION

⟺ Filter   Enter property name or value

	Status	Name ↑	Location	Number of nodes	Total vCPUs	Total memory	Notifications	Labels	
☐	✅	cluster-1	us-central1-c	3	6	12 GB	—		⋮

Figure 9.21: Cluster created

12. In Compute Engine, you can find that the following three instances are created:

Figure 9.22: Compute VMs created

13. Click to **Activate Cloud Shell** as follows:

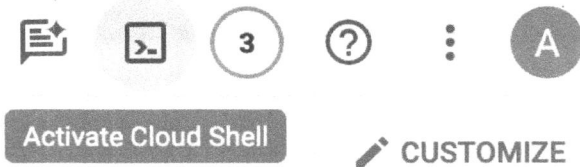

Figure 9.23: Activate the Cloud Shell

14. Cloud Shell is activated as follows:

Figure 9.24: Activated Cloud Shell

15. Create the following files for the application:

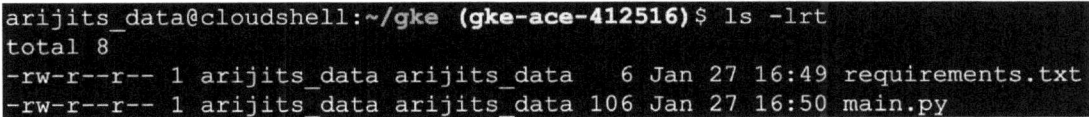

```
arijits_data@cloudshell:~/gke (gke-ace-412516)$ ls -lrt
total 8
-rw-r--r-- 1 arijits_data arijits_data   6 Jan 27 16:49 requirements.txt
-rw-r--r-- 1 arijits_data arijits_data 106 Jan 27 16:50 main.py
```

Figure 9.25: Application related files

16. Add a Docker file and edit the application related files as follows:

```
arijits_data@cloudshell:~/gke (gke-ace-412516)$ ls -lrt
total 12
-rw-r--r-- 1 arijits_data arijits_data   6 Jan 27 16:49 requirements.txt
-rw-r--r-- 1 arijits_data arijits_data 177 Jan 27 17:00 main.py
-rw-r--r-- 1 arijits_data arijits_data 114 Jan 27 17:02 Dockerfile
arijits_data@cloudshell:~/gke (gke-ace-412516)$ cat requirements.txt
Flask
arijits_data@cloudshell:~/gke (gke-ace-412516)$ cat main.py
from flask import Flask

app = Flask(__name__)

@app.route('/')
def func():
    return 'Service1'

if __name__ == "__main__":
    app.run(host='0.0.0.0', port=8080, debug=True)
arijits_data@cloudshell:~/gke (gke-ace-412516)$ cat Dockerfile
FROM python:3
WORKDIR /app
ADD . /app

RUN pip install -r requirements.txt
EXPOSE 8080
CMD ["python", "main.py"]
arijits_data@cloudshell:~/gke (gke-ace-412516)$
```

Figure 9.26: Application files and Docker file contents

17. Create an image and send it to the container repository as follows:

```
arijits_data@cloudshell:~/gke (gke-ace-412516)$
arijits_data@cloudshell:~/gke (gke-ace-412516)$
arijits_data@cloudshell:~/gke (gke-ace-412516)$ gcloud builds submit -t gcr.io/gke-ace-412516/app-image:v1.0
```

Figure 9.27: Create and upload application image

18. **Authorize Cloud Shell** when prompted as follows:

Authorize Cloud Shell

Cloud Shell needs permission to use your credentials for the gcloud CLI command.

Click Authorize to grant permission to this and future calls.

REJECT   AUTHORIZE

Figure 9.28: Authorize Cloud Shell

19. You will get the following success message once you successfully submit it:

```
v1.0: digest: sha256:c702fb64abb633c8b43ed69c0fdddc7d5bcb4f2277f467c874456b8acb1db02c size: 2632
DONE
------------------------------------------------------------------------------------------------
ID: 9677e4d1-3de1-44e4-b06e-4b698b8b8261
CREATE_TIME: 2024-01-27T17:09:10+00:00
DURATION: 1M33S
SOURCE: gs://gke-ace-412516_cloudbuild/source/1706375328.21109-6dca8c0d00b8451e94563fac7a9c1f22.tgz
IMAGES: gcr.io/gke-ace-412516/app-image:v1.0
STATUS: SUCCESS
arijits_data@cloudshell:~/gke (gke-ace-412516)$
```

Figure 9.29: Image creation successful

20. You can go to **container repository** and verify the provided location created, as follows:

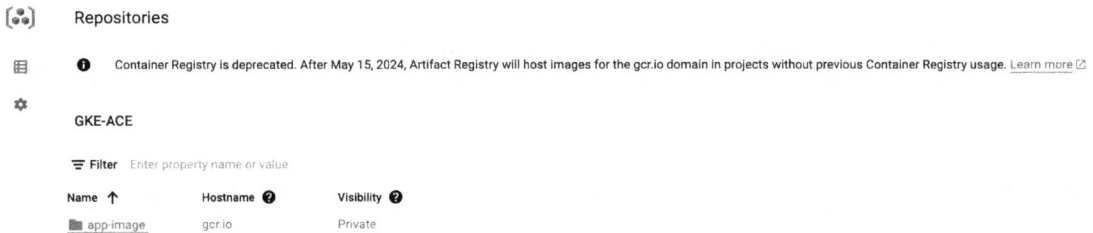

Repositories

ⓘ Container Registry is deprecated. After May 15, 2024, Artifact Registry will host images for the gcr.io domain in projects without previous Container Registry usage. Learn more ☑

GKE-ACE

≡ Filter   Enter property name or value

Name ↑	Hostname ❓	Visibility ❓
📁 app-image	gcr.io	Private

Figure 9.30: Container repository

21. You can find the image under the provided location as follows:

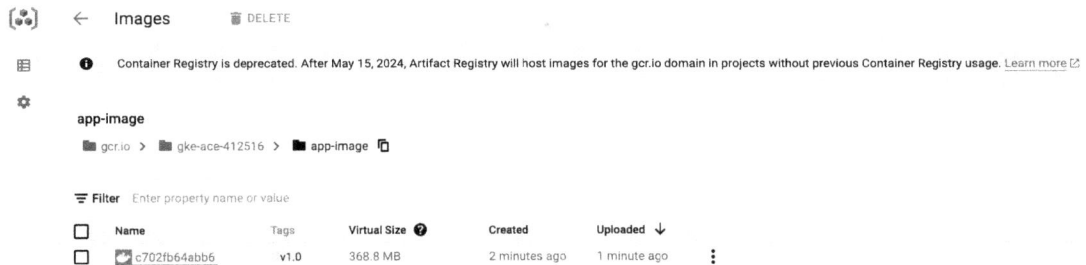

← Images   🗑 DELETE

ⓘ Container Registry is deprecated. After May 15, 2024, Artifact Registry will host images for the gcr.io domain in projects without previous Container Registry usage. Learn more ☑

app-image

📁 gcr.io > 📁 gke-ace-412516 > 📁 app-image 📋

≡ Filter   Enter property name or value

☐	Name	Tags	Virtual Size ❓	Created	Uploaded ↓	
☐	🖼 c702fb64abb6	v1.0	368.8 MB	2 minutes ago	1 minute ago	⋮

Figure 9.31: Container repository (2)

22. Click on **DEPLOY** in the clusters section to create a deployment as follows:

Kubernetes clusters   ➕ CREATE   ➕ DEPLOY   ↻ REFRESH

Figure 9.32: Create deployment

23. Select a container image as follows from the existing figure:

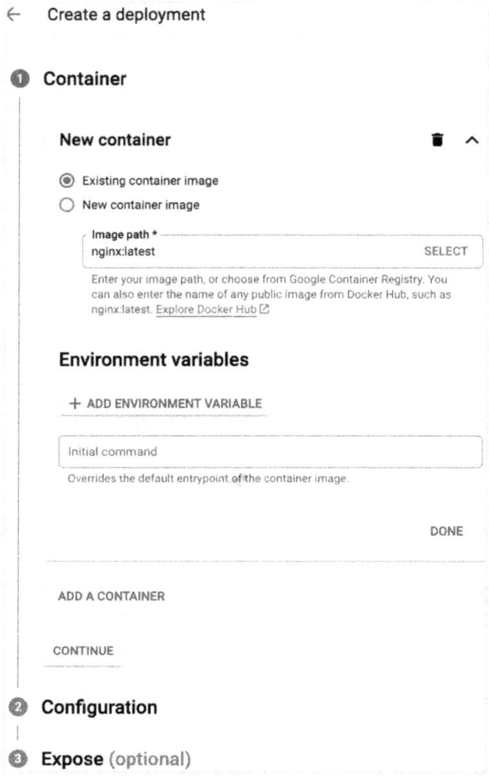

Figure 9.33: *Create deployment (2)*

24. Select the right **image** from **CONTAINER REGISTRY** as follows:

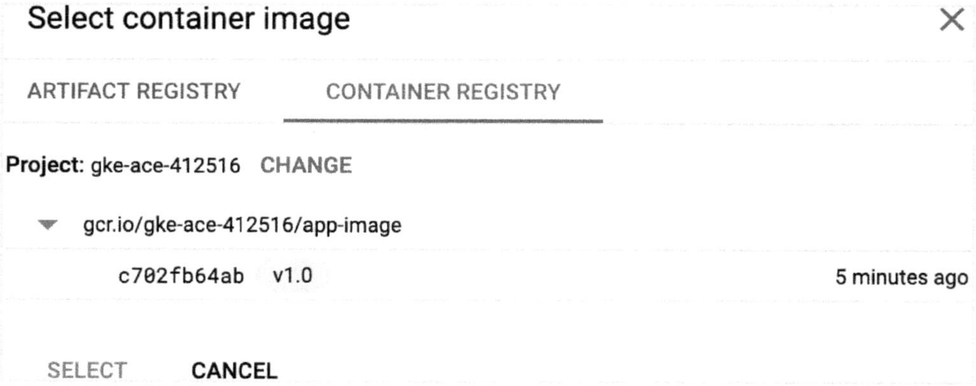

Figure 9.34: *Choose the image*

25. Click on **CONTINUE,** as shown in the following figure:

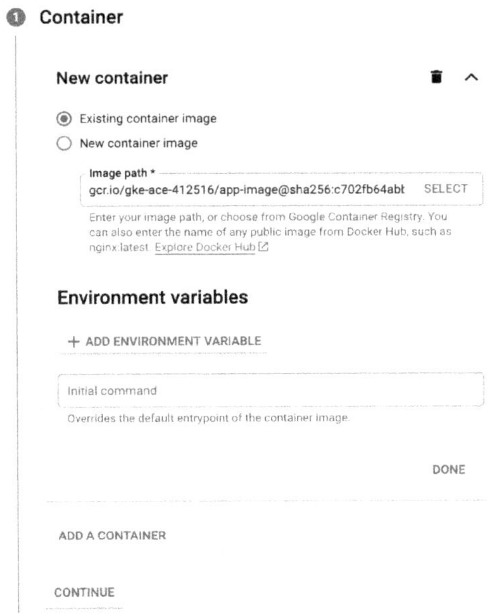

Figure 9.35: Verify the selected image

26. You can provide a **deployment name** and correct the label. Finally, select the cluster and create the deployment as follows:

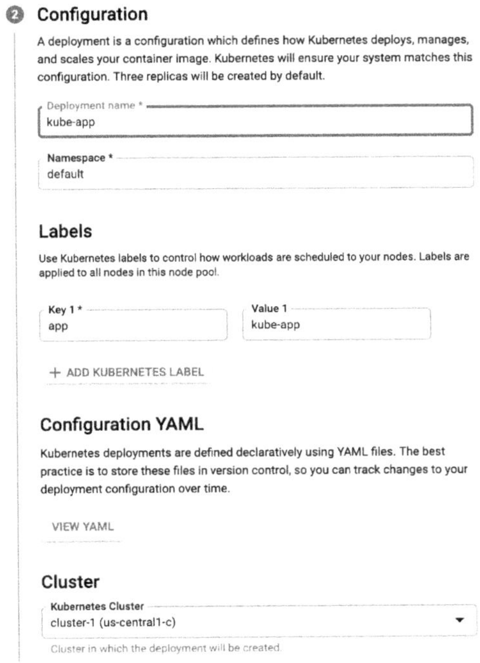

Figure 9.36: Choose the cluster

27. You can see the progress while creating the deployment as follows:

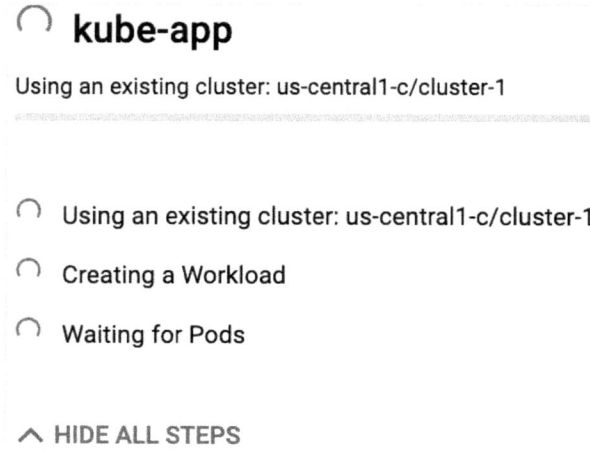

◠ **kube-app**

Using an existing cluster: us-central1-c/cluster-1

◠ Using an existing cluster: us-central1-c/cluster-1

◠ Creating a Workload

◠ Waiting for Pods

∧ HIDE ALL STEPS

Figure 9.37: Creating deployment

28. You can verify the created deployment as follows:

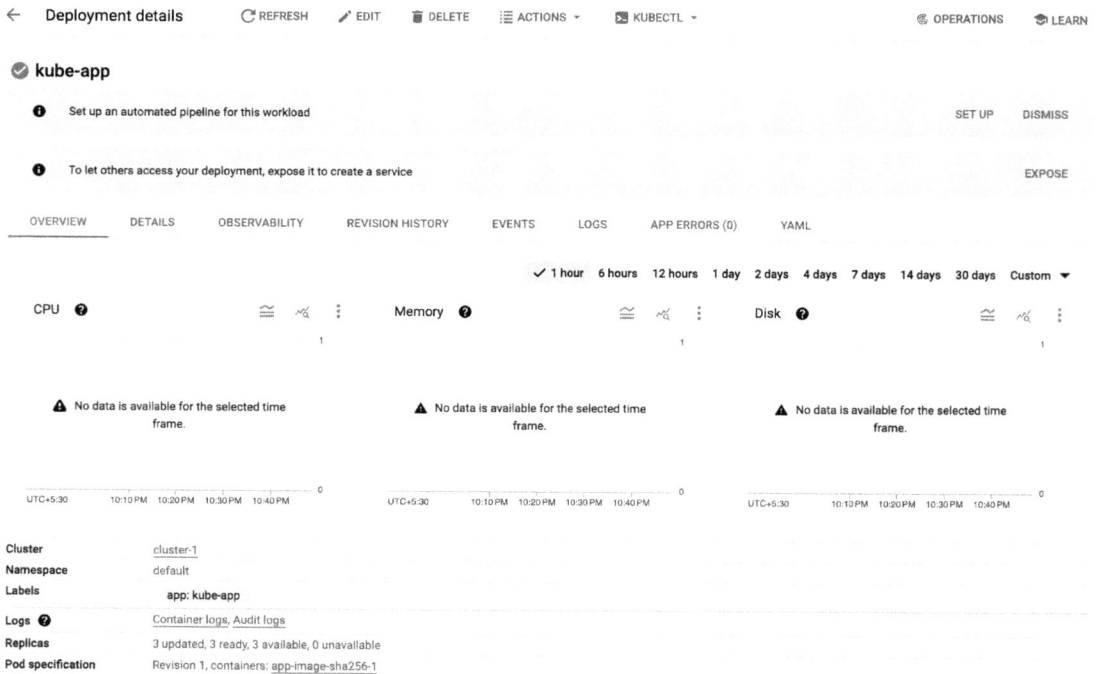

← Deployment details   ↻ REFRESH   ✎ EDIT   🗑 DELETE   ☰ ACTIONS ▾   ▣ KUBECTL ▾   ℰ OPERATIONS   ⚑ LEARN

✓ **kube-app**

ℹ Set up an automated pipeline for this workload   SET UP   DISMISS

ℹ To let others access your deployment, expose it to create a service   EXPOSE

OVERVIEW   DETAILS   OBSERVABILITY   REVISION HISTORY   EVENTS   LOGS   APP ERRORS (0)   YAML

✓ 1 hour   6 hours   12 hours   1 day   2 days   4 days   7 days   14 days   30 days   Custom ▾

CPU ❓   ≅ ⩗ ⋮   Memory ❓   ≅ ⩗ ⋮   Disk ❓   ≅ ⩗ ⋮
                        1   1   1

⚠ No data is available for the selected time   ⚠ No data is available for the selected time   ⚠ No data is available for the selected time
              frame.   frame.   frame.

UTC+5:30   10:10PM 10:20PM 10:30PM 10:40PM   0   UTC+5:30   10:10PM 10:20PM 10:30PM 10:40PM   0   UTC+5:30   10:10PM 10:20PM 10:30PM 10:40PM   0

Cluster   cluster-1
Namespace   default
Labels   app: kube-app
Logs ❓   Container logs, Audit logs
Replicas   3 updated, 3 ready, 3 available, 0 unavailable
Pod specification   Revision 1, containers: app-image-sha256-1

Figure 9.38: Deployment details

29. Click on **EXPOSE** to create service and choose the options as follows:

Port mapping

Port 1	Target port 1	Protocol 1
5000 ❓	8080 ❓	TCP ▼ ❓

+ ADD PORT MAPPING

Service type
Load balancer ▼ ❓

Service name
kube-app-service

EXPOSE   VIEW YAML

* Indicates required field

Figure 9.39: Exposing service

30. You can see the progress of a service being created as follows:

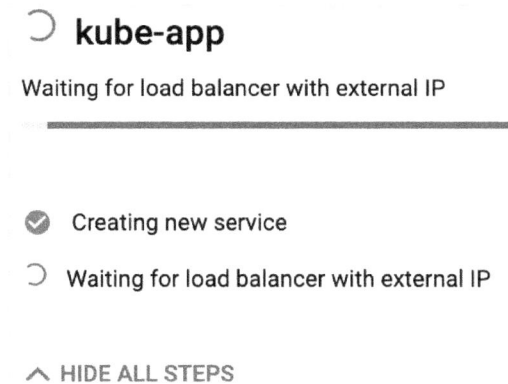

⟲ **kube-app**

Waiting for load balancer with external IP

✅ Creating new service

⟲ Waiting for load balancer with external IP

∧ HIDE ALL STEPS

Figure 9.40: Exposing service (2)

31. You can see the **Service details** dashboard as follows:

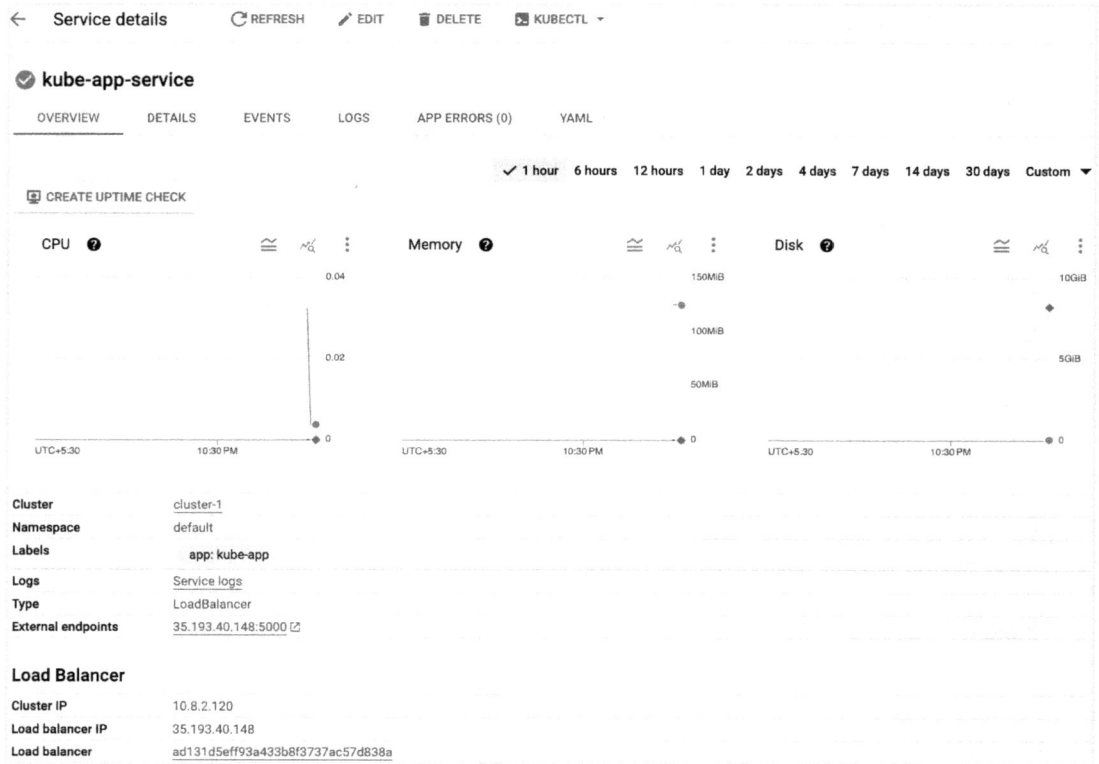

Figure 9.41: kube-app-service dashboard

32. Navigate to the external endpoint as follows:

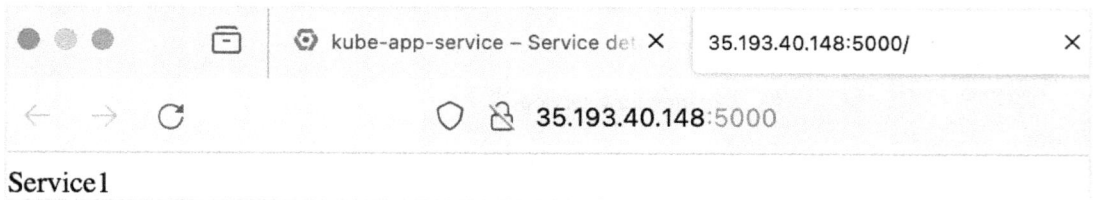

Figure 9.42: Service call via browser

33. Verify clusters, workload, and service as follows:

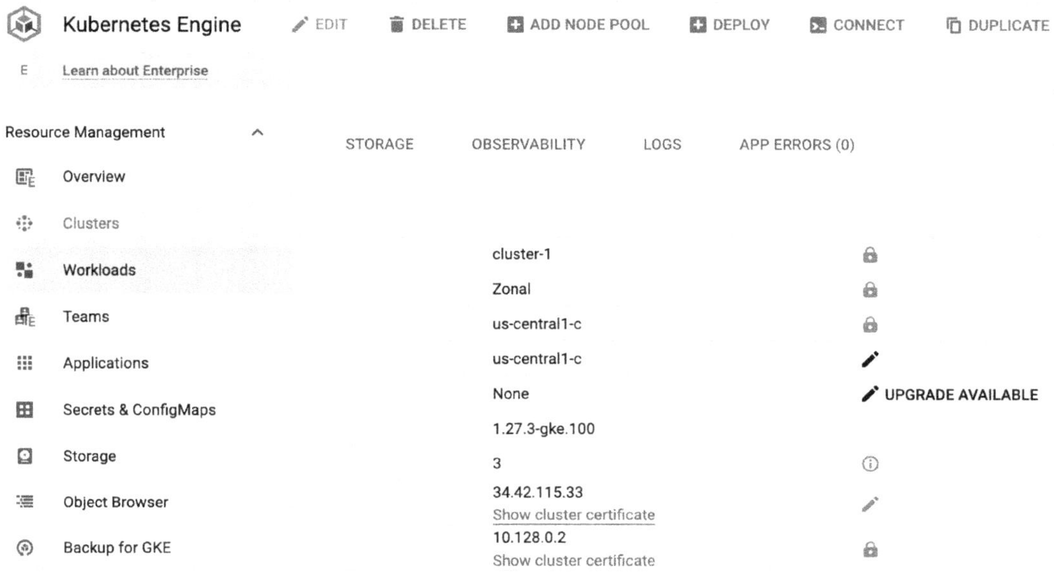

Figure 9.43: Cluster

Verify deployment:

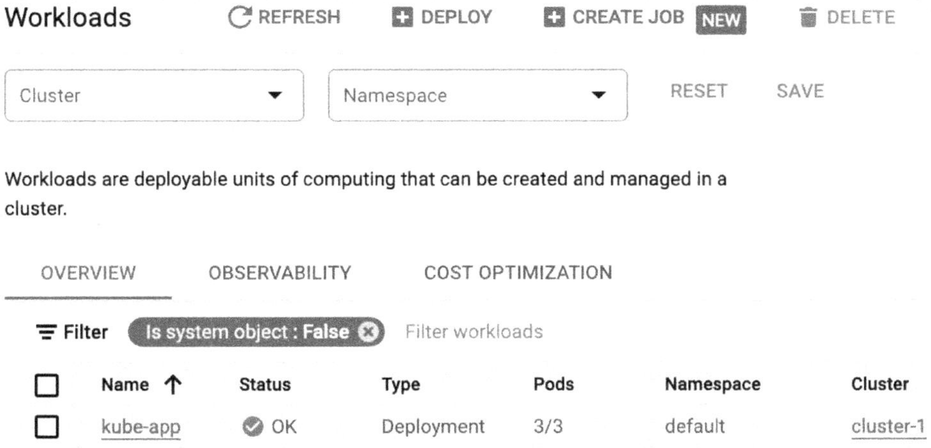

Figure 9.44: Deployment

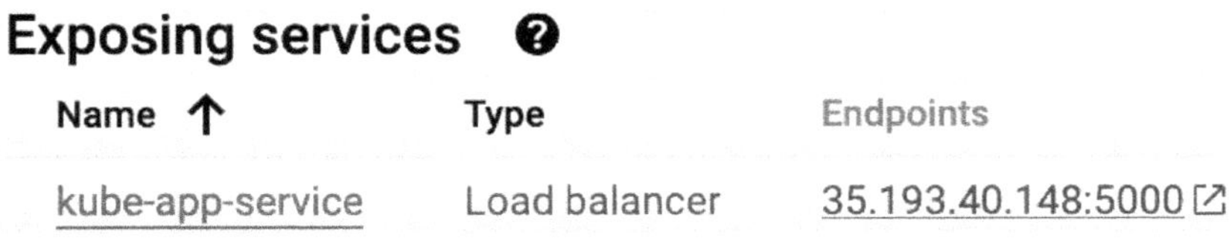

Exposing services ❷

Name ↑	Type	Endpoints
kube-app-service	Load balancer	35.193.40.148:5000 ↗

Figure 9.45: Service

34. Deployment YAML:

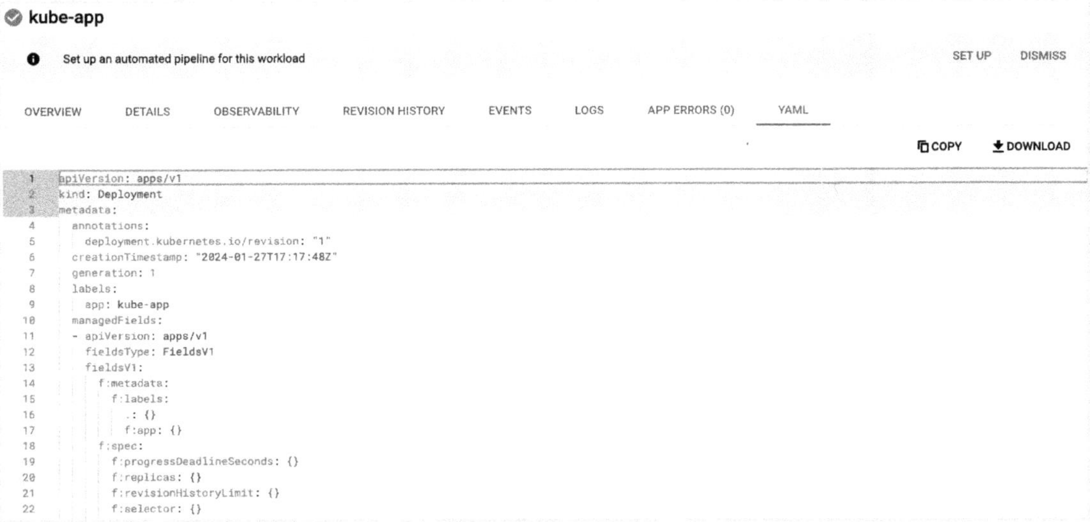

✓ kube-app

ⓘ Set up an automated pipeline for this workload   SET UP   DISMISS

OVERVIEW   DETAILS   OBSERVABILITY   REVISION HISTORY   EVENTS   LOGS   APP ERRORS (0)   YAML

⧉ COPY   ⬇ DOWNLOAD

```
1   apiVersion: apps/v1
2   kind: Deployment
3   metadata:
4     annotations:
5       deployment.kubernetes.io/revision: "1"
6     creationTimestamp: "2024-01-27T17:17:48Z"
7     generation: 1
8     labels:
9       app: kube-app
10    managedFields:
11    - apiVersion: apps/v1
12      fieldsType: FieldsV1
13      fieldsV1:
14        f:metadata:
15          f:labels:
16            .: {}
17            f:app: {}
18        f:spec:
19          f:progressDeadlineSeconds: {}
20          f:replicas: {}
21          f:revisionHistoryLimit: {}
22          f:selector: {}
```

Figure 9.46: Deployment YAML

35. Service YAML:

✓ kube-app-service

OVERVIEW   DETAILS   EVENTS   LOGS   APP ERRORS (0)   YAML

⧉ COPY   ⬇ DOWNLOAD

```
1   apiVersion: v1
2   kind: Service
3   metadata:
4     annotations:
5       cloud.google.com/neg: '{"ingress":true}'
6     creationTimestamp: "2024-01-27T17:20:31Z"
7     finalizers:
8     - service.kubernetes.io/load-balancer-cleanup
9     labels:
10      app: kube-app
11    managedFields:
12    - apiVersion: v1
13      fieldsType: FieldsV1
14      fieldsV1:
15        f:metadata:
16          f:labels:
17            .: {}
18            f:app: {}
19        f:spec:
20          f:allocateLoadBalancerNodePorts: {}
21          f:externalTrafficPolicy: {}
22          f:internalTrafficPolicy: {}
23          f:ports:
24            .: {}
25            k:{"port":5000,"protocol":"TCP"}:
```

Figure 9.47: Service YAML

36. Delete the GKE cluster as follows once you are done with your testing:

✕   1 Kubernetes cluster selected   🗑 DELETE   🏷 LABELS

Run your business critical workloads faster, safer, and easier at enterprise scale

GKE Enterprise combines multi-cluster and multi-team operations with fully managed security, governance, and service networking components. policies, and provide application visibility with actionable insights and an application-aware network for resiliency.

When you're ready to scale beyond a single team or cluster, GKE Enterprise delivers an integrated and consistent way to configure, secure, protect

LEARN AND ENABLE

OVERVIEW   OBSERVABILITY   COST OPTIMIZATION

≡ Filter   Enter property name or value

	Status	Name ↑	Location	Number of nodes	Total vCPUs	Total memory	Notifications	Labels	
☑	⚠	cluster-1	us-central1-c	3 ℹ	6	12 GB		—	⋮

Figure 9.48: Cluster being deleted

37. You can see the following VM instances being auto deleted as the cluster gets deleted:

VM instances   🔧 CREATE INSTANCE   ⬆ IMPORT VM   ↻ REFRESH

INSTANCES   OBSERVABILITY   INSTANCE SCHEDULES

VM instances

≡ Filter   Enter property name or value

	Status	Name ↑	Zone	Recommendations	In use by	Internal IP	External IP	Connect	
☐	⟳	gke-cluster-1-default-pool-a4583344-2wrs	us-central1-c		gke-cluster-1-default-pool-a4583344-grp	10.128.0.5 (nic0)	35.232.115.170 (nic0)	SSH ▾	⋮
☐	⟳	gke-cluster-1-default-pool-a4583344-42dt	us-central1-c		gke-cluster-1-default-pool-a4583344-grp	10.128.0.3 (nic0)	35.224.198.252 (nic0)	SSH ▾	⋮
☐	⟳	gke-cluster-1-default-pool-a4583344-cg5n	us-central1-c		gke-cluster-1-default-pool-a4583344-grp	10.128.0.4 (nic0)	35.232.253.110 (nic0)	SSH ▾	⋮

Related actions

⊕ **Explore Backup and DR** NEW	🖥 **View billing report**	📊 **Monitor VMs**	🗄 **Explore VM logs**	🔲 **Set up firewall rules**
Back up your VMs and set up disaster recovery	View and manage your Compute Engine billing	View outlier VMs across metrics like CPU and network	View, search, analyze, and download VM instance logs	Control traffic to and from a VM instance
🔄 **Patch management**	↻ **Load balance between VMs** 🔗			
Schedule patch updates and view patch compliance on VM instances	Set up Load Balancing for your applications as your traffic and users grow			

Figure 9.49: VMs being auto deleted when cluster got terminated

38. Verify the GKE cluster post deletion, as follows:

Kubernetes clusters   ➕ CREATE   ➕ DEPLOY   ↻ REFRESH

Run your business critical workloads faster, safer, and easier at enterprise scale

GKE Enterprise combines multi-cluster and multi-team operations with fully managed security, governance, and service networking components. Er policies, and provide application visibility with actionable insights and an application-aware network for resiliency.

When you're ready to scale beyond a single team or cluster, GKE Enterprise delivers an integrated and consistent way to configure, secure, protect, i

LEARN AND ENABLE

OVERVIEW   OBSERVABILITY   COST OPTIMIZATION

▼ Filter   Enter property name or value

☐ Status	Name ↑	Location	Number of nodes	Total vCPUs	Total memory	Notifications	Labels	
☐ ⚠	cluster-1	us-central1-c	0	0	0 GB	—		⋮

Figure 9.50: GKE cluster deletion complete

gcloud commands

The following are some useful gcloud commands to keep in mind:

- **Create a GKE cluster:** gcloud container clusters create "CLUSTER_NAME" --machine-type n1-standard-2 --num-nodes 2 --zone "ZONE"

- **List GKE clusters:** gcloud container clusters list

- **Switch to a GKE cluster:** gcloud container clusters get-credentials "CLUSTER_ NAME" --zone "ZONE" --project "PROJECT"

- **GKE cluster resizing:** gcloud container clusters resize "CLUSTER_NAME" --num-nodes 3

- **GKE cluster update:** gcloud container clusters update "CLUSTER_NAME" --zone "ZONE"

- **GKE cluster delete:** gcloud container clusters delete "CLUSTER_NAME" --zone "ZONE"

- **GKE cluster delete configurations:** gcloud config configurations delete "CLUSTER_ NAME"

kubectl commands

The following are some useful kubectl commands to keep in mind:

- **Node's information:** kubectl get nodes -o wide

- **Configurations inside GKE cluster**: kubectl config view

- **Create deployment:** kubectl create deployment "DEPLOYMENT_NAME" --image="IMAGE_NAME"

- **Pod details:** kubectl get pods -o wide

- **Expose service:** kubectl expose deployment "DEPLOYMENT_NAME" --type LoadBalancer --port 80 --target-port 80

- **Service view:** kubectl get services

Conclusion

By the end of this chapter, we learned about Kubernetes and how to work on Google Cloud's version of Kubernetes, i.e., GKE. We have also discussed how a containerized application is deployed on GKE's service under deployment and invoked from outside.

In the proceeding chapters, we will discuss the Cloud Functions and App Engine.

Multiple choice questions

1. **To communicate inside GKE cluster's control plane which command line utility is used?**

   a. gcloud

   b. kubectl

   c. etcd

   d. None of these

2. **GKE can be used in which of the following modes:**

   a. Standard

   b. Autopilot

   c. Both a and b

   d. None of these

3. **In GKE, we need to create deployment first and then service.**

   a. True

   b. False

4. **In GKE, a cluster is a group of Pods**

   a. True

   b. False

5. **If a service needs more than 32 GB of RAM and 8 vCPUs, GKE is preferable over Cloud Run**

   a. True

   b. False

Answers

1.	b
2.	c
3.	a
4.	b
5.	a

Join our book's Discord space

Join the book's Discord Workspace for Latest updates, Offers, Tech happenings around the world, New Release and Sessions with the Authors:

https://discord.bpbonline.com

CHAPTER 10
Cloud Functions

Introduction

We have learned about **infrastructure as a service (IaaS)** and **platform as a service (PaaS)** in the previous chapters (*Chapters 7, 8, and 9*). Now, it is time to learn another concept called **functions as a service (FaaS)**. Google Cloud Functions is a FaaS offering in **Google Cloud Platform (GCP);** it is a serverless execution environment for building applications where other cloud services are required to be integrated with each other within the platform. With Cloud Functions, you can write a simple and single-purpose function that is attached to the events emitted from the system and/or other GCP services. The function is triggered when the event which is attached to the function gets triggered. The code within the function is executed in a fully managed environment. We do not need to worry about infrastructure and managing servers to host or execute Cloud Functions.

Structure

The chapter covers the following topics:

- Functions as a service
- Functions as a service vs serverless applications
- Cloud Functions
- Cloud Functions triggers

- Cloud Functions configurations
- Working with Cloud Functions

Objectives

By the end of this chapter, we will understand the complete concept of Cloud Functions. We will see how to deploy Cloud Functions using Google Cloud console and gcloud commands. We will also learn about the FaaS concept and how to implement it using Cloud Functions. In this chapter, we will learn about various triggers and configurations and see how to integrate with Google Cloud Database like BigQuery. We will also understand the difference between 1st and 2nd generation Cloud Functions.

Functions as a service

FaaS is a cloud computing type that allows customers to execute the code in response to the events, without managing the complex hardware infrastructure generally associated with building and launching applications. Hosting software applications on the internet normally requires provisioning and managing virtual or physical servers and managing operating systems and web servers hosting the processes. With FaaS, the physical hardware, virtual machine, operating system, and web server software management are handled automatically by the cloud service providers. This allows developers to focus completely on individual functions in their code.

Function as a service vs serverless applications

Serverless and FaaS often come with one another, but the truth is that FaaS is a subset of serverless. Serverless is focused on any type of service category like compute, storage, database, messaging, API gateways, etc., where configuration, management, and billing of servers are abstracted from the end user. FaaS, on the other hand, is the most central technology in serverless architectures, which is focused on the event-driven computing paradigm where application code, or containers, only run in response to events or requests.

Cloud Functions

Google Cloud Functions is a serverless execution environment for building and connecting cloud services. With Cloud Functions, you write simple, single-purpose functions that are attached to the events emitted from the cloud infrastructure and services. The function is triggered when an event being watched is fired, and the underlying code is executed in a fully managed environment. There is actually no need to provision any infrastructure or worry about managing servers.

Some of the key features of Cloud Functions

The following are the key features of Cloud Functions:

- Connects and extends services to build complex applications
- End-to-end development and diagnosability
- Develop locally, scale globally
- No server management
- Runs code in response to events
- Pay only for what you use
- Avoid lock-in with open technology

Cloud Functions triggers

We write codes inside the Cloud Functions and expect the code to be executed when an underlying trigger occurs. The triggers can be of two types, one is HTTP triggers, and another is event based triggers.

Currently, we have two versions of Cloud Functions available in GCP, 1st generation and 2nd generation.

Triggers supported in 1st generation

Cloud Functions (1st gen) supports the following types of triggers:

- HTTP triggers
- Event triggers
  - Pub or sub triggers
  - Cloud storage triggers
  - Firestore triggers
  - Google analytics for firebase triggers
  - Firebase realtime database triggers
  - Firebase authentication triggers
  - Firebase remote config triggers

Triggers supported in 2nd generation

Cloud Functions (2nd gen) supports the following types of triggers:

- HTTP triggers
- Event triggers

- o Pub or sub triggers
- o Cloud storage triggers
- o Generalized Eventarc triggers

All event-driven functions in Cloud Functions (2nd gen) use Eventarc for event delivery. In Cloud Functions (2nd gen), pub or sub triggers and Cloud storage triggers are implemented as types of Eventarc triggers. Eventarc does not currently support direct events from firestore, Google analytics for firebase, or firebase authentication. Use Cloud Functions (1st gen) to use these events because Cloud Functions can be triggered by messages on a pub or sub topic. We can integrate Cloud Functions with any other Google service that supports Pub or sub as an event bus. In addition, by using HTTP triggers we can also integrate with any service that provides HTTP callbacks (webhooks).

Cloud Functions configurations

Let us understand Cloud Functions configurations to optimize the behavior. We will see some of the usage using gcloud commands, but the same can be done using the GCP console as well.

- We can control how many instances of particular Cloud Functions can be created using the **max-instances** flag.

```
gcloud functions deploy YOUR_FUNCTION_NAME --max-instances MAX_
INSTANCE_LIMIT
```

- We can avoid a cold start and reduce the latency by setting a minimum number of instances using **min-instances** flag.

```
gcloud functions deploy YOUR_FUNCTION_NAME --min-instances MIN_
INSTANCE_LIMIT
```

- Secret manager can be used with Cloud Functions to store API keys, passwords, etc. The following example is using mounted volume for the secrets configuration file:

```
gcloud functions deploy FUNCTION_NAME \
--runtime RUNTIME \
-- set-secrets 'SECRET_FILE_PATH=SECRET_RESOURCE_PATH:VERSION'

gcloud functions deploy FUNCTION_NAME \
--runtime RUNTIME \
--update-secrets 'SECRET_FILE_PATH=SECRET_RESOURCE_PATH:VERSION'
gcloud functions deploy FUNCTION_NAME \
--runtime RUNTIME \
--clear-secrets
```

- We can set up the key value pairs as environment variables and use the same with Cloud Functions at run time.

```
gcloud functions deploy FUNCTION_NAME --set-env-vars FOO=bar
```

- By default, Cloud Functions has memory allocated as 256 MB (Mega Byte) for Gen 1 and 256 MiB (Mebi-Byte) for Gen 2; one can set the allocated memory while deploying Cloud Function using gcloud command or via console. For the gcloud command, **memory** option is required to set the allocated memory.

```
gcloud functions deploy YOUR_FUNCTION_NAME --memory=MEMORY_LIMIT
```

- For Cloud Functions 1st Gen, the maximum timeout duration is 540 seconds. For 2nd Gen, the maximum timeout duration is 3600 seconds; one can set the timeout using **timeout** option.

```
gcloud functions deploy YOUR_FUNCTION_NAME --timeout=TIMEOUT_DURATION
```

Working with Cloud Functions

We are going to see how Cloud Functions work with a trigger event via Cloud storage bucket and loading the data to BigQuery using a simple Python code.

Let us understand the use case, we have a source file landing into Cloud storage bucket needs to be copied to another bucket using Python automatically. So, when a file lands in the Cloud storage bucket, a Cloud Function will be triggered and code will be executed to copy the file to another bucket.

We will complete the whole requirement using Cloud Functions in a step-by-step process in GCP console:

1. Start with searching Cloud Functions in GCP console's search box.

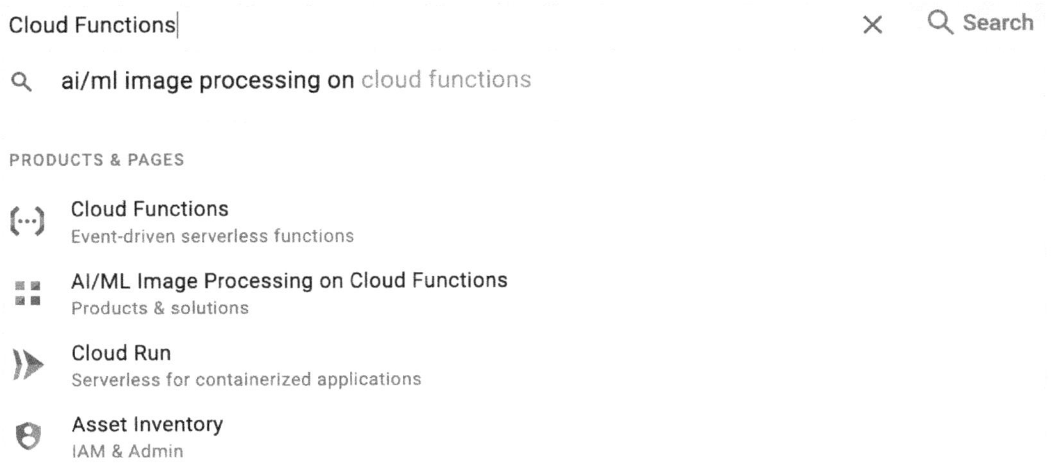

Cloud Functions| ✕   🔍 Search

🔍   ai/ml image processing on cloud functions

PRODUCTS & PAGES

{··}   **Cloud Functions**
       Event-driven serverless functions

▪▪   **AI/ML Image Processing on Cloud Functions**
▪▪   Products & solutions

〉▶   **Cloud Run**
       Serverless for containerized applications

🔒   **Asset Inventory**
       IAM & Admin

Figure 10.1: Search Cloud Functions in GCP console

2. Click on **Create Function** to proceed:

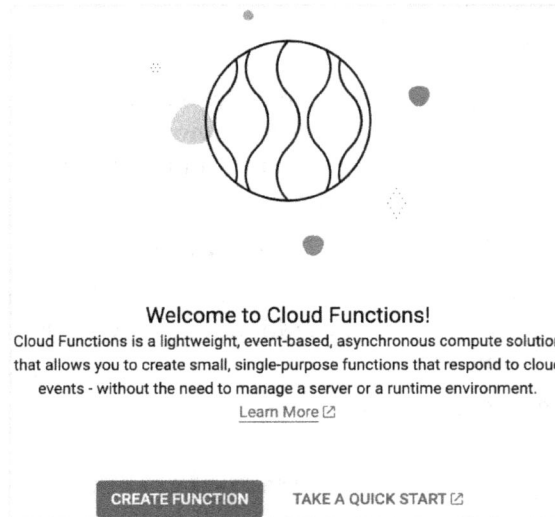

Welcome to Cloud Functions!

Cloud Functions is a lightweight, event-based, asynchronous compute solution that allows you to create small, single-purpose functions that respond to cloud events - without the need to manage a server or a runtime environment.

Learn More ☑

CREATE FUNCTION   TAKE A QUICK START ☑

Figure 10.2: Inside Cloud Functions* window

3. Need to enable the below APIs if not done already.

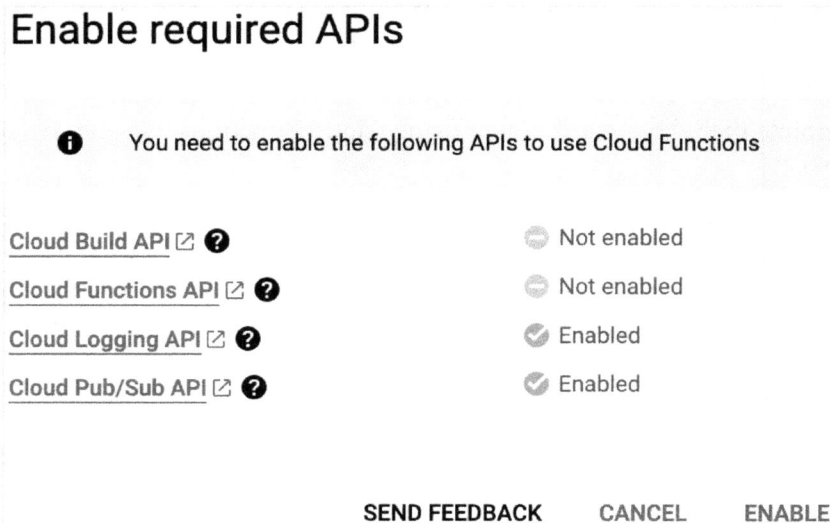

Enable required APIs

🛈   You need to enable the following APIs to use Cloud Functions

Cloud Build API ☑ ❓	⦿ Not enabled
Cloud Functions API ☑ ❓	⦿ Not enabled
Cloud Logging API ☑ ❓	✅ Enabled
Cloud Pub/Sub API ☑ ❓	✅ Enabled

SEND FEEDBACK   CANCEL   ENABLE

Figure 10.3: Required APIs

4. Fill in the details in the following:

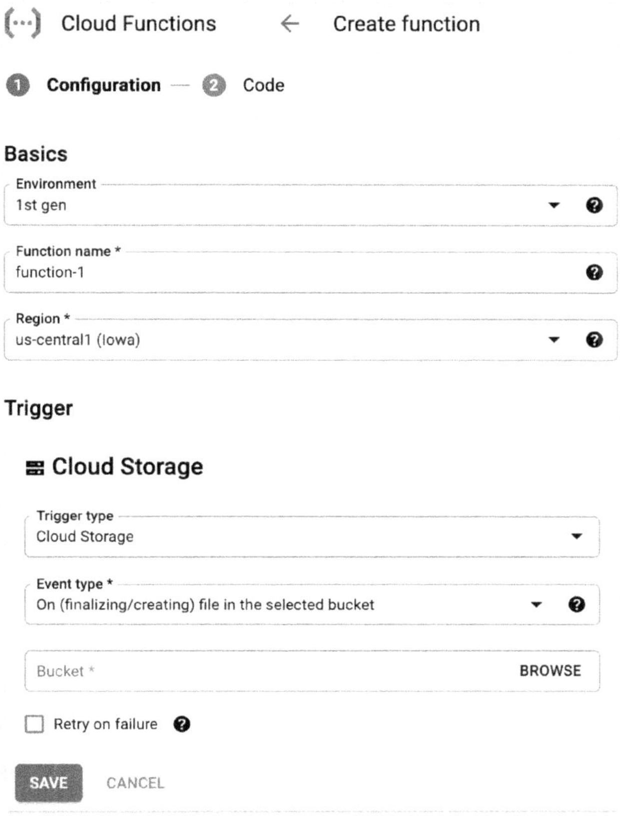

Figure 10.4: Function details

5. Choose the right trigger type:

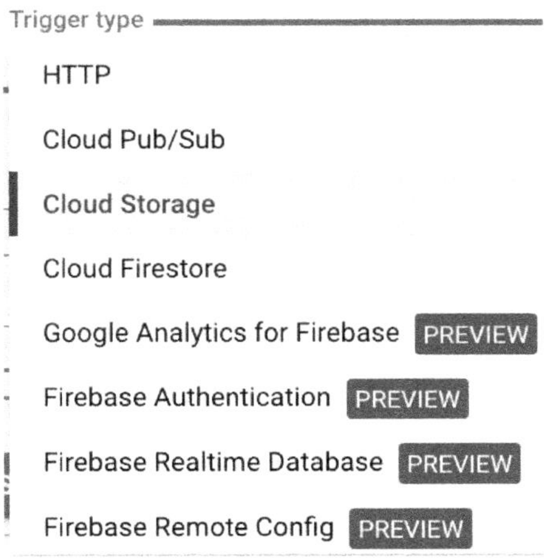

Figure 10.5: Choose the trigger type

6. When Cloud storage has been chosen as **Trigger type**, now choose on what event the function needs to be triggered.

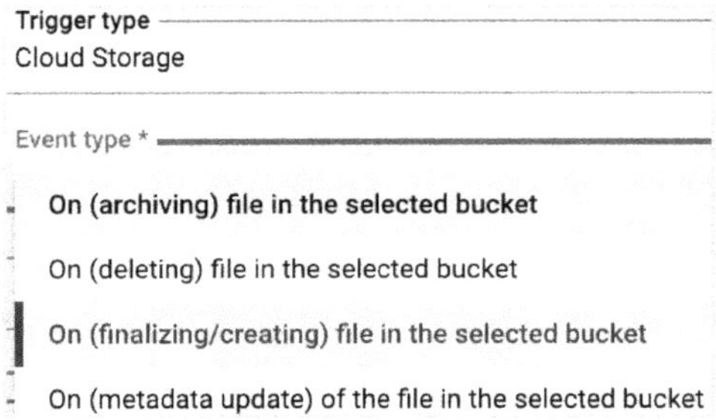

Trigger type
Cloud Storage

Event type *

On (archiving) file in the selected bucket

On (deleting) file in the selected bucket

On (finalizing/creating) file in the selected bucket

On (metadata update) of the file in the selected bucket

Figure 10.6: Event of a trigger

7. Choose the underlying bucket for the trigger:

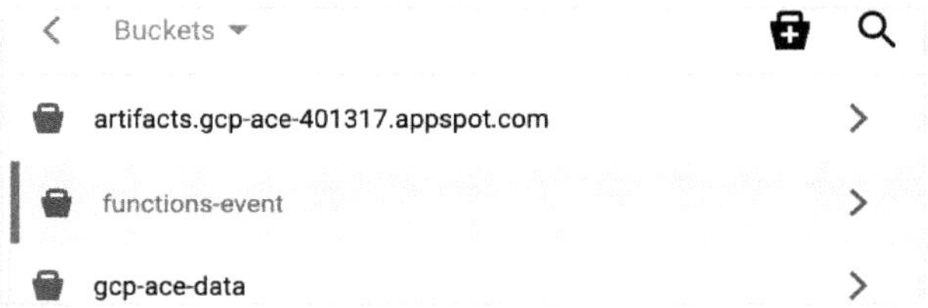

< Buckets ▼

artifacts.gcp-ace-401317.appspot.com >

functions-event >

gcp-ace-data >

Figure 10.7: Choose the bucket

8. Choose the required configurations for runtime, build, connections, and security. You can keep the default settings.

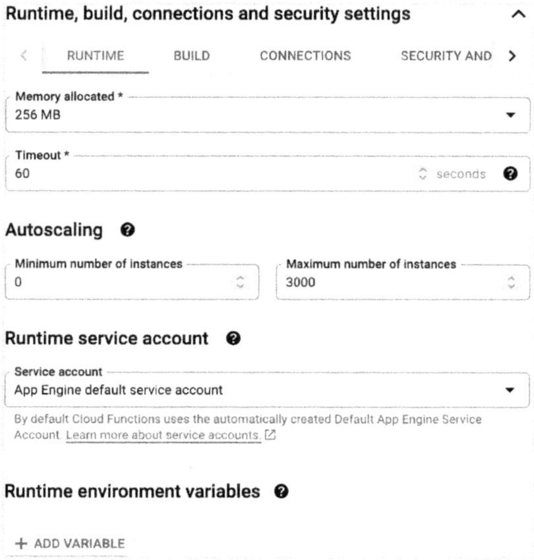

Runtime, build, connections and security settings

< RUNTIME BUILD CONNECTIONS SECURITY AND >

Memory allocated *
256 MB

Timeout *
60   ⌄ seconds ❷

Autoscaling ❷

Minimum number of instances
0

Maximum number of instances
3000

Runtime service account ❷

Service account
App Engine default service account

By default Cloud Functions uses the automatically created Default App Engine Service Account. Learn more about service accounts. ☒

Runtime environment variables ❷

+ ADD VARIABLE

Figure 10.8: Choose the required configurations

9. Configure the connection details as follows:

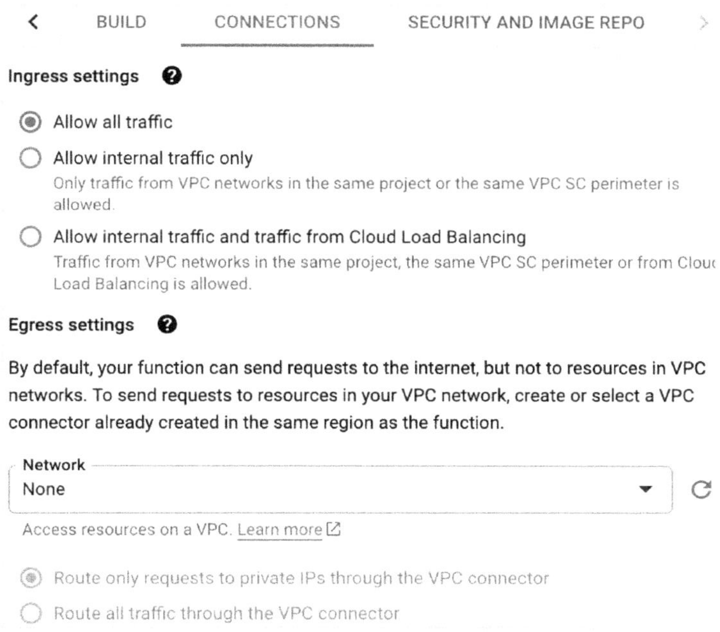

Figure 10.9: Connections in Cloud Functions

10. You can configure security and image repository; in this case, we are going with default options:

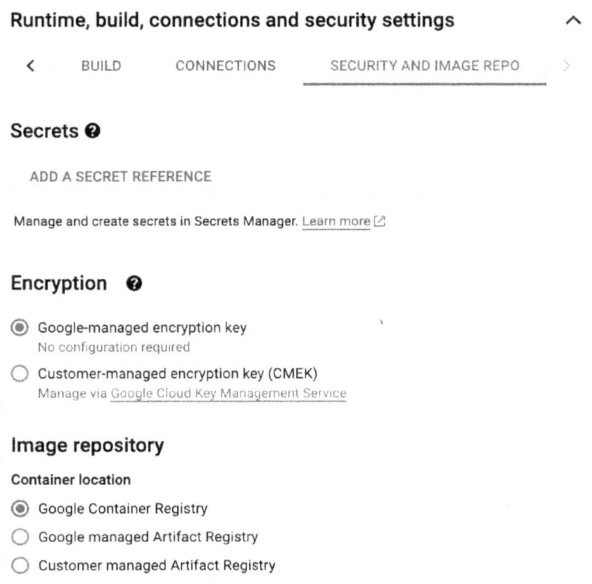

Figure 10.10: Choose the required configurations for security and image

11. Cloud Functions code runtime window:

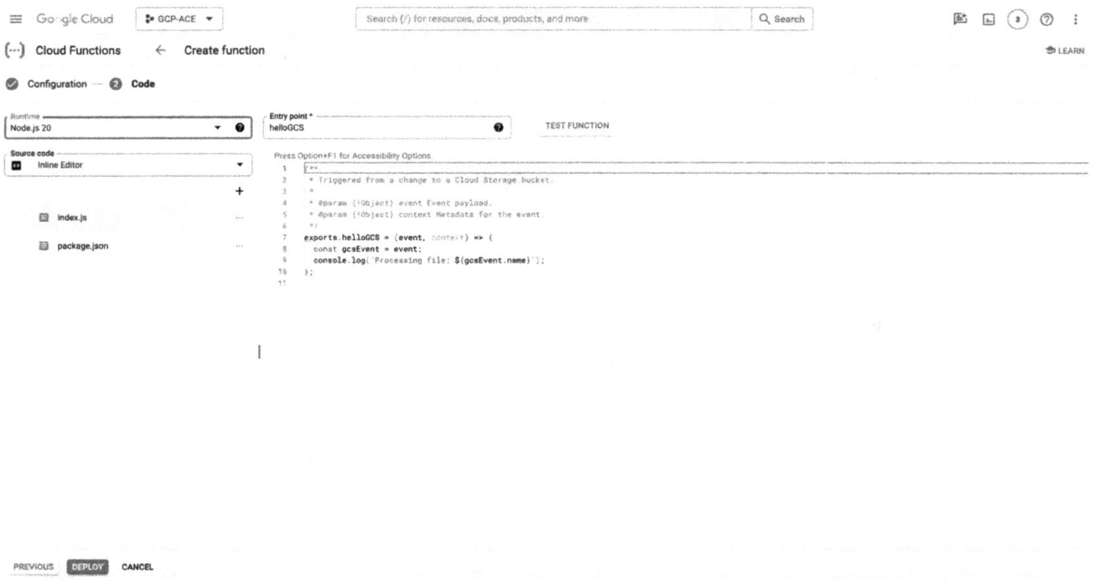

Figure 10.11: Default code runtime window

12. Change runtime to Python 3.11 as shown in the following:

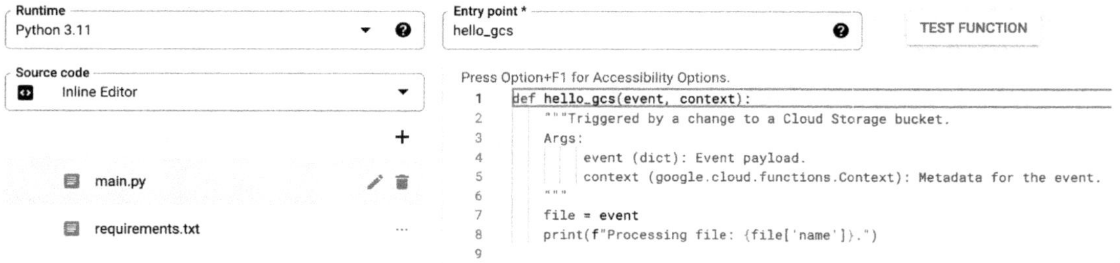

Figure 10.12: Python runtime

13. Replace the code, as shown in the following:

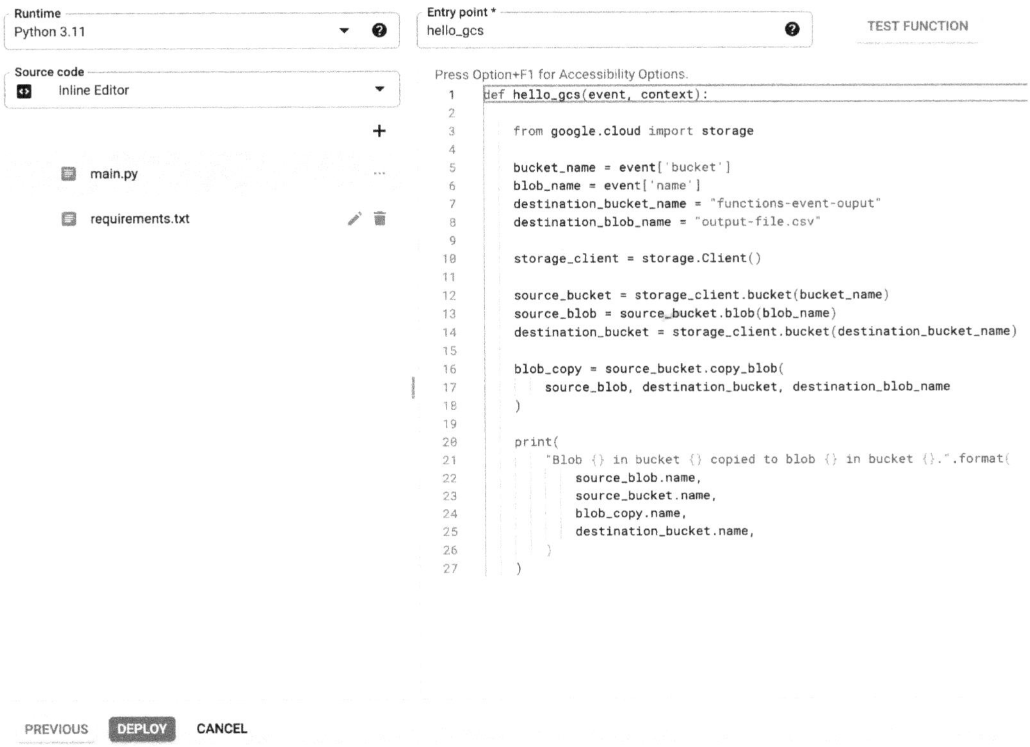

Figure 10.13: Code for use case

Code:

```
1.  def hello_gcs(event, context):
2.
3.      from google.cloud import storage
4.
5.      bucket_name = event['bucket']
6.      blob_name = event['name']
7.      destination_bucket_name = "functions-event-ouput"
8.      destination_blob_name = "output-file.csv"
9.
10.     storage_client = storage.Client()
11.
12.     source_bucket = storage_client.bucket(bucket_name)
13.     source_blob = source_bucket.blob(blob_name)
14.     destination_bucket = storage_client.bucket(destination_
    bucket_name)
```

```
15.
16.     blob_copy = source_bucket.copy_blob(
17.         source_blob, destination_bucket, destination_blob_name
18.     )
19.
20.     print(
21.         "Blob {} in bucket {} copied to blob {} in buck-
    et {}.".format(
22.             source_blob.name,
23.             source_bucket.name,
24.             blob_copy.name,
25.             destination_bucket.name,
26.         )
27.     )
```

14. Change the requirements.txt to include the required library:

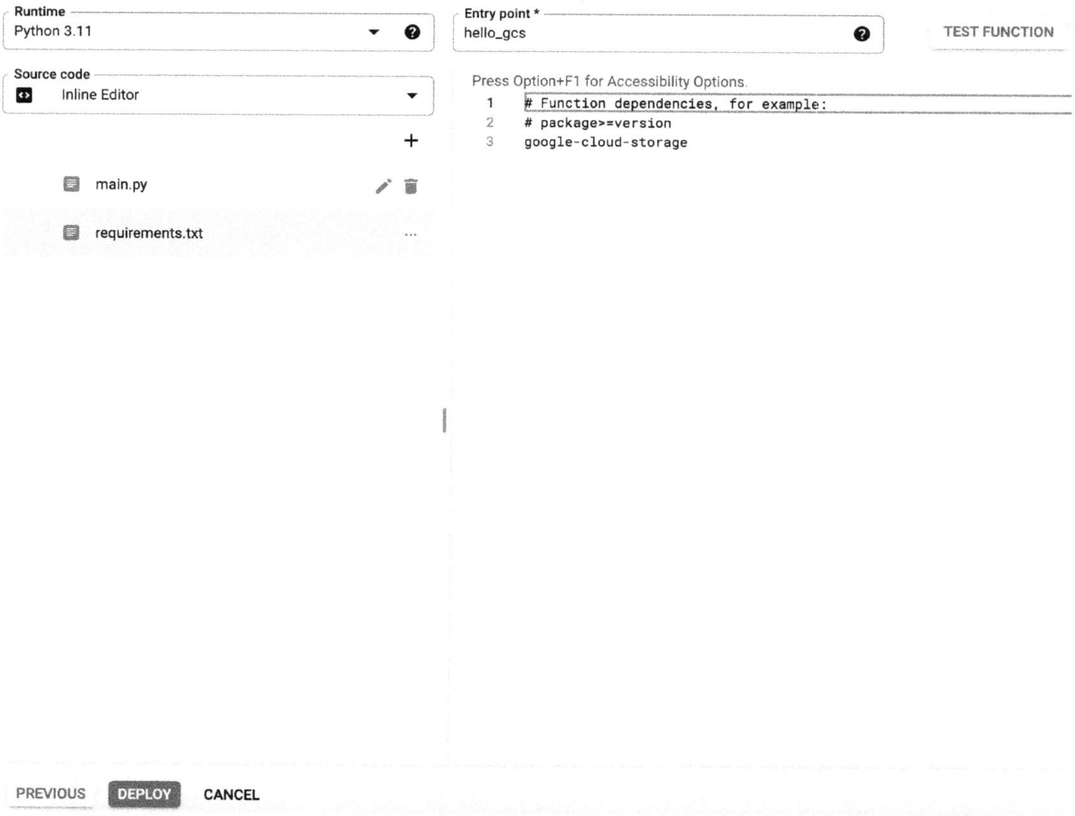

Figure 10.14: Requirements.txt

15. Source bucket **functions-event** has no files initially.

functions-event

Location	Storage class	Public access	Protection
us (multiple regions in United States)	Standard	Not public	None

OBJECTS CONFIGURATION PERMISSIONS PROTECTION LIFECYCLE OBSERVABILITY INVENTORY REPORTS

Buckets > functions-event

UPLOAD FILES   UPLOAD FOLDER   CREATE FOLDER   TRANSFER DATA ▾   MANAGE HOLDS   DOWNLOAD   DELETE

Filter by name prefix only ▾   ☰ Filter   Filter objects and folders

☐	Name	Size	Type	Created ❓	Storage class	Last modified	Public access ❓	Version history ❓

No rows to display

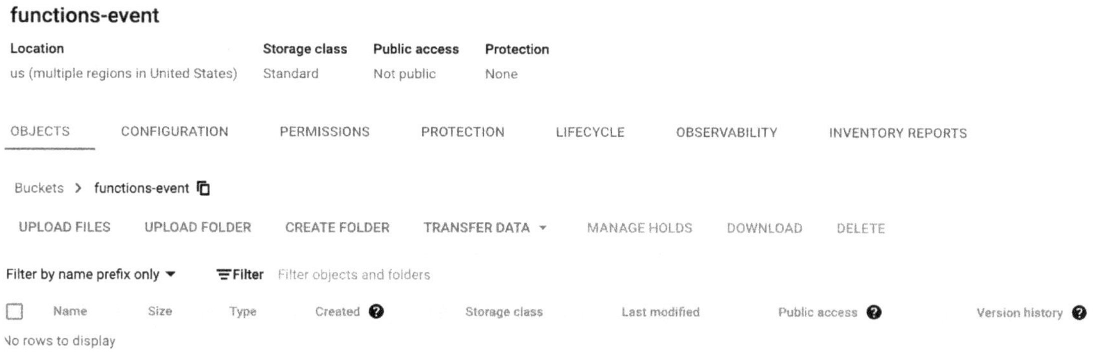

Figure 10.15: Source bucket

16. The target bucket **functions-event-output** has no files initially.

functions-event-ouput

Location	Storage class	Public access	Protection
us (multiple regions in United States)	Standard	Not public	None

OBJECTS CONFIGURATION PERMISSIONS PROTECTION LIFECYCLE OBSERVABILITY INVENTORY REPORTS

Buckets > functions-event-ouput

UPLOAD FILES   UPLOAD FOLDER   CREATE FOLDER   TRANSFER DATA ▾   MANAGE HOLDS   DOWNLOAD   DELETE

Filter by name prefix only ▾   ☰ Filter   Filter objects and folders

☐	Name	Size	Type	Created ❓	Storage class	Last modified	Public access ❓	Version history ❓

No rows to display

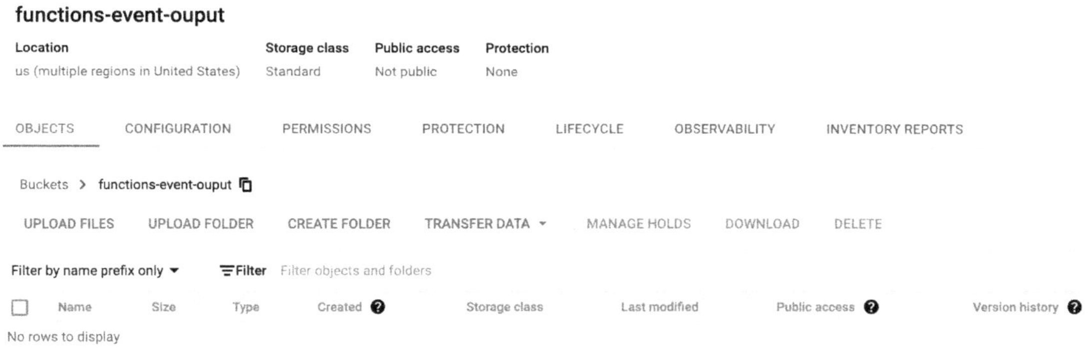

Figure 10.16: Target bucket

17. Now, when a file will be uploaded into the source bucket **functions-event**, the Cloud Functions code will be triggered, and, in this case, the uploaded file will be copied to **functions-event-output** bucket.

The following image shows a file uploaded to the source bucket:

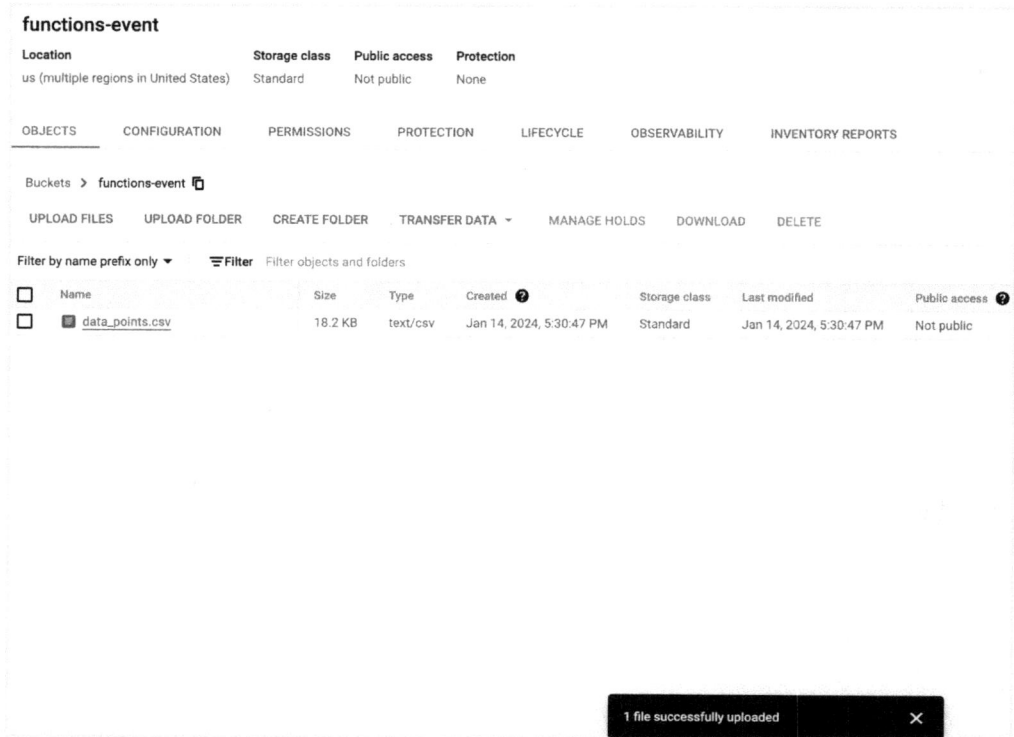

Figure 10.17: File uploaded to the source bucket

In addition to this use case, an uploaded file can also be loaded to other GCP database services like BigQuery.

18. The following image shows metrics of Cloud Function usage:

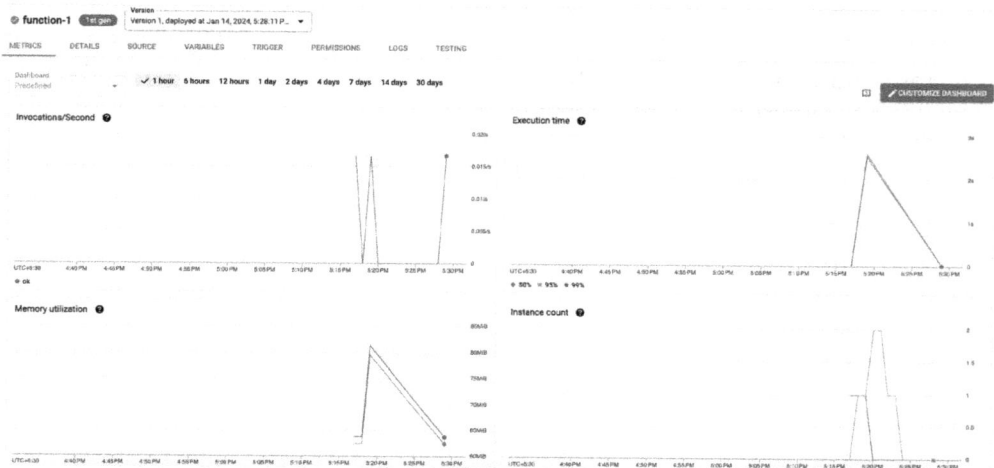

Figure 10.18: Cloud Functions metrics

19. File copied to target bucket.

functions-event-ouput

Location	Storage class	Public access	Protection
us (multiple regions in United States)	Standard	Not public	None

OBJECTS CONFIGURATION PERMISSIONS PROTECTION LIFECYCLE OBSERVABILITY INVENTORY REPORTS

Buckets > functions-event-ouput 🗐

UPLOAD FILES   UPLOAD FOLDER   CREATE FOLDER   TRANSFER DATA ▾   MANAGE HOLDS   DOWNLOAD   DELETE

Filter by name prefix only ▼   ☰Filter Filter objects and folders

☐	Name	Size	Type	Created ❷	Storage class	Last modified	Public access ❷
☐	📄 output-file.csv	18.2 KB	text/csv	Jan 14, 2024, 5:30:51 PM	Standard	Jan 14, 2024, 5:30:51 PM	Not public

Figure 10.19: File copied to the target bucket

Conclusion

We have reached the end of the chapter, and we have learned about FaaS and found out how fully managed Cloud Functions are deployed in GCPs and get invoked when an attached event occurs. This is very helpful in designing event-based systems. In the next chapter, we will learn about the App Engine.

Multiple choice questions

1. **In FaaS, scaling of an application is managed by whom?**

    a. User

    b. Cloud Service Provider

    c. Both

    d. None of These

2. **What is the maximum timeout duration in the 1st Generation Cloud Function?**

    a. 520 secs

    b. 530 secs

    c. 540 secs

    d. 550 secs

3. **The memory option is used to set the memory limit in Cloud Functions.**

    a. True

    b. False

4. **The min-instances option is used to avoid cold start in Cloud Functions.**

   a. True

   b. False

5. **Cloud Functions can integrate with BigQuery.**

   a. True

   b. False

Answers

1.	b
2.	c
3.	a
4.	a
5.	a

Join our book's Discord space

Join the book's Discord Workspace for Latest updates, Offers, Tech happenings around the world, New Release and Sessions with the Authors:

https://discord.bpbonline.com

CHAPTER 11
App Engine

Introduction

In the last chapters, we have learned about compute engine (*Chapter 7*), which is an **infrastructure as a service (IaaS)** offering, Cloud Run (*Chapter 8*), which is a **platform as a service (PaaS)** offering, and Cloud Functions (*Chapter 10*), which is a **function as a service (FaaS)** offering from **Google Cloud Platform (GCP)**. In this chapter, we are going to learn about App Engine, which is another managed serverless PaaS offering from GCP. It is one of the oldest services offered by GCP, and it is mainly used to deploy applications quickly in GCP.

It is an important service for the GCP Associate Cloud Engineer exam. We can expect some questions from this chapter.

Structure

The chapter covers the following topics:

- App Engine
- Types of App Engine
- App Engine components
- Creating an application using App Engine

- Traffic splitting between versions
- Multiple services inside one application
- Request routing to applications, services, and versions

Objectives

We will try to understand the concept of App Engine in this chapter. We will see how to set up the App Engine using Google Cloud Console and using gcloud commands. We will understand about App Engine types such as standard and flexible. We will also get to know about traffic splitting and request routing to services and versions. Finally, we will create an application using App Engine and create multiple services and different versions of the services and split the traffic between versions. In this chapter, we will execute various gcloud commands related to App Engine to deploy Python services under a single application and verify those from the console as well by navigating to the services, versions, and instances tab. We will verify our application by logging into the services using a browser.

App Engine

App Engine is a fully managed and serverless platform for developing and hosting applications at scale. You need to choose from several popular languages, libraries, and frameworks in order to develop applications, and once deployed with a runtime, App Engine will take care of provisioning the servers and scaling application instances based on the demand. The following languages are supported by App Engine:

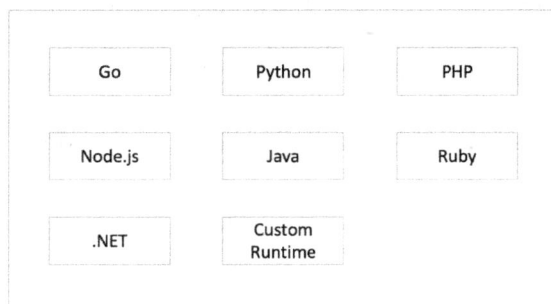

Go	Python	PHP
Node.js	Java	Ruby
.NET	Custom Runtime	

Figure 11.1: Languages for App Engine

Types of App Engine

App Engine can be categorized into two types:

- **App Engine standard**: The standard environment is based on the container instances running inside Google's infrastructure. Containers are preconfigured with any of the available runtimes.

- **App Engine flexible**: The flexible environment runs the applications within Docker containers on a compute engine **virtual machine** (**VM**). The application code can be written in a version of any of the supported programming languages or needs to use custom runtimes.

Comparison between standard and flexible types

Let us compare the following two options under App Engine.

Feature	Standard	Flexible
Instance Startup Time	Seconds	Minutes
Maximum request timeout	Depends on runtime and scaling	60 minutes
Background threads	Yes, with restrictions	Yes
Background processes	No	Yes
SSH debugging	No	Yes
Scaling	Manual, Basic, Automatic	Manual, Automatic
Scale to zero	Yes	No, minimum 1 instance
Writing to local disk	/tmp directory	Yes, ephemeral (disk initialized on each VM startup)
Modifying the runtime	No	Yes (through Dockerfile)
Deployment time	Seconds	Minutes
Automatic in-place security patches	Yes	Yes (excludes container image runtime)
Access to GCP APIs	Yes	Yes
Web Sockets	No	Yes
Supports installing third-party binaries	Yes	Yes
Pricing	Regional	Regional
Location	Based on instance hours	Based on usage of vCPU, memory and persistent disks

Table 11.1: Standard vs Flexible App Engine types

App Engine components

Let us understand the components of App Engine:

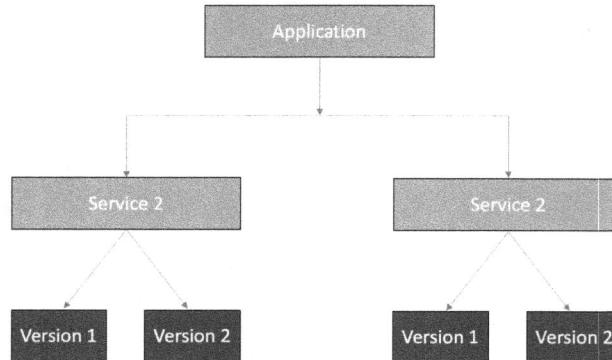

Figure 11.2: App Engine components hierarchy

- **Application**: There can be one application per project in GCP.
- **Services**: These are different microservices under one application or they can be considered as different components of an application also.
- **Versions**: Each service can have multiple versions co-exist in an application. You can split traffic among versions of a service.
- **Instances**: The versions within the services run on one or more instances. By default, App Engine scales an app to match the load. The application will scale up and down automatically to optimize the usage and cost.

Creating an application using App Engine

Let us create an application with App Engine standards in the following step-by-step manner:

1. Search for **app engine** in the GCP console's search box.

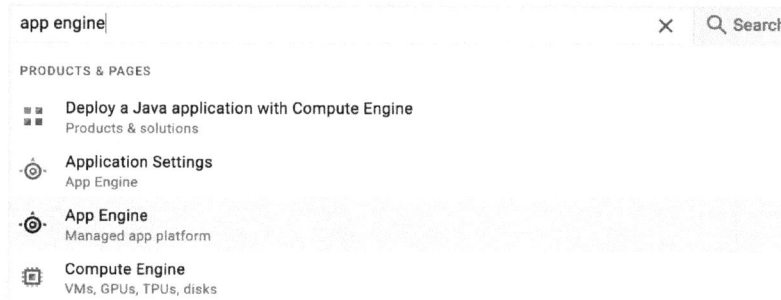

Figure 11.3: Search for App Engine

2. Inside the App Engine page, click on **CREATE APPLICATION**:

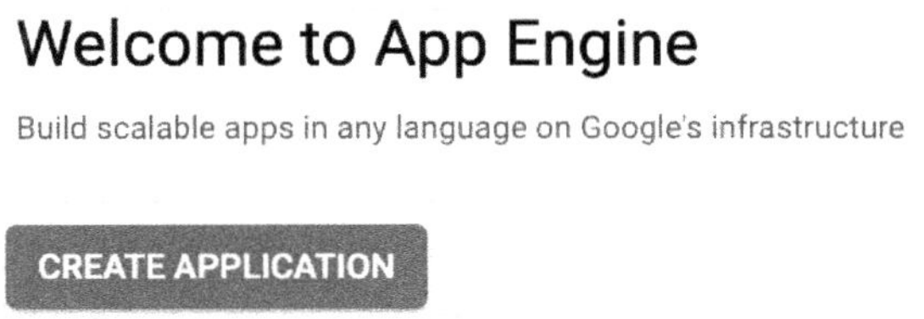

Welcome to App Engine

Build scalable apps in any language on Google's infrastructure

CREATE APPLICATION

Figure 11.4: Create application in App Engine

3. Enable required APIs for App Engine.
4. You need to know the region where you want to deploy the App Engine application.
5. There will be one application in one GCP project.
6. Select a service account, or it will create a new one while creating the application.

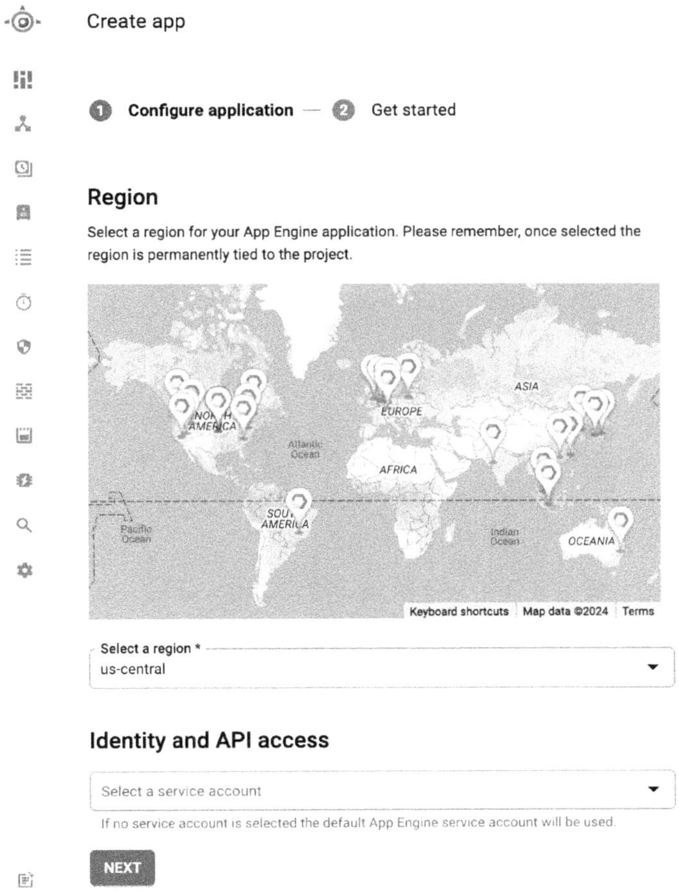

Figure 11.5: Region and service account for App Engine

7. Click on **NEXT** to proceed further:

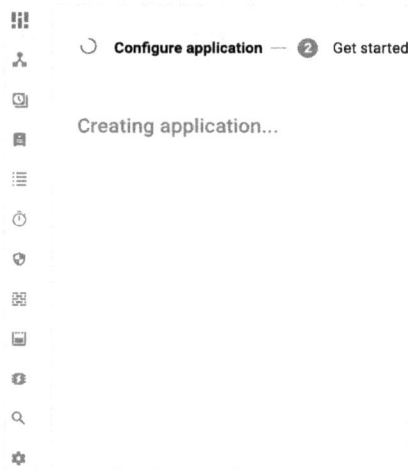

Figure 11.6: Creating App Engine application

8. Click on **I'LL DO THIS LATER**:

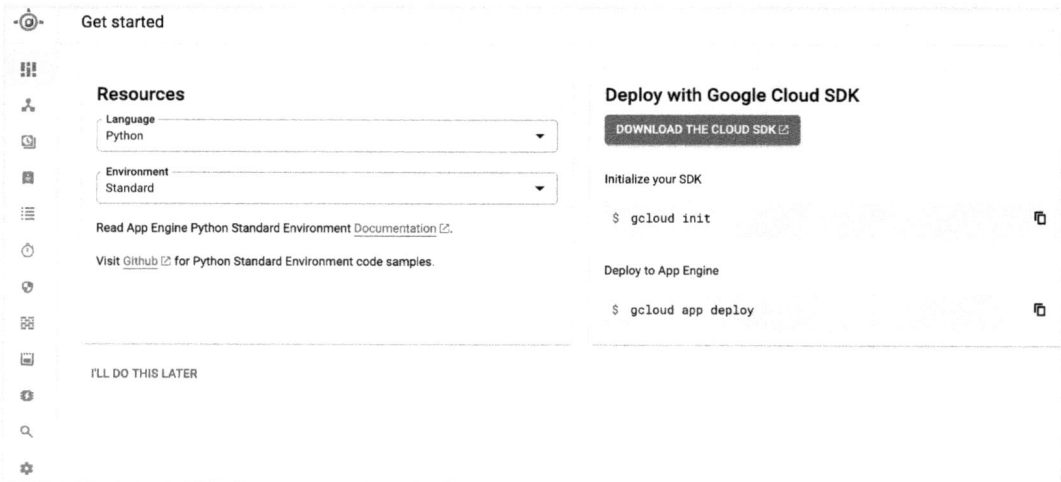

Figure 11.7: After creating the application

9. Activate the Cloud Shell as shown in the following:

Figure 11.8: Activate Cloud Shell

10. Cloud Shell will look like this:

Figure 11.9: Cloud shell is ready

11. Create a directory called **app_engine**.

Figure 11.10: Created app_engine directory

12. Create **service1** directory inside **app_engine** directory:

Figure 11.11: Created service1 directory under app_engine

13. Create the following three files as shown:

Figure 11.12: Create service related files

Python code as **main.py**.

```
arijits_data@cloudshell:~/app_engine/service1 (gcp-ace-401317)$ cat app.yaml
runtime: python311
arijits_data@cloudshell:~/app_engine/service1 (gcp-ace-401317)$ cat main.py
from flask import Flask

app = Flask(__name__)

@app.route('/service1')
def func():
    return 'Service1 and Version1'
arijits_data@cloudshell:~/app_engine/service1 (gcp-ace-401317)$ cat requirements.txt
Flask
arijits_data@cloudshell:~/app_engine/service1 (gcp-ace-401317)$ ▏
```

Figure 11.13: Content of the files

14. Deploy the app like the following:

```
arijits_data@cloudshell:~/app_engine/service1 (gcp-ace-401317)$ gcloud app deploy
Services to deploy:

descriptor:              [/home/arijits_data/app_engine/service1/app.yaml]
source:                  [/home/arijits_data/app_engine/service1]
target project:          [gcp-ace-401317]
target service:          [default]
target version:          [20240120t194242]
target url:              [https://gcp-ace-401317.uc.r.appspot.com]
target service account:  [gcp-ace-401317@appspot.gserviceaccount.com]


Do you want to continue (Y/n)? ▏
```

Figure 11.14: Deploy the application service

15. Select **Y** and wait for the execution to get completed.

```
Beginning deployment of service [default]...
Uploading 1 file to Google Cloud Storage
100%
100%
File upload done.
Updating service [default]...working...▏
```

Figure 11.15: Service getting updated

After completion of deployment.

```
Beginning deployment of service [default]...
Uploading 1 file to Google Cloud Storage
100%
100%
File upload done.
Updating service [default]...done.
Setting traffic split for service [default]...done.
Deployed service [default] to [https://gcp-ace-401317.uc.r.appspot.com]

You can stream logs from the command line by running:
  $ gcloud app logs tail -s default

To view your application in the web browser run:
  $ gcloud app browse
arijits_data@cloudshell:~/app_engine/service1 (gcp-ace-401317)$
```

Figure 11.16: Deployed default service

16. Take the URL and go to the browser and hit the service.

← → C ○ 🔒 https://**gcp-ace-401317.uc.r.appspot.com**/service1

Service1 and Version1

Figure 11.17: Browsing the url of default service

17. Go to the console and investigate the **Services** tab under App Engine.

	Service	Versions	Labels	Dispatch routes	Ingress	VPC access name	VPC egress setting	Last version deployed ↓		Diagnose
☐	default ☒	1			All			Jan 21, 2024, 1:13:44 AM by arijits data@gmail.com		Logs ☒

Figure 11.18: Default service in GCP console

18. **Versions** tab under App Engine:

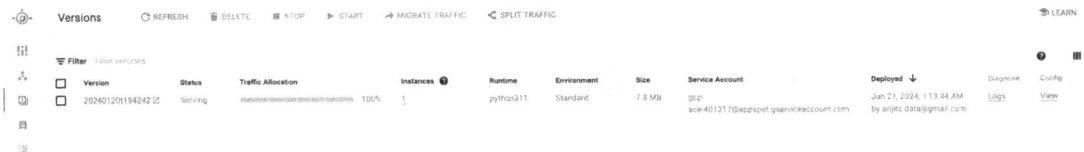

	Version	Status	Traffic Allocation	Instances	Runtime	Environment	Size	Service Account	Deployed ↓	Diagnose	Config
☐	20240120t194242 ☒	Serving	100%	1	python311	Standard	2.8 MB	gcp-ace-401317@appspot.gserviceaccount.com	Jan 21, 2024, 1:13:44 AM by arijits data@gmail.com	Logs	View

Figure 11.19: Version of default service

19. **Instances** tab under App Engine:

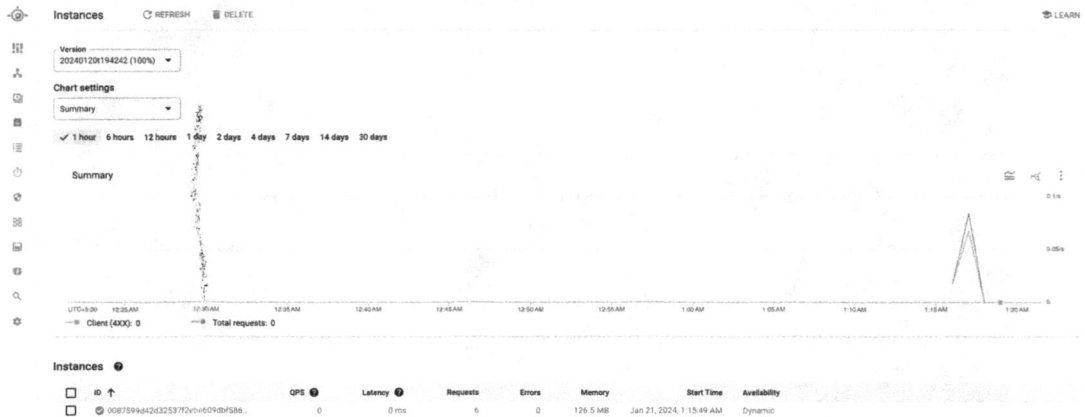

Figure 11.20: Instance of default service

20. You can investigate services, versions and instances using gcloud command like the following:

Figure 11.21: gcloud commands for services, versions and instances

Traffic splitting between versions

Let us understand the traffic splitting between versions:

1. In the **main.py** file, change the return statement to **Version2**.

Figure 11.22: Version 2 of default service

2. Deploy the new version as v2.

```
arijits_data@cloudshell:~/app_engine/service1 (gcp-ace-401317)$ gcloud app deploy --version=v2
Services to deploy:

descriptor:                [/home/arijits_data/app_engine/service1/app.yaml]
source:                    [/home/arijits_data/app_engine/service1]
target project:            [gcp-ace-401317]
target service:            [default]
target version:            [v2]
target url:                [https://gcp-ace-401317.uc.r.appspot.com]
target service account:    [gcp-ace-401317@appspot.gserviceaccount.com]


Do you want to continue (Y/n)?  y

Beginning deployment of service [default]...
Uploading 1 file to Google Cloud Storage
100%
100%
File upload done.
Updating service [default]...working...
```

Figure 11.23: Deployed version 2

3. Verify the app versions list as the following:

```
arijits_data@cloudshell:~/app_engine/service1 (gcp-ace-401317)$ gcloud app versions list
SERVICE: default
VERSION.ID: 20240120t194242
TRAFFIC_SPLIT: 0.00
LAST_DEPLOYED: 2024-01-20T19:43:44+00:00
SERVING_STATUS: SERVING

SERVICE: default
VERSION.ID: v2
TRAFFIC_SPLIT: 1.00
LAST_DEPLOYED: 2024-01-20T19:56:53+00:00
SERVING_STATUS: SERVING
arijits_data@cloudshell:~/app_engine/service1 (gcp-ace-401317)$ ▮
```

Figure 11.24: Verify versions

4. In **main.py** file, now change the version as **Version3**.

```
from flask import Flask

app = Flask(__name__)


@app.route('/service1')
def func():
    return 'Service1 and Version3'
~
~
```

Figure 11.25: Version 3 of default service

5. Now deploy the new version as v3.

```
arijits_data@cloudshell:~/app_engine/service1 (gcp-ace-401317)$ gcloud app deploy --version=v3
Services to deploy:

descriptor:                    [/home/arijits_data/app_engine/service1/app.yaml]
source:                        [/home/arijits_data/app_engine/service1]
target project:                [gcp-ace-401317]
target service:                [default]
target version:               [v3]
target url:                    [https://gcp-ace-401317.uc.r.appspot.com]
target service account:        [gcp-ace-401317@appspot.gserviceaccount.com]


Do you want to continue (Y/n)?  y

Beginning deployment of service [default]...
Uploading 1 file to Google Cloud Storage
100%
100%
File upload done.
Updating service [default]...done.
Setting traffic split for service [default]...done.
Deployed service [default] to [https://gcp-ace-401317.uc.r.appspot.com]

You can stream logs from the command line by running:
  $ gcloud app logs tail -s default

To view your application in the web browser run:
  $ gcloud app browse
arijits_data@cloudshell:~/app_engine/service1 (gcp-ace-401317)$
```

Figure 11.26: Deployed version3

6. Verify the versions using the following command:

```
arijits_data@cloudshell:~/app_engine/service1 (gcp-ace-401317)$ gcloud app versions list
SERVICE: default
VERSION.ID: 20240120t194242
TRAFFIC_SPLIT: 0.00
LAST_DEPLOYED: 2024-01-20T19:43:44+00:00
SERVING_STATUS: SERVING

SERVICE: default
VERSION.ID: v2
TRAFFIC_SPLIT: 0.00
LAST_DEPLOYED: 2024-01-20T19:56:53+00:00
SERVING_STATUS: SERVING

SERVICE: default
VERSION.ID: v3
TRAFFIC_SPLIT: 1.00
LAST_DEPLOYED: 2024-01-20T20:06:34+00:00
SERVING_STATUS: SERVING
arijits_data@cloudshell:~/app_engine/service1 (gcp-ace-401317)$
```

Figure 11.27: Listing all versions using gcloud command

7. Split the traffic based on versions.

```
arijits_data@cloudshell:~/app_engine/service1 (gcp-ace-401317)$ gcloud app services set-traffic --splits=v3=.5,v2=.5 --split-by=random
Setting the following traffic allocation:
 - gcp-ace-401317/default/v3: 0.5
 - gcp-ace-401317/default/v2: 0.5
NOTE: Splitting traffic by random.
Any other versions of the specified service will receive zero traffic.
Do you want to continue (Y/n)?  y

Setting traffic split for service [default]...done.
```

Figure 11.28: Splitting traffic between versions

8. Traffic going to **version 2**.

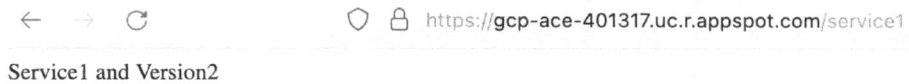

← → C   ○ 🔒 https://**gcp-ace-401317.uc.r.appspot.com**/service1

Service1 and Version2

Figure 11.29: Traffic to version 2

9. Traffic going to **version 3**.

← → C   ○ 🔒 https://**gcp-ace-401317.uc.r.appspot.com**/service1

Service1 and Version3

Figure 11.30: Traffic to version 3

10. Verify the versions in console.

Figure 11.31: All versions in the console

Multiple services inside one application

Let us create another service inside the same application.

1. Create a directory as **service2** and modify the files as the following:

```
arijits_data@cloudshell:~/app_engine/service2 (gcp-ace-401317)$ ls -lrt
total 12
-rw-r--r-- 1 arijits_data arijits_data   6 Jan 20 20:23 requirements.txt
-rw-r--r-- 1 arijits_data arijits_data  37 Jan 20 20:23 app.yaml
-rw-r--r-- 1 arijits_data arijits_data 119 Jan 20 20:24 main.py
arijits_data@cloudshell:~/app_engine/service2 (gcp-ace-401317)$
arijits_data@cloudshell:~/app_engine/service2 (gcp-ace-401317)$
arijits_data@cloudshell:~/app_engine/service2 (gcp-ace-401317)$ cat requirements.txt
Flask
arijits_data@cloudshell:~/app_engine/service2 (gcp-ace-401317)$
arijits_data@cloudshell:~/app_engine/service2 (gcp-ace-401317)$ cat app.yaml
runtime: python311
service: service2
arijits_data@cloudshell:~/app_engine/service2 (gcp-ace-401317)$ cat main.py
from flask import Flask

app = Flask(__name__)

@app.route('/service2')
def func():
    return 'Service2 and Version1'
arijits_data@cloudshell:~/app_engine/service2 (gcp-ace-401317)$
```

Figure 11.32: Another service getting developed for the same application

2. Deploy the new service:

```
arijits_data@cloudshell:~/app_engine/service2 (gcp-ace-401317)$ gcloud app deploy
Services to deploy:

descriptor:                  [/home/arijits_data/app_engine/service2/app.yaml]
source:                      [/home/arijits_data/app_engine/service2]
target project:              [gcp-ace-401317]
target service:              [service2]
target version:              [20240120t202514]
target url:                  [https://service2-dot-gcp-ace-401317.uc.r.appspot.com]
target service account:      [gcp-ace-401317@appspot.gserviceaccount.com]


Do you want to continue (Y/n)?  y

Beginning deployment of service [service2]...
Created .gcloudignore file. See `gcloud topic gcloudignore` for details.
Uploading 2 files to Google Cloud Storage
50%
100%
100%
File upload done.
Updating service [service2]...done.
Setting traffic split for service [service2]...done.
Deployed service [service2] to [https://service2-dot-gcp-ace-401317.uc.r.appspot.com]

You can stream logs from the command line by running:
  $ gcloud app logs tail -s service2

To view your application in the web browser run:
  $ gcloud app browse -s service2
arijits_data@cloudshell:~/app_engine/service2 (gcp-ace-401317)$ █
```

Figure 11.33: Another service is deployed

3. Request to **Service 2**.

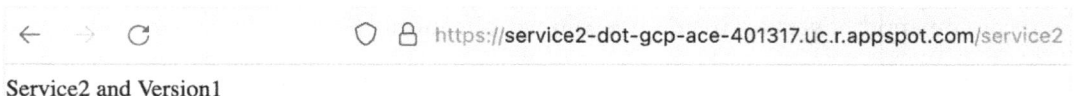

← → C   ○ 🔒 https://**service2-dot-gcp-ace-401317.uc.r.appspot.com**/service2

Service2 and Version1

Figure 11.34: Browsing service 2 url

4. Verify the services from console.

	Service	Versions	Labels	Dispatch routes	Ingress ❓	VPC access name ❓	VPC egress setting ❓	Last version deployed ↓	Diagnose
☐	service2 ☒	1			All			Jan 21, 2024, 1:55:59 AM by arijits.data@gmail.com	Logs ☒
☐	default ☒	3			All			Jan 21, 2024, 1:36:34 AM by arijits.data@gmail.com	Logs ☒

Figure 11.35: Verifying both services together from console

Request routing to applications, services, and versions

Let us understand how the request routing will happen using URLs for applications, services and versions:

https://PROJECT_ID.REGION_ID.r.appspot.com

https://SERVICE-dot-PROJECT_ID.REGION_ID.r.appspot.com

https://VERSION-dot-SERVICE-dot-PROJECT_ID.REGION_ID.r.appspot.com

Figure 11.36: Request routing

Conclusion

We have reached the end of this chapter, we have learned the details related to App Engine services, versions, instances, etc., we have seen how traffic is split between two versions of a service. We have deployed a new service alongside another service inside an existing application. We have understood the differences between App Engine Standard and App Engine Flexible. With this, we are concluding computing services in the GCP section.

Multiple choice questions

1. **App Engine standard can be deployed with the following runtimes.**

   a. Python

   b. Java

   c. Node.js

   d. All of These

2. **Maximum request timeout duration for App Engine flexible is.**

   a. 30 mins

   b. 60 mins

   c. 90 mins

   d. 120 mins

3. **App Engine is a serverless and managed service.**

   a. True

   b. False

4. **Containerised deployment is not possible in App Engine flexible.**

    a. True

    b. False

5. **An application can have multiple services.**

    a. True

    b. False

Answers

1.	d
2.	b
3.	a
4.	b
5.	a

Join our book's Discord space

Join the book's Discord Workspace for Latest updates, Offers, Tech happenings around the world, New Release and Sessions with the Authors:

https://discord.bpbonline.com

CHAPTER 12
Networking in GCP

Introduction

Networking is a very important topic in computer science. It deals with communication between two systems. In the Google Cloud Platform, networking takes place via **Virtual Private Cloud (VPC)**; it is the backbone of various services in GCP to stay connected among each other and communicate internally or outside of GCP. This chapter again holds importance in the GCP Associate Cloud Engineer Exam, and we can expect some conceptual questions from this.

Structure

This chapter covers the following topics:

- Computer networking
- Classless Inter-Domain Routing
- VPC and subnets
- Shared VPC and VPC peering
- Hybrid connectivity

Objectives

We are going to learn about VPC in GCP and how to use it to communicate between VMs in GCP, we will explore custom VPC and create subnets for it. We will understand **Classless Inter-Domain Routing (CIDR)** in order to understand the range on which a VPC and its subnets work. We will learn about different Shared VPC, VPC peering, Cloud VPN, and interconnect.

Computer networking

Computer networking is the way of connecting multiple computers or devices together to enable communication and data exchange between them. It helps users with computers or connected devices to communicate more easily via the Internet or Intranet.

Working of computer network

The basic building blocks of computer networks are nodes and links. A network node can be thought of as equipment for the communication of data, like a modem, router, or equipment data terminal connecting multiple computers. Link in computer networking can be thought of as wires or cables or the free space for wireless networking.

The working of a computer network can be defined as the rules or protocols for sending and receiving data via the links which allow multiple devices to communicate. Each device has an IP address, which identifies devices in the network.

Basic terminologies of computer networks

The following are the basic terminologies of computer networks:

- **Network**: A network is a collection of computers and devices which are connected together to enable communication and data exchange.

- **Nodes:** Nodes are devices or machines which are connected to a network. These include computers, servers, routers, switches, printers, and other devices.

- **Protocol**: A protocol is a set of rules or standards that govern the data transmission process over a network. TCP/IP, HTTP, FTP, etc. are examples of protocols.

- **IP address:** An IP address is a numerical identifier that is assigned to every device on a network. Ideally, it is unique for every device in the network. IP addresses are used to identify devices in the network and enable communication between them.

- **Domain Name System (DNS):** It is a protocol that is used to translate human readable domain names (like *www.google.com*) into IP addresses that computers can understand. Each domain name is associated with the IP address.

Classless Inter-Domain Routing

CIDR is a way of IP address allocation and IP routing which allows an efficient use of IP addresses. CIDR is based on the idea that IP addresses can be allocated based on their network prefix rather than their IP address class, which we were using as the traditional way of IP address allocation.

CIDR addresses are represented with a slash notation, which specifies the number of bits in the network prefix. For example, an IP address of 192.168.1.0 with a prefix length of 28 would be represented as 192.168.1.0/28. This notation indicates that the first 28 bits of the IP address are the network prefix, and the remaining (32 - 28) 4 bits are the host identifier.

Working of CIDR

Let us understand the notation, an IPv4 address consists of 32 bits:

- IPv4 address:

  aaaaaaaa.bbbbbbbb.cccccccc.dddddddd

- If we take the example of 192.168.1.0/28, we can represent it like below:

  aaaaaaaa.bbbbbbbb.cccccccc.ddddxxxx

As it has /28 means (32 − 28) = 4 bits at the last can change between 0 and 1. The previous 28 bits are fixed as 192.168.1, and the last value can be between 0 and (2^4 -1) = 15.

So, it can have 16 IP addresses in the range of:

192.168.1.0, 192.168.1.1, 192.168.1.2, 192.168.1.3, 192.168.1.4, 192.168.1.5, 192.168.1.6, 192.168.1.7, 192.168.1.8, 192.168.1.9, 192.168.1.10, 192.168.1.11, 192.168.1.12, 192.168.1.13,

192.168.1.14, 192.168.1.15.

If we have 192.168.1.0/30 as the range, then we can have only 4 IP addresses in the range, 192.168.1.0, 192.168.1.1, 192.168.1.2, and 192.168.1.3.

Let us look at another example of 0.0.0.0/0; it means all 32 bits can change, so it represents any IPv4 addresses.

Last example, 0.0.0.0/32 means only one IP address, i.e., 0.0.0.0.

These concepts are very important for designing subnets within VPC, which we will learn in the next topic.

VPC and subnets

VPC provides the networking functionality to Compute Engine VMs, GKE, and Serverless workloads. You can think of a VPC network the same way as a physical network, except that it is virtual within the Google Cloud Platform.

A VPC network is a global resource which consists of a list of regional virtual **subnetworks** in data centers connected by a global WAN. VPC networks are logically isolated from each other inside Google Cloud. VPC networks are basically global resources. Each VPC network consists of one or more IP address ranges; these are called **subnets**. Subnets are regional and have IP address ranges associated with them.

Custom mode and auto mode VPC

A network needs to have at least one subnet. **Auto mode VPC** networks automatically create subnets in each region. **Custom mode VPC** networks start with no subnets initially, giving you full control over subnet creation. You can create one or more subnets per region.

Creating resources using VPC and subnets

When you create a resource in GCP, you need to choose a network and subnet. For resources other than instance templates, you need to select a zone or a region. Selecting a zone implicitly selects its parent region. Because subnets are regional objects, the region you select for a resource determines the subnet which it can use:

- When you create an instance, you need to select a zone for the instance. If you do not select a network for the VM, automatically the default VPC network is used, which has a subnet in every other region. If you select a network for the VM, you must select the network which has a subnet in the selected zone's parent region.

- When you create a managed instance group or MIG, you need to select a zone or region, depending on the group type and an instance template. The instance template defines which VPC network to be used. Therefore, when you create a MIG, you must select an instance template with the appropriate configuration; the template needs to specify a VPC network which has subnets in the selected zone or region. Auto-mode VPC networks always have a subnet in every region.

- The process of creating GKE cluster involves selecting a zone or region, a network, and a subnet. You need to select a subnet which is available in the selected zone or the region.

Working VPC and subnets

Let us create custom VPC and subnets:

1. Created a new GCP project called **Learn-VPC** and selected it:

Select a project

NEW PROJECT

Search projects and folders

RECENT   STARRED   ALL

Name	ID
☆ Learn-VPC ❓	learn-vpc-413215
✓ ☆ My First Project ❓	hopeful-adapter-401317

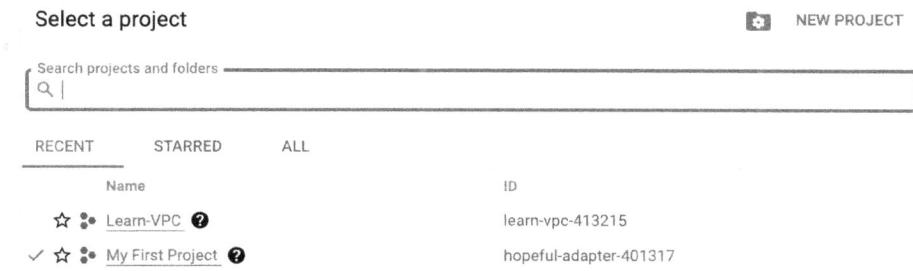

Figure 12.1: New project in GCP

2. Search for "vpc" in search box:

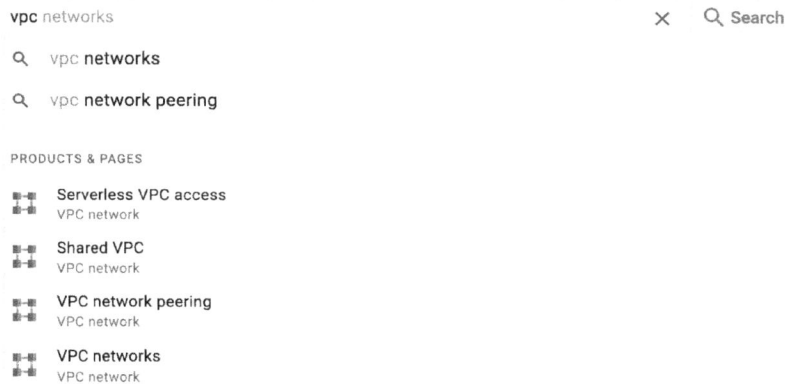

vpc networks   ✕   🔍 Search

🔍 vpc **networks**

🔍 vpc **network peering**

PRODUCTS & PAGES

Serverless VPC access
VPC network

Shared VPC
VPC network

VPC network peering
VPC network

VPC networks
VPC network

Figure 12.2: VPC in GCP

3. Select **VPC networks** from the list.
4. You will be redirected to the **Compute Engine API** page.
5. Enable the API as shown in the below figure:

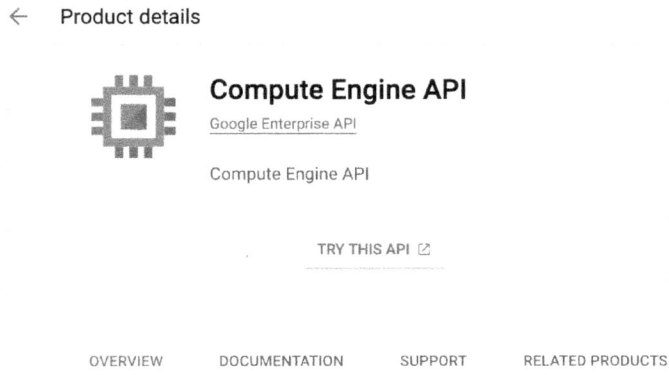

← Product details

Compute Engine API
Google Enterprise API

Compute Engine API

TRY THIS API ⬈

OVERVIEW   DOCUMENTATION   SUPPORT   RELATED PRODUCTS

Figure 12.3: Enabling Compute Engine API

6. On VPC page, you can see a default VPC is already created.

7. The default VPC has 40 subnets total, i.e., one in each region:

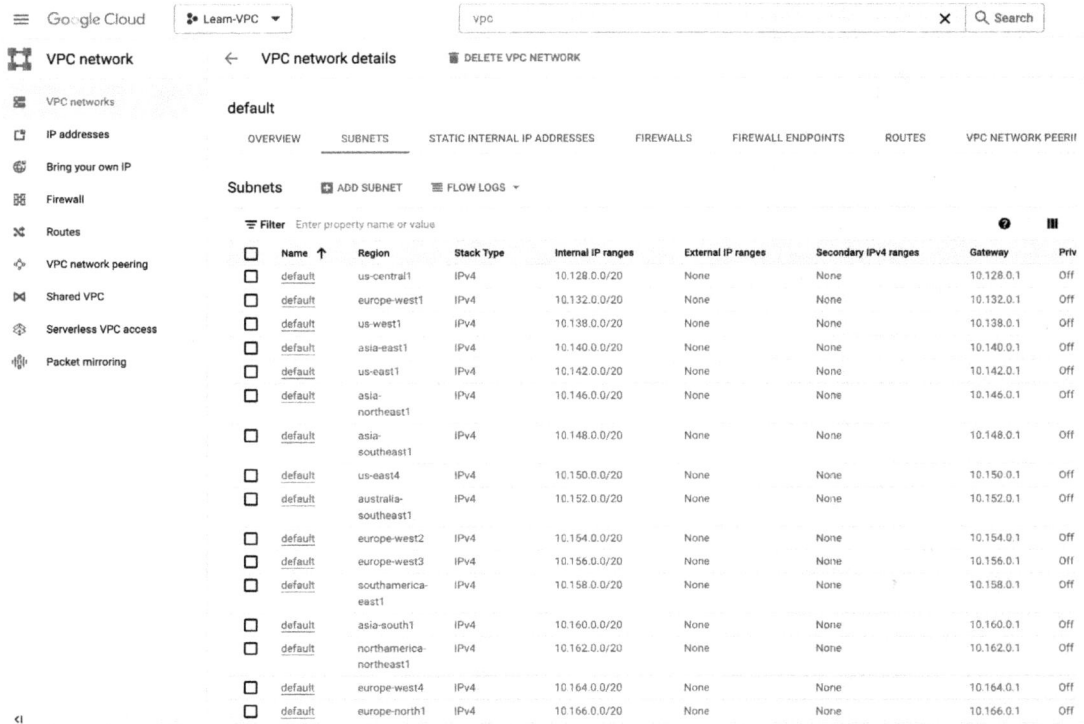

Figure 12.4: Default VPC and subnets in GCP Project

8. Click on **CREATE VPC NETWORK** to get started with creating a VPC network:

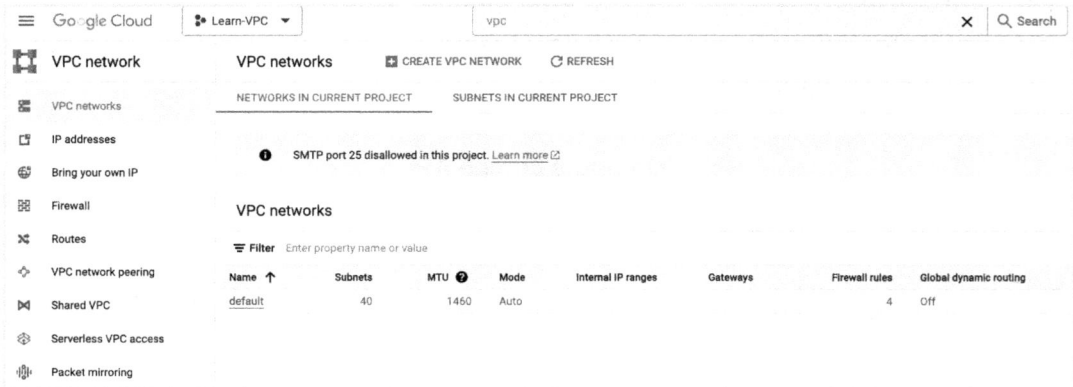

Figure 12.5: Create new VPC in GCP

9. Provide a name and select **Subnet creation mode** as **Custom**:

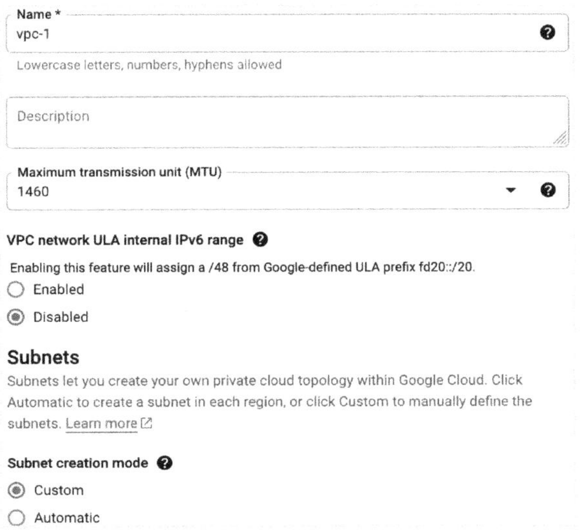

Figure 12.6: Custom subnet creation mode

10. Configure details for subnet.

11. Select region, IPv4 range and keep default settings for others:

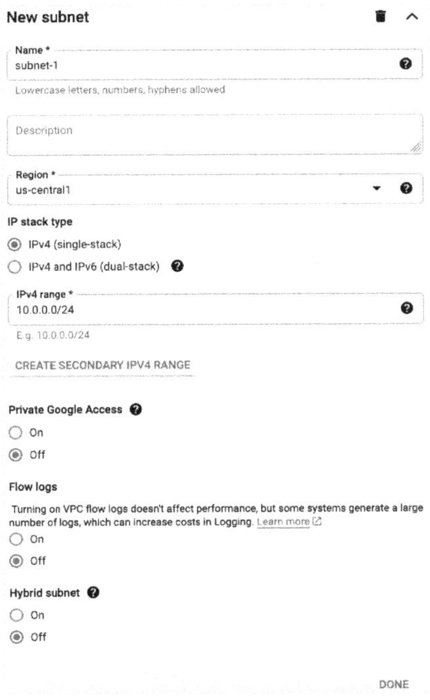

Figure 12.7: New subnet in custom VPC

12. Select Firewall rules as shown, allowing connectivity within subnets, icmp, ssh, and rdp.

13. Keep the **Dynamic routing mode** as **Regional** and click on **CREATE**:

Firewall rules ❓

Select any of the firewall rules below that you would like to apply to this VPC network. Once the VPC network is created, you can manage all firewall rules on the Firewall rules page.

IPV4 FIREWALL RULES

	Name	Type	Targets	Filters	Protocols / ports	Action	Priority ↑	
☑	vpc-1-allow-custom ❓	Ingress	Apply to all	IP ranges: 10.0.0.0/24	all	Allow	65,534	EDIT
☑	vpc-1-allow-icmp ❓	Ingress	Apply to all	IP ranges: 0.0.0.0/0	icmp	Allow	65,534	
☑	vpc-1-allow-rdp ❓	Ingress	Apply to all	IP ranges: 0.0.0.0/0	tcp:3389	Allow	65,534	
☑	vpc-1-allow-ssh ❓	Ingress	Apply to all	IP ranges: 0.0.0.0/0	tcp:22	Allow	65,534	
	vpc-1-deny-all-ingress ❓	Ingress	Apply to all	IP ranges: 0.0.0.0/0	all	Deny	65,535	
	vpc-1-allow-all-egress ❓	Egress	Apply to all	IP ranges: 0.0.0.0/0	all	Allow	65,535	

Dynamic routing mode ❓

◉ Regional
Cloud Routers will learn routes only in the region in which they were created

○ Global
Global routing lets you dynamically learn routes to and from all regions with a single VPN or interconnect and Cloud Router

ℹ Enable DNS API to pick a DNS policy   ENABLE

CREATE   CANCEL

EQUIVALENT COMMAND LINE ▾

Figure 12.8: Firewall rules in custom VPC

14. You can see the new custom **vpc-1** appeared as shown below:

🖿 **VPC network**

VPC networks   ⊞ CREATE VPC NETWORK   ⟳ REFRESH

▤ VPC networks   NETWORKS IN CURRENT PROJECT   SUBNETS IN CURRENT PROJECT

⌗ IP addresses

⊕ Bring your own IP   ℹ SMTP port 25 disallowed in this project. Learn more ↗

▦ Firewall   **VPC networks**

⤧ Routes   ▼ Filter   Enter property name or value

⬥ VPC network peering

⋈ Shared VPC

⬡ Serverless VPC access

⫴ Packet mirroring

Name ↑	Subnets	MTU ❓	Mode	Internal IP ranges	Gateways	Firewall rules	Global dynamic routing
default	40	1460	Auto			4	Off
. vpc-1							

Figure 12.9: New Project in GCP

15. Now, we will create a Compute Engine VM using new VPC and subnet:

16. Search for **compute engine** in the search box:

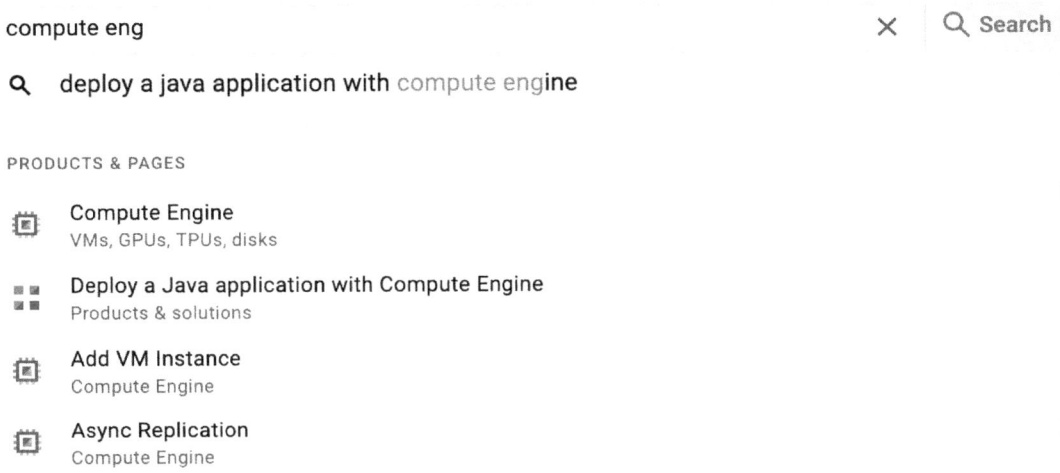

compute eng   ✕ | 🔍 Search

🔍 deploy a java application with compute engine

PRODUCTS & PAGES

▣ **Compute Engine**
    VMs, GPUs, TPUs, disks

▪▪ **Deploy a Java application with Compute Engine**
▪▪ Products & solutions

▣ **Add VM Instance**
    Compute Engine

▣ **Async Replication**
    Compute Engine

Figure 12.10: Search Compute Engine in GCP

17. On landing page, you will get an option as below to create instance:

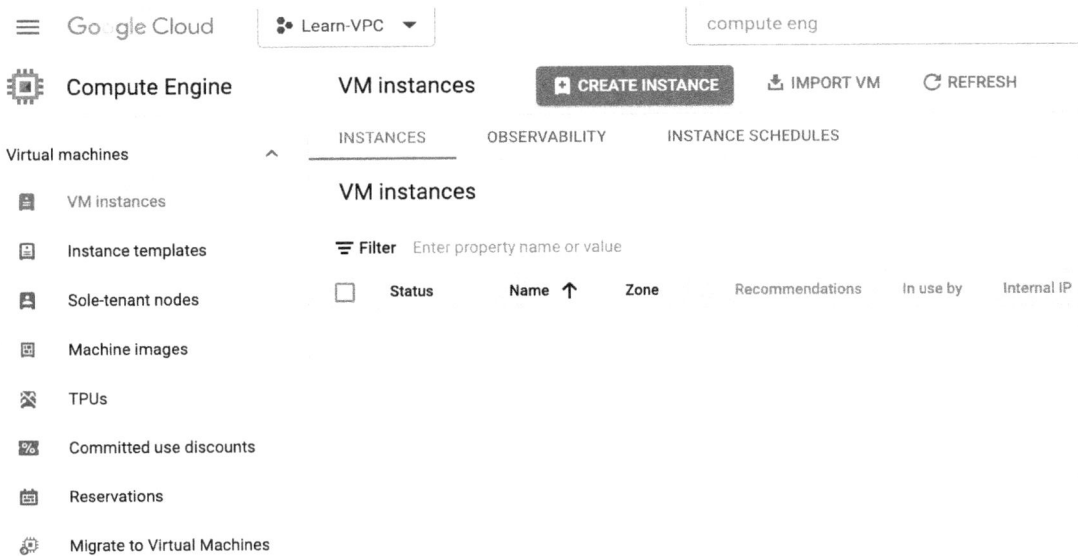

≡ Go﹍gle Cloud   :• Learn-VPC ▼   compute eng

▣ Compute Engine   VM instances   ⬡ CREATE INSTANCE   ⬆ IMPORT VM   ↻ REFRESH

                     INSTANCES   OBSERVABILITY   INSTANCE SCHEDULES

Virtual machines   ∧
                     VM instances

▤ VM instances   ☰ **Filter** Enter property name or value

▣ Instance templates   ☐   Status   Name ↑   Zone   Recommendations   In use by   Internal IP

▤ Sole-tenant nodes

▣ Machine images

🖾 TPUs

▨ Committed use discounts

▣ Reservations

⚙ Migrate to Virtual Machines

Figure 12.11: Inside Compute Engine page

18. Select the configurations as below.

19. Select the **Region** to match with our created subnet.

New VM instance
Create a single VM instance from scratch

New VM instance from template
Create a single VM instance from an existing template

New VM instance from machine image
Create a single VM instance from an existing machine image

Marketplace
Deploy a ready-to-go solution onto a VM instance

Name *
instance-1

∨ MANAGE TAGS AND LABELS

Region *
us-central1 (Iowa)
Region is permanent

Zone *
us-central1-a
Zone is permanent

Machine configuration

NEW: Storage-optimized machine series in Preview
Try the new Z3 series, optimized for high-density storage with expanded Local SSD

TRY NOW ▾

✓ General purpose | Compute optimized | Memory optimized | Storage optimized NEW | GPUs

Machine types for common workloads, optimized for cost and flexibility

	Series ❔	Description	vCPUs ❔	Memory ❔	Platform
○	C3	Consistently high performance	4 - 176	8 - 1,408 GB	Intel Sapphire Rapids
○	C3D	Consistently high performance	4 - 360	8 - 2,880 GB	AMD Genoa
◉	E2	Low cost, day-to-day computing	0.25 - 32	1 - 128 GB	Based on availability
○	N2	Balanced price & performance	2 - 128	2 - 864 GB	Intel Cascade and Ice Lake
○	N2D	Balanced price & performance	2 - 224	2 - 896 GB	AMD EPYC
○	T2A	Scale-out workloads	1 - 48	4 - 192 GB	Ampere Altra Arm
○	T2D	Scale-out workloads	1 - 60	4 - 240 GB	AMD EPYC Milan
○	N1	Balanced price & performance	0.25 - 96	0.6 - 624 GB	Intel Skylake

Monthly estimate
$25.46
That's about $0.03 hourly

Pay for what you use: no upfront costs and per second billing

Item	Monthly estimate
2 vCPU + 4 GB memory	$24.46
10 GB balanced persistent disk	$1.00
Total	$25.46

Compute Engine pricing ↗
∧ LESS

Figure 12.12: Compute Engine Configurations

20. Scroll down to **Advanced options** section:

Observability - Ops Agent ❔
Monitor your system through collection of logs and key metrics.

☐ Install Ops Agent for Monitoring and Logging

Advanced options
Networking, disks, security, management, sole-tenancy

CREATE   CANCEL   ⟨⟩ EQUIVALENT CODE

Figure 12.13: Advanced options in creating Compute Engine

21. Expand the **Network interfaces** section:

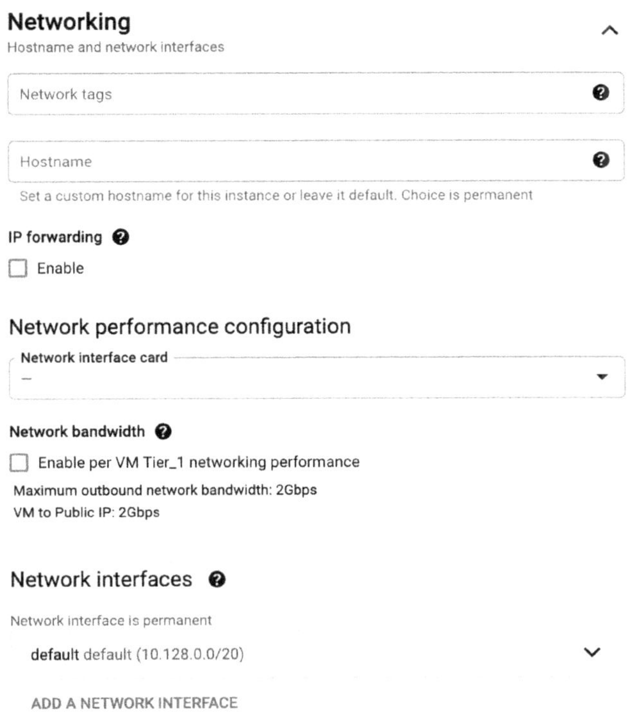

Figure 12.14: *Changing network interfaces*

22. Select **Network** as created **vpc-1** and subnetwork as **subnet-1**:

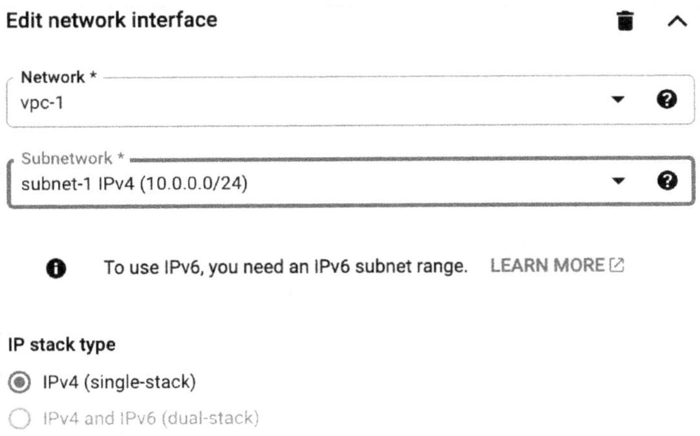

Figure 12.15: *Adding custom VPC and subnet*

23. Finally, create the VM, and it will be using the custom VPC.

24. Verify the same going inside the created VM.

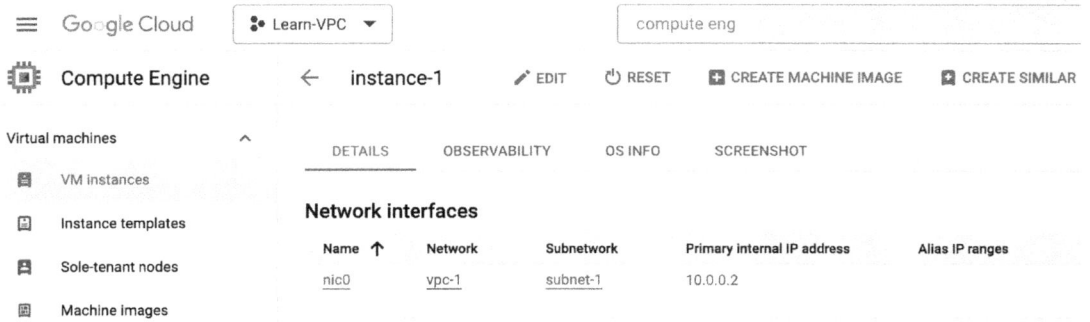

Figure 12.16: Compute Engine VM with custom VPC

Shared VPC and VPC peering

Shared VPC allows an organization to connect the resources from multiple projects to a common VPC network so that they can all communicate with each other securely and efficiently using their internal IPs from that network. When you use the Shared VPC, you designate a project as a host project and normally attach one or more other service projects to it. The VPC networks within the host project are called Shared VPC networks. Eligible resources from service projects can use the subnets in the Shared VPC network.

Google Cloud VPC Network peering connects two VPC networks so that the resources in each network can communicate with each other. Peered VPC networks can be in the same project or different projects of the same organization, or even different projects of different organizations.

Hybrid connectivity

We can extend the on-premises and other cloud networks to GCP with highly available, low latency connections using Cloud VPN or dedicated / partner / cross-cloud interconnect hybrid connectivity options.

Cloud interconnect

Cloud interconnect extends the external network to Google's network through a high-availability, low-latency connection. We can use a dedicated interconnect to connect directly to Google's network. Alternatively, we can use partner interconnect to connect to Google's network through a supported service provider.

When to use cloud interconnect:

- We want to prevent the traffic from traversing through the public internet and our data is very sensitive. Interconnect provides a dedicated physical connection between the data center to GCP, which helps us keep our data traverse completely private.

- We need a very high-speed connection and low latency. Whenever we have large amount of data to be transferred to GCP, it gives us 10Gbps and 100 Gbps connection.

- We need private access to resources in the GCP from our on-premises. It provides a dedicated physical connection, which keeps everything private.

- Need to support very heavy outgoing traffic usually which is called egress traffic from GCP to another destination.

Cloud VPN

Cloud VPN securely extends the peer network to Google's network using an IPsec VPN tunnel. Traffic is encrypted and travels between two networks over the public internet.

When to use Cloud VPN:

- We need public internet access as well, like connecting SAAS product, which are available over the internet only.

- The peering location is not available or suitable to setup an Interconnect.

- We have budget constraints as Interconnect costs $1700 for one 10Gbps link. Cloud VPN is cheaper than Interconnect.

- There are no specific needs to have high speed or low latency.

Conclusion

In this chapter, we have learned about VPC and subnets in this chapter. We have seen how custom VPC subnets are created and used with a Compute Engine VM. We have seen the use cases for VPC peering and Shared VPC and finally understood the usage of Cloud Interconnect and Cloud VPN. In the next chapter, we will cover other networking related topics like firewall rules, load balancing, cloud dns, etc.

Multiple choice questions

1. **VPC can be created in below modes**

    a. Custom

    b. Auto

    c. Both

    d. None of these

2. **192.168.1.0/30 can have _____ IP addresses.**

   a. 1

   b. 2

   c. 3

   d. 4

3. **VPC is a Global resource in GCP**

   a. True

   b. False

4. **Subnets are regional resource in GCP**

   a. True

   b. False

5. **Cloud Interconnect is used for small scale data transfer**

   a. True

   b. False

Answers

1.	c
2.	d
3.	a
4.	a
5.	b

Join our book's Discord space

Join the book's Discord Workspace for Latest updates, Offers, Tech happenings around the world, New Release and Sessions with the Authors:

https://discord.bpbonline.com

CHAPTER 13

Networking in GCP Firewall Rules, Load Balancing, DNS, CDN and NAT

Introduction

In the previous chapter, we completed part 1 of networking in GCP, and now we are going to understand part 2 of networking in GCP, here we are going to learn about firewall rules and load balancers and will see how these help in the movement of network traffic in Google Cloud Platform along with Cloud DNS, CDN, and NAT. These concepts are essential for network-based web applications to work appropriately.

Structure

This chapter will cover the following topics:

- Firewall rules
- Cloud load balancing
- Cloud Domain Name System
- Cloud Content Delivery Network
- Cloud Network Address Translation

Objectives

By the end of this chapter, we are going to learn about firewall rules and different types of load balancer available in Google Cloud Platform. We are going to learn about different types of load balancers. We will set up an application load balancer, a NEG, and a couple of backend services. We will also learn about the concepts of Cloud CDN, DNS and NAT in this chapter.

Firewall rules

Firewall rules are part of the **Virtual Private Cloud (VPC)** networks concept we learned in the last chapter. VPC firewall rules allow or deny connections to or from VM instances in VPC network. Enabled firewall rules are always enforced to protect instances regardless of their configurations and operating systems.

Let us understand some important concepts around firewall rules:

- Firewall rules are stateful, which means if the request is allowed, then the response is automatically allowed.

- Each firewall rule has a priority number assigned, 0 being the highest priority and 65535 being the lowest priority.

- Default implied rules have the lowest priority and can be overridden.

Best practices for firewall rules

When designing and evaluating firewall rules, we need to keep in mind the following best practices:

- Implement the least privilege principles. Block all the traffic by default and allow only the specific traffic you need. This includes limiting rules to just the protocols and ports you need.

- For "allow" rules, restrict those to specific VMs by specifying the service account of the VMs.

- Use hierarchical firewall policy-based rules to block the traffic that should never be allowed at an organization or folder level.

- If you need to create firewall rules based on IP addresses, minimize the number of rules. As an example, it's easier to track one or fewer rules that allow traffic to a range of 10 VMs than to track 10 separate rules.

- Turn on the firewall logging and use firewall insights to verify whether firewall rules are being used properly.

Navigate to **VPC Network** | **Firewall**.

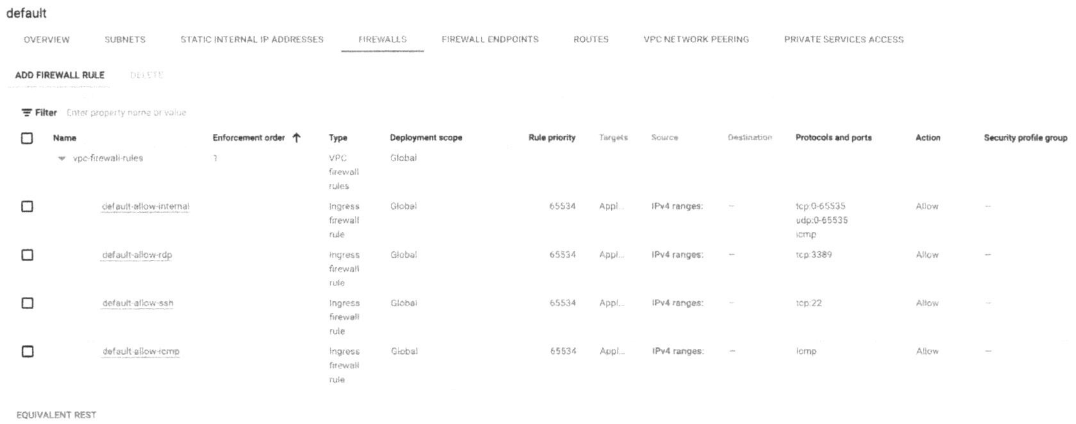

Figure 13.1: *Default firewall rules*

Let us create a Compute Engine VM and write a Python Flask web application inside it, which will use port 5000, so we need to open that port and allow the incoming traffic:

1. Created a VM as **instance-2** using default VPC:

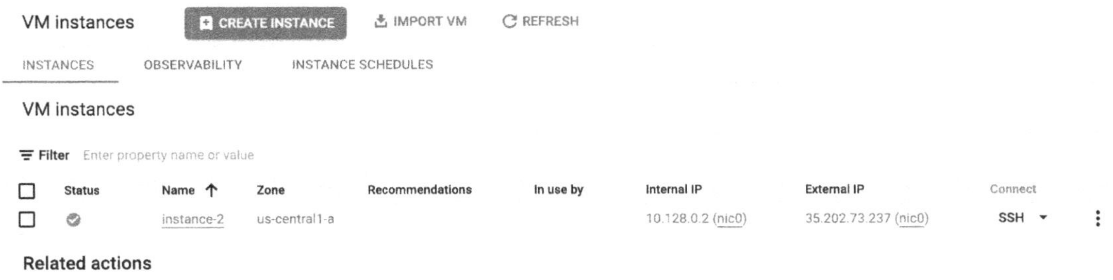

Figure 13.2: *VM created*

As SSH is allowed in default VPC, we can ssh to the VM instance:

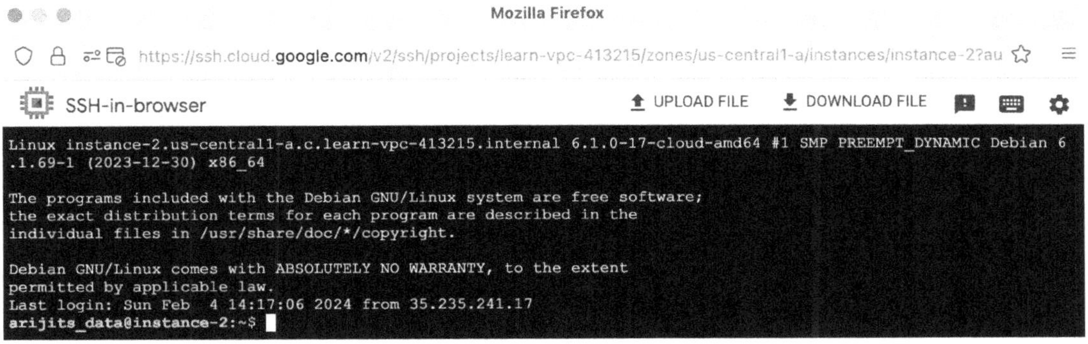

Figure 13.3: *SSH to VM*

2. After installing required libraries, we are going to run the below code:

```
1. from flask import Flask
2.
3. app = Flask(__name__)
4.
5.
6. @app.route('/')
7. def hello():
8.     return '<h1>Hello, World!</h1>'
9.
10.
11. if __name__ == "__main__":
12.     app.run(host="0.0.0.0")
```

Application is ready:

```
arijits_data@instance-2:~$ python3 file.py
 * Serving Flask app 'file'
 * Debug mode: off
WARNING: This is a development server. Do not use it in a production deployment. Use a production WSGI server i
nstead.
 * Running on all addresses (0.0.0.0)
 * Running on http://127.0.0.1:5000
 * Running on http://10.128.0.2:5000
Press CTRL+C to quit
```

Figure 13.4: SSH to VM

3. Try to connect to this application from the browser using the external IP address of the VM, and you will be unable to connect as the firewall rule is not enabled for this port.

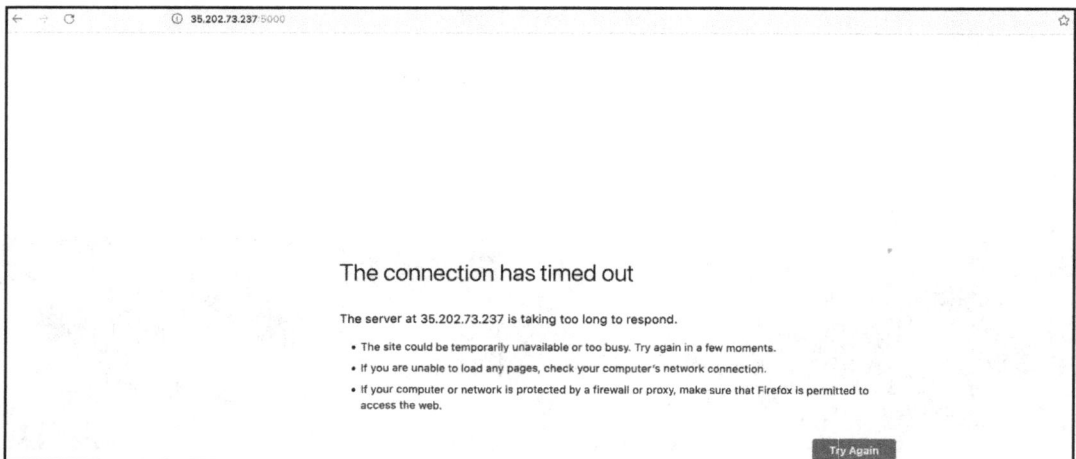

Figure 13.5: Firewall is blocking

4. Now, we will open the port in firewall rules section for default VPC:

    Navigate to **VPC Network | Firewall | Create Firewall Rule**.

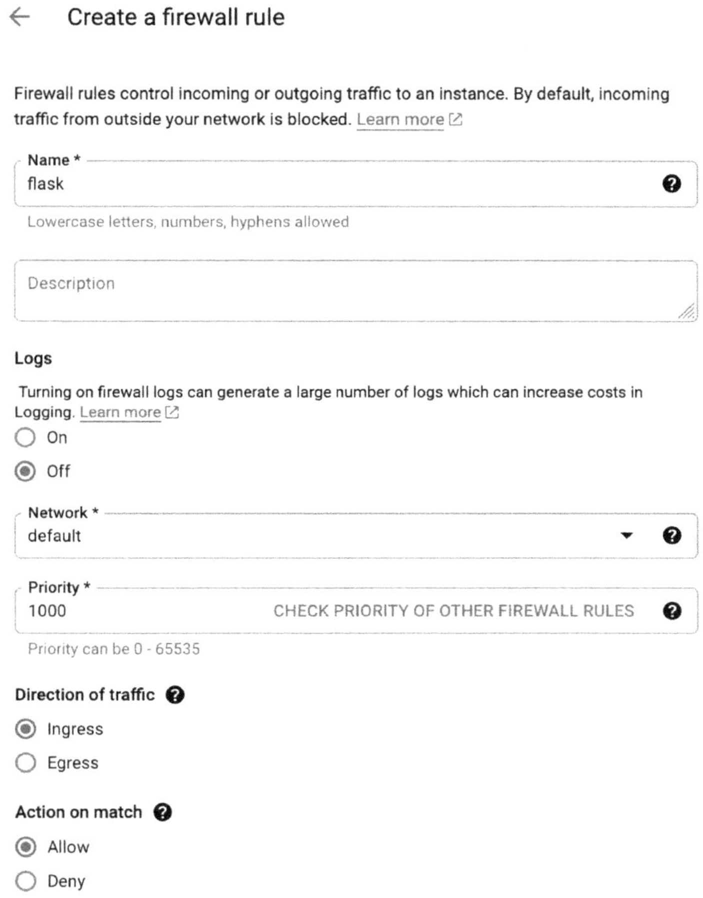

    ← Create a firewall rule

    Firewall rules control incoming or outgoing traffic to an instance. By default, incoming traffic from outside your network is blocked. Learn more ☒

    Name *
    flask   ❓

    Lowercase letters, numbers, hyphens allowed

    Description

    Logs

    Turning on firewall logs can generate a large number of logs which can increase costs in Logging. Learn more ☒
    ○ On
    ◉ Off

    Network *
    default   ▼   ❓

    Priority *
    1000   CHECK PRIORITY OF OTHER FIREWALL RULES   ❓

    Priority can be 0 - 65535

    Direction of traffic ❓
    ◉ Ingress
    ○ Egress

    Action on match ❓
    ◉ Allow
    ○ Deny

    Figure 13.6: *Firewall rule for flask (1)*

5. Keep the configurations as below:
    a. Keep the **Targets** as **All instances in the network**.
    b. Provide **Source IPv4 ranges** as **0.0.0.0/0** to allow all IPs.
    c. Specify the protocol as TCP and port as flask application default port as 5000.
    d. Click on **CREATE**.

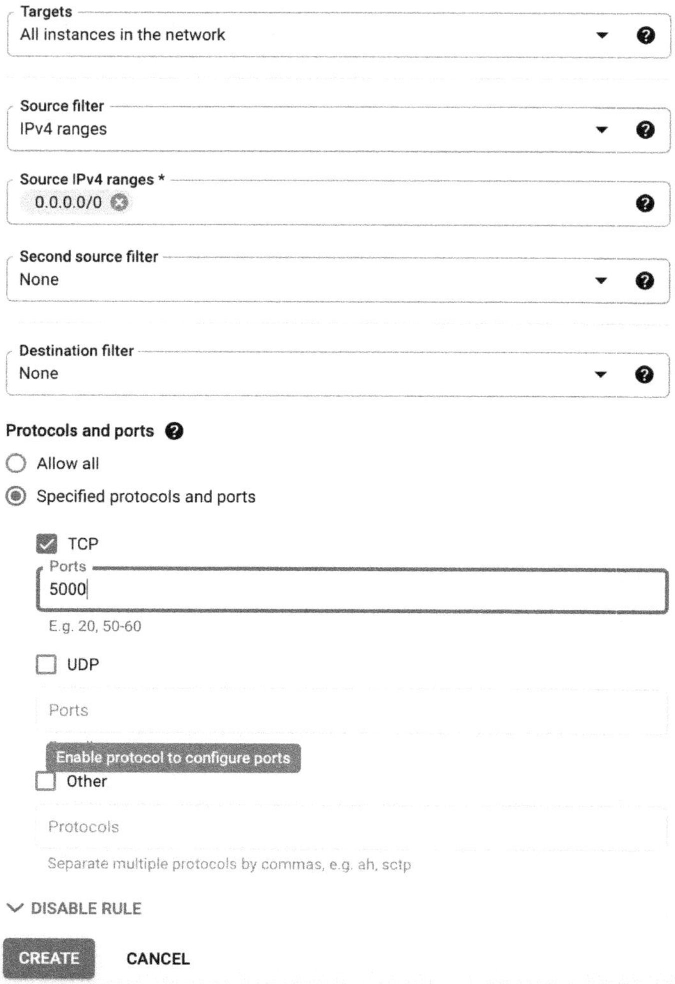

Figure 13.7: Firewall rule for flask (2)

6. Now you can access the web application from browser:

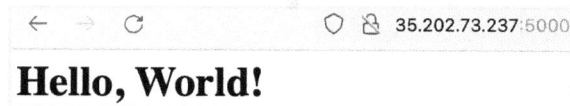

Figure 13.8: Able to access the Flask Web App

Gcloud command to create firewall rule:

```
gcloud compute firewall-rules create flask --direction=INGRESS --priority=1000
--network=default --action=ALLOW --rules=tcp:5000 --source-ranges=0.0.0.0/0
--target-tags=flask-app
```

Cloud load balancing

Load balancer, as its name suggests balances the incoming load of network traffic to multiple instances in single or multiple regions. In GCP, it is a fully distributed and software defined managed service.

The following are the primary features of load balancing:

- Health check
- Auto scaling

In GCP, there are two types of load balancers:

- Application load balancer (HTTP or HTTPS)
- Network load balancer (TCP/SSL) or network load balancer (UDP)

In GCP, we can again divide the load balancers into two categories, i.e., internet facing or internal to GCP load balancers:

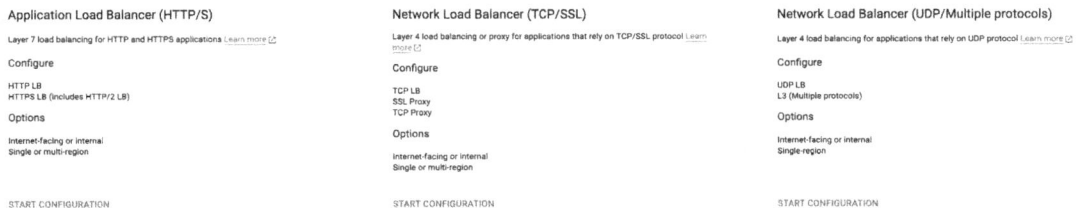

Application Load Balancer (HTTP/S)

Layer 7 load balancing for HTTP and HTTPS applications Learn more ⬁

Configure

HTTP LB
HTTPS LB (includes HTTP/2 LB)

Options

Internet-facing or internal
Single or multi-region

START CONFIGURATION

Network Load Balancer (TCP/SSL)

Layer 4 load balancing or proxy for applications that rely on TCP/SSL protocol Learn more ⬁

Configure

TCP LB
SSL Proxy
TCP Proxy

Options

Internet-facing or internal
Single or multi-region

START CONFIGURATION

Network Load Balancer (UDP/Multiple protocols)

Layer 4 load balancing for applications that rely on UDP protocol Learn more ⬁

Configure

UDP LB
L3 (Multiple protocols)

Options

Internet-facing or internal
Single-region

START CONFIGURATION

Figure 13.9: Types of load balancers in GCP

Networking protocols

Let us understand some networking protocol concepts which will make the load balancer understanding much easier. We will understand these from data transferring perspective.

- **TCP:** Layer 4 protocol, used when reliability is needed more than performance.
- **UDP:** Layer 4 protocol, used when performance is needed more than reliability.
- **TLS:** Same as TCP but with Data Encryption.
- **HTTP:** Layer 7 protocol, for applications like Rest API, email messaging, etc.
- **HTTPS:** Same as HTTP but with SSL encryption.

Working with load balancer in GCP

Let us create a HTTP application load balancer. We also need to create two VM backends; we will be running two flask web apps in those two VM, we will create **network endpoint group (NEG)**, which will point to the Internal IP addresses and ports of these two VMs applications, we need to enable the firewall for the two flask application TCP ports as well.

1. Creating an endpoint group:

   Navigate to **Compute Engine** > **Network endpoint group** (Under **Settings**) and fill the details as below to create NEG.

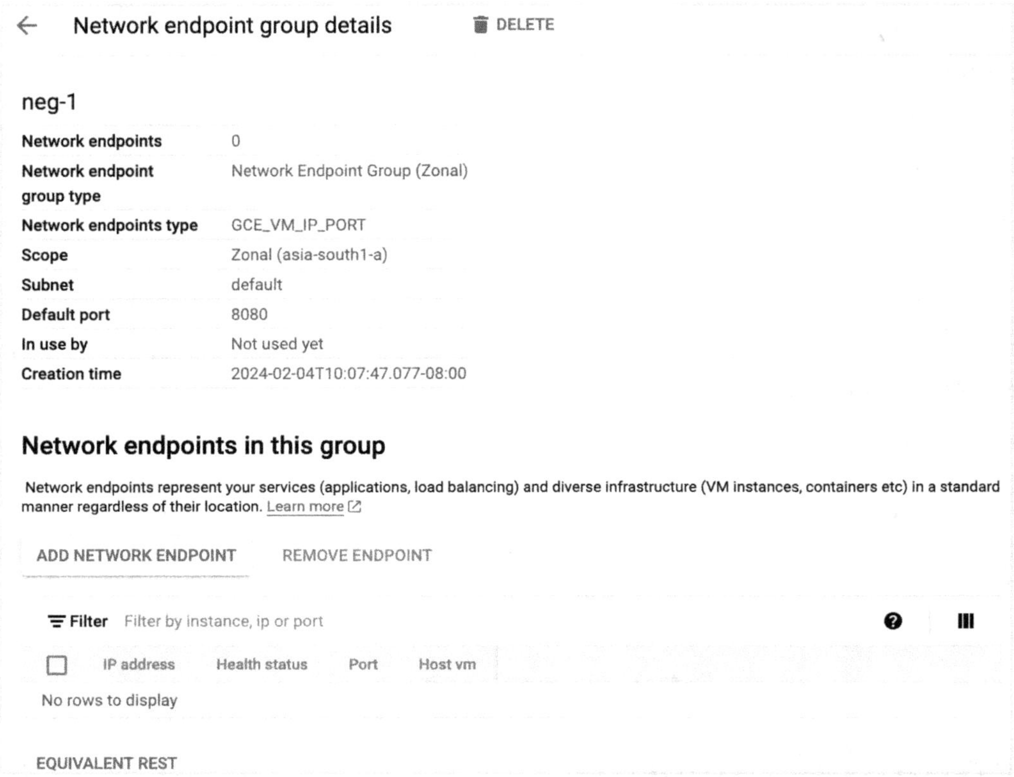

   ← Network endpoint group details   🗑 DELETE

   neg-1

Network endpoints	0
Network endpoint group type	Network Endpoint Group (Zonal)
Network endpoints type	GCE_VM_IP_PORT
Scope	Zonal (asia-south1-a)
Subnet	default
Default port	8080
In use by	Not used yet
Creation time	2024-02-04T10:07:47.077-08:00

   ### Network endpoints in this group

   Network endpoints represent your services (applications, load balancing) and diverse infrastructure (VM instances, containers etc) in a standard manner regardless of their location. Learn more ⤢

   ADD NETWORK ENDPOINT   REMOVE ENDPOINT

   ⇟ **Filter** Filter by instance, ip or port   ❓   ⦀

☐	IP address	Health status	Port	Host vm

   No rows to display

   EQUIVALENT REST

   Figure 13.10: Network endpoint group

2. Create two VM for load balancers backend:

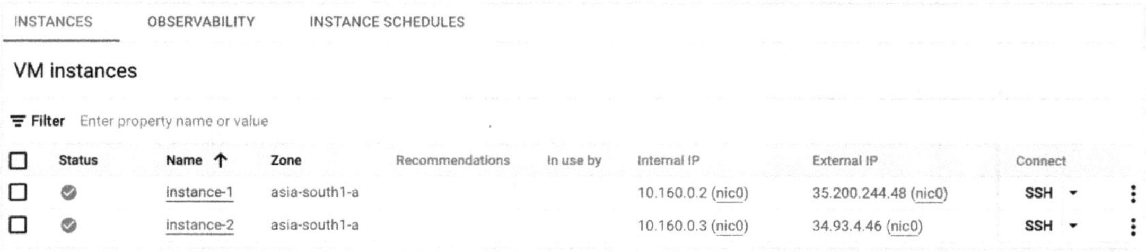

   INSTANCES   OBSERVABILITY   INSTANCE SCHEDULES

   VM instances

   ⇟ Filter   Enter property name or value

☐	Status	Name ↑	Zone	Recommendations	In use by	Internal IP	External IP	Connect	
☐	✓	instance-1	asia-south1-a			10.160.0.2 (nic0)	35.200.244.48 (nic0)	SSH ▾	⋮
☐	✓	instance-2	asia-south1-a			10.160.0.3 (nic0)	34.93.4.46 (nic0)	SSH ▾	⋮

   Figure 13.11: VM Instances for holding the code for backend

3. Add the VM internal IP addresses flask application ports as endpoints:

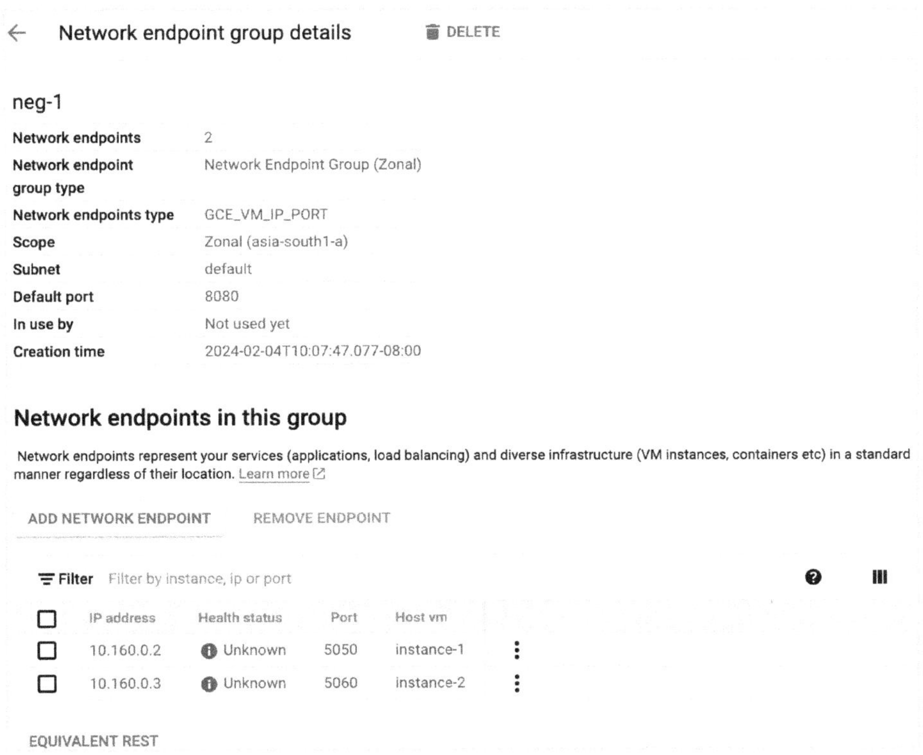

←   Network endpoint group details   🗑 DELETE

neg-1

Network endpoints	2
Network endpoint group type	Network Endpoint Group (Zonal)
Network endpoints type	GCE_VM_IP_PORT
Scope	Zonal (asia-south1-a)
Subnet	default
Default port	8080
In use by	Not used yet
Creation time	2024-02-04T10:07:47.077-08:00

Network endpoints in this group

Network endpoints represent your services (applications, load balancing) and diverse infrastructure (VM instances, containers etc) in a standard manner regardless of their location. Learn more ☑

ADD NETWORK ENDPOINT   REMOVE ENDPOINT

☰ **Filter**   Filter by instance, ip or port   ❷   ▥

	IP address	Health status	Port	Host vm	
☐	10.160.0.2	🛈 Unknown	5050	instance-1	⋮
☐	10.160.0.3	🛈 Unknown	5060	instance-2	⋮

EQUIVALENT REST

Figure 13.12: VM Instances for holding the code for backend

4. Let us start configuring an application load balancer:

Application Load Balancer (HTTP/S)

Layer 7 load balancing for HTTP and HTTPS applications Learn more ☑

Configure

HTTP LB
HTTPS LB (includes HTTP/2 LB)

Options

Internet-facing or internal
Single or multi-region

START CONFIGURATION

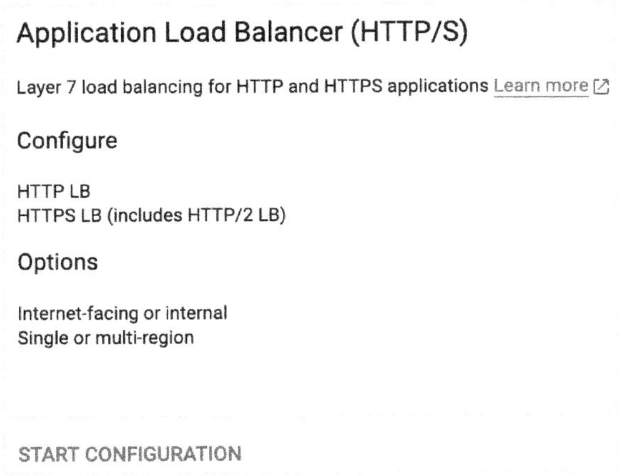

Figure 13.13: Configuring application load balancer

5. Choose from the Internet to my VMs option and classic application load balancer for this demo:

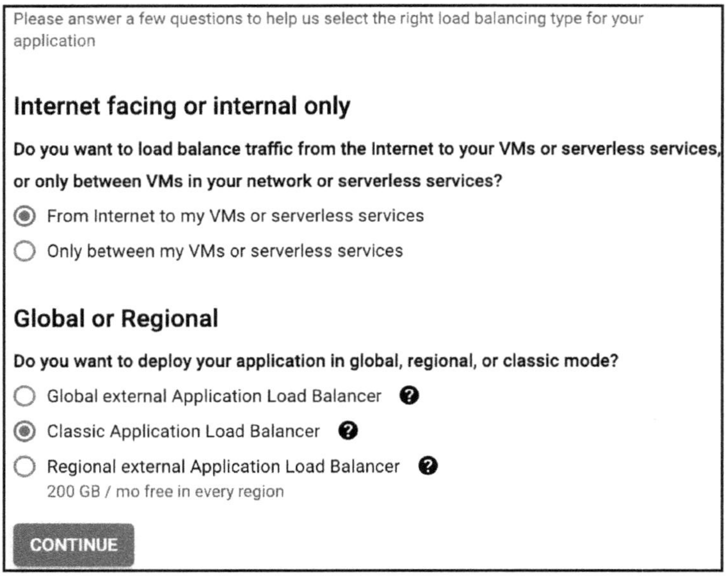

Figure 13.14: Load balancer types

6. Configuring the front end of the classic application load balancer:

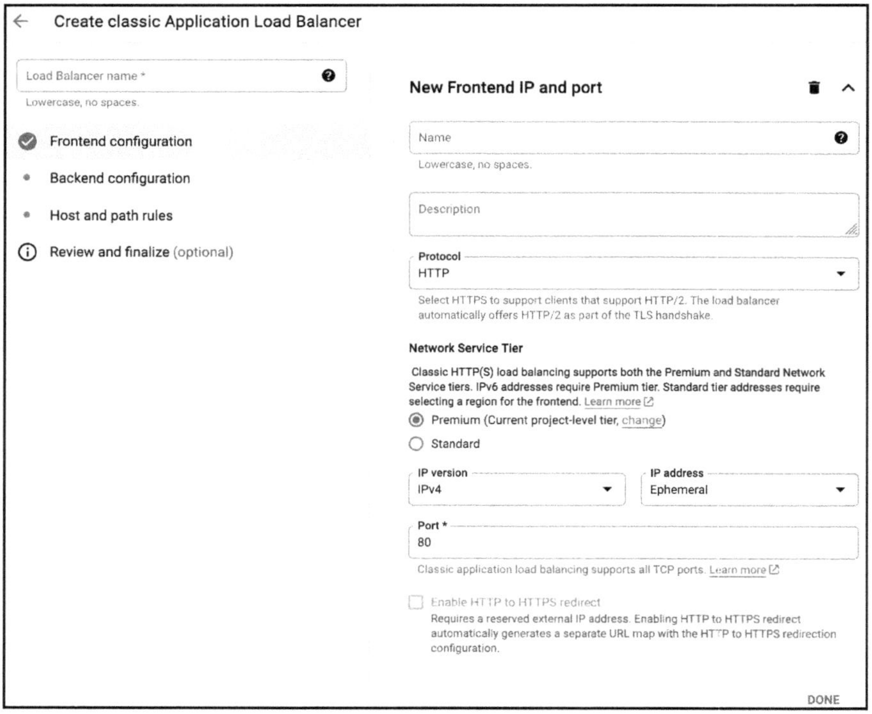

Figure 13.15 Load balancer frontend (1)

At the end of the front-end configuration of the classic application load balancer:

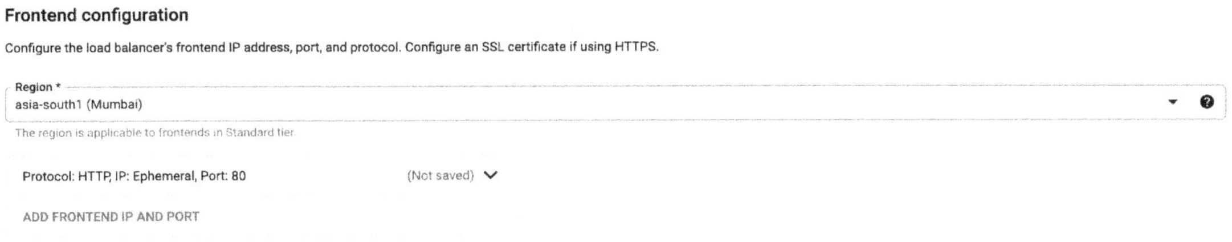

Frontend configuration

Configure the load balancer's frontend IP address, port, and protocol. Configure an SSL certificate if using HTTPS.

Region *
asia-south1 (Mumbai)

The region is applicable to frontends in Standard tier.

Protocol: HTTP, IP: Ephemeral, Port: 80   (Not saved) ∨

ADD FRONTEND IP AND PORT

Figure 13.16: Load balancer frontend (2)

7. At the end of backend configuration. Add the NEG as the backend:

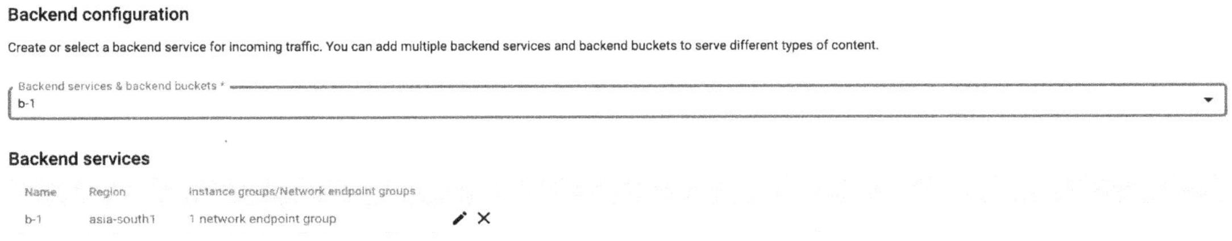

Backend configuration

Create or select a backend service for incoming traffic. You can add multiple backend services and backend buckets to serve different types of content.

Backend services & backend buckets *
b-1

Backend services

Name	Region	Instance groups/Network endpoint groups		
b-1	asia-south1	1 network endpoint group	✎	✕

Figure 13.17: Load balancer backend

8. Keep **Host and path rules** as **Simple host and path rule** and **Backend** as **b-1**:

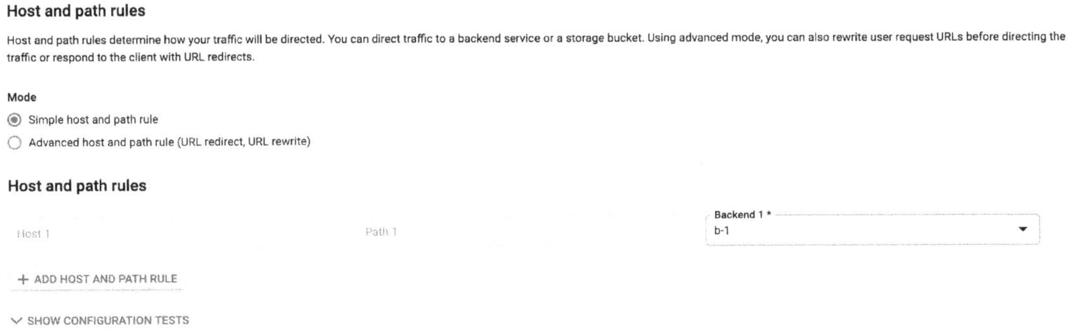

Host and path rules

Host and path rules determine how your traffic will be directed. You can direct traffic to a backend service or a storage bucket. Using advanced mode, you can also rewrite user request URLs before directing the traffic or respond to the client with URL redirects.

Mode

⦿ Simple host and path rule
◯ Advanced host and path rule (URL redirect, URL rewrite)

Host and path rules

Host 1	Path 1	Backend 1 *
		b-1

+ ADD HOST AND PATH RULE

∨ SHOW CONFIGURATION TESTS

Figure 13.18: Host and path rules

9. Review and finalize the load balancer and click on **Create**:

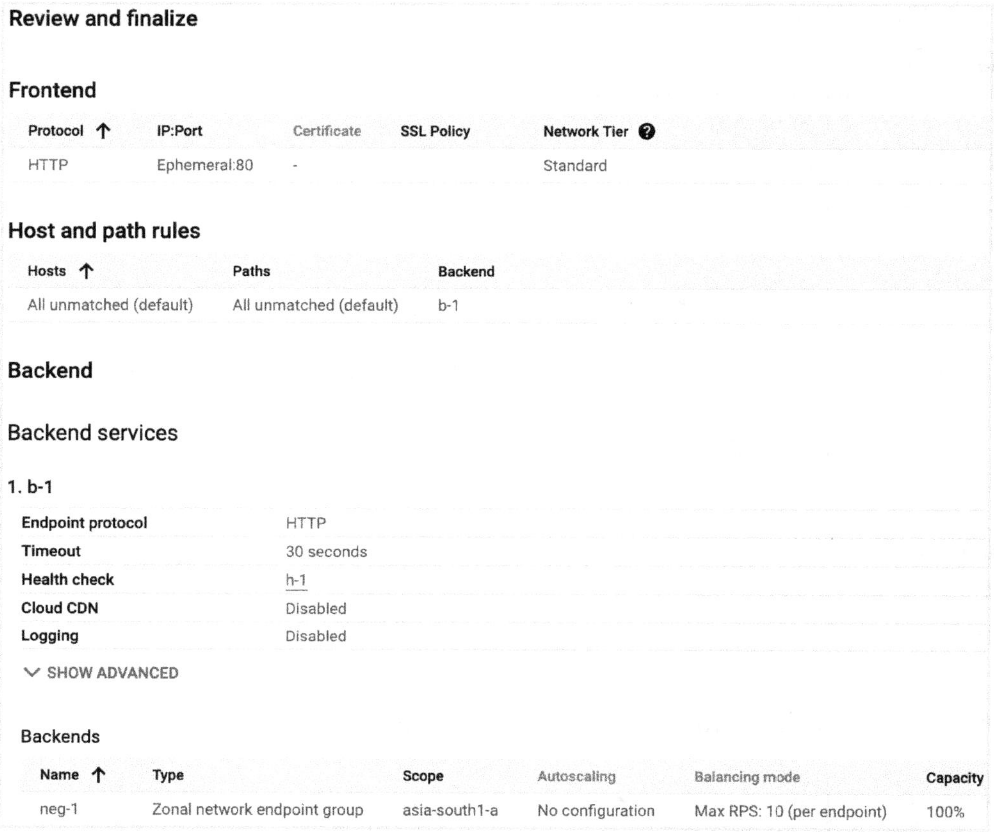

Review and finalize

Frontend

Protocol ↑	IP:Port	Certificate	SSL Policy	Network Tier ❓
HTTP	Ephemeral:80	-		Standard

Host and path rules

Hosts ↑	Paths	Backend
All unmatched (default)	All unmatched (default)	b-1

Backend

Backend services

1. b-1

Endpoint protocol	HTTP
Timeout	30 seconds
Health check	h-1
Cloud CDN	Disabled
Logging	Disabled

∨ SHOW ADVANCED

Backends

Name ↑	Type	Scope	Autoscaling	Balancing mode	Capacity
neg-1	Zonal network endpoint group	asia-south1-a	No configuration	Max RPS: 10 (per endpoint)	100%

Figure 13.19: Review and finalize the load balancer configurations

Keeping two firewall rules for both VM's flask applications:

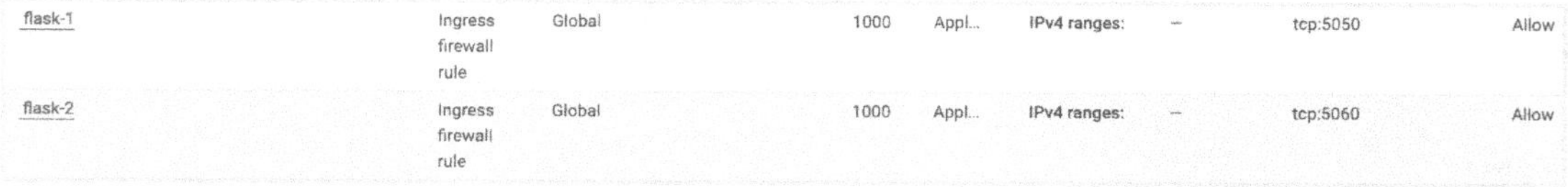

flask-1		Ingress firewall rule	Global		1000	Appl...	IPv4 ranges:	—	tcp:5050	Allow
flask-2		Ingress firewall rule	Global		1000	Appl...	IPv4 ranges:	—	tcp:5060	Allow

Figure 13.20: Firewall rules

Now, load balancer is ready:

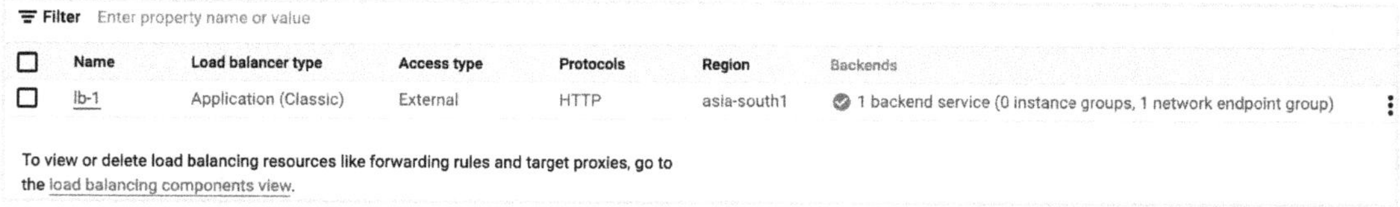

⇌ Filter   Enter property name or value

	Name	Load balancer type	Access type	Protocols	Region	Backends	
☐	lb-1	Application (Classic)	External	HTTP	asia-south1	✅ 1 backend service (0 instance groups, 1 network endpoint group)	⋮

To view or delete load balancing resources like forwarding rules and target proxies, go to the load balancing components view.

Figure 13.21: Load balancer

With load balancer external IP and port we can connect to both services:

← → C   ○ 🔒 35.207.237.28

Hello, World!

Figure 13.22: Service 1

← → C   ○ 🔒 35.207.237.28

Hello, World!!

Figure 13.23: Service 2

The following are the application load balancer types:

Internal load balancer:

It distributes the traffic within a VPC network, and it typically has private IP addresses.

External load balancer:

It distributes the traffic from the internet to a VPC network, and it typically has public IP addresses.

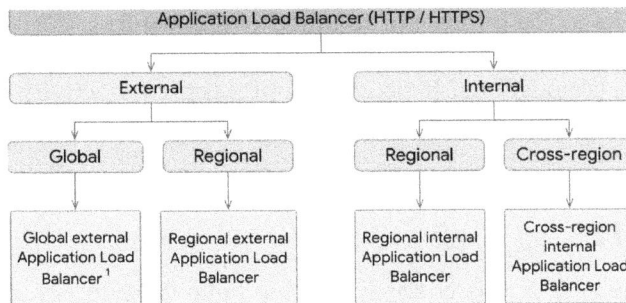

Figure 13.24: Application load balancer

The following are the network load balancer types:

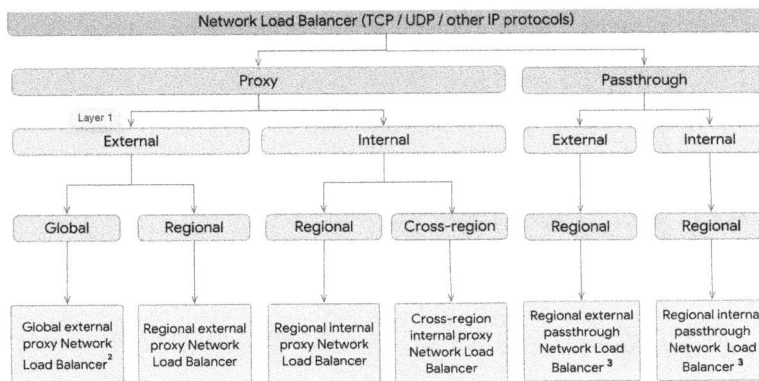

Figure 13.25: Network load balancer

Cloud Domain Name System

Cloud **Domain Name System (DNS)** is a hierarchical distributed database that allows us to store IP addresses and other data and look up them when the request comes. Cloud DNS allows us to publish zones and records in DNS without the need for managing our own DNS servers and software.

Cloud Content Delivery Network

Cloud **Content Delivery Network (CDN)** uses Google's global edge network to serve the content closer to users, which accelerates the websites and applications. Cloud CDN works with global external or classic application load balancers to deliver the content to the users. The external application load balancer provides the frontend IP address and port that receive requests and the backends which respond to the requests.

Cloud Network Address Translation

Cloud **Network Address Translation (NAT)** allows certain resources in GCP to create outbound connections to the internet or to other VPC networks. Cloud NAT supports the address translation for the established inbound response packets. It does not allow any unsolicited inbound connections. It provides outgoing connectivity for Compute VMs, private GKE clusters and Cloud Run, Cloud Functions and App Engine standard via Serverless VPC access.

Conclusion

We have reached the end of this chapter, and we have learned about firewalls and load balancers in this chapter. We have seen how firewall rules can be created and used inside a network to restrict traffic. We have created an application load balancer to understand how it routes traffic to multiple instances. By the end, we have understood the concepts of Cloud DNS, CDN, and NAT. In the next chapter, we will learn Big Data processing, AI related services, deployment, logging, monitoring, etc., at a high level.

Multiple choice questions

1. **Types of network load balancers are:**
   a. Proxy
   b. Pass through
   c. Both
   d. None of these

2. **Backend for load balancers can be.**

   a. GCS Bucket

   b. Services

   c. Both

   d. None of these

3. **In GCP firewall rules, 0 is for lowest priority.**

   a. True

   b. False

4. **HTTPS load balancer is a type of application load balancer.**

   a. True

   b. False

5. **External load balancers can be global or regional.**

   a. True

   b. False

Answers

1.	c
2.	c
3.	a
4.	a
5.	a

Join our book's Discord space

Join the book's Discord Workspace for Latest updates, Offers, Tech happenings around the world, New Release and Sessions with the Authors:

https://discord.bpbonline.com

CHAPTER 14

Big Data Processing, AI, Deployment and Monitoring in GCP

Introduction

This chapter covers the basic details around some of the services related to Big Data processing, artificial intelligence, deployment and monitoring in **Google Cloud Platform** (**GCP**). In various industries, GCP is the preferred choice for Big Data and artificial intelligence. We are going to cover the basic understanding of these services.

Structure

This chapter covers the following topics:

- PubSub
- Big data
- Dataflow, Dataproc, and composer
- Artificial intelligence and machine learning
- Vertex AI
- Cloud Build and Deployment Manager
- Cloud Monitoring and Cloud Logging

Objectives

By the end of this chapter, we will learn the high-level concepts of these topics, we will start with pub/sub and Big Data processing services, then move to the AI and **machine learning** (**ML**) section, where we will understand about Vertex AI, which is a unified ML and AI platform in GCP, we are also going to understand various way of using Vertex AI for different ML problems, and finally, we will learn about deployment and monitoring services in GCP.

Pub/Sub

Pub/Sub is a publish and subscribe (Pub/Sub) service, a messaging system where the senders are decoupled from the receivers of messages. There are several key concepts in Pub/Sub service, lets discuss those.

Components of Pub/Sub

The following are the components of a Pub/Sub service:

- **Publisher:** Creates messages and sends them to a messaging service on a specified topic.
- **Message:** The data which moves via the service.
- **Topic:** A named entity which represents a feed of messages.
- **Schema:** A named entity which governs the format of data of a Pub/Sub message.
- **Subscription:** A named entity which represents an interest in receiving messages on a particular topic.
- **Subscriber:** Receives the messages on a particular subscription.

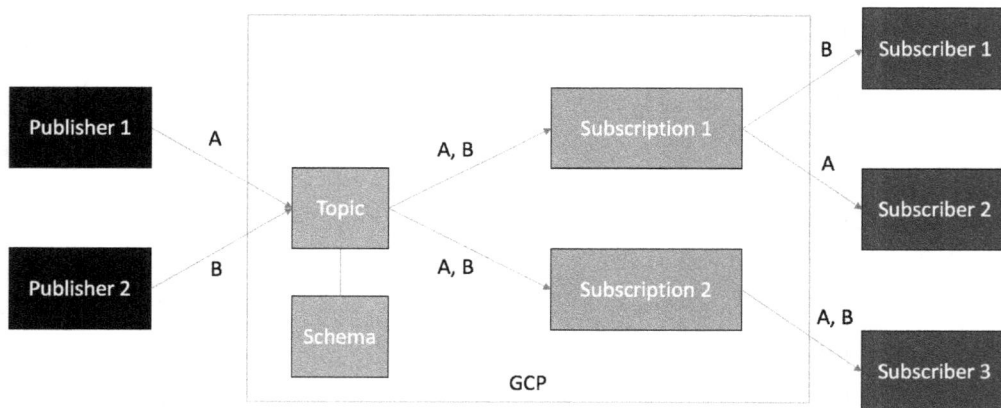

Figure 14.1: How Pub/Sub works

Workflow of the Pub/Sub service

In this section, we will go through the workflow of the Pub/Sub service:

- **Two publisher applications**: Publisher 1 and Publisher 2; send messages to the single Pub/Sub topic. Publisher 1 sends the message A and Publisher 2 sends the message B.

- The topic is attached to two subscriptions (as shown in the image). These are Subscription 1 and Subscription 2 respectively.

- The topic is also attached to a particular schema.

- Each subscription receives the copy of A and B messages from the topic.

- Subscription 1 is connected to two subscriber applications, i.e., Subscriber 1 and Subscriber 2. The two subscriber applications receive a subset of messages from the topic. In this case, Subscriber 1 receives the message B while Subscriber 2 receives the message A from the topic.

- Subscription 2 is connected to a single subscriber called Subscriber 3. Thus, Subscriber 3 receives all messages from the topic.

Big Data

Big Data normally refers to extremely large and/or diverse collections of structured, unstructured, and semi-structured data, which continues to grow exponentially over time. These datasets are actually huge and complex in terms of volume, velocity, and variety, and traditional data management systems cannot store, process, and analyze them.

The amount and availability of data are growing rapidly due to digital technology advancements, such as connectivity, mobility, IoT, and AI. As the data continues to expand, new Big Data tools are emerging to help organizations collect, process, and analyze the data at the speed needed to gain the maximum value from it.

Big Data is heavily used in ML and AI, predictive modeling, and other advanced analytics use cases to solve business problems and make informed decisions.

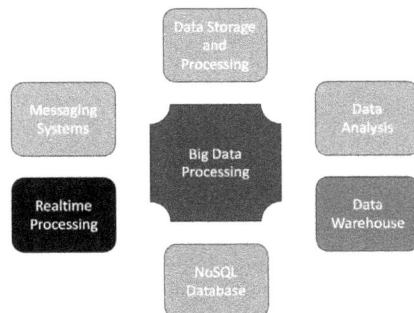

Figure 14.2: Big Data processing

Dataflow, Dataproc, and composer

Let us understand the Big Data processing tools present in GCP. One of them is Dataflow, which is a unified stream and batch processing service based on Apache Beam. Another is Dataproc, which is managed by Hadoop and Spark based cluster service in GCP to process Big Data. Cloud composer is the scheduler, basically a workflow orchestration tool based on Apache Airflow.

Dataflow

Dataflow is a Google Cloud service that provides a unified stream and batch data processing at scale. We can use Dataflow to create data pipelines which read from one or more sources, transform the data, and write the resultant data to a destination.

The following are the typical use cases for Dataflow:

- Data movement- Ingesting data / replicating data across the subsystems.
- ETL workflows which ingest data into a data warehouse like BigQuery.
- Empowering BI dashboards.
- Applying AI / ML capability in real time to the streaming data.
- Processing real-time sensor data or log data at scale.

Dataflow uses the same programming paradigm for both batch and stream processing. Streaming pipelines can work on very low latency. We can ingest, process, and analyze any volume of real-time data. Dataflow guarantees exactly once processing each record.

Streaming data processing using Pub/Sub and Dataflow:

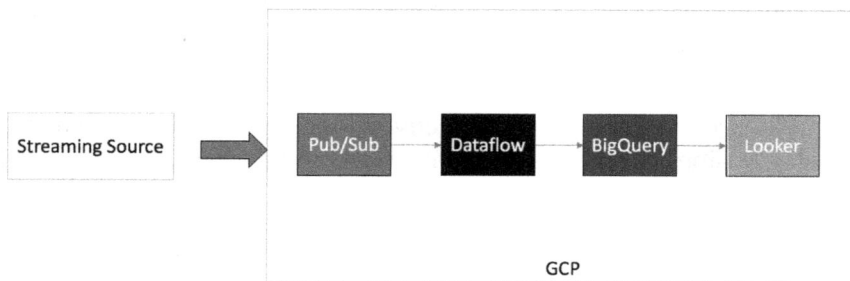

Figure 14.3: Streaming data processing

This shows the following stages:

1. Pub/Sub ingests data from a streaming source system.
2. Dataflow reads data from Pub/Sub and writes to BigQuery. During this, Dataflow may transform or aggregate the data.

3. BigQuery acts as a data warehouse here, allowing the data analysts to run ad hoc queries on inserted data.

4. Looker provides real-time BI analytics or insights from the data stored in BigQuery.

Dataproc

Dataproc is managed Spark and Hadoop service, which helps us to take advantage of open-source data tools for batch processing, querying, streaming, and ML. Dataproc automation helps us to create clusters quickly, manage them easily, and save money by turning clusters off when we do not need them. With less time and money spent on the administration, we can focus on the jobs and data.

When compared to the traditional, on-premises products and similar cloud services, Dataproc has many advantages for clusters of three to even hundreds of nodes:

The following are the reasons why we should use Dataproc:

*   **Cost:** Dataproc is priced at only 1 cent per virtual CPU in the cluster per hour, on top of the other Cloud Platform resources in use. In addition to this low price, Dataproc clusters can include the pre-emptible instances which are having lower compute prices which reduces the costs even further. Instead of rounding the usage up to the nearest hour, Dataproc charges only for what is really used with second-by-second billing and a low one-minute minimum billing period.

*   **Speed:** It can take five to 30 minutes to create the Spark and Hadoop clusters on-premises or via IaaS providers. Dataproc clusters are quick to start, scale, and stop, with each of the operations taking 90 seconds or less on average. It means we can spend less time waiting for the clusters and more hands-on time working with the data.

*   **Integration:** Dataproc has built-in integration with the other GCP services, so we have more than just the Spark or Hadoop cluster—we actually have a complete data platform. For an example, we can use Dataproc to effortlessly load terabytes of raw data directly into the BigQuery for BI reporting.

*   **Managed:** We can use Spark and Hadoop clusters without the need for an administrator. We can easily interact with clusters and Spark or Hadoop jobs using Google Cloud console, Cloud SDK, or Dataproc REST API. When we are done with the data processing tasks inside the cluster, we can simply turn it off, so that we do not need to spend money on the idle cluster.

*   **Simple and familiar:** We do not need to learn the new tools or APIs to use Dataproc, which makes it easy to move the existing projects into Dataproc without the need to redevelop. The software packages for Spark, Hadoop, Pig, and Hive are regularly updated, so we can become more productive.

Composer

Cloud composer is a fully managed workflow orchestration service, enabling us to create, schedule, monitor, and manage workflow pipelines which span across clouds and on-premises data centers. It is built on Apache Airflow, which is an open-source project and operates on the Python programming language.

Workflows, DAGs, and tasks

In data analytics, a **workflow** generally represents a series of tasks for ingesting, transforming, analyzing the data. In Airflow, workflows are created using DAGs which is "Directed Acyclic Graphs".

A **DAG** is a collection of tasks which we can schedule and run, it is organized in a way that reflects relationships and dependencies between tasks. DAGs are created using Python scripts, which can define the DAG structure (tasks and the dependencies) using code.

Each task in a DAG can represent anything—e.g., one task may perform any of the following functions:

- Preparing data
- Monitoring an API
- Sending email
- Running a data processing pipeline

A DAG should not be concerned with the function of each task—its sole purpose is to ensure that each task is executed at the right time, in the right order, or with the right issue handling.

Components of cloud composer

There are mainly four components within cloud composer:

- **GKE cluster**: The Airflow schedulers, workers, and Redis Queue run as GKE workloads on a single cluster, and these are responsible for processing and executing DAGs.
- **Web server**: It runs the Apache Airflow web interface.
- **Database:** It holds the Apache Airflow metadata.
- **Cloud storage bucket:** It holds DAGs, logs, and custom plugins.

Artificial intelligence and machine learning

Artificial intelligence is a very broad field, which refers to the use of technologies to build machines and computers that can mimic the cognitive functions associated with human intelligence, like being able to see, understand, and respond to any spoken or written language or analyze data / make recommendations and many more:

- AI allows a machine to simulate the human intelligence to solve the problems.
- An intelligent system which can perform complex tasks.
- Systems which can solve complex problems like a human.
- Wide scope of applications.
- Human decision-making.
- Can work with any type of data like structured, semi-structured, and unstructured.
- Use logic and decision trees to learn and self-correct.

ML is a subset of AI which automatically enables a machine or a system to learn and improve from the experience. Without doing explicit programming, ML uses algorithms to analyze large amounts of data; it then learns from the insights and makes informed decisions.

- Autonomous learning from past data.
- Increase the accuracy of the output by learning from data.
- Perform specific tasks and deliver accurate results.
- It has a limited scope of applications than AI.
- It uses self-learning algorithms to produce predictive models.
- It can use structured and semi-structured data.
- It relies on statistical models to learn and can self-correct when fed with the new data.

Vertex AI

Vertex AI is a ML platform which allows us to train and deploy ML models and AI applications and even customize **large language models (LLMs)** for the use in our AI-powered applications. It combines data engineering, data science, and ML engineering workflows, enabling us to use a common toolset and scale our applications using Google Cloud.

Vertex AI provides many options for model training and deployment:

- **AutoML** allows you to train tabular, image, text, and / or video data without writing any code or preparing data splits.
- **Custom training** gives you complete control over the training process, including the choice of preferred ML framework, writing your own training code, and choosing the hyperparameter tuning options.
- **Model garden** allows us to discover, test, customize, and deploy on Vertex AI and select open-source models and assets.

- **Generative AI** gives us access to Google's large generative AI models for multiple modalities like text, code, images, and / or speech. We can tune Google's LLMs to meet our needs and then deploy these for use in our applications.

After we deploy our models, we can use Vertex AI's end-to-end MLOps tools to automate and scale the projects throughout the ML lifecycle. These MLOps tools are run on fully managed infrastructure.

Machine learning workflow

Let us understand ML workflow via the below figure. It ideally starts with the Data Preparation step and this cycle continues for model training with new incoming data.

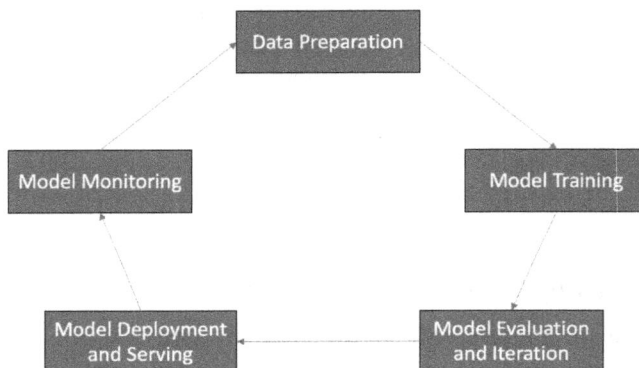

Figure 14.4: Machine learning workflow

Cloud Build and Deployment Manager

After the application is developed, it is time for the application to be deployed in the environment. For this purpose, we have two services Cloud Build and Deployment Manager, which help us in deploying application into GCP.

Cloud Build

Cloud Build is a service which execute the builds on Google Cloud infrastructure. Cloud Build can import source code from Cloud Storage, Cloud Source Repositories, GitHub, or Bitbucket, execute a build to the specifications, and produce artifacts like Docker containers or JARs.

Cloud Build executes the build as a series of **build steps**, where each build step will run in a Docker container. A build step can do anything which a container can do irrespective of the environment.

Deployment Manager

Google Cloud Deployment Manager is an infrastructure deployment service which automates the creation and management of GCP resources. We can write flexible template and configuration files and use them for creating deployments which have a variety of Google Cloud services, such as Cloud Storage, Compute Engine, and / or Cloud SQL, configured in such a way to work together.

You can use Google Cloud Deployment Manager to create a set of GCP resources and manage them as a unit, called a **deployment**. For example, if the team's development environment needs two VMs and a BigQuery, you can define these resources in a *configuration* file, and use the Deployment Manager to create, change, or delete these resources. You can also make the configuration file part of the team's code repository so that anyone can create the same environment with consistent results.

The following are the Deployment Manager fundamentals:

- Configuration
- Templates
- Resource
- Composite types
- Manifest
- Deployment

Cloud Monitoring and Cloud Logging

GCP offers a robust suite of tools and services for monitoring, logging, and gaining operational insight into the applications and services hosted on GCP. Understanding the health, performance, and logs of the applications in real-time is crucial for maintaining the reliability, availability, and performance of cloud-based applications or services.

Cloud Monitoring

Cloud Monitoring provides the visibility into the performance, uptime, and overall health of applications on GCP.

The following are the features of Cloud Monitoring:

- Setting up the custom dashboards and visualizations.
- Create and manage the alerting policies.
- Use uptime checks to verify the availability of the VM instances, URLs, and / or TCP/UDP ports.
- Utilize advanced incident response management with the integration to various platforms.

Cloud Logging

Cloud Logging allows us to store, search, analyze, and monitor log data and events from GCP and other CSPs.

The following are the features of Cloud Logging:

- Real-time log management and analysis.
- Integration with BigQuery, Pub/Sub, and Cloud Storage.
- Create metrics from logs to get deeper insights.
- Retain logs with the custom retention policies.

Conclusion

We have reached the end of this chapter, and we have learned about various topics in this chapter. It starts with Pub/Sub messaging service, then Big Data processing services and Vertex AI, and finally gives a high-level overview of the Deployment and Monitoring process in GCP. In the next chapter, we will build an application using these services in GCP.

Multiple choice questions

1. **To run Apache Spark in GCP, we need to use**

    a. Dataflow

    b. Dataproc

    c. Both

    d. None of these

2. **Cloud Logging can be integrated with**

    a. Pub/Sub

    b. BigQuery

    c. Both

    d. None of these

3. **In GCP, Pub/Sub is asynchronous messaging service.**

    a. True

    b. False

4. **Cloud Dataflow uses Apache Beam.**

   a. True

   b. False

5. **In machine learning workflow, Model training is the first step.**

   a. True

   b. False

Answers

1.	b
2.	c
3.	a
4.	a
5.	b

Join our book's Discord space

Join the book's Discord Workspace for Latest updates, Offers, Tech happenings around the world, New Release and Sessions with the Authors:

https://discord.bpbonline.com

CHAPTER 15

End-to-End Application Lifecycle in GCP Design, Build, Test, Deployment and Monitoring

Introduction

This chapter covers the End-to-End Application lifecycle in **Google Cloud Platform** (**GCP**). We will start from requirement gathering and finish with monitoring of an application. In the middle we will understand the design, elaborated build phase with practical example, testing and deployment of the application.

Structure

The chapter covers the following topics:

- Requirement
- Design and architecture
- Building, unit testing, and deploying the application
- Functionality testing
- Monitoring

Objectives

We will learn the end-to-end lifecycle of an application in GCP in this chapter. We will also understand some of the key concepts while implementing the application.

Requirement

We need to build a simple application which will push reviews/messages from the front end, i.e., client machine's browser, and those will be streamed and reach a dashboard showing the reviews/messages.

Design and architecture

We are going to address this requirement in multiple parts as follows:

- **Front-end:** We will be using React JS for the development of frontend, and it will be deployed within a Compute Engine VM. We will take NGINX plus VM from GCP Marketplace and use this webserver as Reverse Proxy on Compute Engine VM to cater to the incoming requests.

- **Back-end**: We will use Cloud Run as a backend service, which will send the messages to Pub/Sub after receiving a stream of messages.

- **Data pipeline:** Once the message is received by Pub/Sub, it will be read by Cloud Dataflow and transformed and written into BigQuery table.

- **Architecture**: The requirement will be met using the below services.

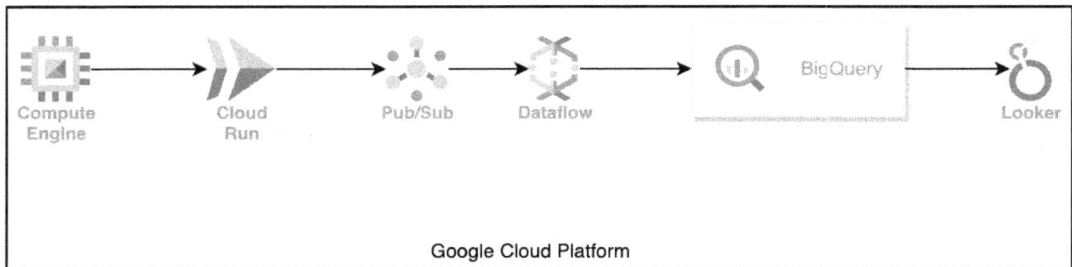

Figure 15.1: GCP Services Architecture for the requirement

Building, unit testing, and deployment

Let us build the application's frontend, backend, and data pipeline in a step-by-step process:

1. We will first code the backend using Python and Flask and then deploy on Cloud Run.

2. Let us assume that data will come to the backend as {"message": "actual text"}.

3. We have created a service account "**e2e-gcp-414110-37d68696dbb7.json**" and assigned the Pub/Sub Admin like below:

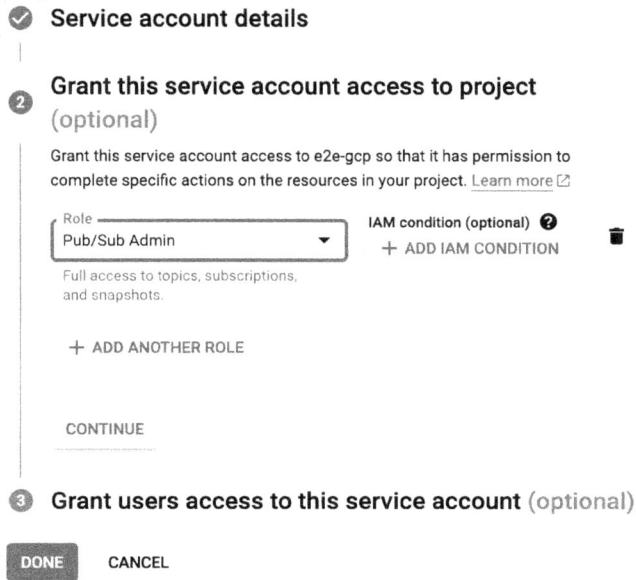

Figure 15.2: Pub/Sub Admin access for local testing initially

4. Created a Pub/Sub topic with a specified schema based on input data and a subscription.

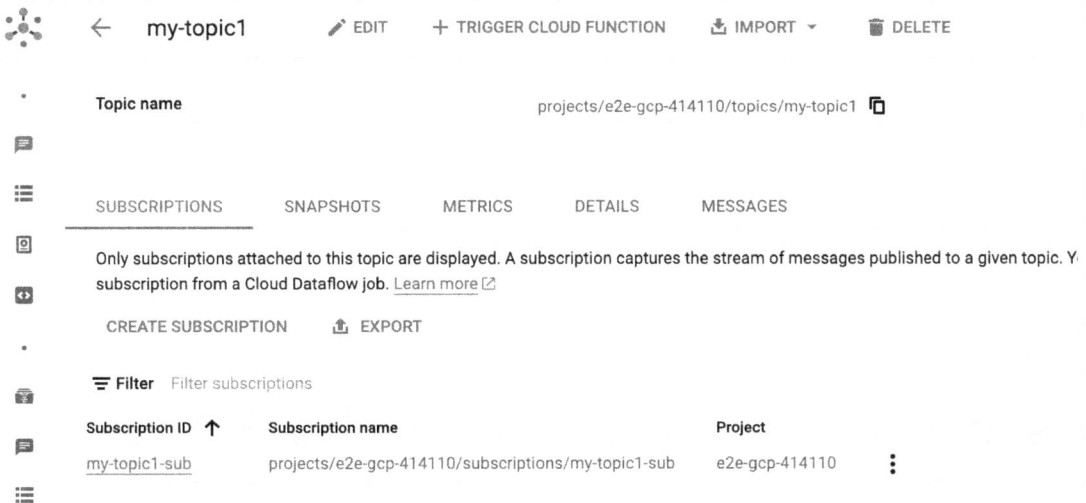

Figure 15.3: Pub/Sub topic and subscription

Schema specified for a topic:

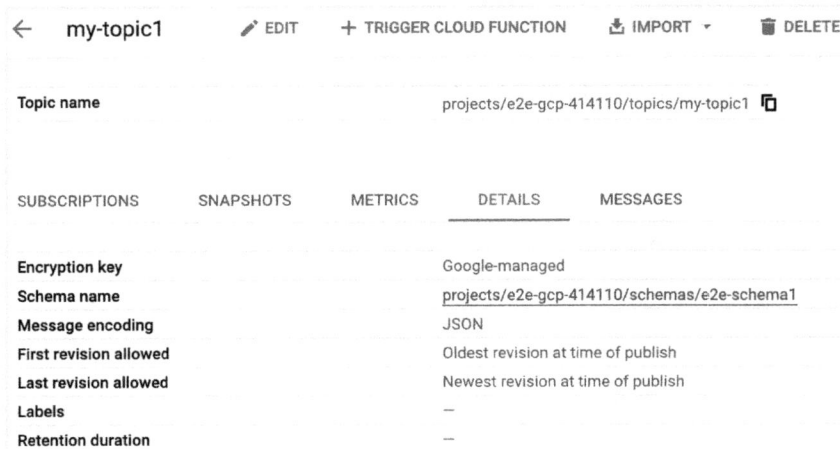

Figure 15.4: *Pub/Sub topic and schema*

Backend code:

```
1.  from flask import Flask, flash, request, redirect, url_
    for, session
2.  from flask_cors import CORS, cross_origin
3.  import os
4.  from google.cloud import pubsub_v1
5.  import json
6.
7.  publisher = pubsub_v1.PublisherClient()
8.  topic_path = publisher.topic_path("e2e-gcp-414110", "my-topic1")
9.  ## Usage of service account
10. os.environ['GOOGLE_APPLICATION_CREDENTIALS'] = '/Users/user1/
    Downloads/e2e-gcp-414110-37d68696dbb7.json'
11.
12. app = Flask(__name__)
13. app.secret_key = os.urandom(24)
14.
15. # cors = CORS(app)
16. CORS(app, expose_headers='Authorization')
17. app.config['CORS_HEADERS'] = 'Content-Type'
18.
19. ## Exception can be handled in the below code block
20. @app.route('/submit', methods=['POST'])
21. def submit():
```

```
22.    input = request.get_json()
23.    print(input)
24.    b_string = json.dumps(input, indent=2).encode('utf-8')
25.    future = publisher.publish(topic_path, b_string)
26.    print(future.result())
27.    op = {"status": "Done"}
28.    return op
29.
30.
31. if __name__ == "__main__":
32.    app.secret_key = os.urandom(24)
33.    app.run(debug=True, host="0.0.0.0", use_reloader=False)
```

5. Now, we will deploy this in Cloud Run based on the below Dockerfile:

Contents of `requirements.txt`:

flask

flask_cors

google-cloud-pubsub

Dockerfile:

```
1.  FROM python:3.11
2.
3.  ENV PYTHONUNBUFFERED True
4.
5.  COPY requirements.txt ./
6.
7.  RUN pip install -r requirements.txt
8.
9.  ENV APP_HOME /app
10. WORKDIR $APP_HOME
11. COPY . ./
12.
13. CMD exec gunicorn --bind :$PORT --workers 1 --threads 8 --time-
    out 0 main:app
```

Testing the Cloud Run URL in Postman:

HTTP **https://pubsub-cr-backend-ba5muso3za-el.a.run.app/submit**

POST ∨	https://pubsub-cr-backend-ba5muso3za-el.a.run.app/submit

Params   Authorization   Headers (9)   **Body** ●   Pre-request Script   Tests   Settings

○ none   ○ form-data   ○ x-www-form-urlencoded   ● raw   ○ binary   JSON ∨

```
1  {
2      "message": "hello, your service is good"
3  }
```

Body   Cookies   Headers (8)   Test Results

Pretty   Raw   Preview   Visualize   JSON ∨

```
1  {
2      "status": "Done"
3  }
```

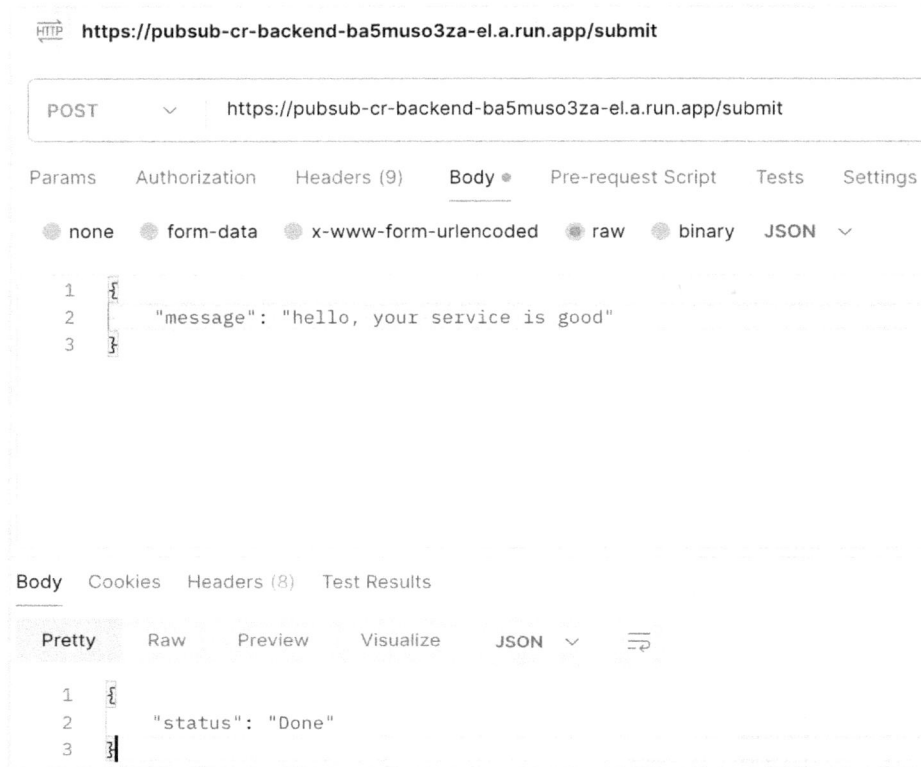

Figure 15.5: Testing Cloud Run URL in Postman

Cloud Run Logs for a successful test:

```
> i   2024-02-12 17:55:56.016 IST   POST 200 799 B 2.4 s PostmanRuntime/7.36.1   https://pubsub-cr-backend-ba5muso3za-el.a.run.app/submit
> *   2024-02-12 17:55:56.577 IST   [2024-02-12 12:25:56 +0000] [1] [INFO] Starting gunicorn 21.2.0
> *   2024-02-12 17:55:56.578 IST   [2024-02-12 12:25:56 +0000] [1] [INFO] Listening at: http://0.0.0.0:8080 (1)
> *   2024-02-12 17:55:56.578 IST   [2024-02-12 12:25:56 +0000] [1] [INFO] Using worker: gthread
> *   2024-02-12 17:55:56.594 IST   [2024-02-12 12:25:56 +0000] [2] [INFO] Booting worker with pid: 2
> i   2024-02-12 17:55:56.598 IST   Default STARTUP TCP probe succeeded after 1 attempt for container "pubsub-cr-1" on port 8080.
> *   2024-02-12 17:55:57.952 IST   {'message': 'hello, your service is good'}
> *   2024-02-12 17:55:58.517 IST   10443066164705999
```

Figure 15.6: Cloud Run success logs

Messages in Pub/Sub topic:

←   my-topic1   ✏ EDIT   + TRIGGER CLOUD FUNCTION   ⬆ IMPORT ▾   🗑 DELETE

Topic name   projects/e2e-gcp-414110/topics/my-topic1 📋

SUBSCRIPTIONS   SNAPSHOTS   METRICS   DETAILS   MESSAGES

PUBLISH MESSAGE   Manually publish a message containing data and attributes with metadata to this topic.

Step 2

Select a Cloud Pub/Sub subscription to pull messages from

Select a Cloud Pub/Sub Subscription to pull messages from *
projects/e2e-gcp-414110/subscriptions/my-topic1-sub

Click Pull to view messages and temporarily delay message delivery to other subscribers. Select Enable ACK messages and then click ACK next to the message to permanently
other subscribers.

⚠   Some messages or columns were truncated due to size. To pull the full message, see this documentation ☑ for an alternative approach.

PULL   ☐ Enable ack messages

☰ Filter   Filter messages

attribute.googclient_schemaencoding	attribute.googclient_schemaname	attribute.googclient_schemarevisionid	body.message
JSON	projects/e2e-gcp-414110/schemas/e2e-sch...	3a4b5361	hello
JSON	projects/e2e-gcp-414110/schemas/e2e-sch...	3a4b5361	hello, your service is good

Figure 15.7: Messages in Pub/Sub topic

Frontend code is written in React JS to build the UI and it calls the Cloud Run backend service.

```
1.  import './App.css';
2.  import { useState } from 'react';
3.
4.  function App() {
5.
6.
7.    const [isSubmitted, setIsSubmitted] = useState(false);
8.    const [dataFlask, setDataFlask] = useState("");
9.    const [message, setMessage] = useState("");
10.
11.   //const handleChange = (event) => {
12.   //  setType(event.target.value);
13.   //}
14.
15.   const handleSubmission = () => {
16.
```

```
17.     const input = { message };
18.
19.     console.log(input);
20.
21.     fetch(
22.          'https://pubsub-cr-backend-ba5muso3za-el.a.run.app/
    submit',
23.          {
24.              method: 'POST',
25.              headers: { "Content-Type": "application/json"},
26.              body: JSON.stringify(input),
27.          }
28.      )
29.          .then((response) => response.json())
30.          .then((dataFlask) => {
31.              setDataFlask(dataFlask);
32.              setIsSubmitted(true);
33.              console.log(dataFlask);
34.
35.          })
36.          .catch((error) => {
37.              console.error('Error:', error);
38.          });
39.   };
40.
41.   console.log(dataFlask);
42.
43.   return (
44.     <div className="content">
45.         <h1>Submit Review</h1>
46.       { !isSubmitted ? (
47.     <div>
48.       <div className="content">
49.       <div>
50.           <label>Review: </label>
51.           <input
52.             type="text"
53.             required
54.             value={message}
```

```
55.              onChange={(e) => setMessage(e.target.value)}
56.            />
57.            </div>
58.        </div>
59.        <button onClick={handleSubmission}>Submit</button>
60.    </div> ) : (
61.    <div className="content">
62.    <div>Submitted</div>
63.    </div> )}
64.    </div>
65.  )
66. };
67.
68.
69. export default App;
```

6. Take Nginx Reverse Proxy VM from GCP Marketplace:

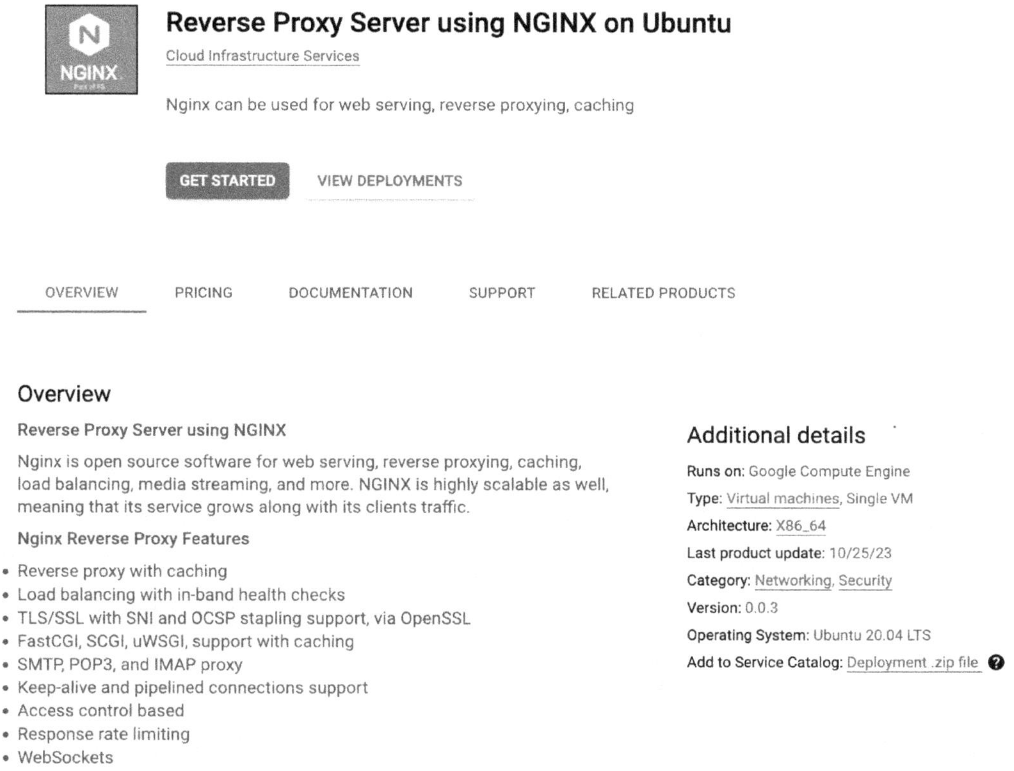

Reverse Proxy Server using NGINX on Ubuntu
Cloud Infrastructure Services

Nginx can be used for web serving, reverse proxying, caching

GET STARTED   VIEW DEPLOYMENTS

OVERVIEW   PRICING   DOCUMENTATION   SUPPORT   RELATED PRODUCTS

Overview

Reverse Proxy Server using NGINX

Nginx is open source software for web serving, reverse proxying, caching, load balancing, media streaming, and more. NGINX is highly scalable as well, meaning that its service grows along with its clients traffic.

Nginx Reverse Proxy Features

- Reverse proxy with caching
- Load balancing with in-band health checks
- TLS/SSL with SNI and OCSP stapling support, via OpenSSL
- FastCGI, SCGI, uWSGI, support with caching
- SMTP, POP3, and IMAP proxy
- Keep-alive and pipelined connections support
- Access control based
- Response rate limiting
- WebSockets

Additional details

Runs on: Google Compute Engine
Type: Virtual machines, Single VM
Architecture: X86_64
Last product update: 10/25/23
Category: Networking, Security
Version: 0.0.3
Operating System: Ubuntu 20.04 LTS
Add to Service Catalog: Deployment .zip file ❓

Figure 15.8: Reverse Proxy Server in GCP Marketplace

Enabling APIs to deploy the Marketplace VM:

New Reverse Proxy Server using NGINX on Ubuntu deployment

Enable required APIs

ⓘ The following APIs are required to deploy a VM product from Marketplace

Compute Engine API ↗ ❓   ☁ Not enabled

Cloud Deployment Manager V2 API ↗ ❓   ☁ Not enabled

Cloud Runtime Configuration API ↗ ❓   ☁ Not enabled

ENABLE   SEND FEEDBACK

Figure 15.9: Enabling APIs for VM

Configuring Marketplace VM:

Deployment name *
nginx-reverse-proxy-1

Zone
us-east1-b   ▼ ❓

Machine type

[✓ General purpose] Compute optimized Memory optimized

Machine types for common workloads, optimized for cost and flexibility

Series
N1   ▼

Powered by Intel Skylake CPU platform or one of its predecessors

Machine type
n1-standard-1 (1 vCPU, 3.75 GB memory)   ▼

	vCPU	Memory
	1	3.75 GB

Boot Disk

Boot disk type *
Standard Persistent Disk   ▼ ❓

Boot disk size in GB *
10   ⌄ ❓

Additional information

Ⓝ **Reverse Proxy Server using NGINX on Ubuntu overview**
Product provided by Cloud Infrastructure Services

Reverse Proxy Server using NGINX on Ubuntu   INR 2,184.98/mo
Usage Fee

⌄ SHOW MORE

Infrastructure fee

VM instance: 1 vCPU + 3.75 GB memory (n1-standard-1)   INR 2,882.95/mo

Standard Persistent Disk: 10GB   INR 39.24/mo

Sustained use discount ❓   - INR 864.89/mo

Estimated monthly total   **INR 4,242.29/mo**

All products are priced in USD and charged in the currency (INR) specified by your Billing Account. The price for this month is calculated with an exchange rate of 1 USD = 83.14 INR

Price estimates based on 30-day, 24hrs per day usage of the listed resources in the selected region. The Estimated Monthly Infrastructure Fee calculation may not reflect all Google Cloud IaaS resources actually created or consumed by this product (or the fees charged for such consumption). Cloud Infrastructure Services may be able to provide a more accurate estimate of monthly GCP IaaS consumption.

Figure 15.10: Configuring the VM (1)

Allowing the traffic and deploying:

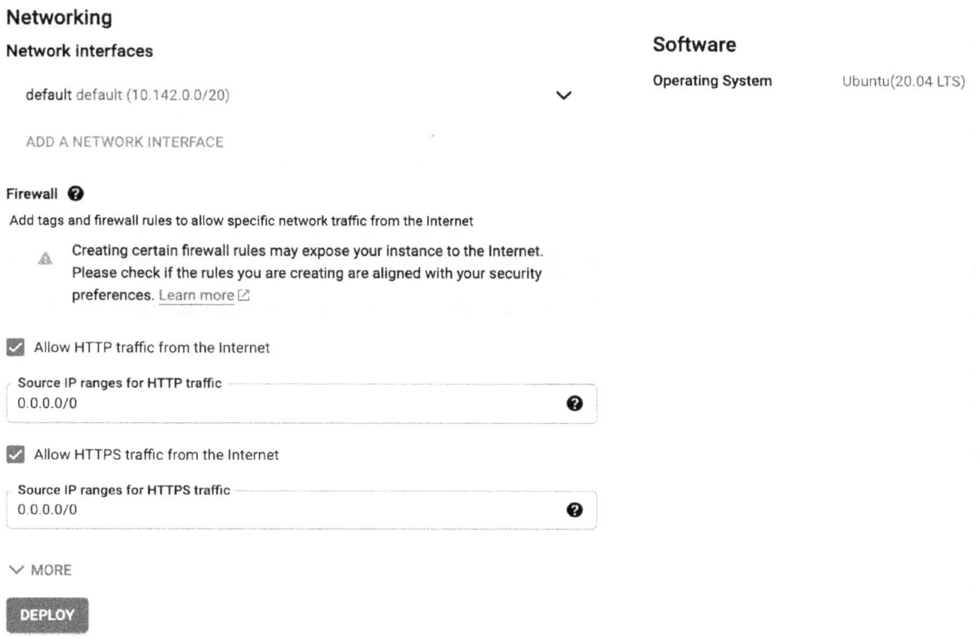

Networking

Network interfaces

default default (10.142.0.0/20)   ˅

ADD A NETWORK INTERFACE

Firewall ❓

Add tags and firewall rules to allow specific network traffic from the Internet

⚠   Creating certain firewall rules may expose your instance to the Internet.
     Please check if the rules you are creating are aligned with your security
     preferences. Learn more ↗

☑ Allow HTTP traffic from the Internet

Source IP ranges for HTTP traffic
0.0.0.0/0   ❓

☑ Allow HTTPS traffic from the Internet

Source IP ranges for HTTPS traffic
0.0.0.0/0   ❓

˅ MORE

DEPLOY

Software

Operating System   Ubuntu(20.04 LTS)

Figure 15.11: Configuring the VM (2)

VM is deployed and can be seen in the instances section for Compute Engine:

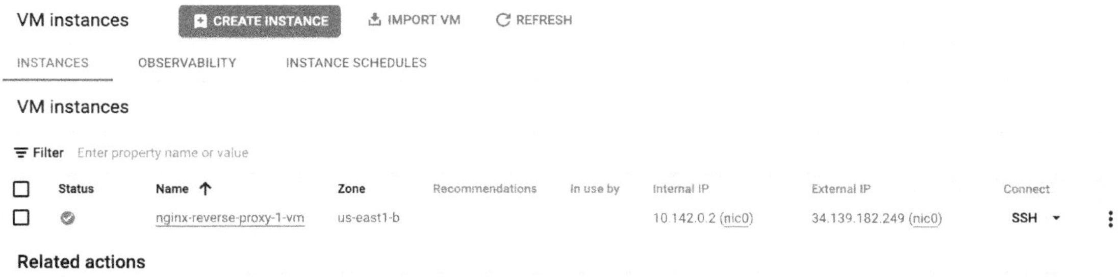

VM instances   ➕ CREATE INSTANCE   ⬆ IMPORT VM   ↻ REFRESH

INSTANCES   OBSERVABILITY   INSTANCE SCHEDULES

VM instances

⚟ Filter   Enter property name or value

	Status	Name ↑	Zone	Recommendations	In use by	Internal IP	External IP	Connect	
☐	⊘	nginx-reverse-proxy-1-vm	us-east1-b			10.142.0.2 (nic0)	34.139.182.249 (nic0)	SSH ▾	⋮

Related actions

Figure 15.12: Deployed VM

7. Take the external IP and hit the browser:

Welcome to nginx!

If you see this page, the nginx web server is successfully installed and
working. Further configuration is required.

For online documentation and support please refer to nginx.org.
Commercial support is available at nginx.com.

Thank you for using nginx.

Figure 15.13: Nginx Welcome Text

8. Now SSH to the VM in GCP console and deploy the React JS built code in **/var/ www/html** directory by simply copying the contents build folder (**Note: command npm run build is used from React JS code base's root directory to build the code. A build folder will be generated after the build process gets completed**).

```
arijits_data@nginx-reverse-proxy-1-vm:/var/www/html$ ls -lrt
total 44
drwxr-xr-x 4 root root 4096 Feb 12 14:35 static
-rw-r--r-- 1 root root   67 Feb 12 14:35 robots.txt
-rw-r--r-- 1 root root  492 Feb 12 14:35 manifest.json
-rw-r--r-- 1 root root 9664 Feb 12 14:35 logo512.png
-rw-r--r-- 1 root root 5347 Feb 12 14:35 logo192.png
-rw-r--r-- 1 root root  644 Feb 12 14:35 index.html
-rw-r--r-- 1 root root 3870 Feb 12 14:35 favicon.ico
-rw-r--r-- 1 root root  517 Feb 12 14:35 asset-manifest.json
```

Figure 15.14: Deployment for frontend

9. Now, the external IP will take us to our frontend application if everything goes fine:

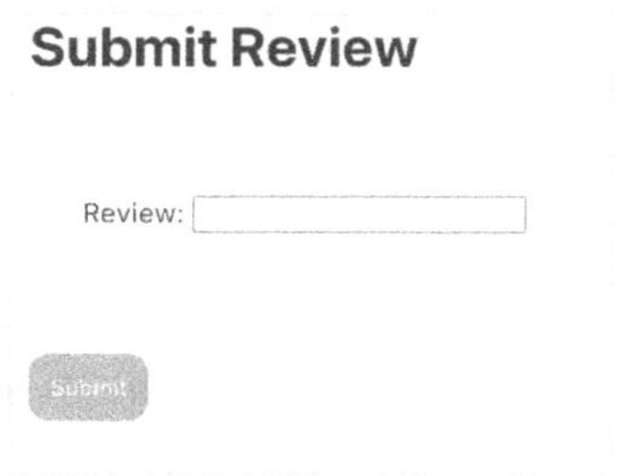

Submit Review

Review: [   ]

Submit

Figure 15.15: Frontend in browser

10. After the submission of a review:

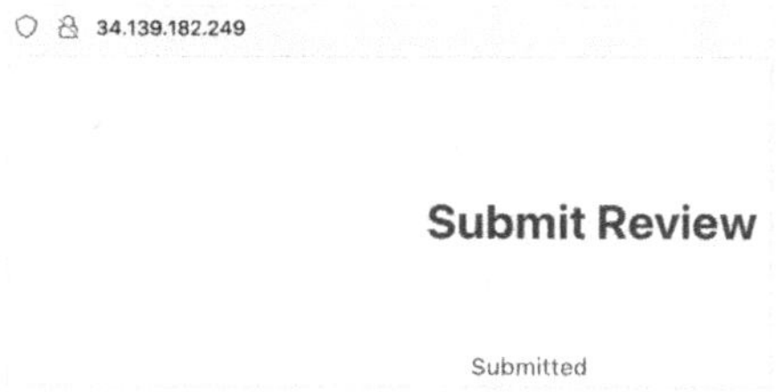

○ 🔒 34.139.182.249

Submit Review

Submitted

Figure 15.16: One review submitted from browser

11. Verifying the message in the GCP console:

›ute.googclient_schemaencoding	attribute.googclient_schemaname	attribute.googclient_schemarevisionid	body.message
N	projects/e2e-gcp-414110/schemas/e2e-sch...	3a4b5361	hello
N	projects/e2e-gcp-414110/schemas/e2e-sch...	3a4b5361	hello, your service is good
N	projects/e2e-gcp-414110/schemas/e2e-sch...	3a4b5361	I am very happy with the service.

Figure 15.17: Verifying the message in Pub/Sub

So till now frontend and backend are working perfectly.

12. Now, let us start with the analytics part. We will create a BigQuery table for this:

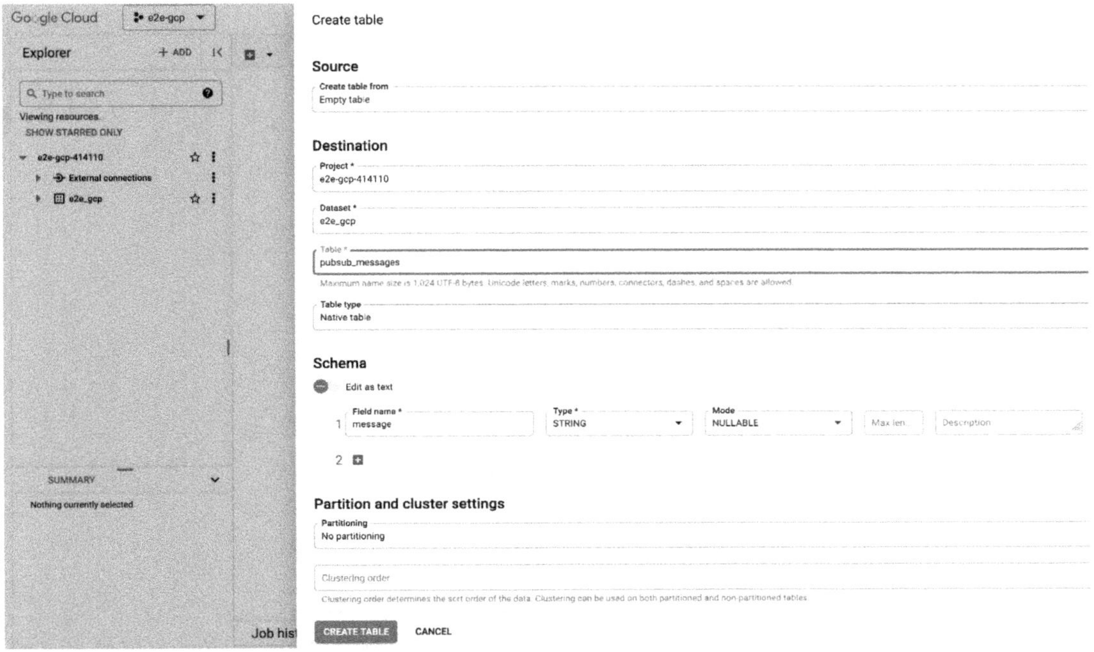

Figure 15.18: BigQuery table

13. Provide the below permissions to GCP project's default Compute Engine service account:

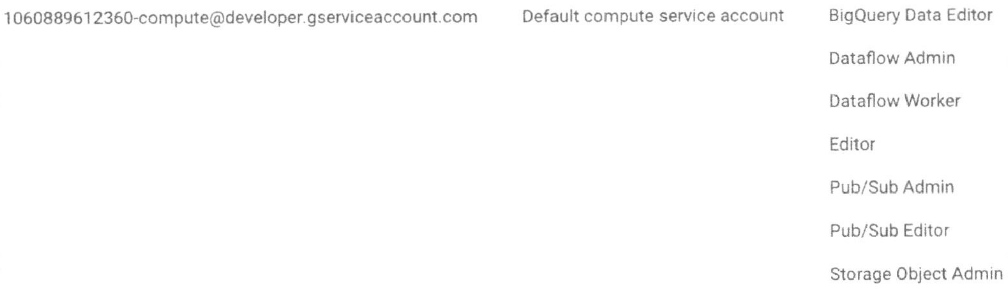

1060889612360-compute@developer.gserviceaccount.com	Default compute service account	BigQuery Data Editor
		Dataflow Admin
		Dataflow Worker
		Editor
		Pub/Sub Admin
		Pub/Sub Editor
		Storage Object Admin

Figure 15.19: Permissions

14. Now, let us create a streaming Dataflow Job to load data to BigQuery from Pub/Sub. Create a Job from template:

Figure 15.20: Dataflow Job (1)

Next, fill in the details as per the below mentioned figure:

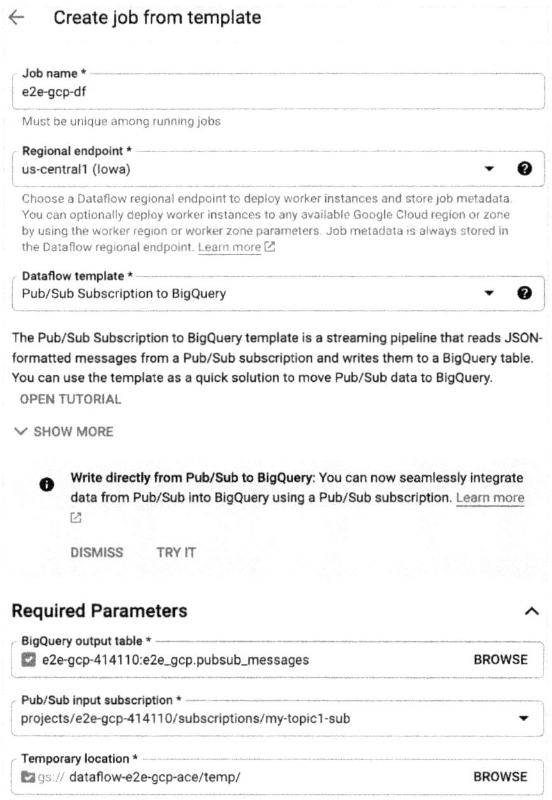

Figure 15.21: Dataflow Job (2)

Dataflow Job is ready:

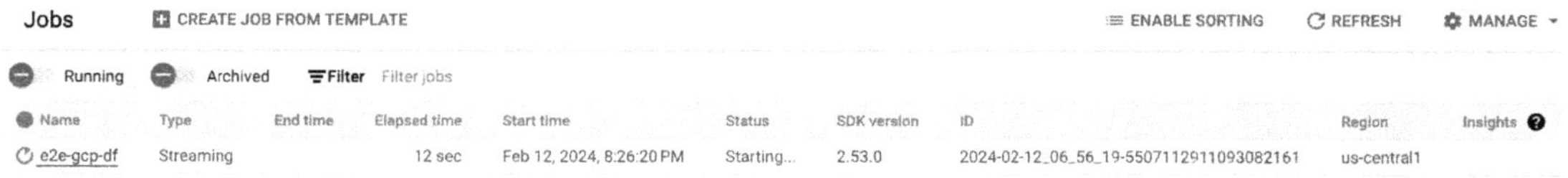

Figure 15.22: Dataflow Job is ready

Inside the Dataflow Job:

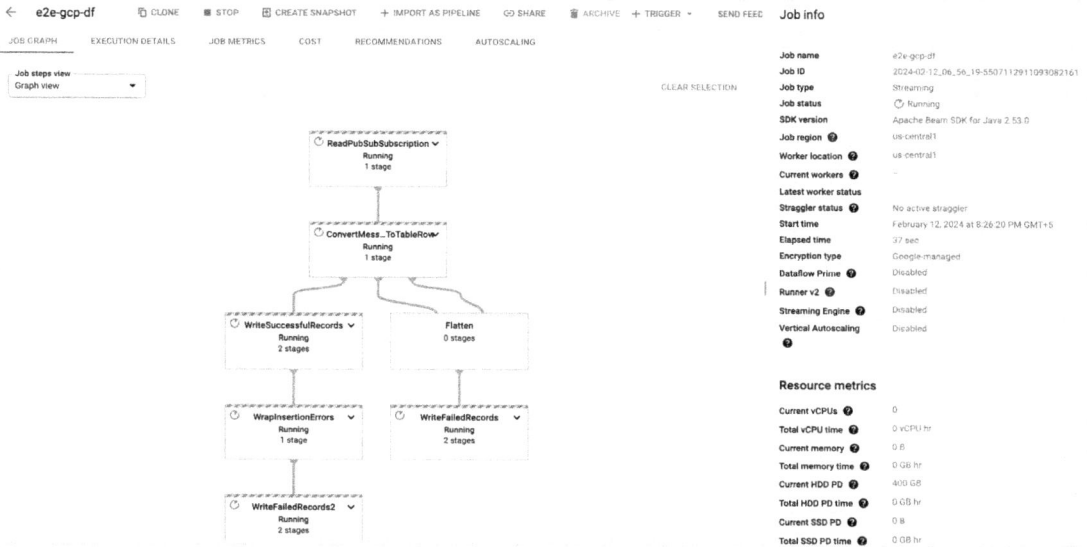

Figure 15.23: *Inside Dataflow Job*

15. BigQuery table is already loaded with data from Pub/Sub automatically after the Dataflow Job started running:

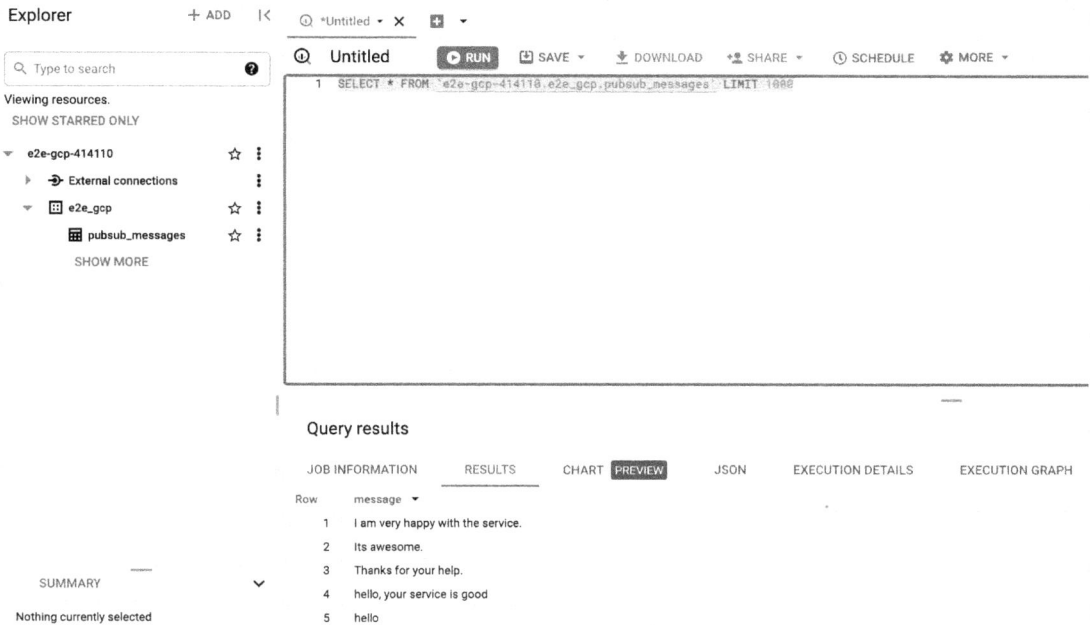

Figure 15.24: *BigQuery table getting loaded*

16. Now, submit a review from frontend and see it in BigQuery:

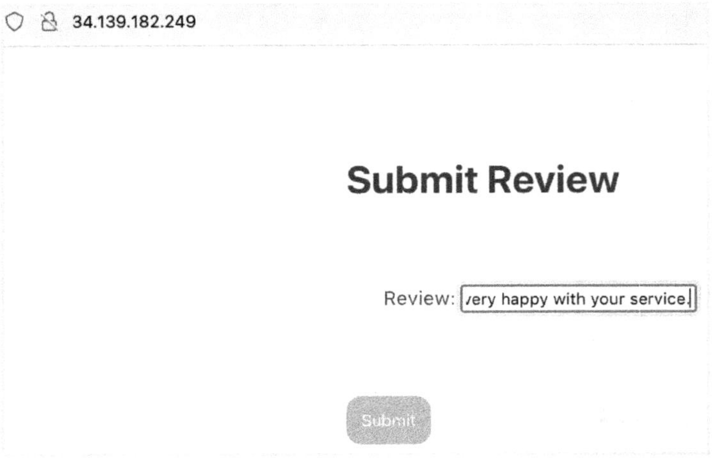

Figure 15.25: Review Submitted from frontend

Now, in BigQuery, you will see the reviews appearing:

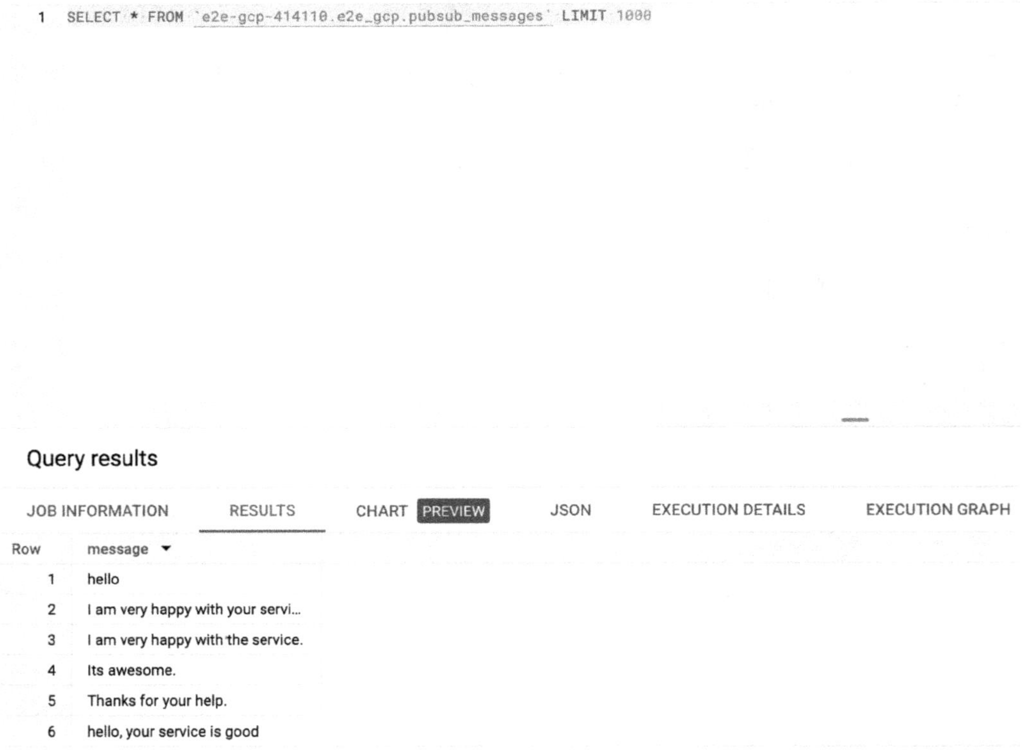

```
1   SELECT * FROM `e2e-gcp-414110.e2e_gcp.pubsub_messages` LIMIT 1000
```

Query results

JOB INFORMATION	RESULTS	CHART	PREVIEW	JSON	EXECUTION DETAILS	EXECUTION GRAPH

Row	message ▼
1	hello
2	I am very happy with your servi...
3	I am very happy with the service.
4	Its awesome.
5	Thanks for your help.
6	hello, your service is good

Figure 15.26: Review verified from BigQuery

Let us build the tabular report in Looker Studio:

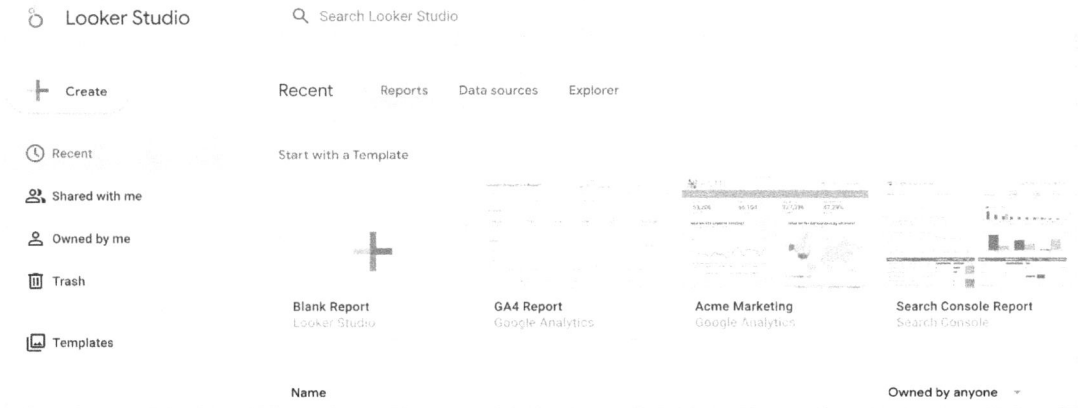

Figure 15.27: Click on blank report to get started

17. Add BigQuery as data to the report:

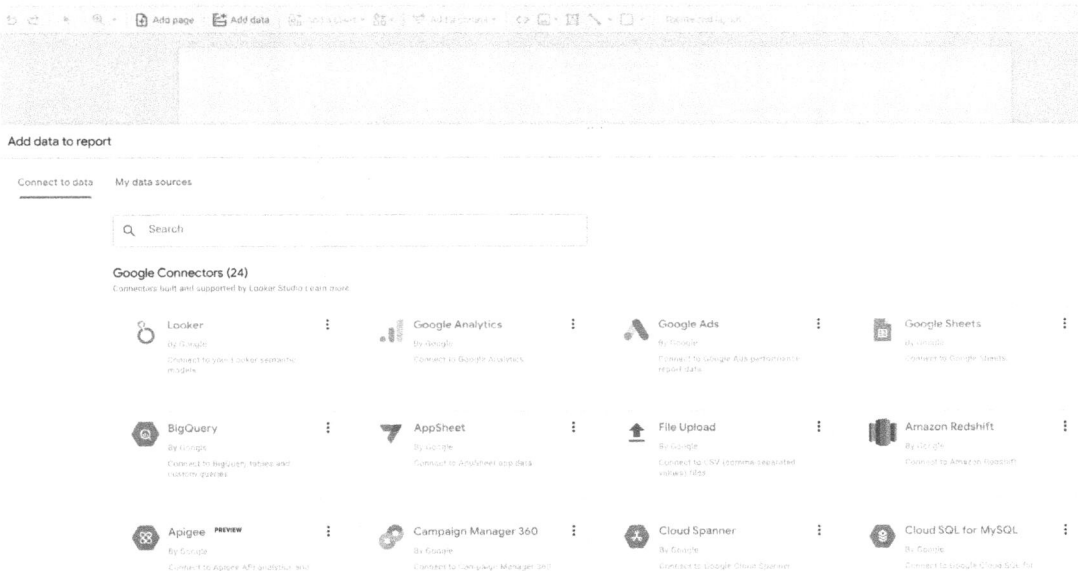

Figure 15.28: Add data in report

18. Pick the project, dataset, and table:

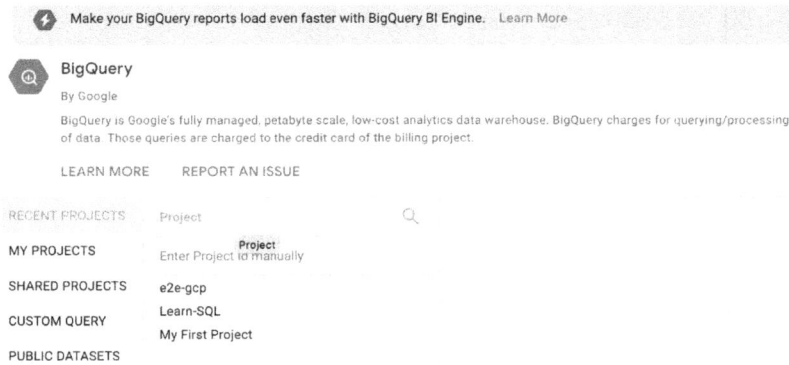

Figure 15.29: BigQuery project

19. Select the dataset and table as mentioned in following figure:

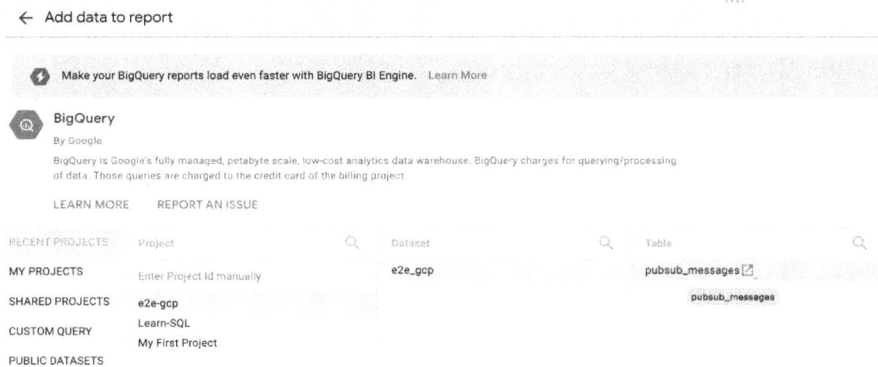

Figure 15.30: BigQuery dataset and table

Functionality testing

Let us test the functionality of this application by inserting a review from the front end application and view it in real time from Looker.

1. Send a review from frontend:

Figure 15.31: Submit another review from browser

2. Verify the result in Looker Studio report:

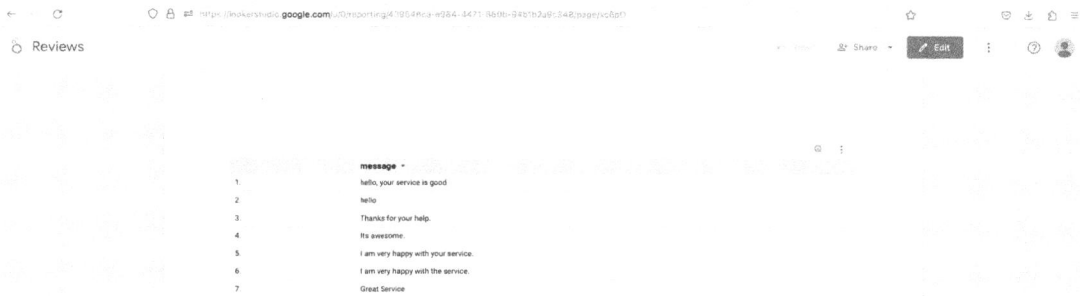

Figure 15.32: *Verify from Looker Studio report*

Monitoring

Let us monitor the application components which we deployed in GCP. Monitoring plays a vital role in the lifecycle of an application. Effective monitoring helps in identifying if there are any bugs present in the software or any improvement is needed or not which in turn improves the usability and user experience of the application / product.

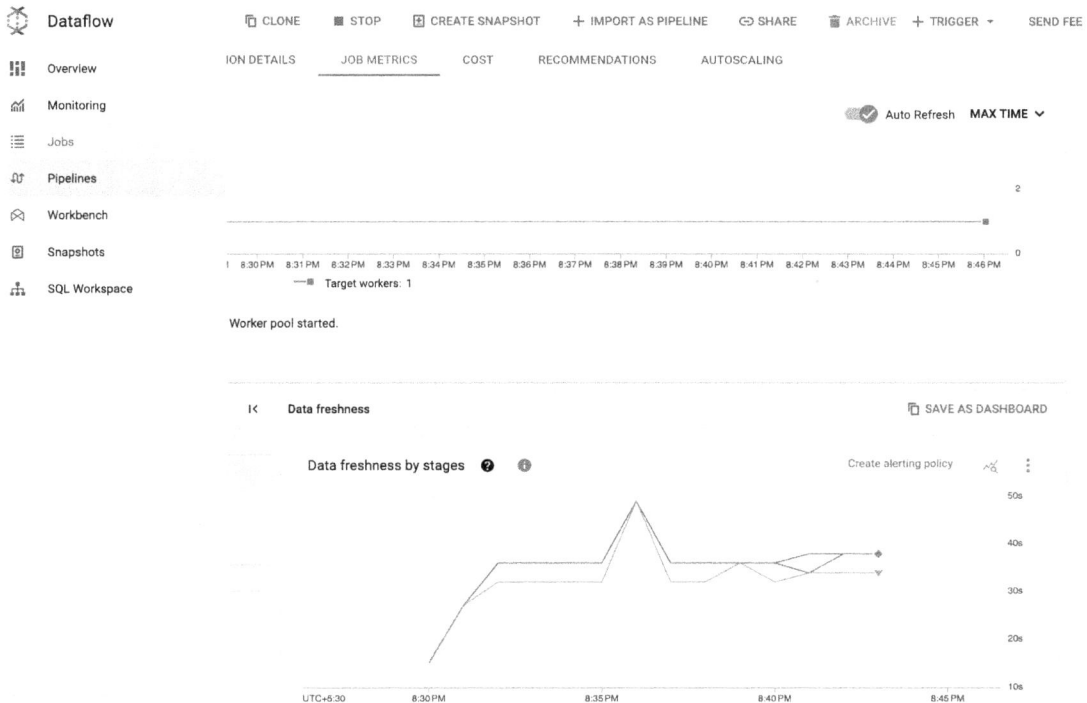

Figure 15.33: *Dataflow Job Metrics*

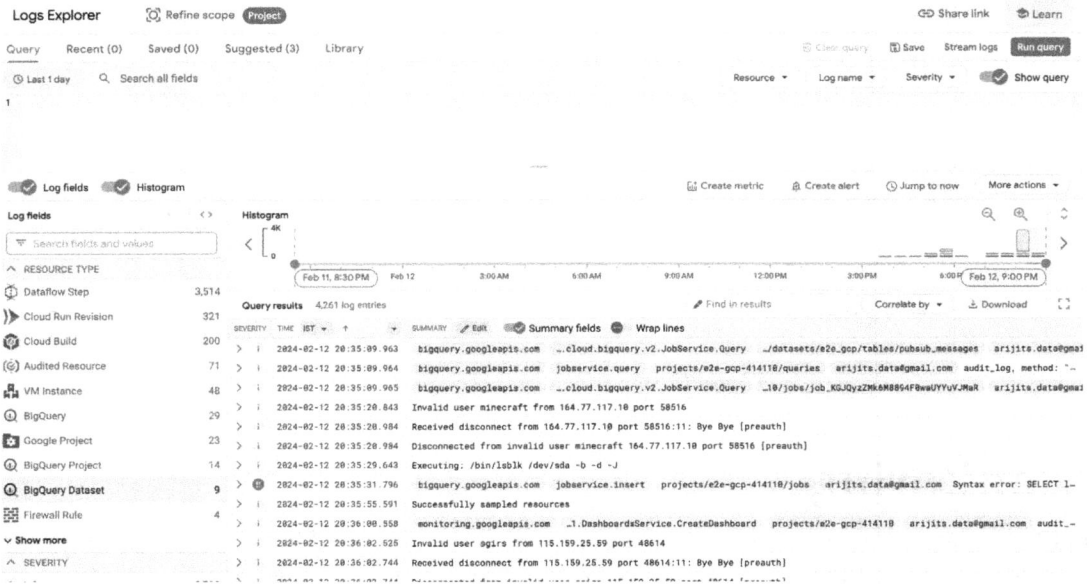

Figure 15.34: Logs Explorer for BigQuery Dataset

BigQuery Monitoring:

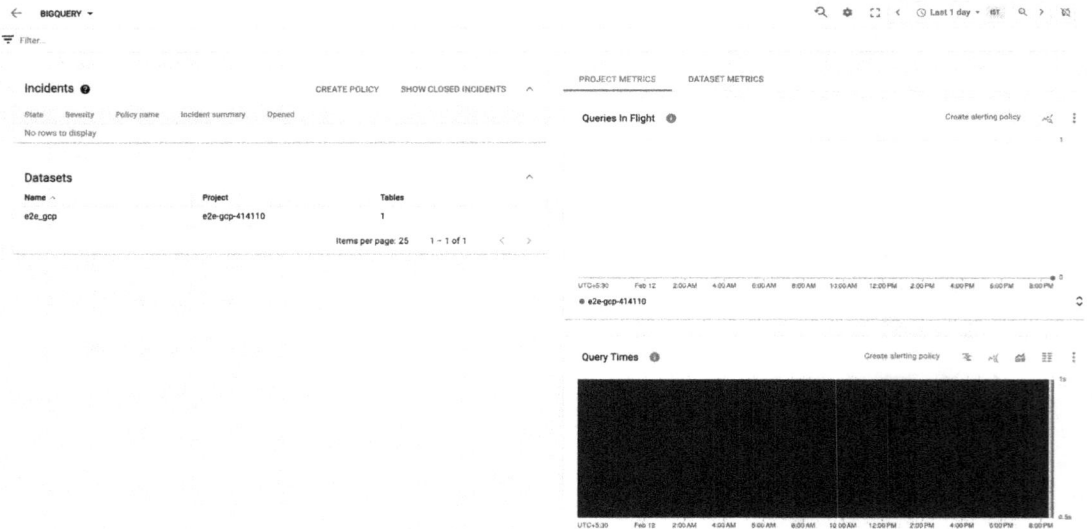

Figure 15.35: BigQuery Monitoring

Trace Explorer for Cloud Run API requests:

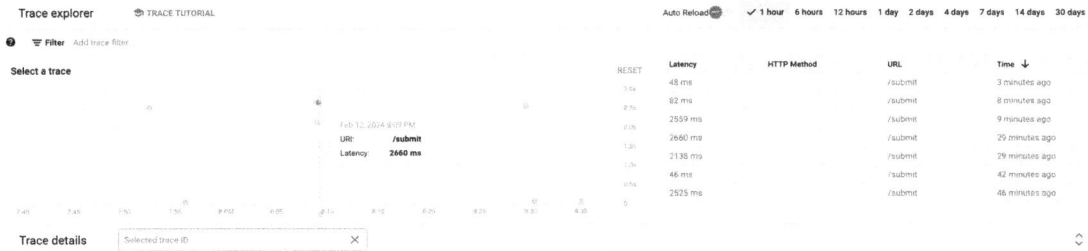

Figure 15.36: Trace Explorer

With these, we have completed the application development lifecycle in GCP.

Conclusion

We have reached the end of the chapter. In this chapter, we have learned how to build a complete application, i.e., frontend, backend, and analytics parts together using GCP services. We have seen how to build, test, and deploy the components of applications in GCP. We have seen how logs and requests can be monitored and these logs can also be exported to BigQuery for further analysis.

Join our book's Discord space

Join the book's Discord Workspace for Latest updates, Offers, Tech happenings around the world, New Release and Sessions with the Authors:

https://discord.bpbonline.com

CHAPTER 16
Specific Topics for GCP ACE Exam

Introduction

This chapter covers the specific topics required for GCP Associate Cloud Engineering certification exam. It will cover topics not specific to any particular area, so completing other chapters is recommended before starting this. It will put emphasis on some of the specific topics on which questions were asked in previous GCP Associate Cloud Engineer exams.

Structure

The chapter covers the following topics:

- GCP database product choice
- Installing and configuring Ops Agent on GCP VM
- Add a GPU to a new instance
- Compute Engine VM snapshots and images
- Cloud Run or Cloud Run for Anthos
- Horizontal Pod Autoscaling for GKE
- Vertical Pod Autoscaling for GKE
- Cloud Foundation Toolkit

- Connecting On-Prem and GCP using Cloud VPN
- Managing users and groups in Cloud identity
- Provisioning and setting up products in Google Cloud's operations suite
- Assessing compute quotas and requesting increases
- Creating and managing short-lived service account credentials

Objectives

We will learn about the above-mentioned topics, which are important from this certification perspective. This final chapter will provide you with knowledge from various areas of the Google Cloud Platform.

GCP database product choice

We have already learned about various database services in GCP. Let us understand the use case of databases in a diagrammatic way:

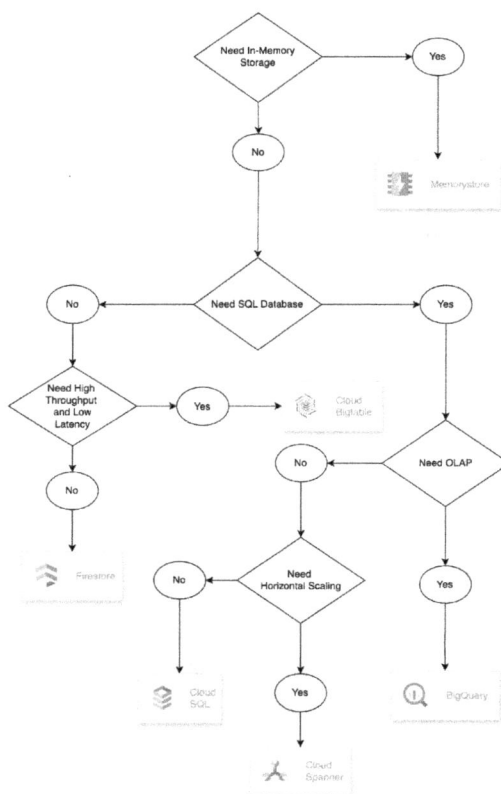

Figure 16.1: GCP database product choice

Installing and configuring Ops Agent on GCP VM

Let us understand the installation and configuration of a Cloud Monitoring agent (Ops Agent) on GCP VM in a step-by-step process:

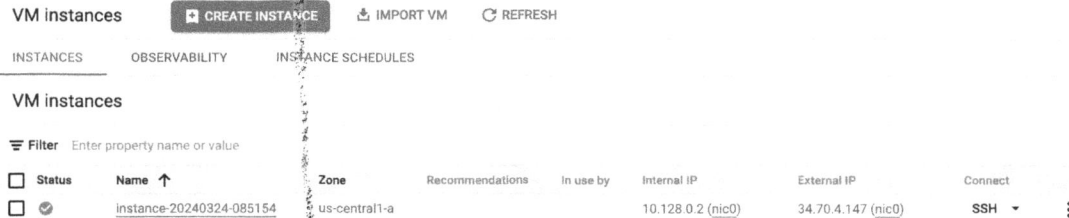

	Status	Name ↑	Zone	Recommendations	In use by	Internal IP	External IP	Connect	
☐	✓	instance-20240324-085154	us-central1-a			10.128.0.2 (nic0)	34.70.4.147 (nic0)	SSH ▾	⋮

Figure 16.2: VM created

1. SSH to this VM in GCP console and download and install the latest version of Ops Agent.

   ```
   curl   -sSO   https://dl.google.com/cloudagents/add-google-cloud-ops-agent-repo.sh
   ```

   ```
   sudo bash add-google-cloud-ops-agent-repo.sh --also-install
   ```

```
Reading package lists... Done
Building dependency tree... Done
Reading state information... Done
0 upgraded, 0 newly installed, 0 to remove and 2 not upgraded.
Get:1 file:/etc/apt/mirrors/debian.list Mirrorlist [30 B]
Get:2 file:/etc/apt/mirrors/debian-security.list Mirrorlist [39 B]
Get:7 https://packages.cloud.google.com/apt google-cloud-ops-agent-bookworm-all InRelease [5112 B]
Hit:8 https://packages.cloud.google.com/apt google-compute-engine-bookworm-stable InRelease
Hit:9 https://packages.cloud.google.com/apt cloud-sdk-bookworm InRelease
Hit:3 https://deb.debian.org/debian bookworm InRelease
Hit:4 https://deb.debian.org/debian bookworm-updates InRelease
Hit:5 https://deb.debian.org/debian bookworm-backports InRelease
Hit:6 https://deb.debian.org/debian-security bookworm-security InRelease
Get:10 https://packages.cloud.google.com/apt google-cloud-ops-agent-bookworm-all/main amd64 Packages [2798 B]
Fetched 7910 B in 1s (7201 B/s)
Reading package lists... Done
Reading package lists... Done
Building dependency tree... Done
Reading state information... Done
The following NEW packages will be installed:
  google-cloud-ops-agent
0 upgraded, 1 newly installed, 0 to remove and 2 not upgraded.
Need to get 94.7 MB of archives.
After this operation, 415 MB of additional disk space will be used.
Get:1 https://packages.cloud.google.com/apt google-cloud-ops-agent-bookworm-all/main amd64 google-cloud-ops-age
nt amd64 2.46.1~debian12 [94.7 MB]
Fetched 94.7 MB in 3s (30.2 MB/s)
Selecting previously unselected package google-cloud-ops-agent.
(Reading database ... 66765 files and directories currently installed.)
Preparing to unpack .../google-cloud-ops-agent_2.46.1~debian12_amd64.deb ...
Unpacking google-cloud-ops-agent (2.46.1~debian12) ...
Setting up google-cloud-ops-agent (2.46.1~debian12) ...
Created symlink /etc/systemd/system/multi-user.target.wants/google-cloud-ops-agent.service → /lib/systemd/syste
m/google-cloud-ops-agent.service.
google-cloud-ops-agent  installation succeeded.
arijits_data@instance-20240324-085154:~$
```

Figure 16.3: Ops Agent Installed on VM

2. Verify the installation with the below command:

```
sudo systemctl status google-cloud-ops-agent"*"
```

Figure 16.4: Status of Ops Agent

Adding a GPU to a new instance

To add GPU to a new instance for deep learning model training, follow the below figure:

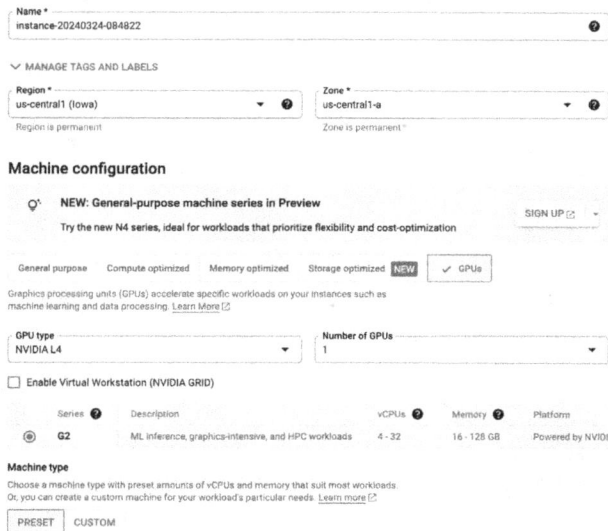

Figure 16.5: Adding GPU to VM

Calculated cost for the same configuration:

Monthly estimate

$516.99

That's about $0.71 hourly

Pay for what you use: no upfront costs and per second billing

Item	Monthly estimate
4 vCPU + 16 GB memory	$107.16
1 NVIDIA L4	$408.83
10 GB balanced persistent disk	$1.00
Total	$516.99

Compute Engine pricing ⬀

∧ LESS

Figure 16.6: Cost of GCP VM with GPU

Compute engine VM snapshots and images

Let us start by creating a snapshot:

Snapshots   ⊞ CREATE SNAPSHOT   📅 CREATE SNAPSHOT SCHEDULE   ⟳ REFRESH   🗑 DELETE

Snapshots are backups of persistent disks. They're commonly used to recover, transfer, or make data accessible to other resources in your project. Learn more ⬀

SNAPSHOTS   ARCHIVE SNAPSHOTS   INSTANT SNAPSHOTS [PREVIEW]   SNAPSHOT SCHEDULES

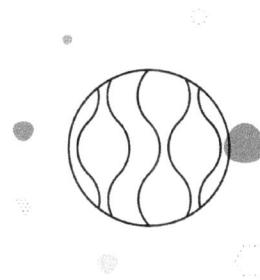

No snapshots to display

Add a new snapshot

CREATE SNAPSHOT   TAKE THE QUICKSTART

Figure 16.7: VM snapshot

1. Click on **CREATE SNAPSHOT** follow the following figure:

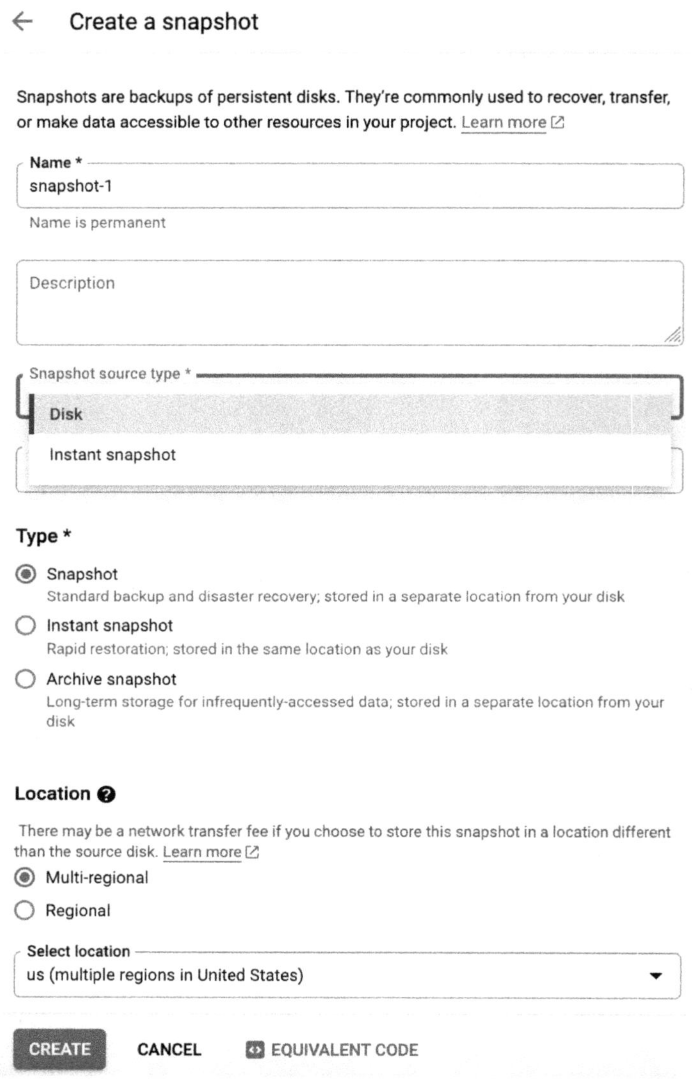

←   Create a snapshot

Snapshots are backups of persistent disks. They're commonly used to recover, transfer, or make data accessible to other resources in your project. Learn more ☑

Name *
snapshot-1

Name is permanent

Description

Snapshot source type *

Disk

Instant snapshot

Type *

⦿ Snapshot
   Standard backup and disaster recovery; stored in a separate location from your disk

◯ Instant snapshot
   Rapid restoration; stored in the same location as your disk

◯ Archive snapshot
   Long-term storage for infrequently-accessed data; stored in a separate location from your disk

Location ❷

There may be a network transfer fee if you choose to store this snapshot in a location different than the source disk. Learn more ☑

⦿ Multi-regional
◯ Regional

Select location
us (multiple regions in United States) ▾

[CREATE]   CANCEL   ⟨⟩ EQUIVALENT CODE

Figure 16.8: Creating disk snapshot

2. To create an image of the disk, follow the below process:

    a. First, the instance needs to be stopped, which is using the disk:

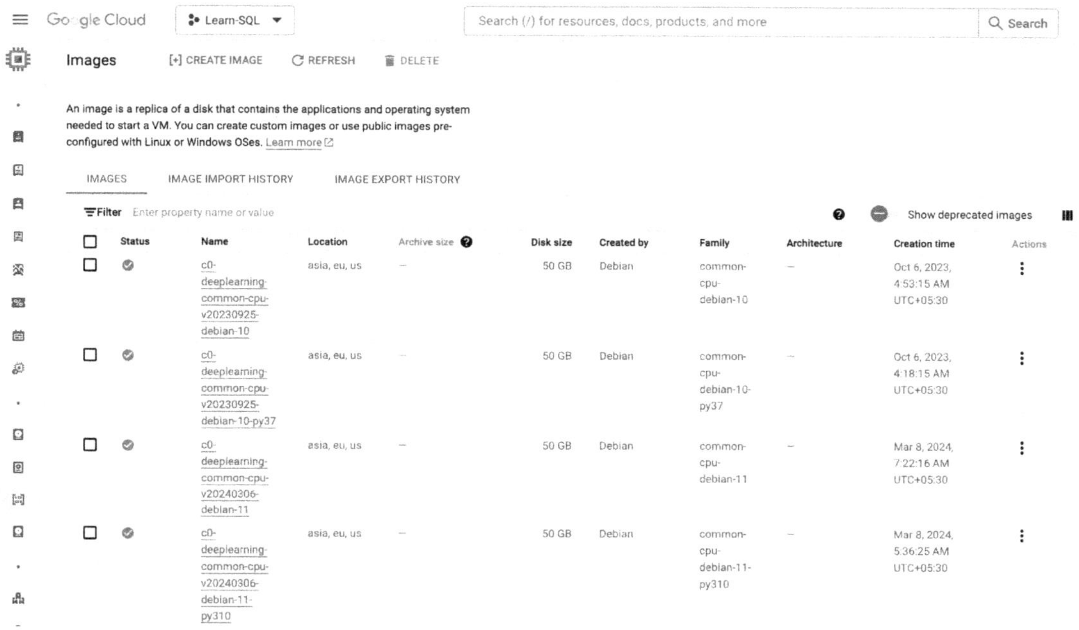

Figure 16.9: VM images

3. Click on **CREATE IMAGE** to get started:

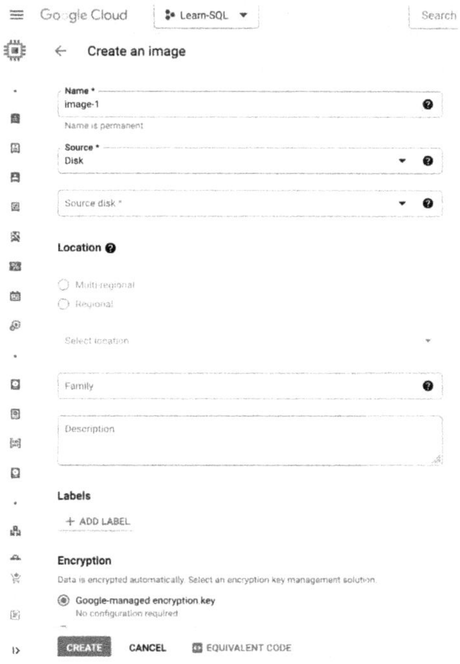

Figure 16.10: Creating disk image

Cloud Run or Cloud Run for Anthos

Cloud Run is a serverless platform for stateless workloads. For this solution, there is no requirement for the infrastructure management. Alternatively, you may have an existing Kubernetes cluster. In this scenario, all the workloads run from this environment. Additionally, you may need some features such as namespace, control over the pod allocation, additional telemetry, etc. In such a case, Cloud Run on Anthos becomes a considered choice. In both cases, the workloads to be deployed will remain the same, so as a developer, the associated effort will not increase despite the visible differences in terms of the deployment platform.

Horizontal Pod Autoscaling for GKE

The Horizontal Pod Autoscaling changes the shape of the Kubernetes workload by automatically increasing or decreasing the number of pods in response to the workload's compute or memory consumption or in response to the custom metrics reported within Kubernetes or from external metrics from the sources outside of your cluster. Each of the configured Horizontal Pod Autoscaler operates using a control loop. A separate HPA exists for each workflow. Each HPA periodically checks the given workload's metrics against all the target thresholds you have configured, and accordingly, it changes the shape of the workload automatically.

Vertical Pod Autoscaling for GKE

Vertical Pod Autoscaling allows you to analyze and set compute and memory resources required by Pods. Instead of having to set up-to-date compute requests and limits and memory requests and limits for the containers in the Pods, you can configure the Vertical Pod Autoscaling to provide the recommended values for CPU/compute and memory requests and limits, which you can use to manually update the Pods, or you can configure the Vertical Pod Autoscaling to automatically update the values. VPA is enabled by default in the Autopilot clusters.

Cloud Foundation Toolkit

The Cloud Foundation Toolkit has many reference templates for the Deployment Manager and Terraform, which reflect the Google Cloud best practices. These templates can be used quickly to build a repeatable enterprise ready foundation in GCP. This allows you to focus on the deployment of your applications. With **Infrastructure as Code (IaC)**, you can easily change the foundation as and when required.

Connecting On-Prem and GCP using Cloud VPN

Cloud VPN facilitates an encrypted connection over the public internet between your on-premises network or other Cloud provider and the VPC in GCP. This connection uses standard IPsec protocol for ensuring secure communication. GCP offers two types of VPN:

- **Classic VPN:** This is suitable for scenarios which do not require high levels of availability.

- **HA VPN:** This is a high availability, high throughput, fault tolerant Cloud VPN solution. Once you choose HA VPN, the two VPN tunnels are automatically created between the connecting gateways.

← Create a VPN

A virtual private network lets you securely connect your Google Compute Engine resources to your own private network. Google VPN uses IKEv1 or IKEv2 to establish the IPsec connectivity. Learn more ☑

VPN options

◉ High-availability (HA) VPN
Supports dynamic routing (BGP) only
Supports high availability (99.99 SLA, within region)
Supports IPv4 and IPv6 traffic
Learn more ☑

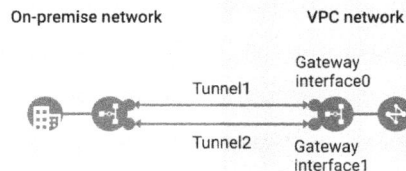

○ Classic VPN
Supports static routing
No high availability
Supports IPv4 traffic only
Learn more ☑

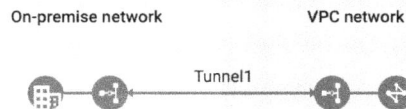

CONTINUE   CANCEL

Figure 16.11: Cloud VPN for hybrid connectivity

Managing users and groups in Cloud Identity

Cloud Identity is an Identity as a Service solution that centrally manages users and groups. We can configure Cloud Identity to federate the identities between Google and other identity providers like Active Directory.

When we adopt Cloud Identity, we can create a Cloud Identity account for each of your users and groups. we can then use IAM to manage access to Google Cloud resources for each Cloud Identity account. We will show this using Google Workspace.

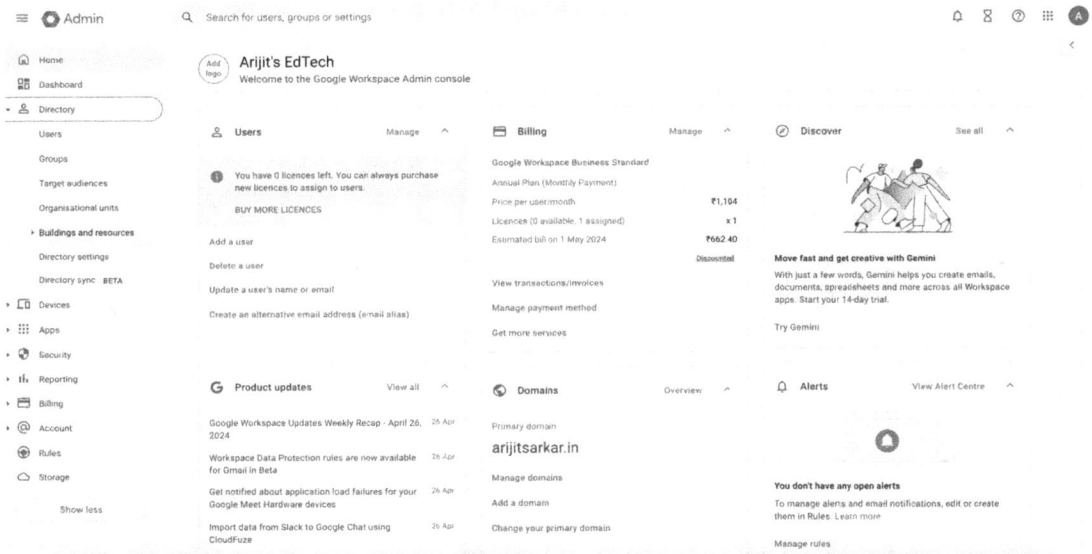

Figure 16.12: Google Workspace Admin Console

1. Create users and groups in Admin Console:

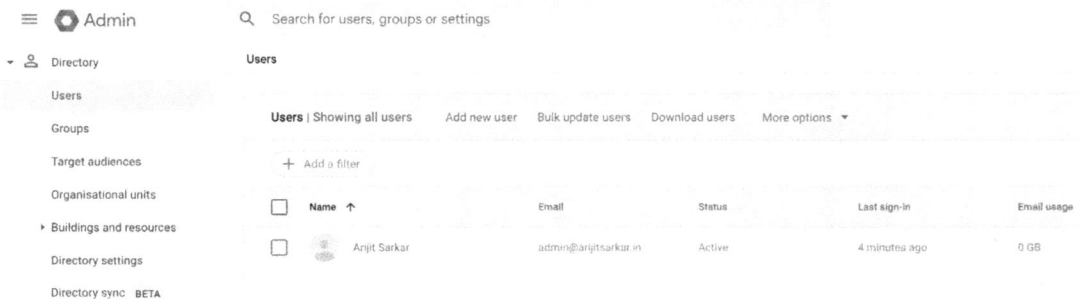

Figure 16.13: Users and groups in Google Workspace Admin Console

2. Provide access to this user in IAM section in GCP:

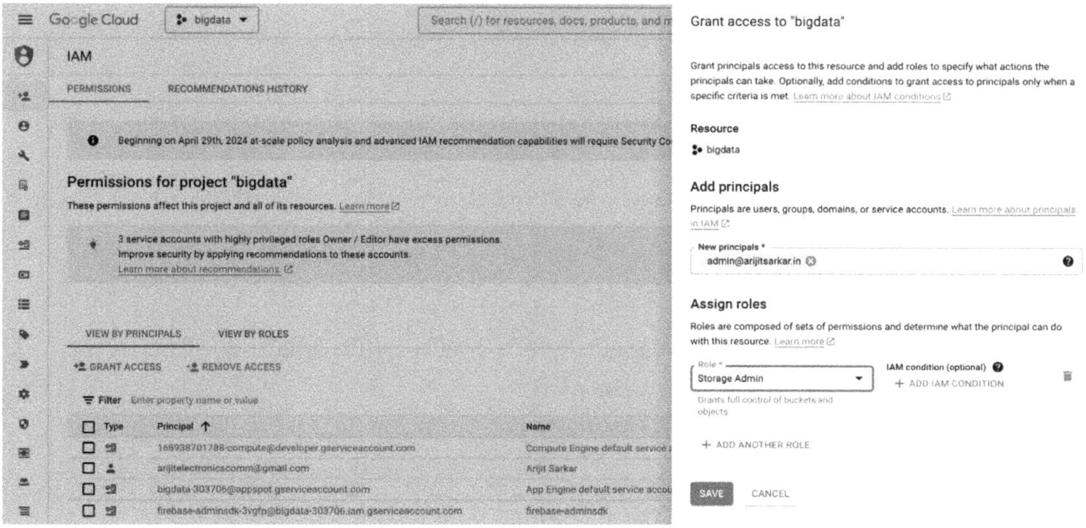

Figure 16.14: User access in IAM

Similar to this, you can create groups and provide access.

Provisioning and setting up products in Google Cloud's operations suite

Let us understand how we can start with GCP's operations suite's Monitoring Dashboard for BigQuery:

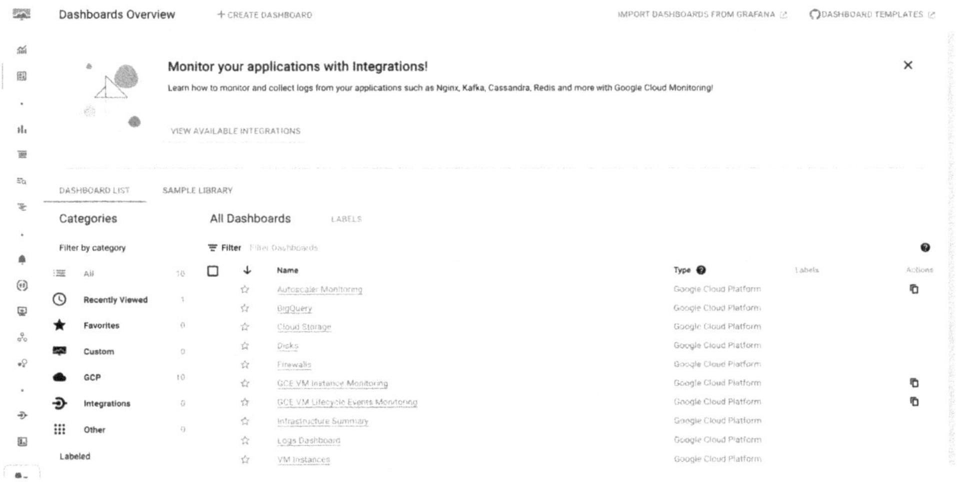

Figure 16.15: Monitoring page

1. Select **BigQuery** from the list:

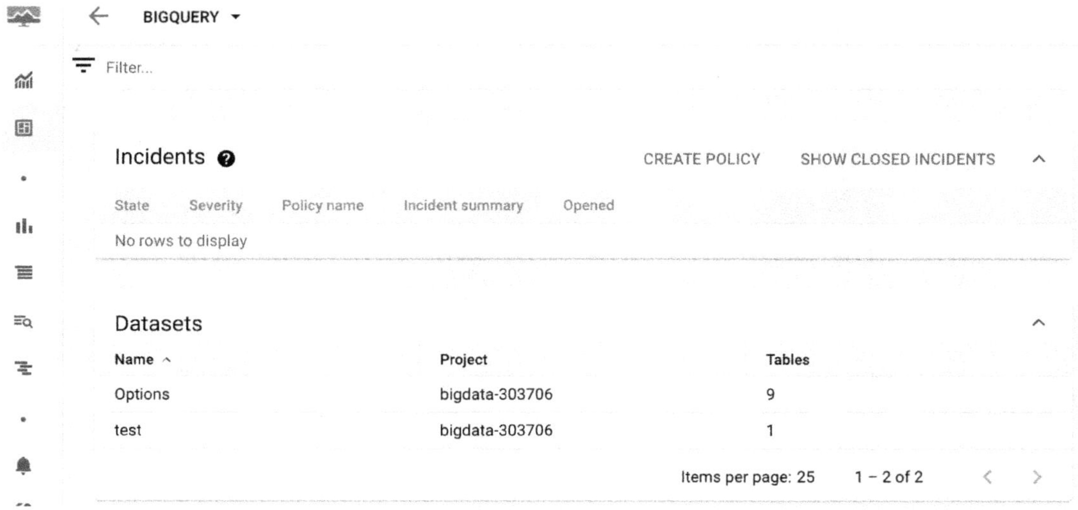

Figure 16.16: You can see the datasets of BigQuery

2. Provide the start date and end date to create the monitoring view and logs:

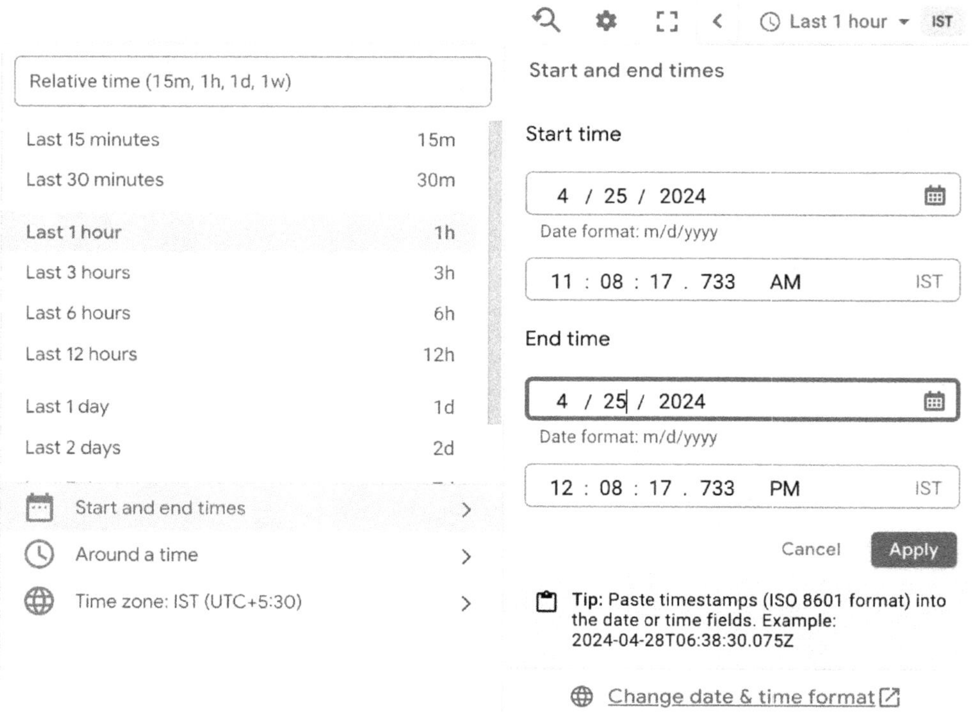

Figure 16.17: Start date and end date to create the monitoring view and logs

The appearance will be similar to the following figure:

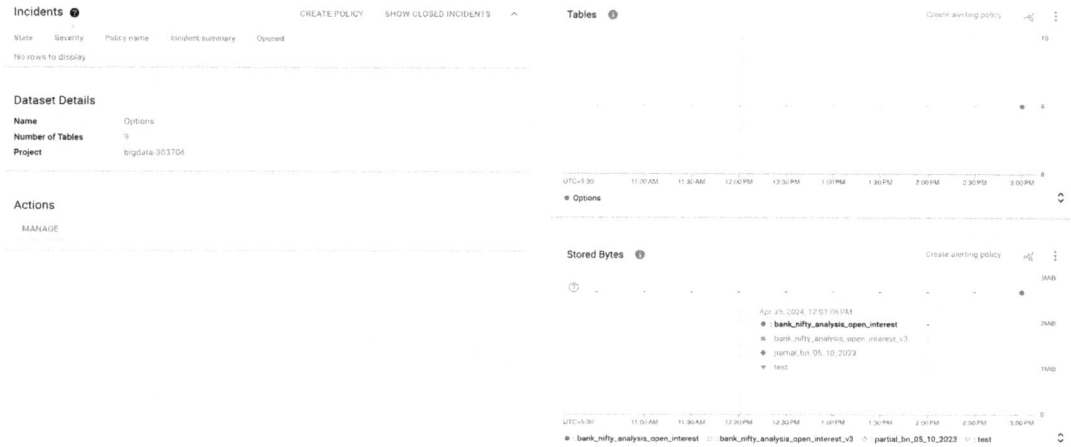

Figure 16.18: Monitoring view

3. You can create policy for alerts like the one below:

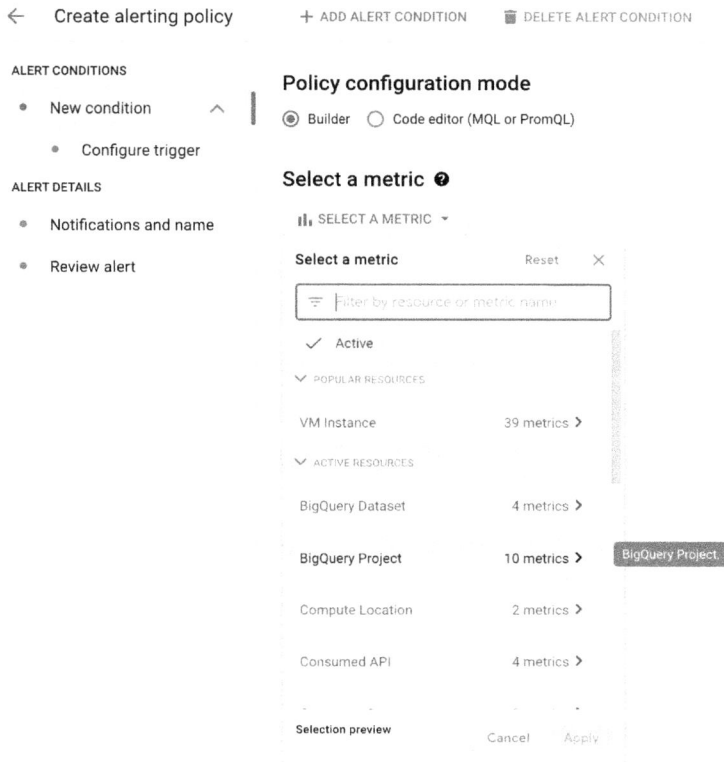

Figure 16.19: Alerting policy

4.   View the logs from **Logs Explorer** for the selected time frame:

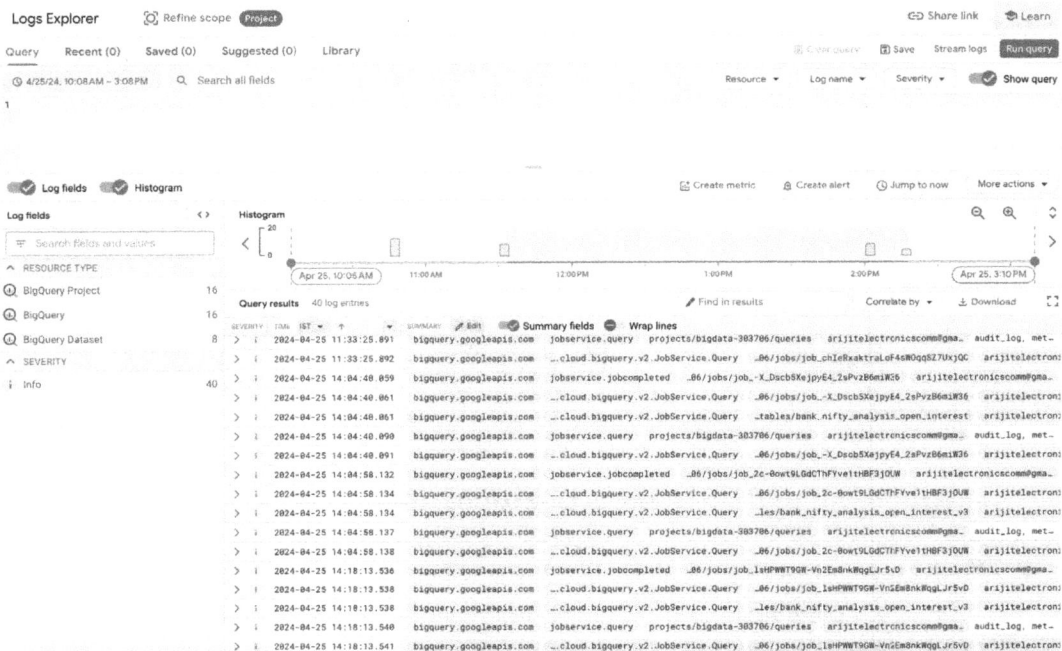

Figure 16.20: Logs Explorer

These logs can be exported to the supported destinations like:

1.   Cloud Logging Bucket

2.   BigQuery Dataset

3.   Cloud Storage Bucket

4.   Another Google Cloud Project

5.   Pub/Sub Topic (via this, it can be sent to 3rd party systems.)

Assessing compute quotas and requesting increases

Cloud Quotas enables customers to manage quotas for all their Google Cloud services. With Cloud Quotas, users can now easily monitor quota usage, create, and modify the quota alerts, and request the limit adjustments for quotas. Quotas are managed via the Cloud Quotas dashboard or Cloud Quotas API.

Google Cloud has three types of quotas:

- **Rate quotas** are typically used for limiting the number of requests which you can make to an API or service. Rate quotas reset after a time interval which is specific to the service like the number of API requests per day.

- **Allocation quotas** are used to restrict the use of resources that do not have a rate of usage, like the number of VMs used by the project at a given point of time.

- **Concurrent quotas** are used to restrict the total number of concurrent operations at any given time. These are usually long running operations like Compute Engine uses the **insert_operations**, which are expected to last more than one hour.

  You can find the Quota in IAM section:

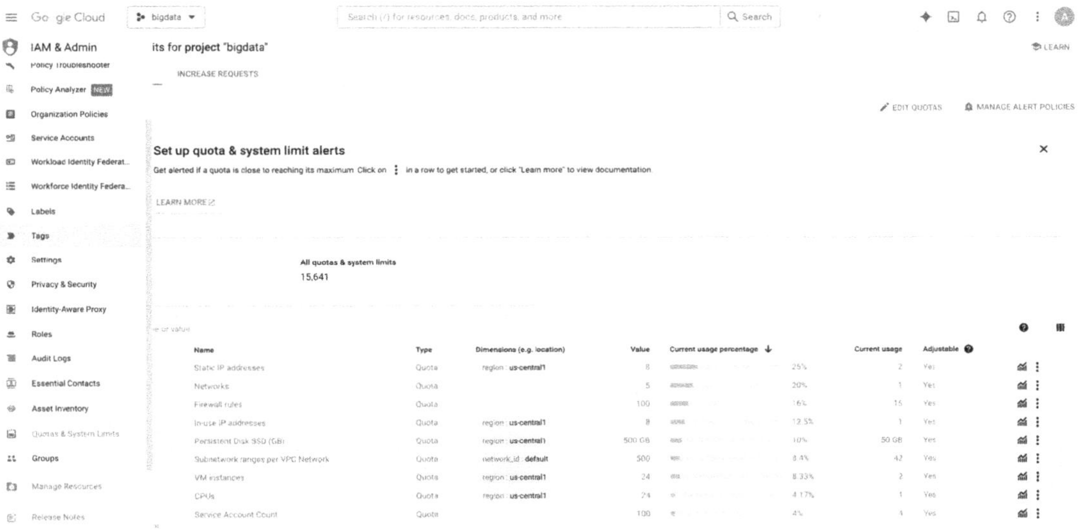

Figure 16.21: Quota and system limits

For organization level accounts, you can increase the quota from **INCREASE REQUESTS** tab.

Creating and managing short-lived service account credentials

You can create the following types of short-lived credentials for a service account:

- OAuth 2.0 access tokens
- **OpenID Connect (OIDC)** ID tokens
- Self-signed **JSON Web Tokens (JWTs)**
- Self-signed binary blobs

Let us understand the process for OAuth 2.0 access tokens:

1.   First, you need two service accounts, one is Caller SA, which will have permission to create short lived access tokens, and second is Priv SA, which will have permissions which should be present in Access Tokens.

2.   Execute the below commands:

```
gcloud auth login CALLER_SA
gcloud auth print-access-token --impersonate-service-account=PRIV_SA
```

3.   Generated token will be valid for 3600 secs maximum (default).

Conclusion

This is a small chapter covering some of the specific topics which we have discussed in previous chapters. With this we have come to the end of this GCP Associate Cloud Engineer exam guide and two sample tests, fowling this chapter, comprised of 20 questions each will provide you an understanding of the questions asked in the examination.

Join our book's Discord space

Join the book's Discord Workspace for Latest updates, Offers, Tech happenings around the world, New Release and Sessions with the Authors:

https://discord.bpbonline.com

CHAPTER 17
Practice Test 1

Practice questions

1. You have been asked to create a custom VPC with a single subnet. The subnet's range should be large enough. Which range should be used?

   a. 0.0.0.0/32

   b. 10.0.0.0/8

   c. 0.0.0.0/0

   d. 192.168.1.0/28

2. You need to deploy an application to the App Engine. You need the number of instances to scale based on request rate. You want at least 2 unoccupied instances always. Which type of scaling should you use?

   a. Manual Scaling with 2 instances.

   b. Basic Scaling when min_instances set to 2.

   c. Basic Scaling when max_instances set to 2.

   d. Auto Scaling when min_idle_instances set to 2.

3. **Your development team needs a new Jenkins server. You need to deploy the server quickly. What should you use?**

    a. First download and then deploy the Jenkins Java WAR to App Engine.

    b. Create a new Compute Engine VM instance and install Jenkins.

    c. Create a GKE cluster and create a deployment using Jenkins Docker image.

    d. Using GCP Marketplace to launch Jenkins solution.

4. **You are analyzing GCP service costs for two separate projects. You want to use this to create service cost estimates grouping by service type, daily, monthly, for the next 1 year using query syntax. What should be done in this case?**

    a. Export the bill to a GCS bucket, and then import into Bigtable for analysis.

    b. Export the bill to a GCS bucket, and then import into Sheets for analysis.

    c. Export the transactions to a local file in local machine and perform analysis using a desktop-based tool.

    d. Export the bill to BigQuery, and then write time and window based queries for analysis.

5. **You are creating an instance of SQL Server 2017 on GCP Compute Engine VM to test features in new version. You need to connect to this instance quickly. What should be done?**

    a. Install RDP client on the local machine. Verify firewall rule on port 3389.

    b. Install RDP client in desktop. Set Windows username and password via GCP Console. Use these for log in to the instance.

    c. Set the Windows password in GCP Console. Verify the firewall rule on port 22. Click the RDP button in GCP Console and provide credentials for login.

    d. Set the Windows username and password via GCP Console. Verify the firewall rule on port 3389. Click the RDP button via GCP Console and provide the credentials.

6. **You have changed a Deployment Manager template and need to confirm whether all the dependencies of all the defined resources are met properly before committing to project. You also want quick feedback on the changes. What should be done?**

    a. Use the logging statements in the Deployment Manager template written using Python.

    b. Monitor the activities of the Deployment Manager execution on the Cloud Logging page in the GCP Console.

c. Execute the template of Deployment Manager for a separate project with the same config and monitor for any failure.

d. Execute the template of Deployment Manager using the preview option in the same project and notice the state of dependent resources.

7. **You have a project for the App Engine application which serves as a development environment. The required testing was successful, and now you need to create a new project to serve as production environment. What should be done?**

a. Utilise gcloud to create a new project and then deploy the tested application to this new GCP project.

b. Utilise gcloud to create a new project and copy the deployed and tested application to this new GCP project.

c. Create the Deployment Manager config file, which copies the current App Engine deployment into the new project.

d. Deploy the application via gcloud and specify the project parameter as the new project name in order to create a new project.

8. **You have highly sensitive data stored in three GCS buckets and the data access logging is enabled. You are willing to verify the activities for a particular user for the buckets. You also need to verify addition of metadata labels and whether any files have been viewed from these buckets. What should be done?**

a. In GCP Console, filter the Activity log to view the information.

b. In GCP Console, filter the Cloud Logging logs to view the information.

c. View the bucket inside the Storage section of GCP Console.

d. Use Cloud Trace to view the information.

9. **You are owning a GCP project and now want to delegate the control to the colleagues in order to manage buckets and/ or files in GCS. You want to follow best practices. Which IAM roles should be granted?**

a. Storage Object Admin

b. Storage Admin

c. Project Editor

d. Storage Object Creator

10. **You need to verify the IAM users and corresponding roles assigned in a GCP project. What should you do in this situation?**

a. Run "gcloud IAM roles list" and review the output section.

b. Run "gcloud IAM service-accounts list" and review the output section.

c. Go to the project and then to the IAM in GCP Console and review members and roles.

d. Go to the project and then to the Roles section in GCP Console and review roles and status.

11. **You have created a GKE cluster and now need to make sure that it always runs the supported and stable version of Kubernetes. What should be done?**

   a. Select Container-Optimized OS as a node image for GKE cluster.

   b. Enable the Node Auto-Upgrades feature for GKE cluster.

   c. Select the latest available cluster version for GKE cluster.

   d. Enable the Node Auto-Repair feature for GKE cluster.

12. **You have 64 GB of data in a single file which you need to upload to a storage bucket. The WAN connection you have is rated at 1 Gbps, and you are alone using the connection. You want to use most of the rated 1 Gbps to transfer the file rapidly. What should be done in this situation?**

   a. Decrease the window size for TCP on the machine initiating the transfer.

   b. Using parallel composite uploads using gsutil.

   c. Change the storage class of the bucket.

   d. Use GCP Console to transfer instead of gsutil.

13. **You have deployed a new version of an application to the App Engine and noticed a bug in that release. Now, you want to immediately revert to the previous version of this application. What should be done?**

   a. Run "gcloud app restore".

   b. In the App Engine section of GCP, select the app which needs to be reverted and then click on Revert.

   c. In the App Engine section, on the Versions page, route 100% of traffic to its previous version.

   d. Go ahead and deploy the original version of application separately and then navigate to App Engine settings, split the traffic between the applications so that the original one serves 100%.

14. **You need to create an autoscaling managed instance group (MIG) for an HTTPS web application and You need to make sure that automatically any unhealthy VMs are recreated. What should be done?**

   a. Configure the health check on the 443 port and use it while creation of the managed instance group.

   b. Select Multi-Zone instead of Single-Zone while creating the required managed instance group.

    c. In the Instance Template, add a label as "health-check".

    d. In the Instance Template, add a start-up script which sends a heartbeat to the metadata server.

15. **You are building an application which will store relational data from users across the globe. CTO of the organization is concerned about the scaling requirements as the size of the user base is not clear. You need to implement a DB solution which can scale along with the user growth while the minimum configuration changes required. Which storage solution should you use?**

    a. Cloud Firestore

    b. Cloud Spanner

    c. Cloud Datastore

    d. Cloud SQL

16. **You need to build a latency-sensitive web application and for this you want to run single-caching HTTP reverse proxy and this reverse proxy does not require CPU utilization. Now you need a 30-GB in-memory cache, and additional 2 GB of memory for the process. How should this reverse proxy implementation be done minimizing the cost?**

    a. Create Cloud Memorystore for the Redis instance with 32-GB capacity.

    b. Run it on GCP VM, and choose a custom machine type with 6 vCPUs + 32 GB of memory.

    c. Run it on Compute Engine VM, choose the instance type as n1-standard-1, and add an SSD persistent disk of 32 GB.

    d. Package it in a container image and run it on GKE, using n1-standard-32 instances as nodes.

17. **You are going to deploy an application which is packaged in a container image, within a GCP project. The application exposes an HTTP endpoint and receives very few requests per day. What should be done keeping the cost minimal?**

    a. Deploy the container on Cloud Run.

    b. Deploy the container on App Engine Flexible.

    c. Deploy the container on Cloud Run on GKE.

    d. Deploy the container on GKE with cluster autoscaling and horizontal pod autoscaling enabled.

18. **You have built an application on GCP that uses Cloud Spanner. The support team needs to monitor the application but at the same time should not have access to the table data.**

You need a solution to provide the correct permissions to the support team, what should be done following the best practices?

    a.   Add the support team group to the roles/monitoring.viewer role.

    b.   Add the support team group to the roles/spanner.databaseReader role.

    c.   Add the support team group to the roles/spanner.databaseUser role.

    d.   Add the support team group to the roles/stackdriver.accounts.viewer role.

19. You are building an application which will run in your datacentre. The application will use GCP services like AutoML and you have created a service account which has appropriate access to AutoML. Now you need to enable an authentication mechanism to the APIs from on-premises. What should be done?

    a.   Set up a direct interconnect between your datacentre and GCP to enable authentication for the on-premises applications.

    b.   Use gcloud to create a key file for the service account which has appropriate permissions.

    c.   Go to the IAM & admin console, grant a user account, the permissions similar to the service account permissions, and finally, use this user account to authenticate from the datacentre.

    d.   Use service account credentials in on-premises applications.

20. You need to add a new auditor to a GCP project. The auditor should be allowed to read, but should not be able to modify all project items. What should be the best way to configure auditor's permissions?

    a.   Select built-in IAM service Viewer role. Add this user's account to this role.

    b.   Create a custom role with the view-only project permissions. Add this user's account to the custom role.

    c.   Select built-in IAM project Viewer role. Add this user's account to this role.

    d.   Create a custom role with view-only service permissions. Add this user's account to the custom role.

Answers

1. B	
2. D	
3. D	
4. D	
5. B	

6. D	
7. A	
8. A	
9. B	
10. C	

11. B	
12. B	
13. C	
14. A	
15. B	

16. A	
17. A	
18. A	
19. B	
20. C	

CHAPTER 18
Practice Test 2

Practice questions

1. **You have a 2-TB CSV file stored inside a Cloud Storage bucket. Data analysts in your team are good only in SQL and they want to access this data. You need to find a cost-effective solution to complete their request as quickly as possible. What should you do?**

   a. Load data in Cloud SQL and run a SQL query against it.

   b. Create a BQ table and load data in BQ. Run a SQL query on this table and drop this after the work is done.

   c. Create an external table in the BQ table, which points to the Cloud Storage bucket, and run a SQL query on the external table.

   d. Create a Hadoop cluster on GCP VM and copy the AVRO file to HDFS by compressing it. Load this file in a hive table and provide access to the Data analysts so that they can run SQL queries.

2. **You need to verify that a GCP service account has been created at a particular time. What should be done?**

   a. Filter the Activity log to see the Config category and filter based on Resource type to the Service Account.

   b. Filter the Activity log to see the Config category and filter based on Resource type to the GCP Project.

   c. Filter the Activity log to see the Data Access category and filter based on Resource type to the Service Account.

   d. Filter the Activity log to see the Data Access category and filter based on Resource type to the GCP Project.

3. **You need to configure a solution for archiving the data in a GCS bucket. You need to keep the cost as minimal as possible. Data with multiple versions should be sent for archival after 30 days and previous versions are typically accessed one time in a month for reporting. The archive data is also sometimes updated at the month-end. What should be done?**

   a. Add a bucket lifecycle rule that archives data from regional storage after 30 days to Coldline Storage.

   b. Add a bucket lifecycle rule that archives data with newer versions after 30 days to Nearline Storage.

   c. Add a bucket lifecycle rule that archives data from regional storage after 30 days to Nearline Storage.

   d. Add a bucket lifecycle rule that archives data with newer versions after 30 days to Coldline Storage.

4. **You need to select and configure a solution to store and archive data on GCP. You also need to support the compliance objectives for the data from one geographic location. This data is typically archived after 30 days and it needs to be accessed once in a year. What should be done?**

   a. Select Regional Storage and add a bucket lifecycle rule that archives data after 30 days to Nearline Storage.

   b. Select Multi-Regional Storage and add a bucket lifecycle rule that archives data after 30 days to Coldline Storage.

   c. Select Multi-Regional Storage and add a bucket lifecycle rule that archives data after 30 days to Nearline Storage.

   d. Select Regional Storage and add a bucket lifecycle rule that archives data after 30 days to Coldline Storage.

5. **You need to find when the users are added to Cloud Spanner specific IAM roles on the Google Cloud Platform project. What should be done?**

   a. Open Cloud Spanner in the console to review the configurations.

   b. Open the IAM & admin in the console to review the IAM policies of Cloud Spanner roles.

   c. Go to the Cloud Monitoring console and review the information regarding Cloud Spanner.

   d. Go to the Cloud Logging console, check the admin activity logs, and filter Cloud Spanner IAM roles.

6. **Finance team in your organization wants to view the billing report for GCP projects. You need to make sure that the finance team does not get any extra permissions in the project. What should be done?**

   a. Add the group for the finance team to roles/billing user role.

   b. Add the group for the finance team to roles/billing admin role.

   c. Add the group for the finance team to roles/billing viewer role.

   d. Add the group for the finance team to roles/billing project/Manager role.

7. **You need to host an application on a Compute Engine VM instance in a project which is shared with other teams. Now, you want to prevent other teams from causing downtime by mistake on the application. What is the best way to prevent this?**

   a. Use a Shielded VM.

   b. Use a Preemptible VM.

   c. Use a sole-tenant node.

   d. Enable deletion protection on the instance.

8. **Your organization has put a one dedicated person to create and manage all service accounts for GCP projects. Now you need to assign this person with the minimum possible role for projects. What should be done?**

   a. Add the user to roles/iam.roleAdmin role.

   b. Add the user to roles/iam.securityAdmin role.

   c. Add the user to roles/iam.serviceAccountUser role.

   d. Add the user to roles/iam.serviceAccountAdmin role.

9. You are building an archival strategy for the data lake and have chosen Cloud Storage to archive the data. Your users need to access this data once a quarter for some of the regulatory requirements. You need to select a cost effective solution. Which storage option should be chosen here?

   a. Cold Storage

   b. Nearline Storage

   c. Regional Storage

   d. Multi-Regional Storage

10. You have a workload running on the Compute Engine, which is critical to the business. You need to ensure that the workload data on the boot disk is backed up at regular intervals. You need to be able to restore the backup as quickly as possible in case of any disaster. You also need older backups to be cleaned up automatically to save the cost. You also need to follow best practices. What should you do?

    a. Create a Cloud Function for creating an instance template.

    b. Create a snapshot schedule for the disk using a desired interval.

    c. Create a cron job to create a new disk from the existing disk using gcloud.

    d. Create a Cloud Task to create an image and export it to the Cloud Storage.

11. Your company has huge amount of unstructured data in various file formats. You need to perform ETL on the data. You also need to make the data available on GCP so that it can be transformed by a Dataflow job. What should be done?

    a. Upload the data to BigQuery.

    b. Upload the data to GCS bucket.

    c. Upload the data into Cloud SQL.

    d. Upload the data into Cloud Spanner.

12. You have an application which receives SSL-encrypted TCP traffic on the port 443. Users of this application are located across the world. You need to minimize the latency for the users. Which load balancing option should be used?

    a. HTTPS Load Balancer

    b. Network Load Balancer

    c. SSL Proxy Load Balancer

    d. Internal TCP/UDP Load Balancer

13. You have an application deployed on general-purpose Compute Engine instance which is experiencing very high disk read throttling on its Zonal SSD Persistent Disk. Usually the application primarily reads large files from disk. The disk size is currently 400 GB. You need to provide the maximum throughput while minimizing costs. What should be done?

    a. Increase the size of the disk to 1 TB.

    b. Increase the allocated CPU to the instance.

    c. Use Local SSD on the instance.

    d. Use Regional SSD on the instance.

14. You need to create a copy of existing custom Compute Engine VM to facilitate an expected increase of application traffic due to a business reason. What should you do?

    a. Create a VM snapshot of your base VM and create your images from that snapshot.

    b. Create a VM snapshot of your base VM and create your instances from that snapshot.

    c. Create a custom VM image from a snapshot and create your images from that image.

    d. Create a custom VM image from a snapshot and create your instances from that image.

15. Your company runs a batch process in an on-premises server within its data centre which takes around 40 hours to complete. The task runs quarterly, it can be performed offline, while it must be restarted if interrupted. Now you want to migrate this workload to the GCP, minimizing the cost. What should be done?

    a. Migrate the workload to a GCP's Compute Engine Preemptible VM.

    b. Migrate the workload to a GKE cluster with Preemptible nodes.

    c. Migrate the workload to a GCP VM, start and stop the instance as needed.

    d. Create an Instance Template with Preemptible VMs On and create a managed instance group from the created template, adjust the required Target CPU Utilization and migrate the workload.

16. You are developing a new application and are looking for a MongoDB installation to store semi structured JSON data. You need to automate the solution as quickly and easily as possible. What should you do?

    a. Deploy MongoDB Atlas through the Google Cloud Marketplace.

    b. Create a new Compute Engine instance and install MongoDB on it.

c. Look for an alternate solution to store the data in a similar NoSQL database.

d. None of these.

17. **You are asked to set up performance monitoring for applications on Google Cloud projects Dev, Test, and Prod together. You need to monitor the CPU, memory, and disk. What should be done?**

a. Enable API and then use default dashboards to view all projects in sequence.

b. Enable API and then share charts from project Dev, Test, and Prod.

c. Enable API and then give the metrics.reader role to projects Dev, Test, and Prod.

d. Enable API, create a workspace under project Dev, and then add projects Test and Prod.

18. **You have created many resources in multiple GCP projects. All the projects are linked to the different billing accounts. In order to better estimate future charges, you need to have a single visual dashboard of all costs incurred. You need to include the new cost data as quickly as possible. What should be done?**

a. Configure Billing Data Export to BQ and visualize the data in Looker Studio.

b. Visit the Cost Table page to get a CSV export and visualize it in the Dashboard using Looker Studio.

c. Fill the resources in the Pricing Calculator to get an overall estimate of the monthly cost.

d. Use the Reports view in Cloud Billing Console to view desired cost information.

19. **You need to store sensitive information in a GCS bucket. Now, for legal reasons, you need to be able to keep a record of all the incoming requests which read any of the stored data. You need to make sure that the solution should comply with the requirements. What should be done?**

a. Enable the Identity Aware Proxy (IAP) API on the project.

b. Scan the bucket using the Data Loss Prevention (DLP) API.

c. Allow only a single Service Account to read the data.

d. Enable the Data Access audit logs for the Cloud Storage API.

20. **You are planning to deploy an ERP system on GCP and it needs to hold the full database in-memory for the faster data access, and you need to configure the most appropriate resources on GCP for this application. What should you do?**

a. Provision of preemptible VM instances.

b. Provision VM instances with GPUs attached.

    c.   Provision VM instances with local SSDs attached.

    d.   Provision VM instances with M1 machine type.

Answers

1. C
2. A
3. B
4. D
5. D
6. C
7. D
8. D
9. A
10. B
11. B
12. C
13. C
14.D
15. C
16. A
17. D
18. A
19. D
20. D

Join our book's Discord space

Join the book's Discord Workspace for Latest updates, Offers, Tech happenings around the world, New Release and Sessions with the Authors:

https://discord.bpbonline.com

Index

www.ingramcontent.com/pod-product-compliance
Lightning Source LLC
Chambersburg PA
CBHW061805210326
41599CB00034B/6881